GRAPHICS FILE FORMATS

GRAPHICS FILE FORMATS

Reference and Guide

C. Wayne Brown and Barry J. Shepherd

MANNING

Greenwich

The publisher offers discounts on this book when ordered in quantity. For more information please contact:

Special Sales Department
Manning Publications Co.
3 Lewis Street
Greenwich, CT 06830
or
73150,1431@compuserve.com
Fax: (203) 661-9018

Design: Christopher Simon   Copyediting: Jody Berman
Cover: Chris Link   Typesetting: Stephen Adams

The illustration appearing on the cover is due to A. Ravishankar Rao,
IBM T. J. Watson Research Center

Recognizing the importance of preserving what has been written, it is the policy of Manning Publications to have the books they publish printed on acid-free paper, and we exert our best efforts to that end.

Library of Congress Cataloging–in–Publication Data

Brown, C. Wayne, 1954–
     Graphics file formats : reference and guide / by C. Wayne Brown
and Barry J, Shepherd.
       p.   cm.
     Includes bibliographical references and index.
     ISBN 1-884777-00-7
     1. Computer graphics.   2. File organization (Computer science)
I. Shepherd, Barry J., 1939–   . II. Title.
T385.B777   1995
006.6—dc20   93-50175
                                                     CIP

Manning Publications Co.
3 Lewis Street
Greenwich, CT 06830

10 9 8 7 6 5 4 3 2 1

Printed in the United States of America

TO MY WIFE, SANDY
— Wayne Brown

TO MY FAMILY
— Barry Shepherd

COPYRIGHTS

Copyrights to entries in the following list of product names are held by their respective owners.
(* Some names may not be subject to copyright)

ADEX
ADRG
Abekas YUV format
AMF
ANIM
ARC/INFO
AT&T ATT
Atari Degas
Autologic*
Atari Spectrum
AVS Image
AVS.dat
AVS Field
Betacam
Betacam SP
BIFF
BMP
BUFR *
CDF*
ChromaLink
Cineon
Claris CAD
CUR
CUT
DataBeam DBX
DEC pixel format
DLG
DMP
DXF
EPS
Erdas LAN / GIS
FITS
FLI
Flux
Freedom of the Press
 Freeway
GEM/IMG
GEM/Metafile
GEM VDI
GF3*
GIF

GRASP
Handshake
HDF
HDS*
HiJaak 2.1
Hi-8
HP-GL
HP-GL/2
HP Paintjet
HP-PCL
HP-RTL
IBM GOCA
ICO
IFF
ILBM
Illustrator 3.0
Image Alchemy
IMG
Inset IGF
IPI
ISIF
Landsat*
LBM
Lotus PIC
LZW encoding
MacPaint
Mac 3D
MapBase
MathCAD MCS
Micrographx DRW
MIF
Moov
Motif
Movie.BYU
MTV / PRT
netCDF
NTSC
OS/2
PackBits
PBM
pbmplus*

PC Paintbrush
PCPAINT/Pictor page
   format
PCX
PDBLib*
PhotoCD
Photoshop
PICT
PICT2
PICTureThis
Plot3D
PLPS
PM Metafile MET
PostScript
PRIM
QDV
QO
QRT
QUBE*
RIB
RIFF
RLE
RPL
SAS
SA4D
SBF
Scodl
Sculpt3D
SFDU*
SFF*
SFIL
Silicon Graphics*
SLD
Stork*
Super 3D
SunRaster
SunVision
SuperPaint
S-Video
S-VHS
Super-VHS

Swivelman 3D
Tango
TARGA
Tektronix Plot 10
TGA
TIFF
TIGER/Line
TWGES
UIL
U-Matic
U-Matic SP
Utah Raster Toolkit
VFF.geometry
VFF image
VFF.movie
VIFF
Vivid
Windows 3.0 Metafile
WMF
WordPerfect Graphic File
WPG
WSS
X bitmap
XBM
Xim
X pixmap
XPM
X window dump
3DGF
32 bit PICT
907 PCI

CONTENTS

APPENDICES

The storage and transmission of graphical data is a crucial part of many current applications. Before 1990 there were no good sources of information on graphical data streams besides the original technical specifications that defined them, and these were (and are) difficult to find and sometimes difficult to understand. Incompatibilities between data formats and the problems associated with transferring data between systems has left many users frustrated and seeking help. This book was written because of these problems.

Wayne Brown began work on the manuscript in the spring of 1991. The task of collecting, organizing, and documenting the many file formats started well, but the size of the task grew quickly. New data formats seemed to be "discovered" daily. The goal of creating a comprehensive resource, one that truly covered all existing graphical data formats, became elusive. After one and half years of serious work, Wayne laid aside the project because the thought of making it "complete" became too overwhelming. Fortunately, Barry Shepherd agreed to complete the work.

Few surveys are ever complete in this day of rapid technological change, especially in this area where new data formats are continually created. This book is not complete in the rigorous sense; but it does contain a significant amount of information that we believe will be useful to many readers. The information in this book has been useful to us.

As of this writing there are several available books related to graphic data formats. Steve Rimmer has written two books about raster data formats in popular use on personal computers. These are *Bit-Mapped Graphics* (1990) and *Supercharged Bit-mapped Graphics* (1992). These books include a significant amount of working C code, and are targeted toward people who want to write software "readers" and "writers" of a particular data format. Another recent work is David Kay and John Levine's book *Graphics File Formats* (1992). It discusses 23 individual data formats in detail, including both raster and vector data streams. Most of their discussion is limited to two-dimensional data. Implementing software "readers" and "writers" of a particular data stream is one emphasis of this work, though no actual code is included. If your goal is software development related to an existing data format, these three books would be valuable resources to you.

This book differs from the above in two respects. First, our goal is to help you understand how graphic data streams differ and why. The book is organized according to data and design issues—not individual formats. Hopefully it will help you make wise decisions related to their implementation and application. If you plan on implementing new data formats in the future, this book can help you make critical design decisions. If you are searching for an appropriate data stream to meet a particular application, this book will guide your search. Second, this book surveys, in detail, 51 different data formats and lists more than 80 others from a broad range of applications. As such the book serves as a general reference to graphical data streams. We hope this book is a useful resource for your work.

We are indebted to the people who helped us collect the information contained in this book. There are too many to call by name. Many times we telephoned total strangers requesting information and invariably received the information we were looking for, or we were directed to someone else who could help. We want to say thanks to all of them.

Wayne Brown would like to thank several people by name. Marjan Bace, the Publisher at Manning Publications, was a pleasure to work with. Thanks to his continual encouragement (and prodding) this book is a reality. And, without Barry Shepherd coming along to finish the work, it would still be an unfinished manuscript sitting on a shelf. Barry was asked to do the impossible: finish someone else's project. He did it with much enthusiasm and great skill due to his knowledge and experience in developing national and international graphic standards. Thanks also to Sam Reynolds who helped greatly with the initial work and who provided an invaluable sounding board. Without Sam's initial support this project would have never been started. Most importantly, Wayne thanks his wife who supported him throughout the long hours needed to complete this project. She is a wife worthy of honor and praise.

We will be happy to hear from our readers. Comments and questions can be sent by e-mail to the addresses below.

C. WAYNE BROWN
wayne@cs.uca.edu

BARRY J. SHEPHERD
72674.445@Compuserve.com

INTRODUCTION

CONTENTS

1.1 THE PROBLEM

Graphical data is stored, manipulated, and transmitted to produce "pictures" or "images." If all graphical data sets produce a similar end result, why are there so many different graphical data formats? And why are so many of these data formats incompatible with each other? The simple answer is because there are many different applications using different types of data in different ways to satisfy different needs. A more complete and detailed answer requires the rest of this book.

When any system is designed, there are always design trade-offs. These trade-offs allow for a certain level of system performance within a restricted range of costs. It is true what they say, "You get what you pay for." There is a wide range of cost/performance ratios in systems that deal with graphical data. In addition to design trade-offs, data formats must meet the specific needs of a broad range of diverse applications while attempting to keep up with the tremendous advances occurring in technology. And you can't forget the politics of the marketplace that causes corporations and standards organizations to do things that they perceive to be in their best interest. The result is a broad spectrum of graphical data formats that is confusing to the average user (and sometimes to the expert as well).

Is *every* graphical data format in existence today actually needed? The simple answer is: No, they are not all needed. If we do not need (or want) them all, how can we distinguish between the ones we should keep and the ones we should abandon? Are some data formats better than other formats? Is there a "best" format? What are the design issues? What trade-offs must be made? Can diverse industries agree on graphical data formats that meet the majority of their needs while compromising on some issues? Is the standardization of graphical data formats really that critical an issue? And, besides all of these BIG questions, what does byte 37 of data format *abc* contain? Lots of questions! And the answers are often difficult to find. This book addresses these questions.

From a user's perspective, file format issues can be very frustrating. If you have a data set in a format that is incompatible with your desired application, it is a nuisance at best; at its worst, it can totally halt a project. Many users wish for a single universal data format that would eliminate their frustrations, eliminate their confusion, and boost their productivity. Such a data format is probably not going to appear any time soon. The issue is not feasibility, but cost-effectiveness. Perhaps someday when we each have a machine on our desk equivalent to today's supercomputers and costing less than today's personal computers, we can standardize on a single graphical data format.

1.2 THE GOALS OF THIS BOOK

Given that we will not have just one universal graphical data format but many formats, can we eliminate the redundant ones? The answer is: We hope so! The following chapters discuss the issues related to the storage, retrieval, and transmission of graphical data. The information provided will hopefully accomplish the following objectives.

- Define, categorize, and synthesize the critical issues related to the design of graphical data formats.

- Identify the features and characteristics of individual data formats that make them "better" than other formats.

- Provide a useful resource for users and software developers who need information on both particular data formats and data formats in general.

- Minimize the creation of new graphical data file formats, when existing ones meet the need. (If software developers become aware of existing formats, then perhaps they will not be so tempted to create new unnecessary ones.)

- Encourage and facilitate the convergence of data formats into a smaller set of commonly used formats.

- Inform inquiring minds who just want to know about these issues.

To accomplish these objectives, this book is divided according to the major issues that separate graphical data formats. Information on each particular data format can be found in the appendices and through references contained in the index.

This book has four major sections: Chapters 2–4, Chapters 5–10, Chapters 11–12, and the appendices. Chapters 2–4 contain a historical, political, and design overview that provide a context in which to discuss graphical data. Chapters 5–10 contain the details of graphical data representation. Chapters 11–12 discuss the relationships between data formats and conversions between them. And finally, the appendices contain a detailed entry on each data format that we consider important—either because it is widely used, because it is a standard, or because its unique properties separate it from other formats.

In picking a data format that meets the needs of your application, we suggest the following approach. Read Chapter 4 on the design trade-offs and implementation issues that affect graphical data streams. Select the issues that are most critical to your application and weigh them according to some priority scale. As you read the other chapters on data types, color, data organization, data encoding, and data compression, make note of the individual data formats that satisfy your critical needs. After having read the chapters, examine the appendix entry for each format that you identified. A thorough review of these summaries will help you narrow your search.

Ideally you might wish that this book would say, "For application X use data format Y." We could make such broad generalizations, but you might hold us accountable for selecting a data format that is not quite right for your specific needs. It is much better that you understand the issues yourself and come to your own conclusions. Our goal is to educate you so that you can make wise choices, not to make choices for you.

1.3 THE BIG PICTURE —
AN OVERVIEW OF CHAPTERS 2-4

Many technologies and industries have come from the desires of people who wish to create and share pictures. As one example, Kodak estimates that 60 billion photographs are taken every year. Pictures are created for a variety of reasons—business correspondence (Faxes), business communications (teleconferencing), personal communications (visual telephones), entertainment (TVs, movies), advertising and education (printing), medicine (X rays), and engineering design (prototypes). Traditionally each of these activities has been based on disjoint technologies. Chapter 2 gives a short history of these technologies with an emphasis on how they are converging on a common digital representation for image data.

Because the creation of pictures has been based traditionally on many different technologies, experts knowledgeable in each technology have created standards. The computer age is bringing about the convergence of once disjoint industries around a common tool—the computer. The computer is mankind's first truly multipurpose machine that can perform a variety of tasks simply through the changing of a program. Yet, even though industries are shedding their older technologies for computers, standards are developed often along old traditional industry lines. The current challenge is to make data formats as flexible as the computers that use them. It is a challenging task. Chapter 3 discusses the standardization of graphical data formats, who the players are, the procedures they use, and suggestions for transforming the process to meet these new challenges.

If data formats are to meet the needs of multiple industries, the issues that mold them must be well-defined and understood. Chapter 4 discusses how design goals affect all data formats. Data formats have many similarities to computer programming languages, but the similarities are often ignored. The principles that form good programming languages need to be applied to the design of data formats if we are to create well-designed data formats.

1.4 THE DETAILS BY TOPIC —
AN OVERVIEW OF CHAPTERS 5–10

Data formats can be divided into two broad views: a conceptual view and an representational view. The *conceptual view* includes three big ideas: the types of graphical data used to create pictures, the organization of this data, and color. The *representational view* includes the assignment of a unique code value for each data item (data encoding), the compression of these values to minimize storage, the low-level organization of these values, and the conversion of these values to appropriate physical phenomenon for their storage or transmission. A summary of these issues are listed below.

Conceptual View	Representational View
• Data types	• Data encoding
• Color theory	• Data compression
• Data organization	• Data organization
	• Conversion to the physical medium

1.4.1   Conceptual View

There are several distinct types of graphical data. The use of each type is determined by both the source of the data and its intended use. Graphical data can be divided into three broad categories:

- *Raster Data*   A group of sampled values, in either 2-dimensional or 3-dimensional space, that represents an image or that can be processed into an image.
- *Geometry Data*   A mathematical description of space, either 2-dimensional or 3-dimensional, that represents the components of an image.
- *Latent Image Data*   Nongraphical data that can be transformed into useful images by some algorithmic process.

These different types of data are discussed in detail in Chapter 5. There is also a variety of other related, nongraphical information that is stored with a graphical data set. Chapter 5 discusses and categorizes all of the data types found in a graphical data set.

The representation of color is an important part of most graphical data sets. Since color is an important issue to understand, all of Chapter 6 is devoted to its discussion.

Most typical data sets consist of a linear list of data values. This is commonly referred to as a *data stream*. The order of the data values within the stream is important for many applications. Chapter 7 discusses how data is organized, both from a conceptual view and a representational view.

1.4.2   Representational View

The design of a data format is based, in part, on the memory, speed, and circuitry components of the hardware systems targeted to use the data. In order to satisfy these hardware issues, data formats organize data in different ways, compress data using a variety of schemes, and encode data in different representations. If all of these issues were disjoint,

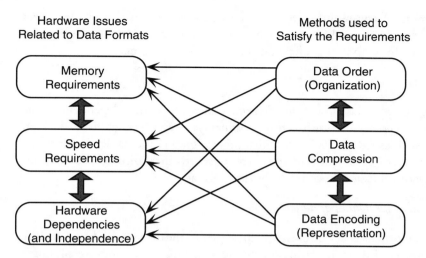

Figure 1.1 Hardware and data set interdependencies

then the design of a data format would be greatly simplified. However, all of these issues are interrelated. For example, the amount of available memory can affect the speed of data access, and the ordering of the data within a data set can affect the efficiency of the data compression, and so on.

Figure 1.1 indicates the interdependencies between a hardware system and a data set. As indicated by the numerous arrows, choosing a particular method has an impact on all other aspects of the data format.

Chapter 7 discusses data organization, Chapter 8 discusses data encoding, and Chapters 9 and 10 discusses data compression. Before you get lost in the details contained in these chapters, let's briefly discuss each of these issues.

Memory Requirements

Some graphical devices have no memory at all, while others have large amounts of memory. The source of data and its intended use determine the memory requirements. A home television has no memory; it takes a stream of data and presents it directly to the screen. The typical television does minimal manipulation on the data stream. As capabilities of data manipulation are added to a system, memory to store at least parts of the data is required. The types and complexities of the data manipulation determine the amount of memory required by a system for a given image size and resolution.

The cost of memory is continually decreasing. A common phrase heard these days among computer professionals is, "Memory is cheap." Compared to earlier technology, memory is indeed cheap. But graphics applications are real memory hogs. While current memory sizes of 4 to 32 MBs are typically sufficient for many graphics applications, it is always easy to find an application where 32 MBs is not enough. Consider, for example, the memory requirements for storing one 9" × 7" raster image in full color at film resolution. A single such image requires 720 MBs of memory.[*] Conventional wisdom holds that you

---

[*] Calculated using 3 bytes of memory per dot and 2000 dots per inch (linear resolution).

always need 20% more of any resource than you currently possess. While memory sizes continue to increase, the 20% need for more seems to stay constant. Memory, or the lack thereof, will be an issue for graphical applications for some time to come.

Speed Requirements

The speed at which a graphical data set must be processed is application dependent. Some applications use hours of computer time to create and manipulate a single graphical data set. Other applications, such as video telephones, must process graphical data sets in real time. In both cases, user expectations of hardware speed are constantly increasing. For some applications, speed is the critical issue that controls the data format.

Hardware Dependencies (and Independence)

The goal of many data formats is device independence; that is, the data set can be used easily on any system, regardless of their similarities or differences. This is a desirable goal, but it does not come for free. Device independence typically decreases processing speed and increases memory requirements. Data sets stored in hardware-specific formats can be accessed faster and typically require less memory. In some cases, the link between a data format and a specific hardware device is what makes the data format useful. Consider for example the Fax format used to send photocopy-type data over ordinary telephone lines. The Fax hardware and data format are interdependent, and they have created a successful and beneficial service to the public.

Data Order Organization

The importance of data order can best be explained by an example. Consider the task of printing a color image using a color raster printer. All raster printers fall into one of two categories: those that create an image in a single pass over the paper, and those that make multiple passes over the paper. The multiple passes consist of a pass for each color ink used to create the image.

Now consider the format of the data needed to print on each of these types of printers. For a multi-pass printer, the data should be organized into "color pages," where the color data for each page is stored contiguously. For a single-pass printer, the data should be stored in a "line" format, such that all of the data required to print an entire line is contiguous in the data set. Refer to the Figure 1.2. If the data is in the correct order for the desired printer, then printing the image is straightforward. If the data is not in the correct order, then we have two options. We can "buffer" the data in memory until it is needed, but the cost of the memory increases the total cost of the system. If we cannot afford the memory, then we can read through the data set a multiple number of times to extract the appropriate data at the appropriate time. This affects the system speed and slows down the printing process.

Other difficulties with the data order can exist. For example, it is common to print in one of two orientations: portrait (vertical) mode or landscape (horizontal) mode.[*] It is

---

[*] The image to be printed is rotated 90 degrees on the page.

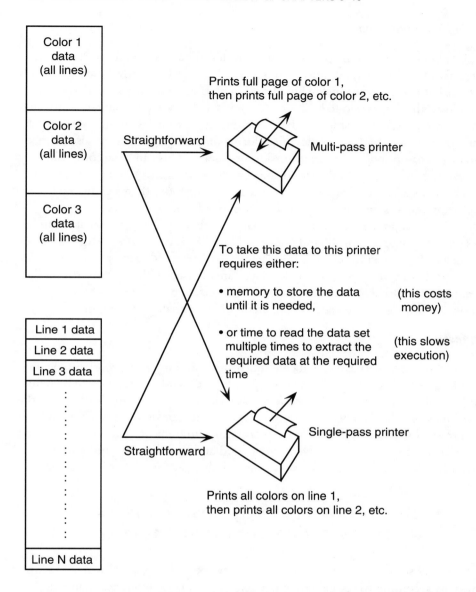

Figure 1.2 Performance considerations of data organization and printer capability

impossible to optimize the organization of a data set to facilitate both printing modes simultaneously.

The order of data is important for other reasons besides printing. For example, the order of data values can be used as an efficient means of associating data values without requiring extra "links" or "pointers." The data order can also affect the amount of achievable data compression for a particular data set. Some data orders facilitate compression more than others. These and other related issues are discussed in Chapter 7.

Data Encoding Representation

Data must be represented in some physical way in order to be stored and transmitted. If a continuous wave form is used, then the medium is called *analog*. Currently, home televisions receive pictures in the form of an analog broadcast signal. If discrete values are used to represent the data, then the data is said to be *digital*. Digital data has several advantages over analog data. Digital data can be copied an infinite number of times without data loss; the accuracy of analog data degrades as copies of copies are made. Digital data can also be made more resistant to corruption during transmission or storage. This can be accomplished by means of checksums or other error detection and correction schemes. A disadvantage to digital data sets is their size; typically they require much more memory than a comparable analog representation unless some encoding or compression scheme is employed.

Most digital data representations use the binary number system. The binary number system uses only two digits, zeros (0) and ones (1). Using these two digits, a large variety of encoding schemes have been developed. If a data set is represented using the same encoding as the target hardware system, then the data can be used without conversion. This speeds up data access. Otherwise, the data must be converted to the representation used on specific hardware slowing the data access. Chapter 8 discusses data encoding issues.

Data Compression

Graphical data sets can be very large, and consequently the amount of memory on a system can limit some graphical applications. Data compression helps solve this problem by reducing the amount of memory required to store a particular data set. It can also increase the time required to access the data because compressed data must be decompressed. Graphical data is compressed for two major reasons: to increase the amount of data that can be sent over a communications channel in a given time period and to reduce the amount of space required to store a data set. Data compression issues are discussed in Chapter 9 and 10.

1.5 THE DATA FORMAT RELATIONSHIPS — AN OVERVIEW OF CHAPTERS 11–12

Once the issues that separate graphical data formats have been discussed, Chapter 11 classifies data formats according to several criteria. There are so many differences between data formats that a single classification scheme does not adequately compare the formats. Therefore several classification schemes are used.

The most commonly requested information about graphical data sets is, "How do I convert format X into format Y?" In some cases the conversion is almost trivial. In others the conversion is essentially impossible. And there are many levels of difficulty in between. Chapter 12 discusses the problems associated with the conversion of data between formats.

1.6 THE DETAILS BY FORMAT — APPENDICES

There are too many details relating to each data format to include them all in a single document. For example, the PostScript "Red Book" is 764 pages, the IGES manual is 515 pages, and the three-part IPI Draft International Standard totals 1140 pages (although only about 240 pages deal with data types and formats). The intent of the appendices is to encapsulate the major aspects of a data format in a couple of pages. Hopefully each synopsis will provide enough understanding to determine whether a particular format would meet the needs of a particular application. If more information on a particular format is needed, the references listed with each format will lead the reader to appropriate sources.

1.7 GENERAL THOUGHTS ON DATA FORMATS

Traditional computer science can be summarized with the following expression:

Data Structures + Algorithms = Data Processing

If we have data relevant to an application in a structure suitable for processing and we have precisely-defined methods for manipulating that data (algorithms), then we can do useful work. Both the structure of the data and the algorithms are important to the entire process. Programming languages have been developed to facilitate the implementation of algorithms. These languages have rich constructs such as iteration, scope of definition, and recursion that enhance the creation of algorithms. On the other hand, the methods for defining data rarely have such sophistication. Data are typically viewed as static entities while algorithms are viewed as dynamic processes.

Let's look at another perspective on data, from the field of Artificial Intelligence (AI). The field of AI has intensely debated the nature of intelligent processing over the years. At one point it was thought that intelligence was the ability to make inferences. That is, given that I know A and B, I can figure out C. The major emphasis of this research was on producing algorithms that could do inferencing. Other researchers have come to believe that much of a human's intelligence is based simply on how much they know. An expert in a field is an expert because of their domain knowledge about the field. For these researchers the emphasis is on their ability to gather and encode this expert knowledge. There is a debate within the AI research community about which is more important—inferencing or domain knowledge. While the debate is still open, a number of researchers think that both are equally important.

So which is more important, data or algorithms? We claim they are equally important. So, is the traditional view of static data and dynamic algorithms appropriate? In some cases it is, but in other cases it is not. The description of data can often be enhanced by using some of the same constructs developed for programming languages. We need to think of data descriptions as languages, and apply some of the theory we know about languages to the description of data.

Is there justification for this view of data formats? Perhaps the best justification is the success of PostScript. PostScript was designed to describe the layout of pages for publishing and thus it supports a rich set of graphical commands and data elements. It is also a fully functional programming language that allows for, among other things, variable definition, iteration, and recursion. While the success of PostScript can be attributed possibly to several factors, the predominant factor is its versatility. PostScript defines a set of tools, a language syntax, and an execution strategy (i.e., it is a *stack-based processor*). Within this framework, software tools can generate PostScript data sets in any way needed to describe their data. For example, a raster image can be a set of static data values, or it can be a set of values generated by a "data procedure." The "data stream" is not restricted to a set of static values. It is a *conceptual data stream* that can be composed of any combination of static and generated values.

Of all the data formats surveyed in this book, PostScript stands alone in its ability to represent conceptual data streams. (A new data format called *RPL* is under development that is similar to PostScript[*] and designed for 3-dimensional applications.) If there is any gap in the spectrum of data formats, it is in the realm of support for "algorithmic data streams." Some examples of algorithmic data streams include fractal-based data, constraint-based data, and grammar-based data.

Our whole concept of data formats needs to be expanded and enhanced. The traditional view of a data stream as a linear list of static values is inadequate for the versatility needed in today's graphical-based systems. Data formats have long been relegated to the sphere of "unimportant and uninteresting." There are as many challenges related to the design of good data formats as there are to good programming languages. It is time more of these important issues are addressed.

---

[*] Both PostScript and RPL are based on the Forth programming language.

CONTENTS

2.1 INTRODUCTION

The creation of pictures has been a human activity since the beginning of humanity. Initially this involved painting or carving on rocks. But while rocks are nice and permanent, they are oftentimes difficult to transport due to their size. Humans like to share their pictures—and the knowledge contained in them. So the search for methods of creating nice pictures on transportable medium was on.

Some of the methods developed to create, manipulate, reproduce, and share pictures are shown in Figure 2.1. The list is in no way complete. A complete list would require a much more technical discussion than we desire to get into here. If you would like to see a more technical list of imaging techniques, refer to [Jacobson76].

Most of these picture-creating methods have developed into major industries, each with their own technologies, clients, and jargon. But an interesting phenomenon has occurred in the past 10 years. Most, if not all, of these once disjoint technologies are merging toward a more unified approach to imaging—the digital approach. This trend can be attributed to many technological advances, the most important of which is the integrated circuit. The integrated circuit has brought phenomenal advances in computing speed and in the digital memory that makes digital imaging economically possible.

Let's look briefly at the history of picture technologies—when they were invented and how they are rapidly changing due to today's technologies. It is beyond the scope of this

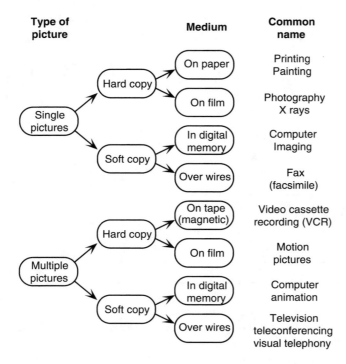

Figure 2.1   Methods for picture creation, manipulation, and reproduction

discussion to do justice to the ingenuity of past inventors. If you are unfamiliar with the development of these technologies, you have missed some fascinating history.[*]

2.2 SINGLE PICTURES

2.2.1 Printing

The technology used in producing multiple copies of an image from an original is called *printing*. Printing mechanisms required the development of three things: paper, ink, and the techniques for transferring the ink to the paper. Paper was invented by the Chinese in the second century, passed on to the Arabs in the 12th century, and spread through Europe in the 13th and 14th centuries. Ink was created a long time ago, but ink with the correct viscosity (stickiness) for printing has evolved only since the 1400s. Printing got its first major push with the invention of the Gutenburg press in 1450.

The four major traditional printing technologies developed since the 15th century are listed below. Each of these is based on a technique for creating a *plate* that can transfer ink to a medium in the appropriate places to form a copy of the original image. For further information see [Cogoli73].

---

[*] A good source of historical information on these topics is [Britannica90].

Traditional Techniques

- *Letterpress*   The plate used to create the image has raised material only where printing is to occur; all other material of the plate is removed below a certain level of the printing surface. Ink is applied to the surface of the plate and paper is pressed against it. Only the raised portions of the plate contact the paper and transfer ink to the paper's surface. The predominantly-used method for creating the plates is by combining moveable type.

- *Intaglio*   This is the reverse process of Letterpress. All areas on the plate where printing is to occur are removed to form small cavities. Ink is applied to the entire plate, and a scraper blade then removes all of the ink not in the cavities. When paper is pressed against the plate, the ink in the cavities adheres to the paper. Any process that uses intaglio printing plates is called *gravure printing*. The term *photogravure printing* is used when the plate cavities are etched into a photographically sensitive plate using a chemical process. The term *plate engraving* is used when the cavities are formed by hand cutting or machine cutting.

- *Screen*   A finely woven cloth is stretched tightly on a frame and a stencil is attached to the cloth. The stencil is cut away in those areas to be inked. The screen is placed over the material to be printed and ink is pressed through the screen. Only those areas where the stencil allows ink through are printed.

- *Offset*   This process is unique from the others in that the surface of the printing plate is smooth. The process works on the premise that water and oil do not mix. A greasy image is placed on the plate that attracts a greasy ink and repels water. The clear areas of the plate are dampened with water such that they are receptive to water but repel ink. The technical name for this process is *lithography*.

Modern Techniques

All of the printing methods just described require physical contact of a plate with the material to be printed. Newer technologies can print a page without physically touching it. Some of these technologies include the following:

- *Electrostatic*   An image is created by placing an electrical charge on the paper where printing is desired. The electrical charge attracts toner, a fine-colored plastic powder, that is then fused permanently onto the paper by heat.

- *Thermal*   An image is created on heat-sensitive paper that changes color in the presence of high temperatures. Heat is applied only to those areas where the image is to be printed.

- *Ink Jet*   An image is "painted" on the paper by ink that is sprayed from a small nozzle.

- *Thermal Dye Diffusion*   Special dyes are used that change from a solid to a gas when heated. The gases are then absorbed by specially coated paper.

These technologies have one thing in common—they have no plate that contains the original image. Therefore the image must be stored in some kind of memory. Digital computer memory meets this need quite well. In almost every case of nonplate printing, the printing is done as a series of dots. Therefore we need digital data formats that can store "pages of dots" to facilitate printing in these new technologies.

Any device that creates images by displaying groups of dots is called a *raster* device. Data formats that store data for these devices are called *raster data formats*. The number of discrete dots per inch (or per mm) that a device can display determines its *resolution*. Higher resolution devices typically produce higher quality images.

The new nonplate printing technologies are capable of matching or exceeding the resolution of the more traditional printing methods. The current advantages of the traditional methods are of printing speed and lower cost per page for high-volume printing. For an electronic printing system to match the speed of a fast offset printer, the system would have to handle terabytes[*] of data per second. Until they can match such speeds, older printing technologies will continue to be used. But even in offset printing, digital data is being used increasingly to create the plates.

Printer Data Formats

The following data formats have been created to share data between printing systems. Sharing data between large printing systems is currently not common. However, it is quite common to share data between "desktop publishers"—people who create publishable material on a personal computer—and larger printing systems. PostScript is by far the current de facto standard for sharing such data.

PUBLISHING SYSTEM DATA EXCHANGE FORMATS

Format	Description
ChromaLink	Data exchange format by Hell Graphics
DDES	Digital Data Exchange Standard A suite of standards for the exchange of raster data, vector data, and text data. (See appendix)
Freeway	Data exchange format by Crossfield
Handshake	Foreign File Transfer Protocol by Scitex
HP-PCL	Hewlett Packard Printer Control Language
MIF	FrameMaker files
PostScript	(See appendix)

One notable exception to the modern techniques is pen plotting. Though a pen plotter touches the page to draw an image, it uses no plates and prints relatively slowly. A pen plotter is designed to draw lines, thus the most logical type of data to drive a pen plot is line data. Pen plotters serve a different purpose than traditional printing and will more than

---

[*] A terabyte is 10^{12} bytes (a trillion bytes).

likely continue on a separate development path. The following lists several of the most common data formats to drive plotters. The HP-GL data format was initially designed for pen plotting, but it is sometimes used as an interchange format.

PLOTTER SYSTEM INTERCHANGE FORMATS

Format	Description
907 PCI	907 Plotter Communications Interface Calcomp, P.O. Box 3250, Anaheim, CA 92801
DMP	Digital Memory Plotter language Houston Instruments, Summagraphics 60 Silvermine Road, Seymour, CT 06483
HP-GL	Hewlett Packard Graphics Language (See appendix)
HP-GL/2	Hewlett Packard Graphics Language/Two (See appendix)

While the above data formats emphasize the sharing of data among different printing systems, some data formats have been created to eliminate the printing step all together. For example, the P.OEM™ PC Publishing System is a method of publishing an entire book in electronic form.

2.2.2 Photography (Film)

In 1826, a French lithographer-inventor, Joseph-Nicephore Niepce, created the first photograph made in a camera. His method was based on an asphalt solution. A little more than 10 years later a British amateur scientist, William Henry Fox Talbot, invented a photographic system that created a positive picture from a negative image. He perfected the process in 1840 using silver iodide paper. This negative-positive photographic system is still the predominant system used today for film photography.

The predominant light-sensitive material used for today's film is minute silver halide crystals suspended in an emulsion. The emulsion is typically composed of silver bromide with some silver iodide. The crystals are sometimes referred to as *grains*. The size of the grains are one of the major contributing factors to the light sensitivity of the film. Large grains are more light sensitive than small grains. The structure of the grains is discontinuous, and if the image is enlarged, the discontinuity can become apparent. An enlarged image is said to be "grainy" if the discontinuities are visible to the naked eye.

The resolution of film is dependent on a complicated interaction between the grain size used to create the film, the amount and kind of light that the film is exposed to, and the developing process used to create a final picture from the film. There is no direct relationship between the grain size of a film and the resolution of a resulting photograph. The resolution of a particular film can be determined through empirical testing by photographing a standard test pattern. The test pattern is composed of groups of parallel lines of varying thickness separated by spaces equal to the line thickness. The resolution of the film is determined by the number of lines per millimeter in the smallest test pattern that can be discerned under magnification on the developed film. Typically, films in use today for photography range in resolution from approximately 1000 to 3000 lines per inch (black and white line pairs) or approximately 40 to 118 lines per mm.

Film has, in essence, the ability to capture the intensity of light at discrete points, where each discrete point is a silver halide crystal. One major difference between film and other imaging systems is the high resolution that film offers. A typical 35-mm color negative has a resolution of approximately 20 million pixels (picture elements—i.e., dots). This compares poorly with the approximately 90,000 pixels of a low-end monochrome digital camera. But the resolution of light-sensitive charge-coupled devices (CCD) for cameras is rising. As of the early 1990s, high-end (expensive) cameras can produce resolutions of 1.3 million pixels. This resolution is sufficient for creating enlargements of up to 4×6 inches from 35-mm cameras. Recently, resolutions as high as 4 million pixels also appeared (2048 pixels $\times$ 2048 pixels).

The major drawback to normal photographic film is that it must be processed chemically to yield a picture. A major advantage of digitally capturing images is that there is no chemical processing required; an image can be viewed immediately for inspection. Additional benefits include the possibility of employing flexible digital-image-processing algorithms and the possibility of making perfect copies, free from any degradation.

One way to solve the resolution problem of digital cameras is to *scan* a stationary object row by row instead of capturing the entire picture instantaneously. A scanner can be built economically because it needs only a single row of densely packed CCDs. Many scanners have been introduced in the marketplace that offer a variety of resolutions and color accuracies. Initially, each manufacturer of these devices created their own proprietary data formats to store the scanned data. Thankfully, a group of farsighted professionals in this field recognized the need to standardize the output from scanners and created TIFF, the Tagged Image File Format.

Standard data formats for the storage of still frame *camera* pictures on other mediums besides film are rare. One group of manufacturers related to electronics, cameras, film, and magnetic media got together in 1983 and agreed to adopt a format developed by Sony. This analog format stores images on a two-inch floppy diskette. It is sometimes referred to as the *Mavica format,* named after the still video camera Sony introduced in 1982.

There has recently been work on employing the PCMCIA interface definition to define credit-card-sized memory devices for use in electronic cameras. This work is progressing in the international standards arena.

The first major consumer product for digital camera images was the Photo CD system by Eastman Kodak Company, 343 State Street, Rochester, NY 14650-0519. It was announced in 1991 and began sales in 1992. It maintains backward compatibility with existing cameras by using photographic film as the original medium for capturing the images. The images are converted to digital form, and multiple copies of each image at several different resolutions are placed on a Compact Disc (CD) at a processing center. The images are compressed using a proprietary "subband encoding scheme." The images can then be viewed on a television screen using a Photo CD player.

Recently other systems that store photo images on CDs have become available. The creation of standard data formats related to the output of digital cameras is currently underway.

The creation of images on film is not limited to visible light. Some films are sensitive to electromagnetic energy outside the range of visible light. The most notable of these technologies is X rays, commonly used in medicine but also used in other industries. X-ray images can be stored in digital data formats that are essentially identical to other digital images. One slight difference is that medical images often require a higher accuracy of representation for each pixel (dot) to insure the accurate interpretation of an image. Most medical digital imaging data formats have been kept proprietary and closely guarded by the manufacturers who have created them. One standard data format for data interchange between different medical systems has been defined.

MEDICAL IMAGE INTERCHANGE STANDARD AND CONTACT

Format	Description
ACR-NEMA DICOM	ACR—American College of Radiologists
	NEMA—National Electrical Manufacturers Association 2101 L Street, N.W., Washington, DC 20037
	DICOM—Digital Imaging and Communications in Medicine ACR-NEMA Standards Publication No 300 1988. Simple interchange data format for 2D bitmap data from CT, MR, ultrasound, PET, etc., images plus specific data associated with the image

2.2.3 Fax

The name *Fax* is a shortened term for *facsimile*. A Fax system transmits a copy of printed or pictorial material through an electrical wire (or radio wave) and faithfully reproduces it on the other end. The first Fax machine was invented by a Scottish inventor, Alexander Bain, in 1842. His "automatic electrochemical recording telegraph" was patented in 1843. The first commercial Fax system began service in 1865 and connected Paris with other French cities. The first photoelectric scanning Fax system was developed in 1902. The first radio transmission of a photograph between Europe and the United States occurred on June 11, 1910.

Fax systems have been a part of commercial businesses for most of the 20th century, but the use of ordinary phone lines for transmission is a fairly recent development (See Costigan71] and Quinn89]). Fax systems have proliferated around the world since the introduction of a set of international standards by the International Telegraph and Telephone Consultative Committee (CCITT) in the mid-1960s. The following CCITT standards for Fax transmissions are based on a minimum document size of 210 mm × 297 mm (approximately 8.27" × 11.69"), which is the International Standards Organization (ISO) document size referred to as A4.

The Fax transmission of images has always been viewed as the transfer of a set of discrete dots. The dots are scanned one row at a time from left to right and from top to bottom. This is essentially the same type of data we saw in the printing and photography discussion. The only real difference is that phone lines have a limited capacity for data transmission. To send more data in less time, the CCITT standards uses *digital data compression* schemes that reduce the amount of data that must be sent. Data compression has become very important to all branches of digital imaging.

STANDARDS FOR FACSIMILE TRANSMISSION

Format	Description
Group I	Transmits a document over normal telephone wires in approximately 6 minutes when either or both stations are unattended. These machines were introduced in 1966 and were standardized in 1968 (See appendix)
Group II	Identical to Group I except that it transmits the document in approximately 3 minutes. The lower transmission time is accomplished by compression modulation. These machines were introduced in the mid-1970s and standardized in 1976 (See appendix)
Group III	Transmits a document over normal telephone wires in approximately 1 minute. Digital compression is used to reduce the amount of data that must be transmitted. A modem converts the data to an analog signal for actual transmission. These machines were introduced in 1974 and standardized in 1980 (See appendix)
Group IV	Transmits a document over digital public data networks (PDNs) in a digital two-dimensional compressed format. Optional encoding in the future will allow for not only black and white images, but also for grayscale and color images (See appendix)
Group V, etc.	Other standards will be defined in the future as digital data communication systems become more widespread and as the bandwidth of the data channels increase

2.2.4 Computer Imaging

The initial use of computers was to calculate and print tables of numbers. Printing was an integral part of the computer's job, because many of the errors found in large numerical tables were due to manual transcribing errors. This initial printing was typically fashioned after typewriters that strike an inked ribbon against paper. Computers have come a long way since these initial machines of the 1940s.

Most of the early attempts to draw pictures using computers were based on "vector"-type cathode ray tubes (CRTs). They are called vector devices because they create pictures by drawing straight line segments (i.e., vectors). Vector type screens such as the Tektronics 1410 storage tube screen were the mainstay of computer graphics for more than two decades. In the 1970s raster-type devices started to be used for graphics. Prior to this, they had been predominantly used only for text output. In the late 1970s and early 1980s there were "screen wars" between vector and raster devices. Raster devices won the battle— mainly due to their ability to fill areas on the screen with solid and shaded colors. Raster devices require their data in the form of discrete dots. Sometimes data is stored in other formats and converted to dots at display time. We will discuss this in greater detail later.

Many graphical data formats have been created to support the storage of data on computer systems. The following lists of data formats are not exhaustive, but they represent many of the data formats used by more than one application, computer system, or group. The lists are divided into categories related to their origin and data types.

Graphical User Interfaces (GUI)

There are many ways that humans interact with computers—too many to list here. One increasingly common method is through a graphical user interface (GUI). Each GUI typically defines several data formats that can be used by all applications using the interface. Currently, the three most predominantly used GUIs are the Macintosh's Finder, Microsoft's Windows for IBM-compatible personal computers, and X Windows for workstations. Data formats defined by these GUIs are listed below.

DATA FORMATS USED BY GUIs

Format	Description
BMP	BitMaP format (Microsoft Windows) (See appendix)
CUR	CURsor resource file (Microsoft Windows) (See appendix)
ICO	ICOn resource file (Microsoft Windows) (See appendix)
PICT	A data format for QuickDraw Commands (Macintosh Finder) (See appendix)
PICT2	An extension of PICT for color data (See appendix)
WMF	Windows MetaFile (Microsoft Windows) (See appendix)
UIL	Motif (GUI built on top of X Windows)
X bitmaps	Monochrome raster data (See appendix)
X pixmaps	Grayscale and color raster data (See appendix)
X window dump	Screen image dump (See appendix)

Computer Applications

Raster data formats that have their roots in computer applications are shown in the following table.

COMPUTER APPLICATION-BASED
RASTER DATA FORMATS

Format	Description
ADRG	Arc Digitized Raster Graphics Defense Mapping Agency Scanned Operational Navigation Charts (ONC)
3DGF	Macromind
CUT	Dr. Halo raster format
DDIF	DEC Digital Image Format Digital Equipment Corporation
GIF	Graphics Interchange Format (See appendix)
IFF	Amiga Interchange File Format (See appendix)
IMG	GEM IMaGe file (See appendix)
IIF	Image Interchange Facility (See appendix)
ILMB	Interleaved Bitmap data chunk (See IIF in appendix)
JBIG	Joint Bilevel Imaging Group (See appendix)
JPEG	Joint Photographic Experts Group (See appendix)
LBM	Deluxe Paint II encoding Electronic Arts, San Mateo, CA
MacPaint	MacPaint Data Format (See appendix)
PCX	PC Paintbrush file format (See appendix)
Photoshop	Adobe
32-bit PICT	An extension to PICT supported by limited systems
PRIM	Photo Realistic Image Manager Byte by Byte Corporation 9442-A Capital of Texas Highway North, Suite 650, Austin, TX 78759 Allows 64 bits per pixel, 16 bits for RGB and Alpha values; includes high compression

COMPUTER APPLICATION-BASED
RASTER DATA FORMATS *(Continued)*

Format	Description
Sun raster 8	Sun Microsystems (See appendix)
Sun raster 24	Sun Microsystems
SuperPaint	Aldus Corporation One Tower Lane, #1130, Oakbrook Terrace, IL 60181
TGA	TARGA file format (See appendix)
VFF image	Visualization File Format for images
VST	(See TGA in appendix)
SunVision	Sun Microsystems

Pictures as Two-Dimensional Geometry

Although most graphical output devices are raster based, pictures can be represented by other forms of data besides raster data. One commonly-used representation is two-dimensional geometry—lines, circles, arcs, polygons, etc. The advantages of storing data in this form are discussed in the chapter on data types. Listed below are some commonly used two-dimensional geometry data formats, often referred to as "vector formats."

DATA FORMATS FOR 2D GEOMETRY DATA

Format	Description
Claris CAD	(MacDraw) Claris 440 Clyde Avenue, Mountain View, CA 94043
Windows Metafile	A list of calls to the Windows graphic library (See appendix)
WPG	WordPerfect Graphics format

Hybrid Data Formats

Some data formats support both raster data and vector data. Some of these formats are listed in the table on the next page.

2.2.5 Commonalities of Single Pictures

What do printing, photography, medical X rays, Fax machines, and computer images have in common? They are all based on raster data; they produce images, with few exceptions, by the display of dots—discrete samples of intensity over an area of interest. And increasingly more of these applications are using digital memory to store their data. We've just identified

DATA FORMATS SUPPORTING RASTER AND VECTOR DATA

Format	Description
CGM	Computer Graphics Metafile (See appendix)
EPS	Encapsulated PostScript (See appendix)
GEM Metafile	(See appendix)
IFF	Interchange File Format Electronic Arts (See appendix)
PostScript	A page description language (See appendix)
WPG	WordPerfect Graphics file format
SPDL	Standardized Page Description Language, an ISO standard (See PostScript in appendix)

more than 60 commonly-used data formats. How are they similar and how are they different? That is what we will discuss.

2.3 MOVING IMAGES

2.3.1 Motion Pictures

Work in the area of moving pictures from the projection of images using film began in the 1860s and beyond. Thomas Edison is often credited with the invention of the first viable motion picture system in 1892, though some people claim he just combined the discoveries of others. His device was called a *kinetograph*. Two major hurdles in the early development of motion pictures were the design of a projection system that eliminated a visible flicker between images, and a lamp with sufficient lighting power to project images onto a distant screen.

Standards have been an issue throughout the evolution of motion pictures. Major characteristics of motion pictures that have been standardized to some degree include: the frame rate of projection, the aspect ratio of the film (i.e., the ratio of its width to height), the type of color-reproduction system used, the type of sound reproduction used, and the synchronization of image to sound.

The *frame rate* of a motion picture is the number of individual images displayed each second during the projection. A variety of frame rates were used for silent films, but the addition of sound to films required the standardization of the frame rate. In 1927, the frame rate for motion pictures was standardized at 24 frames per second. In fact, although only 24 distinct images are shown each second, each image is shown twice so that 48 images are seen each second (although half of them are duplicates). This is still the predominant standard used by film motion pictures today. Other frame rates have been used over the years by specific systems. For example, the Todd-AO system used a frame rate of 30 frames per second and was used to produce such films as *Oklahoma* (1955) and *Around the World in 80 Days* (1956). Another more recent nonstandard system uses 60 frames per second.

The *aspect ratio* of an image is the ratio of its width to its height. Before the mid-1950s, the standard aspect ratio for motion pictures was 1.33 to 1 (or 4 to 3). After that time the United States standardized the aspect ratio to 1.85 to 1, while the European countries standardized on 1.66 or 1.75 to 1. Other aspect ratios have been used over the years— including the Cinerama system with an aspect ratio of 2.75 to 1. Most people feel that a wider picture increases the realism of the motion picture. This perception is due in part to the fact that most action takes place in the horizontal direction. An additional consideration is that the wider screen involves more peripheral vision, which appears to be important to creating a feeling of visual immersion in the scene.

One important issue in motion pictures is the synchronization of the images with sound. One way to encode sound on a film strip is by optical encoding. The decoding and playback of the sound requires a separate mechanism from the projection of the images. Therefore, on a standard 35-mm film strip, optical sound is recorded 21 frames in *advance* of its corresponding image. On a 16-mm print the sound is recorded 26 frames in advance. Another method of sound encoding is on magnetic tape. On a standard 70-mm magnetic sound print, the sound is recorded 28 frames *behind* its corresponding image. On standard 35-mm film print it is 23 frames behind. The synchronization of sound and images is also a problem when the motion picture and sound data are in digital form.

The hope of many film professionals is that some day motion pictures can be produced without film in a digital data format. Currently, film can capture higher resolution, higher-quality images than digital cameras. Film will continue to be the predominant medium for motion pictures until digital cameras can achieve comparable resolutions (at comparable prices). In the meantime, systems have been developed that take film images, transfer them to digital form for editing and incorporation of special effects, and then transfer them back to film for display. Three standards developed for such conversion of data are listed below.

FORMATS FOR MOTION PICTURE TO VIDEO CONVERSION

Format	Description
SMPTE 240M	Video Production System Transfers film images into an analog video tape format (1920×1035 resolution) for editing and then back again to ultra-high resolution film
SMPTE 260M	Video Production System Similar to SMPTE 240M except the data is stored and manipulated in a digital format
Cineon	Cineon digital film system, Eastman Kodak Company Scans 35-mm motion picture film into a digital format for image manipulation; supports a resolution of 4096×3112 at 10 bits per color per pixel

2.3.2   Television

The concept of sending a moving picture over an electrical wire dates back to the 1870s. The initial ideas envisioned a system much like a Fax machine that could send an image decomposed into a group of dots, but every dot in the image would be communicated simultaneously. This idea quickly gave way to the notion of sending the dots of each image in a serial fashion and reconstructing the image after it was received.

The first patent of a complete television system was issued to Paul Nipkow in Germany in 1884. It used a mechanical rotating drum to scan an image, both for sending and receiving. Mechanical systems dominated the research in this area for many years. In 1926 J. L. Baird, a developer in England, gave the first demonstration of true television. His system had a resolution of 30 lines and it updated the screen approximately 10 frames every second. It was crude, but it proved the feasibility of the idea and stimulated further research.

Mechanical systems lacked sensitivity, making it difficult to extend them to higher resolution images. It was recognized by most developers that a good-quality image of reasonable size required at least 100,000 elements and preferably 200,000 elements, assuming a screen approximately 12 inches high was viewed from a distance of 5 to 8 feet. This number can be calculated from the resolving power of the human visual system. For a square image, 200,000 elements requires approximately 447 scan lines, each with 447 elements per line. This was beyond the feasible limits of mechanical systems.

Early Electronic Systems

The idea of a totally electrical system was first proposed by a Scottish electrical engineer, A. Campbell Swinton, in 1908. His idea was to use magnetically deflected beams in CRTs to scan an image. The idea was too advanced for the technology of 1908, but it was implemented by V. K. Zorykin's iconoscope camera tube, which was patented in 1923. Based on these developments, an all-electronic television was demonstrated by the Radio Corporation of America (RCA) in 1932. It initially used 120 scan lines which was rapidly increased to 343.

The Electric and Musical Industries (EMI) of Great Britain began television research in 1931 under the direction of Isaac Shoenberg. Their team developed a complete and practical system by 1935 and launched the first public television service in 1936. Shoenberg was very concerned with the standardization of the image signal. He proposed an image signal using 405 scan lines updated at a rate of 25 times per second. To decrease the visible flickering effect that can occur at this frame rate, the scan lines were *interlaced*. The screen is divided into even- and odd-numbered scan lines. All of the odd scan lines for the screen are updated first, in 1/50th of a second; then the even scan lines are updated. The net effect is a complete new image displayed 25 times per second. The frame rate of 50 updates per second was chosen to match the electrical power line frequency used in Great Britain (50 Hz). If other update frequencies were used, unwanted distortions in the picture (artifacts) would occur due to competing electromagnetic fields. The EMI standard formed the basis for British television up until 1964.

The United States began regular television broadcasts in 1941. The United States standardized on a signal that included 525 scan lines per picture updated 60 times per second, interlaced, resulting in a total update of the screen 30 times per second. The actual refresh rate is 59.94 fields per second, but this exact value is not significant for most television viewers. The update rate of 60 times per second was based on the electrical power line frequency used in North America (60 Hz). Meanwhile, European countries other than England standardized on a signal of 625 lines at 25 frames per second. Most other countries in the world began their television services in the 1950s and chose either the 525 line United States standard or the European 625 line standard—based on the frequency of alternating current their electrical power systems generated.

The idea of color television existed almost from the very beginning of television research, but color was a more difficult problem. Many of the early systems sent three separate signals over three wires (or channels), but these systems were incompatible with the black and white systems of the day. In the early 1950s the United States' National Television Systems Committee (NTSC) began to investigate the standardization of a color signal that would be compatible with the current standard black and white signal. Their system was finalized in 1953 and is now referred to as the NTSC standard. Variations of this method were standardized in different places around the world. The Phase Alternation Line (PAL) standard was adopted by most of Europe, and the System Electronique Couleur avec Memoire (SECAM) was adopted by France and the Soviet Union. The similarities and differences between these systems is discussed in the chapter on color.

HDTV Developments

The current focus of research is on high-definition TV (HDTV). The main emphasis of HDTV is to provide a better-quality image by doubling the resolution in both the horizontal and vertical directions. This requires the transmission of four times as much information per frame. In addition, there is a push to modify the aspect ratio of the image to increase the width of the image area. Several aspect ratios have been proposed, the most common of which is 16 to 9 (1.78 to 1).

The Federal Communications Committee (FCC) in the United States is currently working on standardizing a new HDTV signal to broadcast in the United States. The FCC has stated that the new HDTV signal must fit within the same signal bandwidth that the current NTSC signal does (approximately 6 MHz). The committee focused its study on six proposals, one of which was expected to be chosen as the new standard. Of the six proposals, five used digital encoding. During the evaluation process, the submitting organizations and consortia finally agreed to create a "grand alliance" which would combine the best parts of all of the digital approaches. It is thus almost certain that the next standard for TV broadcast will be a digital encoding of raster data. This is a significant development in the evolution of TV and it will have a major impact on many other industries. Although Europe had an analog-based system (HDMac) in advanced development, and Japan has demonstrated an analog-based system, both of these regions are now looking toward digital-based systems.

Other Services

Many different developers have attempted to transform television into an information service. These systems are called *teletext* services. They provide a one-way communications link to "pages" or "frames" of alphanumeric and graphic information (typically using a standard

COLOR TELEVISION DATA FORMATS

Format	Description
NTSC	National Television Systems Committee (USA) Color TV broadcast signal standardized in 1953
PAL	Phase Alternation Line Broadcast TV signal used in Australia, Africa, Eurasia, and most of Europe
SECAM	System Electronique Couleur Avec Memorie Broadcast TV signal used in France and Russia
ACATS	Advisory Committee for Advanced Television Systems (USA) A HDTV broadcast standard to be approved in 1994

broadcast television signal). Other developers have created interactive television systems that have two-way communication links where viewers can interact with the current TV program. These are called *videotext systems*. If the system supports graphics as well as text information, it is properly referred to as a videotex system. Graphical data formats have been standardized for these systems, one of which is listed below. Up to now, the commercial success of teletext and videotext systems has been limited in the USA (although the PLPS format is currently used as the basis for the Prodigy information service data stream). In France, England, and Germany, there are large videotex installations.

2.3.3 Video Cassette Recording

Recording images (and sound) onto a magnetic tape is called *video recording*. In a production studio, the source and take-up reels are often separate and independent. A *video cassette* places both the source and take-up reels in a single convenient package. There are a variety of formats for the data stored on a video cassette. Typically, they deal with the same raster data, but they use different encodings that provide different levels of data accuracy. Some data formats can produce much higher-quality images on playback. However, the specifics of each encoding is beyond the scope of this discussion. The following list is included for general reference. If you are unfamiliar with the encoding of color data, the descriptions below will not make much sense. Refer to Chapter 6, which discusses color.

VIDEO RECORDING DATA FORMATS

Format	Description
Betacam	High-performance 1/2-inch analog component tape format (this is not the Betamax consumer tape format)
Betacam SP	Like Betacam, but better-quality bandwidth/resolution due to use of metal tape
CAV	$Y, R–Y, B–Y$
Composite	The normal NTSC signal with no modifications

VIDEO RECORDING DATA FORMATS *(Continued)*

Format	Description
D-1	A component (4:2:2) digital video tape format, for editing and post production, using 19-mm cassettes
CCIR 601	Standard for digitizing PAL, NTSC, and SECAM, called D1 in the United States
D-2	A composite digital tape format for editing and post production, using 19-mm cassettes
D-3	A composite digital tape format for editing and post-production, using 1/2-inch VHS-style cassettes
Hi-8	An analog signal that separates a normal NTSC signal into three signals: one for luminance and two for chrominance; stored at higher frequencies on a 8-mm magnetic tape
M-II	VHS version of Betacam, using VHS format metal tapes
RGB	analog encoding; separate channel for each color—red, green, and blue
RS-170 (EIA)	Monochrome video standard ($640 \times 480 \times 8$ bits per pixel) Electronic Industries Association (EIA) 2001 Pennsylvania Ave. NW Ste 1100, Washington, DC 20006-1813, Tel. (202) 457-4900
RS 343-B (EIA)	An old analog video interface standard, specifying (max) video and (black) offset levels
S-Video	Separates the luma and chroma signals of NTSC or PAL
Super-VHS	An analog signal that separates a normal NTSC signal into three signals: one for enhanced bandwidth / resolution luminance, and two for chrominance; also called S-VHS
Type C (1-inch)	Analog composite video studio quality / bandwidth format using 1-inch tape
U-Matic	NTSC video signal on a 3/4-inch magnetic tape
U-Matic SP	"Superior Performance"

D1 was standardized around a "common data rate" so that manufacturers could build digital tape recorders that could handle both the 525 scan line NTSC standard and the 625 scan line PAL standard. That common data rate is 13.5 megapixels per second. If you were to assume that each pixel contained eight bits of resolution for each of the red, green, and blue primary colors, that would be 324 megabits of data per second (unless some data compression technique was employed).

2.3.4 Computer Animation

Computers have not traditionally been able to replay a sequence of images fast enough to produce moving images without noticeable discontinuities of motion, but this is rapidly changing. Many data formats now exist to store and playback moving images, including synchronized sound. A partial list of such data formats follows. The ability to playback the images with totally continuous-appearing motion is often hardware dependent.

DATA FORMATS FOR COMPUTER ANIMATION AND SOUND

Format	Description
ANBM	Animated Bitmap chunk data (See IIF in appendix)
ANIM	Animation editor and file format OXXI Inc., Long Beach, CA
FLI	Flic Files (See appendix)
GRASP	GRAphical System for Presentation (See appendix)
MooV	Apple QuickTime movie (See appendix)
movie.BYU	Animation package and file format Brigham Young University, Provo, UT
MPEG	Motion Pictures Expert Group (See appendix)
QuickTime	Apple animation format (See appendix)
SFIL	Sound file on Apple Macintosh
SLD	SLiDe presentations AutoCAD
Tango	Algorithm animation system
VFF.movie	Visualization File Format for movies SunVision, Sun Microsystems

2.3.5 Commonalties and Issues Related to Moving Pictures

All of the technologies just discussed display a series of images, one after another, to create motion pictures. They all use images based on raster data. It would be nice if a common frame rate and aspect ratio could be agreed upon to make the interchange of data between systems easier, but a single standard is not likely any time soon.

The required frame rate for moving pictures to appear smooth (without flicker) is determined by both the display mechanism and the amount of room light present during viewing. Cinema motion pictures can get by with 24 unique frames per second (with each frame being flashed twice on the screen) because the images are displayed in a dark room at high resolution. When moving images are displayed in a well lit room at lower resolutions, the human eye needs more frames per second to perceive a similar-quality motion picture. Therefore, more than likely, we will have a multitude of frame rates to deal with in the future.

The issue of frame rate becomes less important when images are displayed under digital computer control (and not with a mechanical film projector). Most computers can process a variety of frame rates under software control. The major issue of diverse frame rates is the conversion from one frame rate to another. If you have one moving picture at 25 frames per second, and you want to convert it to another format that requires 30 frames per second, then you have a problem. You need to add 5 frames a second. (This happens when you convert PAL to NTSC). One method of solving this problem is to select frame rates that are even multiples of each other. For example, 30 and 60, or 24, 48, and 72. If such a set of multiple frame rates can be standardized, then data conversions will become much simpler. We discuss this problem further in Chapter 12.

Standardizing on an aspect ratio is important as well, but again, computers are flexible and can process several aspect ratios at once—under software control. The most important issue related to aspect ratio is resolution (i.e., the number of pixels per unit distance). If the resolutions are different in the horizontal and vertical directions, then the picture elements are not square. This causes difficulties in converting data between formats. A more thorough discussion of this is can also be found in Chapter 12.

In conclusion, we have listed more than 40 different data formats for representing moving pictures. Most of these technologies are converging on digital data representations. Hopefully the digital data representations will converge among themselves to simplify the use of the data and conversion between the data formats.

2.4 MODELING THE REAL WORLD

The imaging technologies we have just discussed provide a picture of something. But what if the something you want to see exists only in your mind or is hidden from your normal sight? Some things are too small to see, like molecules. Other things are hidden from normal view, like a person's heart. Still other things are only visions in your mind. Before the advent of computers, physical, touchable models of such things were often built for the purpose of visualizing them. Designing new things was typically done by the building of a prototype— a first of a kind, physical object—that could be analyzed and studied. Physical models constructed of cardboard, clay, plastic, metal, and many other materials are time-consuming to build and difficult to modify once built. Due to the problems of size, physical models are often built to scale, such as a scale model of a new building by an architect. Scale models of a building are good for visualizing the external appearance of its structure, but it is difficult to visualize the building's interior spaces. An alternative approach to visualizing such things would be nice.

One alternative approach to visualization that does not require physically constructed models is a mathematical approach. The ability to describe an object mathematically has existed to varying degrees for a long time. Geometrical line drawings have been used to describe objects for most of man's existence. Euclid gave us Euclidean geometry around 300 BC, but it took the creation of computers to make three-dimensional mathematical models of physical objects realistically possible. These models are not "graphical data" in the sense of pictures or images—they are mathematical representations of space. We can create images from these mathematical models through a variety of techniques. Creating an image from a mathematical model of space is called *rendering*. It is common to store data that represents *both* a model and rendered images of that model. We have already discussed images; we need to discuss the storage of mathematical models of space.

There are many ways to mathematically model the real world. This makes the development of a single data format difficult. In addition, different applications store different types of application-specific data. Engineering design systems store material characteristics, while mapping systems store boundary divisions. Consequently, many different data formats exist to store this type of data.

It is common for applications to store a mathematical model along with related application data about that model mixed together in a single data format. This is regrettable, since it makes the model data difficult to extract for use in other applications. One thesis of this book is that model data can and should be stored disjointly from application-specific data. Disjoint does not mean unrelated; links can exist between the model data and the application data, but the model can be extracted from the data set easily while ignoring the application-specific data. This is discussed in the data types and data organization chapters.

Figure 2.2 shows *some* of the applications that use the modeling capabilities of digital computers. It is not a complete list of applications nor is it a unique division of the sometimes overlapping fields. A complete list would be quite long.

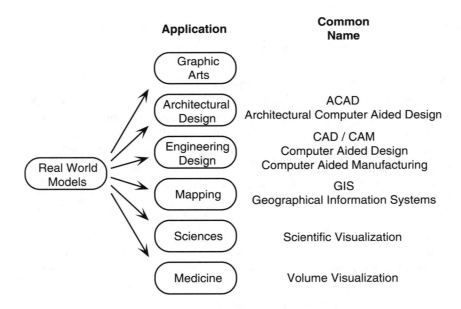

Figure 2.2   Application domains for real-world models

2.4.1 Graphic Arts, Architectural Design, and Engineering Design

There are some generic modeling software packages on the market that can create 2D and 3D models, but most of the more successful software systems are specialized to meet the functionality needed by specific applications. Each system has its own proprietary data format that makes sharing data between systems difficult. Two data formats, DXF and IGES, were designed specifically to interchange data between systems. Most modeling software systems support one or both of these data formats.

MODELING SYSTEM DATA INTERCHANGE FORMATS

Format	Description
DXF	Drawing Interchange File (See appendix)
IGES	Initial Graphics Exchange Standard (See appendix)
STEP	Evolving ISO product data interchange standard

Some professionals might take issue with grouping graphics arts, architectural design, and engineering design into a single category. They do indeed require different types of data. Engineers require very accurate data to facilitate the manufacturing of designed artifacts, often within tolerances of 0.001 inch or less. The typical goal of Graphic Arts professionals is producing quality printed images from 2D and 3D models. The accuracy of these models is often not important—only the quality of the rendered images produced from the model. Architectural models are somewhere in between. They need certain levels of accuracy to create working drawings, but not with the tolerances required by engineers. Architects require high-quality images of their designed spaces. In any event, DXF has become the predominant data format for exchanging 3D modeling data between diverse systems.

The success and widespread use of certain software modeling systems have made their data formats popular. Other software systems will often accept these popular data formats. The following is a partial list of such data formats.

MODELING SYSTEM OUTPUT DATA FORMATS

Format	Description
AMF	ASCII Model File
3DGF	MacroMind
Illustrator 3.0	Adobe
ISIF	Intergraph Standard Interchange Format Intergraph Corporation, Huntsville, AL, 35894-0001 Tel. (800) 826-3515 An ASCII formatted text file for 2D and 3D vector data

MODELING SYSTEM OUTPUT DATA FORMATS *(Continued)*

Format	Description
Mac 3D	Challenger Software
MiniCad 3D	Graphsoft, Ellicott City, MD
.obj	WaveFront
PHIGS A.F.	Programmer's Hierarchical Interactive Graphics System Archive File
RIB	RenderMan Interface Byte-stream (See appendix)
RPL	Octree Corporation 7337 Bollinger Road, Cupertino, CA 95014 Tel. (408) 257-9013 A Forth- and PostScript-like language for the description of 3D objects
SAS	SAS Institute, Cary, NC Mainframe format like DXF under Unix
Sculpt3D	Byte by Byte
Super 3D	Silicon Beach
SwivelMan 3D	(Sometimes referred to as 3D Pro)
TWGES	Computervision, Framingham, MA VersaCAD
VFF.geometry	Visualization File Format for 3D geometry SunVision
WS (Workspace)	Cubicomp

2.4.2 Mapping

Some data formats that support map production contain two-dimensional surface data while other data formats support three-dimensional elevation data as well. The important issue (buzz word) for mapping data is *topology*. Topology data captures the spatial relationship between features (e.g., roads, oil wells, or water meters) in a data set. This information is not always a part of other data formats. Of the following list of mapping data formats, the ARC/INFO data formats are the de facto standards due to their prominence in the industry.

2.4.3 Sciences

The broad range of scientific endeavors is reflected in the large and diverse set of data formats found in the scientific community. The data formats included in the list below were created to share and exchange data between scientific researchers. The list of data formats is abbreviated from [Treinish91]. The data in these files is often related to two-dimensional and three-dimensional spaces and is more often than not visualized in a graphical form. Refer to Section 2.5 on viewing abstract data for more discussion related to scientific data formats.

FORMATS FOR GEOGRAPHIC AND TOPOGRAPHIC DATA

Format	Full Name
ARC/INFO	ARC is a vector-based data format that stores locational data. INFO is a relational database management system. They are tightly linked to provide a Geographic Information System (GIS) ESRI—Environmental Systems Research, Inc. 380 New York Street, Redlands, CA 92373, Tel. (714) 793-2853
DLG	Digital Line Graphs 2D United States Geological Survey (USGS) map data including base categories of transportation, hydrography, contours, and public land survey boundaries
DEM	Digital Elevation Model 3D USGS map data to model and display terrain
Digest	Digital Geographic Information Working Group Geographic information data exchange on magnetic tape between participating NATO countries
GIRAS	Geographic Information Retrieval and Analysis USGS land use/land cover maps including political units, hydrologic units, census and county boundaries, etc.
GBF/DIME	Geographic Base Files/Dual Independent Map Encoding 2D line segments and census geographic statistical codes for most metropolitan areas (used in 1980 census). United States Census Bureau
MapBase	Map Base Digital street map—each linear feature represents political, census and zip code boundaries. ETAK
TIGER/Line	Topologically Integrated Geographic Encoding and Referencing 2D data to support census surveys and programs (used first in the 1990 census). United States Census Bureau
VPF	Vector Product Format US Defense Mapping Agency (DMA, Reston VA), with other military mapping agencies in UK, Canada, and Austria. Generic model for geographic databases

FORMATS FOR EXCHANGE OF SCIENTIFIC DATA

Format	Description
BUFR	Binary Universal Form for Representation Standard interchange format for meteorology and oceanography data in Europe ECMWF
FITS	Flexible Image Transport Service (See appendix)
GF3	General Format 3 Intergovernmental Oceanographic Commission (IOC) For the transport of data for oceanographic and atmospheric sciences applications; developed in the UK

**FORMATS FOR EXCHANGE OF
SCIENTIFIC DATA** *(Continued)*

Format	Description
GRIB	GRIdded Binary form For the storage and exchange of weather data National Weather Service (USA)
HDS	Hierarchical Data System For the storage of scientific data in VAX/VMS environments Starlink Project, Rutherford Appleton Laboratory
QUBE	Hypercube File and PSD (Planetary Data Systems) Label Extensions Standard interchange for data in planetary astronomy
SBF	Solar Energy Research Institute (SER) Broadband Format A tape archive data format to support solar physics and meteorological applications
SFF	Standard File Format or Standard Format File A unified interchange format for computer data (a flat file organization for collections of rows and columns of data) European Space Agency
SFDU	Standard Format Data Unit A proposed international standard interchange mechanism for any data on any media CCSDS
VIFF	Visualization and Image File Format Used by the KHOROS visualization software system KHOROS, Room 110, Department of EECE, University of New Mexico, Albuquerque, NM 87131

2.4.4 Medicine

Volume data from devices such as CATs (Computed Axial Tomography), PETs (Positron-emission Tomography), and MRIs (Magnetic Resonance Imaging) are becoming more important in medicine. In most cases volume data can be conceptualized as a series of 2D slices of raster data concatenated together to form a "volume." There are currently many volume data formats, but none has currently emerged as a de facto standard. The DICOM standard listed previously might fill this void in the future. A few volume data formats are listed below. Many of the scientific data formats listed in Section 2.5 support volume data as well.

SOME FORMATS FOR VOLUME DATA INTERCHANGE

Format	Description
AVS.dat	Application Visualization System volume data format This is a restricted type of AVS.fld data format (See appendix)
VFF.volume	Visualization File Format for voxels SunVision

2.5 VISUALIZING ABSTRACT DATA

Some data are not normally considered graphical data, and yet they are used to generate images. Data from a spreadsheet are a good example. The data in the spreadsheet are not "graphical data"—they are, for example, the sales figures for March or the inventory of a warehouse. Yet pictures are routinely created from such data. Can any data set be converted into an image? Probably! All that is required is a "model" that explains how to map the latent image data into a two-dimensional or three-dimensional space. The important issue is the definition of the model and a method to implement the model (i.e., an algorithm).

All data are, in some sense, "graphical" data. That is, it is possible to generate a graphical image that captures some set of relationships in the data set. For example, a histogram can be created to show the number of times each individual word in a text file is used. This is an extreme example, but it is not too far off the mark. It is quite common to use graphical techniques to visualize abstract data that has no inherent graphical properties. What should the structure of such data be? The data structures must support not only the graphical visualization of the data, but also its other common uses—such as analysis and manipulation tasks.

The most common form for business data is a two-dimensional grid, such as a spreadsheet or a relational data base. The data stored in these structures can be easily converted to graphical form using appropriate mapping from data to graphics. The casual observer can see that the mappings to graphics are not unique. Most spreadsheet applications can take a two-dimensional set of values and create line charts, bar charts, pie charts, and a variety of other charts. The number of data formats that organize data into two-dimensional grids is too numerous to mention here. As we just said—given that more and more data is being visualized in a graphical form—many data formats can be viewed as supporting graphical data. If we took that view of data formats, this book would need to cover most data formats known to man. The number of such formats is probably growing nearly as fast as the human population. We graciously decline the task of surveying all known data formats.

Is it possible to define a set of data structures, besides the two-dimensional grid, that will support a wide range of data in a broad range of applications? Some data formats have been developed that attempt to do this. One major driving force behind their development has been the increasing use of supercomputers by scientists. Supercomputers can quickly generate enormous amounts of data. It is difficult to analyze such data without visual techniques. To avoid having to reinvent the wheel every time a new data set needs to be visualized, researchers have been developing "generic visualization tools" to visualize a broad range of scientific data. There has been some success in these efforts, but there is still much work that needs to be done. The term *scientific visualization*, which was coined in 1987, is often used to describe research in this area.

The following data formats have been created to facilitate data visualization for scientific applications. They typically support a range of data types and organizations—not just a single type or organization.

FORMATS FOR SCIENTIFIC VISUALIZATION DATA

Format	Description
CDF	Common Data Format Standard data format for space and earth science systems; allows for data structured as multidimensional blocks National Space Science Data Center (NSSDC) NASA Goddard Space Flight Center, Greenbelt, Maryland 20771 Tel. (301) 286-6695 (See netCDF)
Flux	Data format used in the apE visualization system (See appendix)
HDF	Hierarchical Data Format (See appendix)
netCDF	Network Common Data Format (See appendix)
PDBLib	A tool for managing and accessing data from many applications on different systems Lawrence Livermore National Laboratory
Plot3D	Supports a number of CFD (Computational Fluid Dynamics) visualization and analysis applications NASA Ames Research Center

One of the important issues addressed by several of the data formats above is the need for a hierarchical structure instead of a "flat" structure. A hierarchical structure allows complex data types to be constructed from a set of predefined data types. The importance of hierarchical data structures is often debated. What are the other important issues? What kinds of data types should these formats support? These are still open questions yet to be answered fully.

2.6 SYNTHETICALLY GROWN WORLDS

Given the computational power of modern computers, it is possible to create pictures (and data that can be converted into pictures) through procedural or algorithmic means. Some professionals use the term *artificial life* to describe research in this area of graphics. Some examples include fractals, L-systems, and behavioral animation. Data formats are needed to store the data related to these types of generated images. No common data formats currently exist. As these types of data become more important in applications, some common data format will be needed.

2.7 SUMMARY

Many once diverse industries are converging in the use of computers as their primary technology for creating and reproducing pictures. Some people are very excited about this convergence while others are fearful and apprehensive. This convergence offers the possibility of creating completely new markets and enhancing our standard of living. It also foreshadows the death of older technologies, which means the loss of jobs, income, and entire industries. We offer no predictions for the future other than that the convergence is already upon us. It will be interesting to watch the convergence unfold in the coming years.

3

STANDARDIZATION

CONTENTS

3.1 INDUSTRY STANDARDS VERSUS INFORMATION STANDARDS

In the past, individual industries, with their application-specific technologies, have created their own industry standards (which are often given stamps of approval from official standards organizations). Standardization based around specific industries is a logical organization when each industry has disjoint technologies. But as the history chapter points out, industries that were once unrelated in technology are now converging to similar digital technologies. Standardization along industrial divisions is still proceeding, and the result is an over abundance of similar but different graphical data standards. This is an unfortunate situation. If we can produce a small set of standards that satisfy the broad range of industries associated with the production and interchange of graphical data, then the economies of scale that the standardization produces will benefit everyone.

3.2 AN INTRODUCTION TO STANDARDIZATION

Standards are important to everyone. They provide a commonality on which we base much of our lives and our economies. Where would we be without a standard frequency for electrical current or a standard side of the road on which to drive? Everyone recognizes the need and the value of standards, but how we get those standards is often obscure, and what they should standardize is often hotly debated. Even the very definition of standards is sometimes disagreed upon.

As a minimum definition, a standard is something that a lot of people use. A more stringent definition requires a standard to have an approval from an official governing body. These two definitions characterize the two major approaches for creating standards. One approach is through large marketplace acceptance which produces *de facto* standards. Another approach is through formal Standards Organizations, such as the International Standards Organization (ISO) and the American National Standards Institute (ANSI). The following discussion is broken down along these lines and contains:

- How "official" standards are created and the graphical data formats that have come out of these organizations
- How de facto standards are created and the graphical data formats that are widely accepted as de facto standards
- A comparison of official and de facto standards
- Suggestions on how we can improve the standardization process in the future

Before we begin the details of this discussion you should understand that the creation of standards is not solely an issue of technology. If it were, then establishing a standard would be a relatively painless process. No, standard making is a political, economic, and technological activity. The best technology does not always become the standard technology because political and economics concerns weigh heavily into the process. For example, new standards are often required to be backward compatible so that people will not lose the investment they have in their current systems. Backward compatibility also provides a relatively smooth transition from existing products (based on an old standard), to new products (based on a new standard).

3.3   OFFICIAL STANDARDS

Our goal is to discuss the standardization of graphical data formats.[*] We would hope that everyone already understands how standards come into existence, but we are afraid that some do not. Therefore, the following discussion includes an overview of the standardization process. This is a slight diversion from the main focus of this book, but few sources contain this information due to the fact that it spans traditional industry boundaries. We hope that this information can encourage the transformation of the standardization process from being industry based into being information based.

There are many organizations in the world today whose purpose is the creation of standards. A partial list of such organizations is contained in Sections 3.3.1 through 3.3.3. We then discuss the process used to create standards by four of the major standards-making bodies: ISO, IEC, ITU, and ANSI.

---

[*] For a good overview of information standardization in general refer to [Cargill89] and [Arnold90].

3.3.1 Major Standards Organizations

The International Electrotechnical Commission (IEC) develops international standards relating to electromechanical systems, while the International Organization for Standardization (ISO) develops international standards for all other areas. ISO is a completely voluntary organization that was established in 1946. IEC was founded in 1906 and is also a completely voluntary organization. Both organizations are an association of members, one from each country desiring to be involved in the standards process. Each member has one vote when ballots are taken to approve a standard, and each member is expected to contribute resources and personnel to standards projects. ISO and IEC have a well-defined set of procedures by which standards are developed. In fact, they do not develop standards at all; they simply standardize the process of making standards and provide the structure needed to make a level playing field for all interested parties.

ISO and IEC are divided into Technical Committees (TCs), each on a different subject or application. ISO has 163 TCs (as of 1992), ranging in scope from Textiles (TC38) to iron ores (TC102) to the analysis of gases (TC158). IEC has 61 TCs. Each TC is typically divided into Subcommittees (SCs) consisting of Participating Members (P-Members) who have voting rights and Observer Members (O-Members) who cannot vote. Each SC is often divided into Working Groups (WGs). Each specific project is assigned to a different WG. Each WG develops a document specification that meets the approved goals of its project. This document is then voted on by the P-Members of the SC—one vote per member. WGs are further divided into Rapporteur Groups (RGs) that progress a specific project between the committee meetings (i.e., they do the actual work).

The International Telecommunications Union (ITU) is a treaty organization under the United Nations. It is organized into committees, but it functions much differently than the ISO and IEC. Until a recent reorganization, two of its committees have been involved with graphical data—the International Telegraph and Telephone Consultative Committee (CCITT) and the International Radio Consultative Committee (CCIR). This division of committees was based on the data transmission medium—CCITT dealt with data transmitted through wires while the CCIR dealt with data broadcast through the air. The CCITT was organized into various study groups (SGs) that are divided into working parties (WPs).

The CCITT approved standards (which they call Recommendations) by meeting once every four years at Plenary Assemblies. The result of the 1988 Plenary Assembly was the publication of its proceedings, which are referred to as the "blue books."[*] The blue books contain 60 separately bound volumes and over 20,000 pages. Each volume contains a set of recommendations. Each recommendation is designated by a single letter followed by a period and a number. For example, T.4 is the recommendation for Fax group 3, and X.25 is a recommendation for data communication networks.

The CCIR had a similar structure as the CCITT. It made recommendations at Plenary Assemblies that met once every four years. Their sequence was two years between the CCITT schedule; that is, they met in 1982, 1986, 1990, etc. The reorganization of the

---

[*] Each year's plenary results are designated by a different color. The proceedings of 1984 were the "red books."

ITU has placed all standards activities that were in either the CCITT or CCIR into the ITU-TS, or International Telecommunications Union Telecommunications Standards bureau.

The American National Standards Institute (ANSI)[*] is organized into committees much like the ISO. The committees are divided by industry and technology. In nearly all cases, each committee functions as a Technical Advisory Group (TAG), responsible for focusing US input into the international standardization process. There is generally a direct correlation between ANSI TAGs and ISO TCs. They usually work closely together but sometimes they are completely disjoint. The exact procedures for creating standards within ANSI are different than the ISO and IEC procedures, but there are similar stages of voting and draft revision by interested parties. Currently most of ANSI's computer graphics standards are being developed through participation of TAG members on relevant ISO SCs.

Each of these organizations—ISO, IEC, ITU, and ANSI—interact with each other when their interests coincide. There appears to be an increasing amount of cooperation and interaction between them in recent years, predominantly due to the convergence of information-related technology.

In years past it was common for individual countries to adopt international standards only after making modifications to them. These variances between standards often made them incompatible. In recent years increasing cooperation between national and international standards-making bodies is eliminating some of these incompatibilities. Hopefully this trend will continue.

3.3.2 International and Regional Standards Groups

One of the major problems associated with graphical data standards is the broad range of applications and technologies that use graphical data. The number of standards-making bodies, trade organizations, user groups, consortia, companies, and individuals involved is overwhelming. To create a comprehensive list of those involved is nearly impossible. The following is an attempt to list many of the players, recognizing that some of them have been left out. If you like acronyms, you will love this list.

INTERNATIONAL STANDARDS GROUPS

ISO   International Organization for Standardization

IEC   International Electrotechnical Commission

ITU   International Telecommunications Union

CCIR   The International Radio Consultative Committee; a subcommittee of the ITU (now part of ITU-TS)

CCITT   The International Telegraph and Telephone Consultative Committee; a subcommittee of the ITU (now part of ITU-TS)

---

[*] ANSI is unique among national standard-making bodies in that it is not affiliated with the US government. Most national standard-making bodies are branches of their respective governments.

INTERNATIONAL STANDARDS GROUPS   *(Continued)*

CIE   Commission Internationale de l'Eclairage (International Commission on Illumination)

IAU   International Astronomical Union

IFIP   International Federation for Information Processing

IPA   International Prepress Association

IPTC   International Press Telecommunications Council

REGIONAL STANDARDS GROUPS

CEN   European Committee for Standardization

CENELEC   European Committee for Electrical Standardization

CEPT   European Conference of Postal and Telecommunications Administrations

ETSI   European Telecommunications Standards Institute

ECMA   European Computer Manufactures Association

There are too many national standards organizations that contribute to international standards activities to list here; most countries of the world have at least one. The following is a list of the voting members of the ISO/IEC JTC1/SC24 subcommittee on computer graphics. An explanation of this committee is given later in this chapter.

NATIONAL BODIES ACTIVE ON JTC1 SC24

ONORM	Osterr. Normalisatie	Austria
ABNT/CB-21		Brazil
		China
CSN	Urad pro normalizaci mereni	Czechoslovakia
DS	Dansk Standardiseringsraad	Denmark
AFNOR		France
DIN	Deutsches Institut fur Normung	Germany
MSZH	Magyar Szabvanyugyi Hivatal	Hungary
JISC	Japanese Industrial Standards Committee	Japan
NNI	Nederlands Normalisatie Institut	Netherlands
		Romania
BSI	British Standards Institution	UK
ANSI	American National Standards Institute	USA

The observer, nonvoting members of the ISO/IEC JTC1/SC24 subcommittee are Australia, Belgium, Bulgaria, Cuba, Finland, Iceland, Italy, Republic of Korea, India, Iran, Philippines, Portugal, Poland, Singapore, Sweden, Turkey, and Yugoslavia.

3.3.3   US Standards Groups

In the United States, there are many organizations interested in the development of standards related to computer graphics and data interchange. Some of these groups operate under the procedures developed by ANSI or create standards that may not be progressed into the international arena. Other groups try to focus industry consensus and use that information to influence existing standards-developing organizations. The groups are separated below into two classes: government bodies, and trade and professional organizations.

US GOVERNMENTAL BODIES INVOLVED WITH STANDARDS

ACATS	Advisory Committee for Advanced Television Systems A committee under the FCC
CALS	Computer-aided Acquisition and Logistics Support A program administered by the DOD
DOD	Department of Defense
FCC	Federal Communications Commission
FIPS	Federal Information Processing Standards A program administered by NIST
NASA	National Aeronautics and Space Administration
NIST	National Institute of Standards and Technology, U.S. Department of Commerce (Formerly known as NBS, the National Bureau of Standards)
NSF	National Science Foundation
NSSDC	National Space Science Data Center, NASA

US TRADE AND PROFESSIONAL ORGANIZATIONS
INTERESTED IN STANDARDS

ACR	American College of Radiologists
ACM	Association for Computer Machinery
AFCEA	Armed Forces Communications and Electronics Association
CBEMA	Computer and Business Equipment Manufacturers Association
EIA	Electronic Industries Association
IEEE	The Institute of Electrical and Electronics Engineers, Inc.
IMA	Interactive Multimedia Association
MMCF	Multi-Media Communications Forum
NAB	National Association of Broadcasters

NAPM   National Association of Photographic Manufacturers

NCGA   National Computer Graphics Association

NEMA   National Electrical Manufacturers Association

NPES   Association for Supplies of Printing and Publishing Technologies

OMF   Open Media Framework

PPA   Professional Photographers of America

SIST   Society for Imaging Science and Technology

SMPTE   Society of Motion Picture and Television Engineers

TIA   Telecommunications Industry Association; associated with the EIA

Each of these organizations is involved with the standardization of graphical data. They
each approach the problem from different industry perspectives and needs. Figure 3.1 gives
an overview of this diversity. The chart covers raster data only. We emphasize that this is
not a complete list.

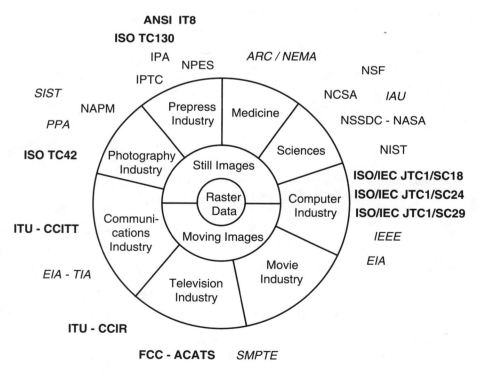

Figure 3.1   Groups involved in creating standards for raster data

The sheer number of organizations involved with graphical data makes the creation of standards a confusing process. Add to this each organization's subcommittees and technical working groups, and one can get very confused. It would require volumes of books to explain all of these organizations, their specific involvement in the process, and their rules and procedures. Refer to each individual organization for details.[*]

Before we leave the topic of who creates standards, it is important to note the role that government agencies play in the process. In the US, two groups stand out: the Federal Information Processing Standards (FIPS) program under the Computer Systems Laboratory (CSL) of the US Department of Commerce and the Computer-aided Acquisition and Logistics Support (CALS) group under the Pentagon. Both groups adopt standards for federal government use and in some cases they promote the development of new standards. Currently GKS, CGM, and PHIGS are recognized FIPS standards. CALS has defined a subset of IGES (designated MIL-D-28000A) for military use that is supported by various vendors. Though sometimes standards are created and then not used, the adoption of standards by large government programs such as FIPS or CALS increases the chance that a standard will be widely used.

3.3.4 How a Standard Is Created

The following gives an overview of the ISO process for developing a standard. This does not include every detail, but it gives you an idea of the process.

New Work Item Proposal (NP)   5–8 months
A new project proposal (base document) is submitted to one of the member bodies of the ISO or directly to an ISO subcommittee. A 3-month ballot is taken. At least five of the voting members must commit to work on the project or it dies from lack of support.

Working Drafts (WD)   6–18 months
One or more working drafts are created by a Working Group assigned to the project. Rapporteur Groups are assigned to figure out the details of each working draft, and then the Working Group comes to a consensus on which working draft best meets the design criteria of the project.

Committee Draft (CD)   12–14 months
The essentially complete working draft is registered as a CD, either by a resolution at a subcommittee meeting or through a 3-month letter ballot. Then a 3 month approval and comment ballot is taken from all national bodies that are members of the subcommittee. All comments must be addressed by an editing committee, a subcommittee meeting, or a Working Group meeting. If substantial changes are made, it must go through the CD process again.

Draft International Standard (DIS)   9–12 months
When the CD is technically stable and the document is in an ISO/IEC-acceptable format, a 6-month ballot is taken by votes from both the member bodies of the subcommittee and the member bodies of the Technical Committee.

---

[*] A useful resource for tracking down some of these organizations can be found in most libraries: *The Encyclopedia of Associations*, 26th edition, Deborah M. Burek, ed., Gale Research Inc., 1992.

International Standard (IS)   3–6 months

Any comments from the DIS ballot must be addressed. If substantial changes are made, another DIS vote is taken that is restricted to 3 months. A final vote is then taken by all ISO/IEC councils. On approval, ISO publishes the final document as an International Standard.

Total time required: 35–58 months

In addition to creating standards, there is a formal process for changing existing ISO and IEC standards by Addenda. This process follows much the same path as the process just described. The stages include a Working Draft (WD), a Proposed Draft Addendum (PDAD), a Draft Addendum (DAD), and an Addendum (AD). Up to three Addenda can be added to a standard before it must be totally revised and republished. ISO also has rules that require all standards to be reviewed once every five years. During a review, a standard can be reaffirmed (renewed without change), revised, or withdrawn.

Each standard developed within ISO is assigned a unique number as its identification code. For example, ISO 8632 is the Computer Graphics Metafile standard. The date of publication (or last review) is often appended to the number, such as ISO 8632-1992.

3.4 EXISTING GRAPHICS-RELATED STANDARDS PROJECTS

3.4.1   ISO and JTC1 Graphics Standards

Figure 3.2 summarizes the major activities related to graphical data that are being pursued by ISO/IEC and ITU. ANSI committees are also included in the chart because they are among the dominant players in ISO and IEC processes, and information about ANSI's structure was available to the authors. Many other national standards-making bodies are also involved in the process. Two of the dominant players besides ANSI are Germany's DIN and Japan's JISC.

ISO and IEC realized that a common joint approach to the development of information technology would be beneficial to both organizations. In the fall of 1987 they formed their first joint committee and called it Joint Technical Committee 1 (JTC1) on Information Technology. JTC1 is organized into many different subcommittees. Officially Subcommittee 24 (SC24) is responsible for computer graphics and image processing projects. However, the term *computer graphics* means different things to different people and in actuality there are many projects related to graphical data outside of SC24. These projects are shown in Figure 3.2. To help make things clear, they are also listed in a slightly different format in the following table. The fact that each organization has a different name for the same project adds considerable confusion when discussing the projects.

Because of the need for coordination between many of these groups, ISO/IEC formed the Joint Technical Advisory Group 2 (JTAG2) in 1990. Its job is to coordinate the development of imaging standards (e.g., raster-based data) between international committees. It is made up of representatives from the various TCs that are developing imaging standards. They held their first meeting in December 1991, and they plan to meet twice each year in the future. In addition to the groups (and standards) mentioned above, there are also representatives from photography, cinematography, video, and ITU-TS (the earlier CCITT and CCIR).

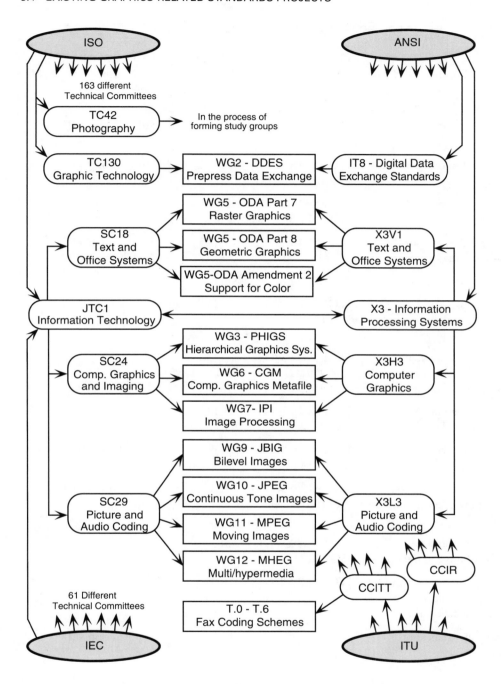

Figure 3.2 Formal international standards groups working on graphics-related standards

RELATED PROJECTS IN ISO/IEC, ANSI, AND CCITT

Project Description	ISO/IEC group ID Number	ANSI group ID Number	CCITT group ID Number
Information Technology (IT)	JTC1	X3	
Open Document Architecture (ODA)	JTC1 SC18	X3V1	Study Group VIII
ODA specification for raster graphics	JTC1 SC18 WG7 ISO 8613-7	X3V1.3	Study Group VIII T.411
ODA specification for 2D geometric data	JTC1 SC18 WG8 ISO 8613-8	X3V1.3	Study Group VIII T.411
ODA amendment 2 for the support of color in documents	JTC1 SC18	X3V1.3	Study Group VIII T.411/Amd 2:1992
Computer Graphics SC	JTC1 SC24	X3H3	
Image Processing and Interchange (IPI)—Image Interchange Facility (IIF)	JTC1 SC24 WG1 ISO 12087-3	X3H3.8	
Programmer's Hierarchical Interactive Graphics System (PHIGS)—Parts 2 and 3	JTC1 SC24 WG3 ISO 9592-2 ISO 9592-3	X3H3.1 X3.144-1988	
Computer Graphics Metafile (2D geometric data)	JTC1 SC24 WG5 ISO 8632:1992	X3H3.3 X3.122	
JBIG—lossless compression and encoding of raster data	JTC1 SC29 WG9 ISO 11544	X3L3	Study Group VIII T.82
JPEG—lossy compression and encoding of continuous tone raster data	JTC1 SC29 WG 10 ISO 10918	X3L3	Study Group VIII T.81
MPEG—compression and encoding of moving images	JTC1 SC29 WG11 ISO 11172	X3L3	
MHEG—compression and encoding for multimedia and hypermedia data	JTC1 SC29 WG12	X3L3	
Fax group 1 specification			Study Group VIII T.2
Fax group 2 specification			Study Group VIII T.3
Fax group 3 specification			Study Group VIII T.4
Fax group 4 specification			Study Group VIII T.6

RELATED PROJECTS IN ISO/IEC, ANSI, AND CCITT *(Continued)*

Project Description	ISO/IEC group ID Number	ANSI group ID Number	CCITT group ID Number
ISO TC130—Graphics Technology (prepress)	ISO TC130	IT8	
Digital Data Exchange Standards (DDES)	ISO TC130 WG2	IT8	
DDES—color picture data on magnetic tape	ISO TC130 WG2 ISO 10755	IT8.1	
DDES—line art data on magnetic tape	ISO TC130 WG2 ISO 10756	IT8.2	
DDES—2D geometric data on magnetic tape	ISO TC130 WG2 ISO 10757	IT8.3	
DDES—on-line transfer of color proofs	ISO TC130 WG2 ISO 10758	IT8.4	
DDES—monochrome image data on magnetic tape	ISO TC130 WG2 ISO 10759	IT8.5	

In a similar way, ANSI has boards that coordinate the activities of different standards-making bodies within the United States. Eight such boards exist, but we are only interested in the two related to graphical data: the Image Technology Standards Board (ITSB) and the Information Systems Standards Board (ISSB). Each board is made up of companies and organizations that are interested and involved in creating related standards.

The Image Technology Standards Board (ITSB) is made up of the members shown in the table below (as of July 1992):

MEMBERS OF THE ANSI IMAGE TECHNOLOGY STANDARDS BOARD

AIIM—Association of Information and Image Management

DOD—Department of Defense

Dupont

IBM—International Business Machines

IEEE—The Institute of Electrical and Electronics Engineers, Inc.

IPA—International Prepress Association

Kodak

NAPM—National Association of Photographic Manufacturers

NPES—Association for Suppliers of Printing and Publishing Technologies

Polaroid

**MEMBERS OF THE ANSI IMAGE TECHNOLOGY
STANDARDS BOARD** *(Continued)*

PPA—Professional Photographers of America

SIST—Society for Imaging Science and Technology

SMPTE—Society of Motion Picture and Television Engineers

Xerox

3.4.2 Other Graphic Standards

Some other significant graphical data standards are listed below. They are listed separately because of their origins.

ADDITIONAL SIGNIFICANT GRAPHICS STANDARDS

Data Format	Origin
D1	Sony certified as CCIR Recommendation 601 a digital encoding standard for broadcast TV data; its parameters allow for NTSC, PAL, and SECAM signals
IGES	NIST—National Institute of Standards and Technology (USA); also accepted as a standard (Y14.26) by ANSI Initial Graphics Exchange Specification
NTSC	FCC—the Federal Communications Commission (USA) broadcast TV signal in North America, South America, Japan
PLPS	ANSI and CSA—Canadian Standards Association a standard for teletext and videotex services. It forms the basis of the Prodigy information service communications format

Several standards are currently under development that will possibly have a major impact on graphical data formats. These include:

GRAPHICS-RELATED STANDARDS CURRENTLY UNDER DEVELOPMENT

Data Format	Origin
ACTS	FCC—the Federal Communications Commission (USA) A committee to determine the USA standard for broadcast HDTV. The decision is expected in early 1994
SPDL	ISO 10180 A combination of ANSI, ISO, and ECMA with major input from Adobe Systems Incorporated and Xerox. Standard Page Description Language. This is basically a more structured form of PostScript. It defines a "wrapper" around normal PostScript Level 2 data

GRAPHICS-RELATED STANDARDS CURRENTLY UNDER DEVELOPMENT *(Continued)*

Data Format	Origin
STEP	ISO 10303 NIST—National Institute of Standards and Technology (USA) Standard for the Exchange of Product Model Data. An effort to produce a suite of standards related to engineering design and manufacturing—some of which will undoubtedly contain graphical data. Its projected initial release is in 1994. It is being developed under ISO, in TC184/WG4

3.5 DE FACTO STANDARDS

If a company or an individual creates a product that is widely accepted by users, then the sheer number of users makes it a de facto standard. Other vendors must support this standard to stay competitive in the marketplace. De facto standards have become common in the computer industry. Some examples include PostScript, TIFF, and DXF. Some professionals argue that marketplace forces are the most natural process for establishing standards. Only "Good" products will be widely purchased thus establishing standards for the entire industry—the survival of the fittest. Some professionals go so far as to say that official standards-making bodies are not needed, and in fact, they are excess baggage to the industry.

The fact of the matter is, sometimes the marketplace chooses the best technological systems and sometimes it does not. For example, the marketplace chose VHS cassette tapes over the better technological choice of Beta cassette tapes. The VHS format won the market because it was released to many companies as an open standard, while the Beta format was initially kept proprietary. The marketplace established the de facto standard due to political and economic issues and not due to superior technology.

An economic theory proposed by Brian Arthur[*] and specifically applied to standards by Eileen McGinnis[†] seems to explain nicely how the marketplace often chooses standards. The theory is called *economic positive feedback* and it works as follows. Given a new technology, many vendors will begin to introduce systems that exploit that technology. Each system begins initially to capture an approximately equal share of the market. At some point one system will gain a slight advantage over the other systems and bring in excess capital funds. These funds are then used to enhance the system, giving it an advantage over the other systems. This feedback loop continues and the system gains prominence as further enhancements generate further sales and income. If the system that obtained the initial advantage was the best technological system, then all is well. But if the system was not the best, or if the extra capital funds are not used for system enhancement but rather for marketing and promotions, then the marketplace has been diverted down an inferior path. As we stated earlier, the establishment of standards depends on economic and political issues as well as technological issues.

---

[*] *Scientific American,* February 1990, pages 92–99.

[†] "Desperately Seeking Standards," SIGGRAPH '91 Panel Proceedings, 1991.

Some de facto standards in the marketplace today are listed below. The list is not complete—many users have their own particular set of de facto standards that are relevant to their particular applications.

**POPULAR DE FACTO STANDARDS FOR COMPUTER
GRAPHICS FILE FORMATS**

Data Format	Origin
ARC/INFO	Environmental Systems Research Institute (ESRI) de facto standard for mapping systems (GIS)
BMP, ICO, WMF	Microsoft Corporation de facto standard for PCs using Microsoft's GUI—Windows
DXF	AutoDesk Inc. de facto standard for 3D geometry data (especially CAD)
GIF	CompuServe Incorporated de facto standard for raster images shared on bulletin boards
IFF	Electronic Arts de facto standard for Amiga computer users
PhotoCD	Kodak A new format for the storage of high-resolution photographic still images; it may or may not become a de facto standard
PICT	Apple Computer, Inc. de facto standard for Macintosh users
PostScript	Adobe Systems Incorporated de facto standard page description language
TIFF	A consortium headed by Aldus de facto standard for raster images captured by scanners and used in desktop publishing
X pixmap, X bitmap, X window dump	Project Athena, Massachusetts Institute of Technology de facto standard for workstations using the X Window System

3.6 A COMPARISON OF OFFICIAL AND DE FACTO STANDARDS

Which is the better approach to standards development—official standards-making bodies or market forces? There are strong opinions and arguments on both sides. The following chart summarizes many of these arguments. Realize that the truthfulness of the arguments on both sides are sometimes debated.

One interesting aspect of the arguments is that both sides claim that the opposite approach inhibits innovation. Who is right? The truth of the matter is, a standard captures the state of a technology and freezes it in time. Often the technology is represented by

COMPARISON OF DE FACTO AND OFFICIAL STANDARDS

De Facto Standards	Official Standards
Advantages	**Disadvantages**
• Can be created quickly	• Require too much time to develop (ranging from 3 to more than 5 years)
• Minimal compromises in the design keep the design focused (because it is designed by a small set of individuals)	• Compromises in the design weaken the technical merit of the standard (because it is designed by committee)
• Standards can be specific enough to meet application-specific needs	• Conflict of interests between members of the committee from competing companies weakens the standard
	• Standards are too complex
	• Standards are too generic to satisfy a broad spectrum of users
Disadvantages	**Advantages**
• Reviewed by a small number of experts	• Reviewed by a large, diverse set of experts to guarantee completeness
• Due to a lack of review, ambiguities and therefore differences in resulting implementations can occur	• Final result is an unambiguous, precisely defined standard
• Prejudiced ownership of the standard can give one company unfair advantages in the marketplace	• Control of the standard is outside the realm of a single company
• Ownership by one company prohibits other companies from enhancing or amending the standard	• The standard can be enhanced and amended in an orderly fashion to benefit all concerned
• More than one standard often exists	• A single standard exists
Claims	**Claims**
• Inhibits innovation	• Inhibits innovation

common (accepted) practice, which is older. In some cases, such as the JPEG and JBIG standards, the technology is actually developed in the standards committee. However, in either case, the technology that the standard is based on typically continues to advance while the standard remains the same. Whether this is good or bad depends primarily on what the standard standardizes.

According to Bob Scheiffler who was the principle designer of the X Windows system, a "system should provide hooks, rather than religion."[*] Said in another way, a standard should provide for the mechanisms needed to accomplish a given task, but not dictate the policies on how those tasks are actually accomplished. If standards are implemented in this way, they do not inhibit innovation. In fact, they provide a stable base from which innovation can flourish. If the base was not there, then it would require constant reinvention,

---

[*] Quoted from an article by Gary Wayne, "Graphics Output, Open or Standard?" *Computer Graphics World,* August 1991.

redevelopment, and refinement and any innovation beyond the basic functions would be inhibited.

On the other hand, if a standard emphasizes not only mechanism, but also the exact policy on how those mechanisms are to be used, then the standard can indeed inhibit innovation. A standard such as this basically says, "This is how it's done. Forget about doing it any other way." We want to avoid these kinds of standards. Therefore, the major issue is to distinguish between what should be standardized and what should not be, not who does the standardizing.

In the future, standards should come from those best suited to provide them, with equal participation from both standards organizations and the marketplace. The breakdown might fall along the following lines.

De facto standards will be created when:

- The investment required to create the standard and validate it by providing an implementation is not overwhelming for a single company. These are typically software-related standards. If more than one standard exists, the initial investment can still be regained.

Official standards should be created when:

- The financial investments are too high for a single company to bear (e.g., the development of a High Definition Video Standard (HDTV)). These are typically hardware related standards.

- There is little financial incentive to standardize, but the need for standardization exists.

3.7 DIRECTIONS FOR THE FUTURE

We can improve the process of making graphical data standards by implementing the following:

- Use modern telecommunications to speed the process of standard specification.

- Use modern telecommunications to open the standards-making process to include more people.

- Reorganize the standards process based on technology rather than on specific industries.

- Learn how to talk to each other across traditional industry boundaries where words do not always have the same meaning.

The cost and time involved in the creation of standards are currently very large. Richard Solomon estimates the cost of standards development at the CCITT, which is just one committee of the ITU, at between one billion and two billion dollars a year.[*] Probably no one knows the combined costs for all standards-making organizations in the world, but a

---

[*] "HDTV: Technologies and Directions," SIGGRAPH '91 Panel Proceedings, 1991.

simple projection suggests an astronomical figure. Adopting standards is big business. We need to streamline the process to reduce the time and expense involved. One such step would be the increased use of modern telecommunications such as conference telephone calls, video teleconferences, and electronic mail. These technologies can speed the dissemination of information and reduce the time needed for voting.

Traditionally only those with large financial resources have been involved with creating standards. The travel costs to committee meetings can be quite large, not to mention the salaries of the members while they are at the meetings. The end result is that committees are made up of people from large companies who can afford the costs or from small companies or consultants who have focussed on the subject matter of the committee. With electronic mail and other telecommunications, more people can be included in the process. This is not to say that a committee of thousands is a good thing—it is not. But standards are sometimes finalized before the people that will be affected by them have seen (or heard) of the standard. Mass communications can allow for a broader range of review during the review cycles.

The standards process needs to be based on technology rather than on specific industries. This has already happened to some extent with the JTC1 committees of ISO. They are intended to be generic committees that produce standards for all industries that use information. The problem is that these generic committees do not always meet the needs of particular applications. The creation of generic standards that meet a broad range of application needs will require knowledge and understanding that spans industry boundaries, mixed with lots of listening and patience. The problems are not trivial, but they are solvable.

Standardization groups seem to have an affinity toward creating their own unique jargon. This adds confusion to the standardization process and often makes the standards difficult to understand by implementors. This is unfortunate but it is often necessary. When a diverse group of experts come together to agree on a standard, they must communicate clearly and unambiguously about the issues. It is not uncommon for two experts to use the same term to describe different things—especially in a dynamic and growing technological area. To agree on the exact meanings of a term sometimes requires the creation of a new term that does not carry the baggage of inferred meanings associated with the previously-used term. The definition of terms is always a problem for dynamic technological areas. We sometimes have to accept new definitions for terms to remove ambiguities of meaning among professionals. Agreeing on terms and their definitions is difficult at times; it requires work and compromises.

3.8 CONCLUSION

When playing chess, we can only make one move at a time, but each move must be part of a larger plan or we will lose. We must have vision. We must try to take the small steps of standardization in view of the long-range possibilities. In the design of graphical data standards, many of the choices that we make now will be with us for a long time. Hopefully we will make good choices. In hindsight, consider the positive impact to today's systems if the world had standardized on one frequency for alternating electrical current instead of two (i.e., 50 and 60 Hz).

CONTENTS

4.1 INTRODUCTION

Most data formats are designed to meet well-defined goals. The major design goals form constraints on the type of data the format will support, the types of data encodings that will be used, and the overall data organization of the format. Given that different data formats are designed to meet different goals, it is easy to see how so many different data formats have come into widespread use. Even when format designs start with similar goals, there is typically more than one way to satisfy the goals.

4.2 A SURVEY OF DESIGN GOALS

Before we do an analysis of design goals, let's consider some examples. Examine the following arbitrary list of design goals. Do not let any of the terminology confuse you. All of the terminology will be explained in more detail in the remainder of the book. Simply try to grasp the diversity of goals presented and the constraints they place on the resulting data formats.

4.2.1   CGM Design Goals[*]

The Computer Graphics Metafile (CGM) is a standard developed by ISO/IEC JTC1 SC24 for encoding "picture" data. The following explicitly-stated design goals helped to guide its development.

- *Completeness*   In any area of the Standard, the functionality specified by the Standard should be complete in itself.

- *Conciseness*   Redundant elements or parameters should be avoided.

- *Consistency*   Contradictory elements should be avoided.

- *Extensibility*   The ability to add new elements and generality to the Standard should not be precluded.

- *Fidelity*   The minimal results and characteristics of elements should be well defined.

- *Orthogonality*   The elements of the metafile should be independent of each other, or any dependencies should be structured and well defined.

- *Predictability*   The Standard should be such that the recommended or proper use of standard elements guarantees the results of using a particular element.

- *Standard Practice*   Only those elements that reflect existing practice, that are necessary to support existing practice, or that are necessary to support proposed standards should be standardized.

- *Usefulness*   Functions should be powerful enough to perform useful tasks.

- *Well Structured*   The assumptions that elements make about each other should be minimized. An element should have a well-defined interface and a simply stated unconditional purpose. Multipurpose elements and side effects should be avoided.

4.2.2   JPEG's Design Goals[†]

The Joint Photographic Experts Group (JPEG) on the encoding and compression of continuous-tone raster-based still images, working as ISO/IEC JTC1 SC29 WG10, stated the following design goals for its work.

- *Current*   Develop a standard that is at or near the state of the art with regard to compression ratios and image quality.

- *User Controllable*   The compression encoder should contain parameters that allow applications to choose trade-offs between image quality and compression ratios.

- *General Purpose*   Applicable to practically all continuous-tone digital images; not restricted by image dimension, color spaces, pixel aspect ratios, etc.

---

[*] Computer Graphics—Metafile for the storage and transfer of picture description information, ANSI X3.122-1986, Part 1, page 2.

[†] Wallace, Gregory K., "The JPEG Still Picture Compression Standard," *Communications of the ACM*, April 1991, **34**, 4, 31.

- *Tractable* Tractable computational complexity to make software implementations feasible.

- *Flexible* Provide a suite of encodings that allow for three different data orderings and one lossless compression mode.

4.2.3 MPEG's Design Goals[*]

The Moving Picture Experts Group standard for the digital encoding of video and audio sequences, working as ISO/IEC JTC1 SC29 WG11, defined the following design goals for its work.

- *Real-Time Playback* The data must be compressed into approximately 1.5 Mbits for each second of video playback and still produce an acceptable image quality.

- *Random Access* Any frame in a sequence of video frames should be accessible in approximately 1/2 second.

- *Fast Forward/Reverse Searches* Display a sequence of video frames while skipping over some specified number of frames between each displayed frame.

- *Reverse Playback* Allow the video signal to be played in reverse.

- *Audio-Visual Synchronization* The video signal should be accurately synchronizable to an associated audio source. The video and audio should be able to be resynchronized at periodic times in a video sequence.

- *Robustness to Errors* Catastrophic behavior in the presence of errors should be avoidable.

- *Coding/Decoding Delay* Since image quality and delay can be traded off to a certain extent, the algorithm should perform well in a range of acceptable delays. Delay is to be considered a parameter.

- *Editability* The ability to construct editing units of short duration that are coded only with reference to themselves so that an acceptable level of editability in compressed form is obtainable.

- *Format Flexibility* Support a large set of formats in terms of raster size (width, height) and frame rate.

- *Cost Trade-Offs* The algorithms must be implementable in a small number of integrated circuit chips, given the technology of 1990. The encoding process must be performed in real time.

4.2.4 TIFF's Design Goals[†]

The Tag Image File Format (TIFF) for the storage of continuous-tone raster images was developed by Aldus Corporation with the following design goals.

---

[*] Le Gall, Didier, "MPEG: A Video Compression Standard for Multimedia Applications," *Communications of the ACM*, April 1991, **34**, 4, 50–51.

[†] *Aldus TIFF Developer's Toolkit*, Aldus Corporation, 1990, pp. 5–6.

- *Extendibility*   Accommodate new image types without invalidating older ones, and allow for the inclusion of proprietary and application-specific information.

- *Portability*   Provide a format that is independent of hardware and operating environments.

- *Revisability*   Provide a file structure that allows images to be easily revised "in place," without having to read the entire file into memory.

4.2.5 PostScript Design Goals[*]

PostScript was developed by Adobe Corporation as a page-description language designed originally for desktop publishing. It had the following design goals.

- *Device Independence*   The description of the image or page should not be based on any particular hardware device, and it should be transmittable over any communication channel without loss or misinterpretation of data.

- *Resolution Independence*   The description of the image or page should be independent of any particular device's resolution. The image will be constructed at the appropriate resolution at print time for the device used to do the printing.

4.3 CONFLICTING DESIGN GOALS

The sample design goals listed above are all quite different. They approach the design of each data format from different perspectives, with different functional requirements and with different priorities. Let's see if we can make some sense out of all of these different goals.

For some formats, the major emphasis is on functionality. By functionality we mean the ability to store certain types of data to meet certain accuracy and usage criteria. The functionality emphasis is on whether the format is "complete"; that is, it can store every type of intended data with no ambiguities. Every data format contains some level of emphasis on functionality. Some data formats go beyond basic functionality to include an emphasis on device memory requirements, speed requirements, device independence, robustness, and extendibility. Let's define these and other related issues:

- *Memory*   The presence or absence of memory is emphasized by some formats. For example, the TIFF format has a design goal of modifying a raster image in place, without reading the entire image into memory. This is important for systems that have limited memory.

- *Accuracy*   The accuracy of a data set is sometimes critical and sometimes negotiable. In some cases the accuracy of data can be decreased to save memory. In other cases, such as engineering design or medical images, very strict tolerances on the data must be maintained. Accuracy can refer to geometry (coordinate) information or intensity/color information.

---

[*] Adobe Systems Inc., *PostScript Language Reference Manual, Second Edition*, 1990, pp. 13–14.

- *Speed*   The ability to display a data set at a certain speed is critical to certain applications. For example, video sequences must display 24 to 30 data sets per second or a viewer will observe noncontinuous motion. Directly related to speed is the data capacity of a communications channel. To satisfy speed requirements, data sets must often be compressed into sizes the communication channel can accommodate.

- *Device Independence*   The emphasis of some formats is a data format that is not tied to any particular hardware device. Data in such a format can be transported from one device to another much more easily than device-dependent formats.

- *Robustness*   Some formats are concerned with the accuracy of the transportation medium for the data. For example, a television signal broadcast is susceptible to corruption due to interference. A robust format contains several layers of defense against corruption so that if part of the data is corrupted, the errors do not cause a total failure of the data set to produce an image.

- *Extendibility*   Extendibility is defined in two different ways. The simplest definition states that a data format can be modified to allow for new types of data and features in the future. In this simple form an old implementation that reads the format will not be able to read the new format. A more stringent definition states that a format can be extended without invalidating previously implemented readers of the format. Older readers will not be able to take advantage of the new data, but they will know how to skip over any data they do not recognize.

- *Compatibility*[*]   Compatibility with prior versions of a data set definition is often needed for access and migration considerations. However, compatibility carries a penalty in performance and increased size of both code and data. For standards based on "existing practice" there is also the possibility of simplifying migration from existing (nonstandard) commercial products, in order to increase the acceptance of the standard.

- *Modularity*   A modular data set definition is designed to allow some of its functionality to be upgraded or enhanced without having to propagate changes through all parts of the data set. This makes it easier to track advances in technology.

- *Plugability*   Plugability is related to modularity. It permits the user of an implementation of a data set reader or writer to replace a module with private (non-shipped) code. As with modularity, it does require that the data set reader or writer be implementable as a framework that can contain the modules, and this implies some additional overhead.

- *Openness*   The whole idea of a standard is that it be implemented by multiple providers and employed by a large number of users. This is not likely to happen if there are major license fees that must be paid before a standard can be implemented. A truly open standard also has an open process for its development and enhancement.

---

[*] Compatibility with other relevant standards is required by ISO procedures. So is compatibility with existing (prior) versions of a standard that is being revised.

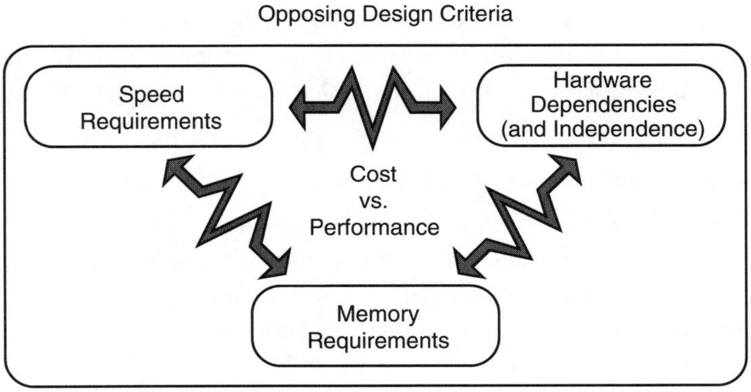

Opposing Design Criteria

Figure 4.1 Opposing design criteria and trade-offs

- *Scalability* The design should be applicable to both small and large data sets and small and large (potentially parallel) hardware systems. Thus, access time should increase no more than linearly with increasing data set size. Access time should decrease with the addition of processors, preferably in a linear relationship. There should be no arbitrary limits on data set size.

All of these are good goals, and it would be extremely nice if they could all be satisfied by a single data format. Regrettably, they cannot be. For example, given current technology, it is not possible to have both real-time access to data and have device-independent data. Real-time access requires special and specific hardware devices. Therefore, the result of this set of conflicting goals is a large set of diverse data formats to meet different needs and to satisfy different levels of cost-to-performance ratios.

Viewed from a hardware perspective, the ideal situation would allow instantaneous access to a data set with limited memory requirements and no device dependence. But these are opposing design criteria. Typically device-independent formats require more access time as compared to device-specific formats. Device-independent formats also typically require conversion to a device's native data format, and this conversion can require additional memory. In addition, the speed of data processing often depends on the amount of memory available for the process. See Figure 4.1.

The goals of extendibility and robustness are very similar.[*] They both require that a data reader recognize and skip unknown data and resume reading data at some subsequent location in the data stream when it recognizes valid data. The techniques for accomplishing this are discussed in Chapter 7.

4.4 PRINCIPLES OF GOOD DESIGN

A data format is, in a sense, a language definition used to store and communicate information. There are many similarities between general-purpose languages and data formats. Both require a syntax description that state their rules of grammar. The grammar rules allow the

---

[*] They are different in that robustness would distinguish an unknown data item from an erroneous data item using some type of error-detection or error-correction scheme.

data, or language, to be interpreted correctly. Both a data set and a language must be "read" to extract the information it contains. The information should be unambiguous, useful, and complete. The following list is a heavily-edited copy of principles for good language design from [MacLennan83].

- *Consistency*   Be consistent in the methods of defining data, organizing data, encoding data, and compressing data.

- *Defense in Depth*   Have a series of defenses so that if an error isn't caught through one mechanism, it will probably be caught by another. As a minimum, erroneous data values should not cause the entire data set to be unreadable. (Reliability)

- *Efficiency*   Use computer resources wisely (e.g., memory, CPU time, and communication channels).

- *Extendibility*   Allow for change. The one thing a designer can be sure of is that the data format will need to change in the future to meet the needs of changing technology.

- *Information Preservation*   The data should allow for the representation of all information the user might know.

- *Localized Cost*   Users should pay only for what they use; avoid distributed costs. Certain data types should be allowed by the data format but not required.

- *Modularity*   Large data sets should be organized into smaller units that enhance its organization, access, and usefulness to more than a single application when possible.

- *Orthogonality*   Independent data should be defined by independent structures.

- *Portability*   Avoid features or facilities that are dependent on a particular machine or a small class of machines, when possible.

- *Reusability*   Data should be usable again and again without loss of accuracy, and it should be usable by applications other than its primary intended application.

- *Simplicity*   A data set should be as simple as possible.

- *Structure*   The static structure of the data should correspond in a simple way to the dynamic use of the data.

- *Zero-One-Infinity*   The only reasonable numbers are zero, one, and infinity. Avoid arbitrary limits on the size and number of data values allowed in a data set.

The following chart relates these principles to the major aspects that define a data set. The bullets indicate the areas most affected by each principle. Some of the principles are important only to one aspect, while others are important to them all. We will discuss these principles, where they apply, throughout the remainder of this book.

APPLICABILITY OF VARIOUS DESIGN PRINCIPLES TO ASPECTS OF DATA STREAMS

Design Principles	Data Type	Data Organization	Data Encoding	Data Compression
Consistency	•	•	•	•
Defense in Depth		•	•	•
Efficiency	•	•	•	•
Extendibility		•	•	•
Information Preservation	•			•
Localized Cost		•	•	
Modularity		•		
Orthogonality	•	•		
Portability	•	•	•	•
Reusability	•	•	•	•
Simplicity	•	•	•	•
Structure		•		
Zero-One-Infinity	•		•	

As in the previous discussion on goals, all of these principles of good design cannot be typically met at the same time—they are not independent principles. A designer might have to fudge on the Simplicity principle to satisfy the principle of Information Preservation, or fudge on the Portability principle to satisfy the Efficiency principle. Even though the principles sometimes oppose each other, they should not be totally ignored unless there is a compelling reason to do so.

4.5   A MINIMAL GROUP OF DATA FORMATS

We end this chapter with an example. A hammer is designed to drive a nail into a solid object. But, have you ever noticed how many different kinds of hammers exist? There are framing hammers, tack hammers, roofing hammers, claw hammers, heavy hammers, and lightweight hammers. They each have the same purpose, but they meet different user needs. Graphical data sets are not much different. They are designed to meet specific user needs, and their structure varies to meet those needs.

We ask the question, "Does this mean we will always have literally hundreds of different graphical data formats (and the confusion they bring)?" We hope not. As the industry matures, it will hopefully synthesize the best-designed formats within certain categories. What are the issues that will define these categories? Our list includes 13 design goals. A set of ten data format categories based on these design goals is shown in Figure 4.2. The following discussion explains the diagram.

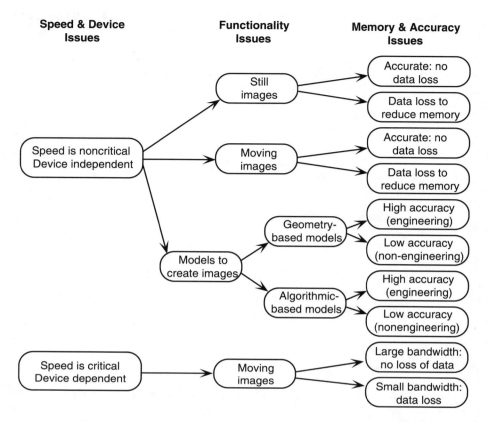

Figure 4.2   Functional grouping of a minimal set of graphic data streams

All data formats, if designed correctly, should be robust and extendible. Therefore these two design issues should not distinguish separate data format categories. Speed and device independence are natural opposites. If speed is the critical design issue you typically need device-dependent data; if speed is not critical you might as well have a device-independent data format. These arguments form our first category division, as shown in Figure 4.2.

Functionality is key to any data format—you must be able to store application-dependent data that meet a user's needs. Application data should be separated from graphical data. In doing so the graphical data becomes distinctive within a data set and becomes more accessible to a wider set of users. We will discuss the separation of graphical and nongraphical data further in the data organization chapter. Based on functionality, our categories are divided into still images and moving images, both being based on raster data and model data. The speed category includes only moving images because this is the only category that is typically time critical.

Design issues involving memory and data precision are often interrelated. In some cases data precision can be lowered to reduce memory requirements. In other applications no loss of data can be tolerated. The trade-off between memory and precision forms a category division for each of the functional divisions. The result is ten distinct design categories. Given the flexibility of computers, it is possible that some of these could be combined into single formats.

Is it possible that only ten data formats could support all graphical data for all applications? Let the debate begin.

5

DATA TYPES

CONTENTS

This chapter categorizes and describes the data types found in graphical data streams. It includes tables that list which data streams include which data types. We suggest that you skip most of the tables on the first reading. This way you will get a good overview of the topic without getting bogged down in the details. The tables are good reference materials that can be examined as the need arises.

We have read, analyzed, and searched well over 5,000 pages of documents to create the information in this chapter. Our intent was to tabulate this information as accurately as possible. However, given the volume of information it is likely we have missed some things. In addition, the data streams are constantly being upgraded and enhanced. Please use the information in this chapter only as a starting point in your study of graphical data streams. Refer to the appendices for further details.

5.1 TYPES OF DATA

In Chapter 2, we defined a *digital image* as a set of discrete samples uniformly spaced over an area of interest, where each sample represents the intensity or color of light. For the remainder of this book the term *picture* and the term *image* refer to a digital image (unless noted otherwise). The data used to create pictures can be divided into three broad categories, which we define below. The names for these categories are not standard from one industry to another or from one application to another. Therefore, defining what the terms mean is very important.

5.1.1   Graphical Data

A *raster data set* contains a set of discrete samples from within some space. If the space is only two dimensional, it is a 2D raster data set. A 2D raster data set that contains color samples over a uniform spacing or grid is called a *digital image*. If the space is three dimensional, it is a 3D raster data set. Many applications refer to 3D raster data as *volumetric data*. Raster data sets from N-dimensional spaces are common in scientific fields (where N is any number greater than 3). Such data sets are sometimes referred to as *vector fields*.

A *geometric data set* contains a mathematical or geometrical representation of objects in 2-, 3- or N-dimensional space. For example, a line segment can be represented by specifying its two geometric endpoints in Cartesian coordinates. An image can be created from this data by generating all of the points that lie between the two endpoints. Generating the points that create an image is called *rasterization* or *rendering*. The terms *object data*, *vector data*, and *model data* are also used to describe this type of data.

A *latent image data set* contains data that is not initially intended for graphical output but from which pictures are produced. For example, numbers in a computer spreadsheet can be used to create graphical charts, and scientific visualization techniques can create images from data collected in scientific experiments. In both of these examples, the initial data is not inherently "graphical," but useful images can be created from the data. The word *latent* means lying hidden and undeveloped. In the broad sense, *all* data formats are latent image data sets. All they lack is an algorithm that maps the data to an image.

Figure 5.1 diagrams the relationships between these categories of graphical data and a resulting image. Minimal processing is required to produce images from raw 2D raster data.[*] The other data types require various amounts of processing to produce an image. The amount of processing is dependent on the quality of the image desired, on the data structures used to organize the data, and on the complexity of the data. Some of the more widely used processes for generating images have names such as *rasterization, rendering, volume rendering*, and *surface rendering*.

Raster data and geometric data are the two most common types of data used to create pictures. However, they come from different sources, and they are used in different ways. Raster data sets are typically *captured*. Some examples include light rays coming through a camera lens, a 2D photocopy scanner, and a 3D CAT scan used for medical imaging. On the other hand, geometric data sets are typically *created*. They can be formed by computer algorithms designed to generate geometric shapes or by computer users who enter geometric data under the control of a drawing tool. In some cases a user can choose which type of data to work with. In other cases the data type is predefined by the application.

Few data sets contain only graphical data. The next sections categorize the other types of data typically found within a graphical data stream.

5.1.2   Meta Data

Most data streams include within themselves information that describes them. This "data about the data" is often referred to as *meta data*. It is used, among other things, to interpret

---

[*] By "raw raster data" we mean the sampled data values that make up the raster data set, not its compressed or encoded form.

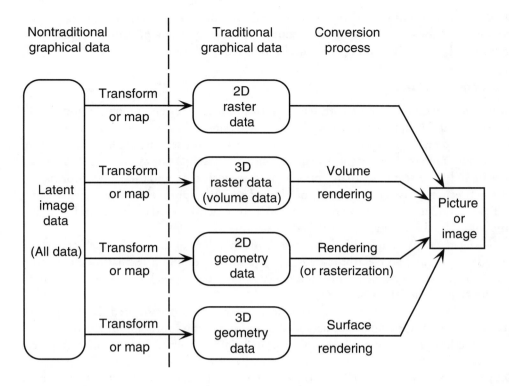

Figure 5.1 Mapping various types of data to produce a picture

the data set correctly, include historical documentation about the data, and attach attributes to data elements. We categorize meta data into three distinct types: interpretation data, attribute data, and documentation data.

Interpretation data allows a data set to be processed and interpreted correctly. Some data formats are so predefined that they contain very little interpretation information. For example, the NTSC signal that supplies data to your TV has minimal amounts of interpretation data; everything is already predefined. On the other hand, some data formats allow for a variety of data types and organizations. Parameter values within such a data stream specify which variation of the data format a particular data set contains. A totally "self-documenting" data stream often contains a significant amount of interpretation data. (Refer to Chapter 7 for a detailed discussion of self-documenting data streams.)

Attribute data specifies the appearance of objects within an image. It is most often found in geometry data streams where the presentation of each geometric primitive requires color, style, and other such information. For example, a line segment typically requires a width (or "weight"), a style (solid, dashed, dotted, etc.), and a color if it is to be displayed correctly within an image. Most geometric primitives have a standard set of attributes associated with them, such as the font, size, style, and orientation attributes associated with text primitives and the "fill" and border attributes associated with polygons.

Documentation data includes information such as a data set's creation date, its author, copyright restrictions, its title, and/or its source. It is not typically presented visually with the graphical data, but it could be if an application required it.

5.1.3   Nongraphical Data

In addition to the graphical data within a data stream, there is often nongraphical data. We divide "other data" into two distinct types: associated data and unassociated data.

Associated data is the nongraphical information associated with the graphical elements of a data set. This type of data is typically very application specific. For example, TIGER Census files include line segments that represent voting precinct boundaries. The information about the precinct must be associated, or "linked to," the appropriate line segments that delimit the boundary. Other examples include the product design data found in IGES files and the sound tracks included in MPEG data streams.

Unassociated data is nongraphical data that is independent of the graphical elements in a data set. For example, an electronic mail message might contain a textual message and a picture of the message's author. The data is related on a conceptual level, but there are no explicit links or relationships between them.

There are an unlimited number of possible associated and unassociated data types. For that reason we do not include such data in the summary tables throughout the rest of this chapter. One important issue related to associated data is how to link it to its graphical counterparts. Another important issue related to unassociated data is how to separate or extract graphical data when it is "buried" within a complex data stream. We discuss some of these issues in Chapter 7 as they relate to data organization schemes.

5.1.4   Data Stream Identification

One important piece of data within a data stream should be an identification tag. This allows software systems to automatically identify a data stream and send it to appropriate software (or hardware) interpreters. Not all files contain an identification tag, but ideally they should. Some data formats rely on a file name suffix for their identification. This is a poor scheme because file names can be accidentally changed by a user. Two identification tags are typically needed: a signature and a version number.

Signature

Sometimes known as a magic number, this tag is a unique set of bytes that distinguishes a signature data stream from all other possible data streams, both graphical or nongraphical. It is typically the first few bytes within a data stream.

IDENTIFYING "MAGIC NUMBERS" FOR SOME DATA FORMATS

Data Format	Name of Data Used in Implementation	Comments
CGM	Begin Metafile	Value depends on type of encoding
GIF	GIF87a or GIF89a	In ASCII, includes version number
HDF	0E031301	First four bytes of file (shown in hex)
PostScript	%!	In ASCII
TIFF	MM or II	In ASCII, MM for Motorola-based "most significant byte first," II for Intel-based "least significant byte first"

Version Number

It is often useful to declare to which version of a data format specification a data stream adheres. Most data formats evolve over time to include new features and, in some cases, discontinue the support of old features. In these cases a version number simplifies the task of interpreting a data stream correctly.

VERSION INFORMATION FOR SOME DATA FORMATS

Data Format	Name of Data Used in Implementation	Comments
CGM	Metafile Version	Value depends on type of encoding
PostScript	PS-Adobe-$V.R$	In ASCII, where V is the version number and R is the release number
	%%LanguageLevel	Indicates that the data set contains operators defined in a certain level of implementation (currently level 1 and 2 are defined)
	%%Version	Specifies the version and revision number of a data set or a resource used by the data set

5.2 RASTER DATA

5.2.1 Raster Sample Data

A raster data set is a group of discrete samples of a space. Two major criteria determine the kinds of data that must be stored for a raster data set: the location of the samples and the size of the samples. Samples can be taken at uniform intervals or at nonuniform intervals, and samples can measure equal or nonequal portions of space. These options are shown as a chart in Figure 5.2 along with the common technical names for each type of raster data. It is beyond our purposes here to explain each type of sampled data in detail. Refer to [Foley90] for a detailed description.

Grid spacing

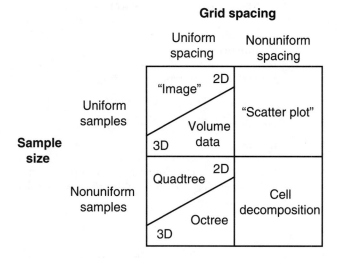

Figure 5.2   Characteristics and names for common raster data types

Three examples of raster data spaces are shown in Figure 5.3. The two most commonly used uniform grids are the hexagonal and rectangular grids. The different types of uniform grids are important in the processing of raster data sets, but they have little impact on the requirements of a data format. Hopefully the example of nonuniform raster data in the figure helps you visualize the added complexity of such data.

Given the four types of raster data shown in Figure 5.2, there are four corresponding storage requirements. For all cases we must store the sample values. Using a uniform grid allows us to infer a sample's location by its ordering within a data set. For nonuniform grids, we must also store the location of each sample. And for samples of different sizes, we must also store the sample size. These storage requirements are summarized in Figure 5.4. The typical nonscientific user will only have dealings with *uniform grid, uniform size* type raster data. Nonuniform samples occur most often in scientific studies, as for example, scatter charts represented in either Cartesian or polar coordinate systems.

A uniform grid, uniform size raster data set is typically stored as a 2-dimensional, 3-dimensional, or *N*-dimensional array. The dimensionality of the array is determined by the dimensionality of the sample space. If each sample requires multiple values the array

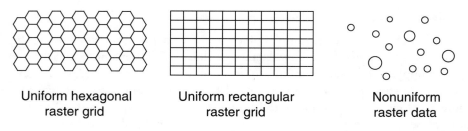

| Uniform hexagonal raster grid | Uniform rectangular raster grid | Nonuniform raster data |

Figure 5.3   Different spatial arrangements of raster data

Sample size		Grid spacing: Uniform spacing	Grid spacing: Nonuniform spacing
	Uniform samples	**Store** Sample value	**Store** Sample value Sample location
	Nonuniform samples	**Store** Sample value Sample size (typically as a tree structure)	**Store** Sample value Sample location Sample size

Figure 5.4 Storage requirements for different types of raster data

dimension is incremented by one. For example, samples in a 3-dimensional space using five distinct values per sample would typically be stored using a 4-dimensional array (i.e., 3 + 1).

A comparison of raster data formats is included in Chapter 11. Note however that, of the 34 raster data formats we survey in this book, only the AVS Field format explicitly addresses nonuniform raster data sets.

Before we leave our discussion on raster data, we should emphasize again the major characteristic of raster data. Raster data is discrete; it is noncontinuous; it is digital data. There is no information in between the samples. Algorithms can infer in between values, but these are only guesses. This can be illustrated by examining a 2D raster image. As the number of samples per unit distance grows, an image becomes less grainy and more pleasing to the human eye. This is because the "gaps" between data values become too small to see. If you "zoom in" on a raster data set, the image becomes "blockish" because the data set contains no information about the areas between the samples. Figure 5.5 illustrates a typical display of a zoomed in section of a raster image.

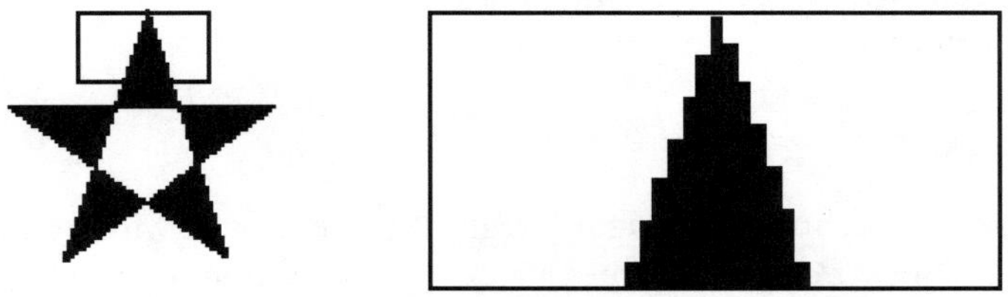

Original Raster Image

Enlarged Rectangular Region
Notice the blockiness

Figure 5.5 The effect of enlarging a raster image, with no smoothing

Some common terms related to raster data are defined below.

Raster Device   Any device that produces a picture by displaying an array of samples. Some examples include, television, dot-matrix printers, ink-jet printers, and laser printers.

Pixel   A single sample of a 2D raster data set. Pixel is an abbreviation for *picture element*. Another equivalent name to pixel is *pel*.

Voxel   A single sample of a 3D raster data set. Voxel is an abbreviation for *volume element*.

Bit Map   Memory used to store 2D raster images. A bit map usually refers to a set of pixels that are each represented by a single bit (binary digit) of memory. This restricts each pixel to only one of two color values. In loose usage, the term *bitmap* refers to any set of pixels, regardless of the number of bits used to represent each pixel.

Pixel Map   Memory used to store 2D raster images. This term is typically used when more than one bit of memory is used to store each pixel value.

Raster Interpretation Data

Most raster data formats allow for a variety of raster data sets. The following information about the data set allows the samples within the data set to be interpreted correctly. Each type of data is explained in more detail below.

DATA WHICH IS INCLUDED TO HELP INTERPRET A RASTER DATA SET

Size	Number of samples in each direction
Sample representation	Number of values per sample, number of bits per value
Sample interpretation	What the values mean
Sample ordering	In what order the samples are organized
Device information	The resolution (and sometimes the calibration) of the device that took the original samples
Positional information	Where to place the array of samples within a larger context
Miscellaneous information	(See below)
Data compression	Type of compression used to reduce storage requirements

Size of Raster Data Set

Most 2-dimensional raster data sets define a rectangular region specified by a width and a height. Likewise a 3-dimensional raster data set defines a rectangular volume specified by a width, height, and depth. In the case of the CGM standard, a skewed rectangular region (i.e., a parallelogram) is allowed. The dimensions are specified in pixel units (i.e., samples).

HOW RASTER DATA SET SIZE IS SPECIFIED

Data Format	Name of Data Used in Implementation	Comments
BMP	Width of bit map	In pixels
	Height of bit map	In pixels
CGM	nx, ny	Parameters of a "cell array." A cell array is a parallelogram delimited by three points "nx" is the number of divisions along the "top" of the parallelogram "ny" is the number of divisions along the "side" of the parallelogram
GEM/IMG	Scan-line width	In pixels
	Number of scan-lines	Each scan line is one pixel high
GIF	Width of Image	In pixels
	Height of Image	In pixels
ICO	Image width	In pixels (only 16, 32, or 64 allowed)
	Image height	In pixels (only 16, 32, or 64 allowed)
OS/2	Width of bit map	In pixels
	Height of bit map	In pixels
PCX	Horizontal resolution	
	Vertical resolution	
PostScript	Width	In pixels
	Height	In pixels
RLE	xsize	Number of pixels in the horizontal direction
	ysize	Number of pixels in the vertical direction
TIFF	ImageWidth	Number of pixels in the horizontal direction
	ImageLength	Number of pixels in the vertical direction
TARGA	Image width	In pixels
	Image height	In pixels

Sample Representation

Each sample is represented by a single value or an ordered N-tuple set of values. Each value is usually expressed to some specified precision. The samples typically represent color or light intensity values. The number of values and their precision determine the range of colors that can be represented for each pixel displayed. If some of the terminology below is unfamiliar, refer to the chapter on color for a full discussion of the terms.

HOW DATA FOR EACH SAMPLE IS DESCRIBED (COMPONENTS AND SIZE)

Data Format	Name of Data Used in Implementation	Comments
BMP	Number of planes	Must be 1
	Bits per pixel	# of bits per pixel value (1, 4, 8, or 24)
CGM	Local color specifier	# of bits per cell color (1, 2, 4, 8, 16, 24, or 32)
PostScript	bits/comp	# of bits used to represent one component value (1, 2, 4, 8, or 12)
	ncomp	# of distinct component values used to represent one pixel (1, 3, or 4)
TIFF	BitsPerSample	# of bits used to represent each pixel sample
	SamplesPerPixel	1 sample for monochrome images, 3 for RGB

Sample Interpretation

The value of a pixel can mean different things to different systems. For example, on a Macintosh computer in one-bit/pixel mode, a 1 represents black and a 0 represents white. On a DOS-based computer (or a Macintosh in grayscale or color mode) a 1 represents white while a 0 represents black—the exact opposite representation. To correctly use each sample value for a given system you must know its correct interpretation. Sample interpretation is directly related to color representation. Refer to the chapter on color for a thorough discussion.

HOW THE MEANING OF SAMPLE (COLOR) INFORMATION IS SPECIFIED

Data Format	Name of Data Used in Implementation	Comments
BMP	Color palette size	Number of RGB values in color table
	# of important colors	Number of color tables entries that are critical to the display of the data; all other entries can be ignored if the color table is too full
	Color table	Array of RGB values each value is 8 bits
CGM:1992	Local color precision	Indicates either an indexed color table or direct color (RGB)
	Color spaces	RGB, CIELAB, CIELUV, CMYK, and RGB related are supported
	Color calibration	For primaries, white point, and transformation of color spaces by matrices and lookup tables
PostScript	setcolorspace	Pixel values represent colors in one of the following color spaces: CIEBasedABC, CIEBasedA, RGB, CMYK, Gray, Separation, or Indexed (table lookup)

HOW THE MEANING OF SAMPLE (COLOR) INFORMATION IS SPECIFIED   *(Continued)*

Data Format	Name of Data Used in Implementation	Comments
TIFF	Photometric Interpretation	Is bit 0 black or white, color palette or full color?
	GrayResponseUnit	Accuracy of values in the GrayResponseCurve
	GrayResponseCurve	Grayscale lookup table, which specifies dot densities
	ColorMap	A color palette for color table lookups
	ColorResponseCurves	"Gamma" correction lookup tables for RGB values

Sample Ordering

While most raster data sets represent a rectangular region, not all data sets store the sample values in the same order. The most commonly used pixel order stores each row from left to right and stores the rows from top to bottom. Some formats predefine the ordering and allow no options. Other formats allow a variety of orderings. Refer to Chapter 7 for details.

SPECIFICATION OF SAMPLE ORDERING OF RASTER DATA

Data Format	Name of Data Used in Implementation	Comments
BMP	Byte offset to data	From the beginning of the file
PostScript	multi	A true/false value; if true then each component of a pixel value is retrieved from a different source (in parallel); if false then all components of a pixel are retrieved from the same source.
TIFF	RowsPerStrip	The image is typically divided into horizontal strips
	StripByteCounts	# of bytes in each strip, after compression
	StripOffsets	Where each image strip data is located in the file
	PlanarConfiguration	Single or multiple image planes

Device Information

This data describes aspects of the original device used to create the raster data set. If the data is moved to another device, then it can be displayed in a closer approximation to the original. Two examples of adjusting data to match the characteristics of a device include adjusting the size of individual pixels and adjusting the space between adjacent pixels. The *resolution* of a raster device is measured in pixels per unit distance. If the resolution is different in the horizontal and vertical directions, then the pixel spacing is not square. (You can think of pixels as being rectangular, but output devices normally produce round or oval pixels.) If raster data is transferred from one device to another with a different pixel spacing, then the software can compensate to some extent for the differences, but only if the original resolution is stored with the data set.

SPECIFICATION OF INPUT DEVICE (SCANNER) CHARACTERISTICS

Data Format	Name of Data Used in Implementation	Comments
BMP	Horizontal resolution	In pixels per meter
	Vertical resolution	In pixels per meter
PostScript	Matrix	Specifies a general linear transformation matrix that can include translation, rotation, reflection, and shearing
TIFF	ResolutionUnit	Dots per inch or dots per centimeter
	XResolution	Dots per unit in the ImageWidth direction
	YResolution	Dots per unit in the ImageLength direction

Positional Information

An image represented by raster data must be positioned on a computer screen, on the page of paper, or in relationship to other data. Some data formats do not include this data, assuming that the position of the image will be specified by other data and software that use the image.

POSITIONING INFORMATION FOR RASTER IMAGES

Data Format	Name of Data Used in Implementation	Comments
PostScript	matrix	Specifies a general linear transformation matrix that can include translation, rotation, reflection, and shearing
CGM	3P	3 (x, y) points define both the size and the position of the cell array
TIFF	XPosition	Offset of left side of image from left side of page
	YPosition	Offset of top of image from top of page

Data Compression Information

Many of the data formats allow the data to be compressed using one or more of the schemes discussed in Chapter 9. Typically a "flag" value denotes whether compression is used and which scheme is used if more than one is allowed.

MISCELLANEOUS INFORMATION FOR INTERPRETING RASTER DATA

Data Format	Name of Data Used in Implementation	Comments
PostScript	%%BoundingBox	Specifies the printable area of a page; all printing is clipped to this bounding rectangle
	%%DocumentData	Either Clean7Bit, Clean8Bit, or Binary; this specifies the range of values to be expected within each byte of the data set
	%%Emulator	Indicates that the data set contains an invocation of the stated emulator
	%%Extensions	Indicates the extensions that must be present in an interpreter if the data set is to be interpreted successfully
	%%Orientation	Either landscape or portrait
	%%Pages	The number of virtual pages that a data set describes
	%%PageOrder	Either ascending, descending, or special
TIFF	NewSubfile Type	Specifies relationships of an image to other images in the same file, e.g., a low-resolution image of a large image

SPECIFYING COMPRESSION TECHNIQUE USED

Data Format	Name of Data Used in Implementation	Comments
BMP	Type of compression	
CGM	(encoding specific)	Includes options for run length encoding and tiling
PostScript	filter	Type of compression used
TIFF	Compression	Type of compression used
	Group3Options	Bit-encoded parameters controlling compression
	Group4Options	Bit-encoded parameters controlling compression

5.2.2 Raster Documentation Data

An image title can be much more than just informative. Suppose the title truly describes the content of an image. If so, then a full text retrieval system can search a list of titles to find images that contain the content of interest to the user in some context.

SPECIFYING RASTER DATA TITLE INFORMATION

Data Format	Name of Data Used in Implementation	Comments
CGM	Begin Metafile	Title not required or standardized
PostScript	%%Title	Title of the data set; useful for printing banner pages on printouts

SPECIFYING RASTER DATA TITLE INFORMATION *(Continued)*

Data Format	Name of Data Used in Implementation	Comments
TIFF	ImageDescription	User comments about image, image subtitle, etc.
	PageNumber	Page # of multiple page documents (e.g., facsimile)

For some applications, information about the author of the raster image data can be vital. Unless an image declares itself to be free of copyright claims, the author can negotiate the copyright terms or identify the owner of the copyright if it is someone other than themselves. The use of copyright-protected material without permission of the owner is illegal in the United States and many other countries.

SPECIFYING RASTER DATA AUTHOR INFORMATION

Data Format	Name of Data Used in Implementation	Comments
CGM	Metafile Description	Any description allowed, not standardized
PostScript	%%Copyright	Copyright information about the data set
	%%Creator	Who created the data set; this is usually the software used to create the data set
	%%For	Indicates the person or company, for whom the data set is being printed
	%%Routing	Provides information about how to route a printed document back to its owner; it may contain a mail address or an office number
TIFF	Artist	Person who created the image
	DocumentName	Document name from which this image was scanned
	PageName	Page name from which this image was scanned

DATE AND TIME INFORMATION SPECIFICATION

Data Format	Name of Data Used in Implementation	Comments
CGM	Metafile Description	Any description allowed, not standardized
PostScript	%%CreationDate	Date and time of data set creation; no format of the data is specified
TIFF	DateTime	Date and time of image creation

Information about the device used to create (scan) an image can help a receiving application program correct the resolution or color balance of an image. The make and model can act as a substitute for detailed calibration information, provided the receiving application recognizes the source device that is specified.

SPECIFYING DEVICE INFORMATION

Data Format	Name of Data Used in Implementation	Comments
CGM	Metafile Description	Any description allowed, not standardized
TIFF	HostComputer	Computer system used to create the original image
	Make	Manufacturer of the scanner, video digitizer, etc.
	Model	Model name/number hardware, if any
	Software	Name and version of software that created the image

5.2.3 Raster Associated Data

Raster data sets rarely contain associated data. As mentioned earlier, raster data is simply a set of samples. How these individual samples relate to each other is not usually known. For example, suppose we have a raster image obtained by scanning a photograph. The photograph contains a car and other background scenery. Now suppose that we ask a software tool to change the color of the car automatically! The software has to distinguish which pixels are associated with the car. This is a very difficult problem in the general case.

Some applications require that the relationships between samples be found. One example is the distinction between bone and flesh in a medical MRI data set. Once we have identified a set of samples as an "object," we can associate other data with that object. When pixels are grouped into related sets, the resulting information is often converted to geometric-type data. For that reason we refer you to the following discussion on geometric-associated data.

5.3 GEOMETRY TYPE DATA

Geometric representations of space differ from raster-based representations in that they are continuous; there are no gaps between sample locations. There are two major approaches to geometric descriptions of space. One approach stores the boundaries of an object. They are naturally referred to as *Boundary Representation (B-reps)* schemes. If all of the boundaries are flat surfaces (i.e., planar) the representation is called *polygonal.* If the boundaries include nonplanar surfaces the representation is called a *curved surface* representation. Another approach defines a set of solid geometric primitives, such as cubes, spheres, cylinders, toruses, etc., and represents complex objects in space as combinations, intersections, and differences of these primitives. This scheme is called Constructive Solid Geometry (CSG). These schemes are shown in Figure 5.6.

CSG descriptions of space are the simplest to store. Typically a tree structure defines how a set of solid primitives are combined into a more complex object. Each node in the tree stores three things: which solid primitive to use, a transformation that positions and orientates that solid in space, and which operation to apply to it and the already created model. Using this scheme, complex objects can be defined with minimal storage requirements. Of the data formats surveyed in this book, only IGES supports CSG data. For this

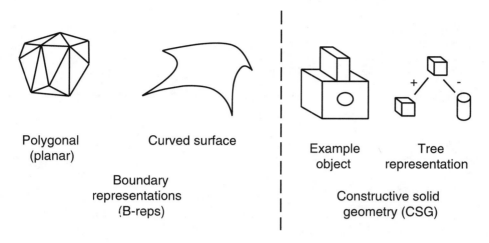

Polygonal   Curved surface
(planar)

                    Boundary
                 representations
                    (B-reps)

                                                     Example   Tree
                                                     object   representation

                                                         Constructive solid
                                                          geometry (CSG)

Figure 5.6   Techniques for describing the geometry of objects

reason we do not discuss CSG data further in this chapter. Refer to the IGES literature for more details.

The most common geometry-based data formats in use today are boundary representation schemes. The remainder of our discussion concentrates on these schemes.

There is a great range of things that can be represented or modeled by geometric data. In addition to physical objects that are designed, analyzed, and manufactured, there are also physical processes, such as weather, galaxy formations, and molecular interactions. Our primary focus in the following discussion is the geometric data itself and not the physical object or process it represents.

5.3.1   Geometry Coordinate Data

Geometric "objects" or "primitives" are typically defined by specifying coordinates (i.e., points) in space. These coordinates define both the shape of the object and its position. The number of coordinates and the meaning of each coordinate varies for each primitive object. Most geometric-based data streams support a minimum set of primitives, including points, line segments, curves, areas, and text. There is great variety in how these objects are specified, as you will see in the tables that follow.

Point

The most basic entity of graphical data is the point. It specifies a position in 2-dimensional or 3-dimensional space. Often, the coordinates associated with a single point are grouped together in a *points table*. It is also possible to store a vector of all the first component values followed by all the second component values, and so on.

FORMATS OF POINT COORDINATE DATA

Data Format	Name of Data Used in Implementation	Comments
CGM	POLY MARKER	Given a list of points, it displays a marker symbol at each point
DXF	Point	(x, y, z) plus an angle specifying the rotation of the X axis from the UCS (User Coordinate System)
	Vertex	(x, y, z) plus possibly five other flag data variables. A vertex is a point along a path defined by a combination of line segments, arcs, and curves
IGES	Point Entity	(x, y, z) plus a pointer to a subfigure used to draw the point
PostScript	moveto	(x, y), set this absolute point as the current point
	rmoveto	(dx, dy), set this relative distance from the current point as the new current point
Windows 3.0 Metafile	MoveTo	(x, y) is set as the current position

Line Segment

A line segment is specified by its two endpoints. Specifying both endpoints for all line segments is wasteful of memory in cases where many of the line segments join at their endpoints. For the sake of efficiency some formats define a *last referenced point*. Using this scheme, line segments are specified by a single point with the other point being inferred as the last referenced point. The use of a last referenced point has some drawbacks. The data stream cannot be easily reorganized because the ordering of line segments cannot be changed. (Changing their order would cause line segments to reference the wrong point as their last referenced point). This is a classic example of the conflicts that arise between design goals. One goal is the efficient use of memory, while another goal is the ability to organize data according to the needs of an output device. It is not always possible to do both at the same time.

Another approach, which works in many cases, draws multiple connected line segments in a single primitive. It used $N + 1$ coordinate values to draw N line segments (N must be greater than or equal to 1). This approach presents problems if a line segment must be inserted, deleted, or moved.

FORMAT FOR COORDINATE DATA FOR LINES

Data Format	Name of Data Used in Implementation	Comments
CGM	POLYLINE	Given a list of points, it draws a line segment between each two successive points in the list
	DISJOINT POLYLINE	Given a list of points, it draws a line segment between the first and second point, between the third and fourth point, etc.
DXF	Line	Draws a line given two points (x1, y1, z1) and (x2, y2, z2)
	Trace	A set of three lines specified by four points, (x, y, z), drawn with a thick width
GEM/Metafile	line	A list of (x, y) coordinates to be connected by straight line segments
HPGL	PA (plot absolute)	Takes a list of absolute points and creates lines by connecting them. PU (pen up) and PD (pen down) commands can be intermixed with the points list to skip line segments
	PR (plot relative)	Takes a list of relative displacements and creates lines by connecting the associated points. PU (pen up) and PD (pen down) commands can be intermixed with the displacement values to skip line segments
IGES	Line Entity	Creates a line given two points, (x1,y1,z1) and (x2,y2,z2)
PostScript	lineto	Draws a line to the specified point from the last referenced point
	rlineto	Draws a line in the specified direction (dx,dy) from the last referenced point
Windows 3.0 Metafile	LineTo	Draws a line from the current position up to but not including the specified point (x, y)

Circle

Circular arcs are entities that have a constant distance from a center point. The constant distance is called the *radius* of the arc. A full arc defines a total rotation of 360 degrees about the center point. A partial arc is any single continuous subset of a full arc. The general methods listed below define circular arcs for various data formats. Refer to their associated diagrams in Figure 5.7 for a visual description of each method.

1 A center point and a radius (full arcs only).

2 A center point, a starting point and an ending point. The arc is created by moving counterclockwise.

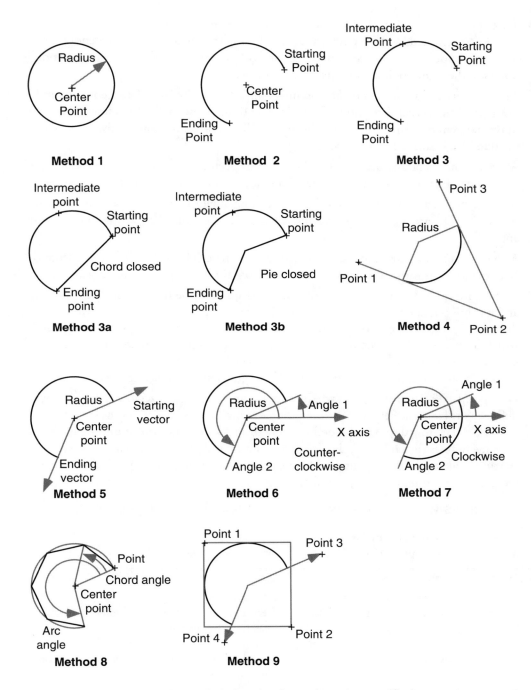

Figure 5.7   Various ways that a circle (or circular arc) can be specified

3   Three points. The points should not be on the same line (i.e., not collinear).

3a   An arc defined by three points and closed using the chord between the endpoints.

3b   An arc defined by three points and closed by connecting the starting and ending points to the center point. This creates a pie shape.

4   Three points and a radius. The first point is implied to be the last referenced point and is not part of the actual definition of the arc. The three points define two lines. The arc is drawn tangent to the two lines with the given radius. The center point is always inside the included angle formed by the two lines.

5   A center point, a radius, and a starting and ending vector. The starting point is calculated using the radius, and the arc is created by moving counterclockwise to the ending vector.

6   A center point, a radius, and a starting and ending angle. The angles are measured from the X axis. The arc is created by moving *counterclockwise* from the starting to the ending angle.

7   A center point, a radius, and a starting and ending angle. The angle is measured from the X axis. The arc is formed by moving *clockwise* from the starting to the ending angle.

8   Two points and two angles. The first point is assumed to be the current "pen" position and it is not included in the arc command. The second point is the center of the arc. The distance between the two points determines the radius. The first angle is the arc angle, which determines the sweep of the arc. If the arc angle is positive then it is drawn counterclockwise. If it is negative then it is drawn clockwise. The second angle is the cord angle, which determines the length of the line segments used to create the arc.

9   Four points. The first two points define a bounding rectangular region. The third point defines a ray from the center of the bounding rectangle. This ray defines the starting angle of the arc. The fourth point also defines a ray from the center of the bounding rectangle. This ray defines the ending angle of the arc. The arc is drawn counterclockwise from the starting angle to the ending angle. The arc fills the bounding rectangle. If the bounding rectangle is not square, an ellipse is formed.

VARIOUS WAYS THAT A CIRCLE (OR CIRCULAR ARC) CAN BE SPECIFIED

Data Format	Name of Data Used in Implementation	Comments
CGM	Circle	Method 1
	Circular arc 3 point	Method 3
	Circular arc 3 point close	Method 3, plus a chord connection or a pie connection (see diagrams 3a and 3b)
	Circular arc center	Method 5
	Circular arc center close	Method 5, plus a chord connection or a pie connection (see diagrams 3a and 3b)
DXF	Circle	Method 1
	Arc	Method 6, if Angle 2 is positive Method 7, if Angle 2 is negative

VARIOUS WAYS THAT A CIRCLE (OR CIRCULAR ARC) CAN BE SPECIFIED *(Continued)*

Data Format	Name of Data Used in Implementation	Comments
GEM/Metafile	Arc GDP Circle GDP Pie GDP	
HPGL	AA (arc absolute)	Method 8, where the center point is specified exactly
	AR (arc relative)	Method 8, where the center point is specified relative to the starting point
	CI (circle)	Method 1, plus a chord angle that determines the accuracy of the drawn arc, as in Method 8
	WG (wedge)	Method 6, except the sweep angle is referenced from the starting angle, not the X axis. This fills the pie shaped region but does not draw the edges of the wedge
	EW (edge wedge)	Same as WG except the edges of the wedge are drawn
IGES	Circular arc entity	Method 2, plus a displacement along the Z axis (IGES is a 3D format)
PostScript	arc	Method 6, plus it connects the last referenced point to the arc starting point
	arcn	Method 7, plus it connects the last referenced point to the arc starting point
	arct (arcto)	Method 4
Windows 3.0 Metafile	arc	Method 9

It is hard to believe that something as simple as a circle can be represented in so many different ways. It is straightforward to transform one representation into another representation, but why are there so many different representations? The various representations address four issues: accuracy, closed versus open shapes, orientation, and degenerate arcs.

The CGM standard includes more than one arc definition to allow for the exact representation of certain coordinates while calculating others. For instance, in Method 3, as shown in Figure 5.7, three points on an arc are specified and a corresponding center point is calculated. The reverse is done in Method 5; the center point is specified, and the starting and ending points are calculated. An application that needs exact[*] endpoints for the arc can use Method 3. An application that needs an exact center point can use Method 5. An application that needs both an exact center point and exact endpoints is out of luck in the CGM standard.

---

[*] Points along an arc cannot be calculated *exactly* because the sine and cosine functions are transcendental (i.e., their fractional parts repeat forever), and most computers limit the precision of their calculations to a fixed number of digits.

The CGM standard includes two additional partial arc entities that have their starting and ending points connected to form closed shapes that are automatically filled with a fill pattern. They can be closed by connecting a chord between the endpoints (Method 3a) or by connecting each endpoint to the center point of the arc to create a pie shape (Method 3b). The same result could be accomplished by an arc command followed by separate line segments to close the arc, and a separate fill command to fill the arc. If a closed arc is needed in an application, the single command that specifies all the required data is the more convenient method. In addition, the single command is more compact in its representation because it does not have to include the additional line segments and fill command. This convenience and compactness is gained at the expense of CGM format complexity (i.e., five different arc specifications).

An arc is an arc, regardless of whether it is created by sweeping through a counterclockwise or clockwise rotation. However, one direction or the other must be implied or specified to create the correct arc. This is not an issue with data formats that assume each individual entity is distinct and separate from the other entities. But some data formats have the concept of a pen that draws graphical entities in a continuous path. This concept is employed in both the PostScript and HPGL data formats. For these formats, arcs must be created in both clockwise and counterclockwise directions. PostScript includes two separate commands to allow for this. HPGL simply uses a positive angle for counterclockwise rotation and a negative angle for clockwise rotation.

Anytime there is data, there is potential for bad data. For example, consider the arc definition used in Method 2. It is quite possible that the radius calculated using the starting point is different from the radius calculated using the ending point. Robust software that "correctly" deals with all such possible cases of bad data is difficult and time consuming to implement. Most of the arc representations minimize redundant data. This reduces the number of ways incorrect data can be generated. How incorrect representations in a data set are dealt with is application dependent.

As in most design situations, there are trade-offs that must be made. For encoding circular arcs, the following two extreme choices are possible: a *compact representation* that stores a minimal set of values or a *verbose representation* that stores every possible characteristic of an arc. The compact representation will minimize the memory required to store the arc, but we must calculate some arc parameters. Ideally they can be calculated to the accuracy required by the specific application using the data. The verbose representation uses memory inefficiently by storing redundant information, but each value is potentially of greater accuracy, as compared to a calculated value.

Conic Arc

Some data formats define a single generic conic arc, of which a circular arc is one simple case. Method 9 described in the previous circular arc section, is an example of this scheme. The more typical approach is to define a separate primitive for conic arcs. A conic arc is a curve defined by the equation $Ax^2 + Cy^2 + Dx + Ey + F = 0$. If $AC = 0$ the equation defines a parabola. If $AC > 0$ the equation defines an ellipse. If $AC < 0$ the equation defines a hyperbola. If $AC > 0$ and D and E are both zero the equation defines a circle.

DATA FORMATS THAT DEFINE CONIC ARCS

Data Format	Name of Data Used in Implementation	Comments
CGM	ELLIPSE	Given three points, the first point is the center point and one point on each of the conjugate axes
	ELLIPTICAL ARC	Same as ELLIPSE, except a starting and ending vector specify a partial arc
	ELLIPTICAL ARC CLOSE	Same as ELLIPTICAL ARC, except the shape is closed with a chord or by connecting the endpoints of the arc to the center point (pie shaped)
	HYPERBOLIC ARC	Defined by a center point, start point, and endpoint
	PARABOLIC ARC	Like HYPERBOLIC ARC, plus transverse and conjugate radii endpoints
GEM/Metafile	Elliptical arc GDP Ellipse GDP Elliptical pie slice GDP	
IGES	CONIC ARC	Supports ellipses, parabolas, and hyperbolas around the origin, with optional start and endpoints

Curve

A curve is a smooth nonstraight "line" defined by three or more noncolinear points. There are many methods for creating curves, such as parametric cubic curves, Hermite curves, Bezier curves, uniform nonrational *B*-splines, nonuniform nonrational *B*-splines, nonuniform rational *B*-splines (NURBS), and Catmull-Rom interpolating splines. Occasionally two methods will generate the same identical curve from identical definition points, but typically different methods generate different curves. Refer to [Mortenson85] or [Foley90] for more information about curve generation.

DATA FORMATS THAT DEFINE CURVES

Data Format	Name of Data Used in Implementation	Comments
CGM	NONUNIFORM *B*-SPLINE	Spline order, number of control points, control points, list of knots, and parameter start and end values
	NONUNIFORM RATIONAL *B*-SPLINE	Like nonuniform *B*-spline, with the addition of weights for the control points
	POLYBEZIER	If discontinuous, then four control points for each Bezier curve. If continuous, then three control points for each curve, plus one additional point
DXF	Polyline	A list of vertexes that are connected by line segments, arcs, a quadratic *B*-spline, a cubic *B*-spline, or a Bezier curve

DATA FORMATS THAT DEFINE CURVES   *(Continued)*

Data Format	Name of Data Used in Implementation	Comments
IGES	PARAMETRIC SPLINE	Selects one of six different planar or nonplanar splines, with break points and 12 coordinates for each segment
	RATIONAL *B*-SPLINE	Planar or nonplanar rational *B*-spline defined by knots, weights, and control points
	Curve on a parametric surface	The trace of a curve defined or projected onto a parametric surface
PostScript	curveto	Adds a section of a cubic Bezier curve to the current path, or to user path
	rcurveto	Adds a section of a cubic Bezier curve, specified relative to the current position, to the current path or user path

Composite Element

A graphical object that is composed of more than one "primitive" object is called a *composite element*. A composite element allows a group of graphical elements to be treated as a single object for the purposes of copying, deleting, transforming, pattern filling, etc.

SPECIFICATION OF COMPOSITE ELEMENTS (ENTITIES WHICH ARE COMBINATIONS OF THE ABOVE SIMPLER ENTITIES)

Data Format	Name of Data Used in Implementation	Comments
CGM	Begin/End compound	Groups a set of line, curve, and arc line primitives together
IGES	Composite Curve	Groups together a set of segments of lines, circular arcs, conic sections, and splines
PostScript	newpath/closepath	Groups together a set of segments of lines, circular arcs, and portions of Bezier cubic curves
	stroke	Makes the current path visible

Text

The idea of placing textual data within a graphical image is straightforward in concept but quite complicated in application. The text is stored as a sequence of character codes, and a position is always associated with the text to locate it within the image. Other criteria that determine the appearance (and location) of the characters in the text string include font type, point size, style, line and character spacings, orientation, foreground and background colors, boundaries, and more.

INFORMATION USED TO SPECIFY TEXT

Data Format	Name of Data Used in Implementation	Comments
CGM	TEXT	Given a positioning point, a flag variable, and a text string
	RESTRICTED TEXT	Same as text, along with a delta width and delta height that form a bounding parallelogram for the text
	APPEND TEXT	Given a flag and a text string. The text is appended to previous "nonfinal" text strings to be displayed as a single unit
	GENERALIZED TEXT PATH	Places a text string along a possibly curved path
DXF	Text	Text string and reference location, with numerous associated attributes
GEM/Metafile	Text	
	Justified graphics text GDP	
HPGL	LB (label instruction)	Given a sting of characters, this plots the string starting at the current point using the current character set
	WD	Write-characters to the display
IGES	General note	Specifies one or more lines of text. See also information on dimensions
PostScript	show	Produces a string of upright characters
	xshow	Like show, but uses provided x offset information instead of the width in the font table
	yshow	Like show, but uses provided y offset information instead of the height in the font table
	xyshow	Like show, but uses provided x and y offset information instead of the width and height in the font table
	widthshow	Like show, but adds provided x and y offset information to the width and height in the font table, for one specified character
	ashow	Like show, but adds provided x and y offset information to the width and height in the font table, for all characters
	awidthshow	Combines ashow and widthshow
	kshow	Executes a user-provided procedure between each of the characters in a string
	charpath	Produces the set of paths of the outlines of the characters in its input. The paths can then be stroked or filled

INFORMATION USED TO SPECIFY TEXT   *(Continued)*

Data Format	Name of Data Used in Implementation	Comments
PostScript	glyphshow	Paints a named character from the current character font
	x, y scale	Sets scale up/down values in x and y for subsequent output
	rotate	Sets a rotation angle for subsequent output
	x, y translate	Moves subsequent output in x and y

Surfaces (2D)

A surface is an enclosed area of space in two dimensions. It is defined typically by specifying its boundaries or edges.

**SPECIFICATION OF SURFACES
(FACES, POLYGONS) IN TWO DIMENSIONS**

Data Format	Name of Data Used in Implementation	Comments
CGM	POLYGON	Given a list of points, it creates a closed region bounded by line segments. Each two successive points in the list forms an edge of the region, with the last point connected to the first point
	POLYGON SET	Given a list of points, it creates one or more closed regions. Each point has a matching edge flag that determines whether the next edge is visible and whether it closes the current region
	RECTANGLE	Given two points that specify the diagonally opposite corners of a filled rectangular region
DXF	Solid	Four points that define a filled region (a quadrilateral or a triangle)
GEM/Metafile	fill area fill rectangle rounded rectangle GDP filled rounded rectangle GDP	
HPGL	EA (edge rectangle absolute)	Given a single point that is taken as the opposite corner of the rectangle, the current point is taken as the starting point of the rectangle. It draws the edge of the rectangle
	ER (edge rectangle relative)	Same as EA except the specified point is relative to the current point
	RA (rectangle absolute)	Defines a solid-filled rectangle

**SPECIFICATION OF SURFACES
(FACES, POLYGONS) IN TWO DIMENSIONS** *(Continued)*

Data Format	Name of Data Used in Implementation	Comments
HPGL	RR (fill rectangle relative)	Same as RA except the specified point is relative to the current point
	EW (edge wedge)	Draws the edge of a circular pie segment based on radius, start and end angles, and chord angle
	WG (fill wedge of circle)	Like EW, but the wedge is filled in
	EP	Edges of a polygon boundary
	FP	Fills a polygon interior
IGES	plane entity	A plane in 3D space, which can be unbounded, bounded by a closed curve, or negative (a hole, bounded by a closed curve)
PostScript	newpath/closepath	Groups a set of segments of lines, circular arcs, and portions of Bezier cubic curves
	fill	Fills the area enclosed by the current path, as determined by the even-odd rule or the winding rule
	ufill	Fills a cached user path
	rectstroke	Draws the boundary of one or more rectangles of specified width and height located at specified X, Y
	rectfill	Like rectstroke, but the rectangle is filled in

Surface (3D)

A surface can be defined in 3D space, but it has no volume. It typically delimits a side of a 3D object. The surface is defined by specifying its boundaries or edges. However, the interior points of a 3D surface do not necessarily lie on a flat plane. A surface can be curved in space. The curvature of the interior points can be controlled by several means, including tangent vectors at the boundaries, control points in the interior of the surface, or simply by the curvature of the boundary edges themselves. Refer back to the section on curves. All of these curve generation methods can be applied to 3D surfaces. Surfaces created using different schemes are typically not identical at all points along their surface.

HOW TO SPECIFY SURFACES (FACES, POLYGONS) IN 3 DIMENSIONS

Data Format	Name of Data Used in Implementation	Comments
CGM	POLYGON	Given a list of points, it creates a closed region bounded by line segments. Each two successive points in the list forms an edge of the region, with the last point connected to the first point

HOW TO SPECIFY SURFACES (FACES, POLYGONS) IN 3 DIMENSIONS

Data Format	Name of Data Used in Implementation	Comments
CGM	POLYGON SET	Given a list of points, it creates one or more closed regions. Each point has a matching edge flag that determines whether the next edge is visible and whether it closes the current region
	RECTANGLE	Given two points that specify the diagonally opposite corners of a filled rectangular region
DXF	Solid	Four points that define a filled region, (a quadrilateral or a triangle)
	3Dface	Four points that define the corners of a face
IGES	Plane entity	A plane in 3D space, that can be unbounded, bounded by a closed curve, or negative (a hole, bounded by a closed curve)
	Parametric spline surface	A u by v grid of parametric polynomial patches
	Ruled surface	Defined by connecting "equivalent" points on two parametric curves with straight lines
	Surface of revolution	Defined by rotating a line about an axis between starting and ending angles (up to a full circle)
	Tabulated cylinder	Defined by moving a line segment parallel to itself, along a curve
	Rational B-spline surface	A general family of surfaces, including the types defined above and more general cases
	Trimmed parametric surface	Specified by the exterior boundary curve and zero or more interior boundary (hole) curves, defined on a parametric surface

Subfigure

The term *subfigure* typically refers to a group of related 3D graphical primitives that compose a small part of a larger 3D model. Subfigures allow a group of graphical elements to be treated as a single object for the purposes of copying, deleting, transforming, etc. They increase memory efficiency because the geometric description of a subpart only needs to be stored once. A subfigure can be replicated many times by only storing a transformation for each *subfigure instance*. Each transformation specifies position and orientation for that instance. Storing data in this way also facilitates the modification of subfigures. If a subfigure is stored only once, then its definition can be changed once and the changes will be automatically propagated to all of its instances.

SPECIFICATION OF SUBFIGURES (SUBPARTS, COMPOSITE FIGURES, BLOCKS)

Data Format	Name of Data Used in Implementation	Comments
CGM	segment	A collection of primitives and attributes that can be copied with 2D scaling, rotation, and translation
DXF	Shape	A combination of lines, circles, and arcs that can be positioned as a unit. The shape data includes an insertion point, a size, shape name, rotation angle, relative X scale factor, and an obliquing angle (an angle of rotation outside the plane of definition)
	Block	The definition of an entity as composed of other lines, arcs, text, etc.
	Insert	The positioning of a block, specified by a block name, a rotation angle, an insertion point, X, Y, and Z scale factors, and X Y direction array counts and spacing
HPGL	BL	Buffer a label for later use
	BP	Buffer a plot for later use
	PB	Plot a label from the buffer
	RP	Replot a buffered plot n times
IGES	Subfigure definition	Identifies a set of entities that can include primitives or other hierarchically nested subfigures
	Singular subfigure instance	Specifies 3D translation and scale at which a subfigure should be included. Able to use conditional and arithmetic operations on input parameters to define geometry in terms of IGES entities (primitives)
	Macro definition	Invokes a specified macro with the needed parameters
	Macro instance	
PostScript	def	Permits a named path to be defined
	x, y scale	Sets scale up/down values in x and y for subsequent output
	rotate	Sets a rotation angle for subsequent output
	x, y translate	Moves subsequent output in x and y
	stroke	Makes a path visible
	userpath	User defined paths that can be cached

Dimensions

Line segments, arrows, and text are often combined into single entities to represent dimensional data in 2D drawings and 3D models. The style used to display dimensions varies between applications and typically varies between data streams.

HOW DRAFTING DIMENSION INFORMATION IS SPECIFIED

Data Format	Name of Data Used in Implementation	Comments
CGM	Registered values for attributes	CGM is application independent, but new line types and symbols can be defined and registered
DXF	Linear dimension	Specifies an inside or outside dimension, with leader lines
	Angular dimension	Labels size of an angle, with required leader lines
	Angular dimension (3 point)	Labels size of an angle, with required leader lines, and center location
	Diameter dimension	Labels diameter, with leader line
	Radius dimension	Describes a radius, with leader line
	Ordinate dimension	Indicates dimensions from a common base line, parallel to X or Y axis
IGES	Angular dimension	Labels size of an angle, with required leader lines
	Diameter dimension	Labels diameter, with leader line
	Flag note	A note in a "flag" box, with zero or more leader lines
	General label	A general note (see text table above) with one or more leader lines
	Linear dimension	Specifies an inside or outside dimension, with leader lines
	Ordinate dimension	Indicates dimensions from a common base line, parallel to X or Y axis
	Point dimension	Text with optional enclosing circle or hexagon and a leader line
	Radius dimension	Describes a radius, with leader line, general symbol text, with an associated geometric symbol, and zero or more leader lines

5.3.2 Attribute Data

Attributes control the appearance of geometry primitives. A different set of attributes applies to each class of primitive object.

SPECIFYING ATTRIBUTES FOR POINT OR MARKER PRIMITIVES

Data Format	Name of Data Used in Implementation	Comments
CGM	Marker type	Symbol used to display the point
	Marker size	Size of marker symbol
	Marker color	Color of the marker symbol
	Symbol size	Scale factor relative to the design size of the (external) symbol
	Symbol orientation	Orientation of the (external) symbol
	Symbol color	Color of the (external) symbol

SPECIFYING ATTRIBUTES FOR POINT OR MARKER PRIMITIVES   *(Continued)*

Data Format	Name of Data Used in Implementation	Comments
DXF		Color, thickness (if nonzero), point display mode, point display size
GEM/Metafile	Set polymarker color index Set polymarker type Set polymarker height	
HPGL	DL	Defines a downloadable character in terms of coordinates and pen control (up/down) operations
	SP (select pen)	Includes width and color
	SM	Selects character for character mode plotting
IGES	PTR in point	Identifies (optional) symbol to be drawn, with color and line weight
PostScript	setfont	Identifies the "current" font from those available
	definefont	Names a font (including family name or appearance, size, italic angle, and weight) as available
	scalefont	Changes font size
	makefont	Provides rotation and different scaling in X and Y
	setcolorspace	Specifies a color space by setting its parameters, or by name (devicegray, deviceRGB, deviceCMYK, or Pattern
	setcolor	Sets the current color, by giving values for its parameters as needed by the current color space
	setrgbcolor	Equivalent to setcolorspace to deviceRGB followed by red, green, and blue components of a setcolor operation
	setgrey	Equivalent to setcolorspace to devicegray followed by a gray value between 0 (black) and 1 (white)
	sethsbcolor	Equivalent to setcolorspace to deviceRGB followed by hue, saturation, and brightness values between 0 and 1, which are converted to equivalent RGB values
	setcmykcolor	Equivalent to setcolorspace to deviceCMYK followed by cyan, magenta, yellow, and black values between 0 and 1
	sepattern	Equivalent to setcolorspace to pattern followed by color components if needed
	makepattern	Selects a user-specified procedural description of a tile or icon used in paint operations. It can specify its colors when defined, or as components when called

SPECIFYING LINE AND CURVE PRIMITIVE ATTRIBUTES

Data Format	Name of Data Used in Implementation	Comments
CGM	Line type	Solid, dotted, dashed, etc.
	Line width	Width at which a line is drawn
	Line color	Color of the line
	Line cap	Shape of the ends of a line (round, butt, triangle, projecting square)
	Line join	How two lines join (miter, round, bevel)
	Line type continuation	How (or if) a line's type is continued at a corner
	Line type initial offset	Where drawing starts within a line type definition
DXF		Line type reference, color, thickness and starting and ending width
	LTYPE	Number and length of dashes and total length of line type pattern
GEM/Metafile	Set polyline color index	
	Set polyline line type	
	Set user defined line type pattern	
	Set polyline line width	
	Set polyline end style	
HPGL	LT (line type)	Specifies a pattern number and, optionally, a pattern length
	SP (select pen)	Includes width and color
	PT (pen thickness)	Selects pen thickness
IGES	Line font definition	Defines spacing of visible components in a nonsolid line
	Line font	Selects a line appearance
	Line weight	Relative weight between maximum and minimum values supported by IGES
	Line widening	Enables lines to be widened, with ends and corners being rounded or square
	Color	The relative amounts of red, green, and blue in a color
PostScript	setlinewidth	Sets width for following stroke operations. Zero is thinnest possible line
	setlinejoin	Specifies shape of corner of two joined lines as miter, round, or bevel
	setlinecap	Specifies shape of line ends as butt, round, or projecting square
	setdash	Sets the length of dashes and gaps in a repeating pattern. The starting offset/phase can also be set
	setcolorspace	Specifies a color space by setting its parameters, or by name (devicegray, deviceRGB, deviceCMYK, or Pattern

SPECIFYING LINE AND CURVE PRIMITIVE ATTRIBUTES *(Continued)*

Data Format	Name of Data Used in Implementation	Comments
PostScript	setcolor	Sets the current color, by giving values for its parameters as needed by the current color space
	setrgbcolor	Equivalent to setcolorspace to deviceRGB followed by red, green, and blue components of a setcolor operation
	setgrey	Equivalent to setcolorspace to devicegray followed by a gray value between 0 (black) and 1 (white)
	sethsbcolor	Equivalent to setcolorspace to deviceRGB followed by hue, saturation, and brightness values between 0 and 1, which are converted to equivalent RGB values
	setcmykcolor	Equivalent to setcolorspace to deviceCMYK followed by cyan, magenta, yellow, and black values between 0 and 1
	setpattern	Equivalent to setcolorspace to pattern followed by color components if needed
	makepattern	Selects a user-specified procedural description of a tile or icon used in paint operations. It can specify its colors when defined, or as components when called
	setflat	Sets the maximum difference/distance between a curve and the set of straight line segments that approximate it (from 0.2 to 100)

SPECIFYING ATTRIBUTES OF TEXT PRIMITIVES

Data Format	Name of Data Used in Implementation	Comments
CGM	Text font index	Selects the font for presentation
	Text precision	Specifies one of three levels of text presentation fidelity
	Character expansion factor	Modifies the width to height ratio of the font from the design value
	Character spacing	Additional intercharacter spacing (may be positive or negative)
	Character height	Specifies character height
	Text path	Direction of successive characters (left, right, up, down)
	Text alignment	Relative positioning of a block of text with respect to a positioning point
	Character orientation	Sets the direction of the character baseline and character "up" vector (possibly not orthogonal)

SPECIFYING ATTRIBUTES OF TEXT PRIMITIVES *(Continued)*

Data Format	Name of Data Used in Implementation	Comments
DXF	Text Attributes	Height, rotation angle of baseline, relative X scale, obliquing angle, text style name, horizontal justification type, vertical justification type, horizontal and vertical mirroring, linetype, color, thickness (if nonzero)
GEM/Metafile	Set text font	
	Set text color index	
	Set graphic text alignment	
	Set graphic text special effects	
	Set character height	
	Set character baseline value	
HPGL	CP (character plot)	Specifies the number of spaces and lines for text output formatting
	ES (extra space)	Specifies extra space between characters and lines of text
	CA (character set alternate)	Names the alternate character set
	CS (character set standard)	Names the standard character set
	DI (direction instruction)	Sets the absolute direction of labels
	DL (downloadable character)	Defines a downloadable character
	DR (direction relative)	Sets the relative direction of labels
	DT (define label terminator)	Defines the ASCII code used to terminate strings of characters
	LO (label origin)	Sets the label origin, such as left justified, right justified, etc.
	SI (set absolute character size)	Width and height of character
	SL (set character slant)	From vertical
	SR (set relative character size)	Both width and height
	SA (select alternate character set)	
	SS (select standard character set)	
	SP (select pen)	Includes width and color
IGES	TEXT define box	Height and width of character string
	TEXT rotate internal	Specifies horizontal or vertical text
	TEXT slant angle	Produces italic-like text
	TEXT rotation	Direction of text baseline
	TEXT mirror	Reflects text about the baseline or the perpendicular to the baseline
	color	The relative amounts of red, green, and blue in the text color

SPECIFYING ATTRIBUTES OF TEXT PRIMITIVES *(Continued)*

Data Format	Name of Data Used in Implementation	Comments
PostScript	setfont	Identify the current font from those available
	definefont	Names a font (including family name or appearance, size, italic angle, and weight) as being available
	scalefont	Changes font size
	makefont	Provides rotation and different scaling in X and Y
	setcolorspace	Specifies a color space by setting its parameters, or by name (devicegray, deviceRGB, DeviceCMYK, or Pattern
	setcolor	Sets the current color by giving values for its parameters as needed by the current color space
	setrgbcolor	Equivalent to setcolorspace to deviceRGB followed by red, green, and blue components of a setcolor operation
	setgrey	Equivalent to setcolorspace to devicegray followed by a gray value between 0 (black) and 1 (white)
	sethsbcolor	Equivalent to setcolorspace to deviceRGB followed by hue, saturation, and brightness values between 0 and 1, which are converted to equivalent RGB values
	setcmykcolor	Equivalent to setcolorspace to deviceCMYK followed by cyan, magenta, yellow, and black values between 0 and 1
	setpattern	Equivalent to setcolorspace to pattern followed by color components if needed
	makepattern	Selects a user-specified procedural description of a tile or icon used in paint operations. It can specify its colors when defined, or as components when called

SPECIFYING SURFACE (FACE, POLYGON) PRIMITIVE ATTRIBUTES

Data Format	Name of Data Used in Implementation	Comments
CGM	Interior style	One of: hollow, solid, pattern, hatch, empty, geometric pattern, or interpolated
	Fill color	Color for hollow, solid, or hatch styles
	Hatch index	Identifies the (cross) hatch fill style
	Pattern index	Identifies which pattern to use
	Interpolated interior	Identifies the shading to be used in the interior as parallel, elliptical, or triangular

SPECIFYING SURFACE (FACE, POLYGON) PRIMITIVE ATTRIBUTES   *(Continued)*

Data Format	Name of Data Used in Implementation	Comments
DXF		Color, starting and ending widths of lines, visibility of edges, thickness (if nonzero)
GEM/Metafile	Set fill color index Set fill interior style Set fill perimeter visibility Set fill style index 89Set user defined fill pattern	
HPGL	FT (fill type)	Specifies a type of fill and a spacing and an angle
	PT (pen thickness)	Determines the spacing between lines drawn to fill in a solid
	SP (select pen)	Includes width and color
	UF	Creates user-defined fill type
IGES	Color	The relative amounts of red, green, and blue in a color
	Line font	Selects a line appearance
	Line weight	Relative weight between maximum and minimum values supported by IGES
	Sectional array	Predefined hatch patterns with specifiable angles and spacing
PostScript	setpattern	Equivalent to setcolorspace to pattern followed by color components if needed
	makepattern	Selects a user-specified procedural description of a tile or icon used in paint operations. It can specify its colors when defined or as components when called
	setcolorspace	Specifies a color space by setting its parameters, or by name (devicegray, deviceRGB, DeviceCMYK, or Pattern
	setcolor	Sets the current color by giving values for its parameters as needed by the current color space
	setrgbcolor	Equivalent to setcolorspace to deviceRGB followed by red, green, and blue components of a setcolor operation
	setgrey	Equivalent to setcolorspace to devicegray followed by a gray value between 0 (black) and 1 (white)
	sethsbcolor	Equivalent to setcolorspace to deviceRGB followed by hue, saturation, and brightness values between 0 and 1, which are converted to equivalent RGB values
	setcmykcolor	Equivalent to setcolorspace to deviceCMYK followed by cyan, magenta, yellow, and black values between 0 and 1

SPECIFYING SURFACE (FACE, POLYGON) PRIMITIVE ATTRIBUTES *(Continued)*

Data Format	Name of Data Used in Implementation	Comments
PostScript	setpattern	Equivalent to setcolorspace to pattern followed by color components if needed
	makepattern	Selects a user-specified procedural description of a tile or icon used in paint operations. It can specify its colors when defined or as components when called

HOW TO SPECIFY SUBFIGURE (SUBPART, COMPOSITE FIGURE, BLOCK) ATTRIBUTES

Data Format	Name of Data Used in Implementation	Comments
CGM	Copy segment	Provides orientation, rotation, and scale of a copied segment
	Inheritance filter	Permits current attribute values to override specified attribute values contained w ithin a copied segment
DXF		Attributes relevant to the type of block to be inserted can be overridden in the insert command
PostScript		Graphic context (line width and style, fill pattern, color, rotation/scale/translation) can be modified before a saved path is stroked or filled

WAYS TO SPECIFY ATTRIBUTES OF DRAFTING DIMENSION PRIMITIVES

Data Format	Name of Data Used in Implementation	Comments
DXF		Arrow size, dimensioning suffix, dimension line color, extension line color, dimensioning tick size, plus all the text attributes
IGES		Drafting dimensions are based on the general text entity. See IGES text attributes above

5.3.3 Geometry Documentation Data

It is important for geometry-based data streams to document their title, author, origin, copyright information, etc., but such information is often lacking.

5.3.4 Geometry Associated Data

It is not possible to identify all associated data for geometry-based data streams, since each application area has its own set of information it must associate with the graphical data. Application-specific data is one of the major reasons why there are so many different graphical data formats. Ideally a single geometric data-representation scheme could be standardized, and application-specific data could be attached to it. Regrettably, as applications have created their own application-specific data types, they have also created their own geometric data representations.

One example of associated data can be found in the IGES data format. IGES is the dominant format used to share associated data related to manufactured products. It defines data types for electrical/electronic attributes and properties, for user definable attribute tables, and for finite element model (FEM) results. Other examples include the census data included in TIGER files and topology data included in ARC/Info data files.

One important set of attribute data for 3D geometry data streams is the desired 2D views that will be used to create images of the data set. Some examples of *viewing* data are listed below.

VIEW SPECIFICATION

Data Format	Name of Data Used in Implementation	Comments
DXF	ViewPort	
HPGL	IP (input P1 and P2)	Sets the scaling points in the upper left and lower right of the drawing surface in plotter units
	IW (input window)	Two points specify the upper left and lower right limits of the plotting area

SPECIFICATION OF MISCELLANEOUS GEOMETRY DATA

Data Format	Name of Data Used in Implementation	Comments
HPGL	DF (default instruction)	Returns the plotter to default conditions
	IM (input mask instruction)	Specifies which errors are responded to and what conditions will cause a positive response to a serial or parallel port in an HP-GL environment
	IN (initialize plotter)	Sets the plotter to the default state
	PS (paper size)	Selects the paper size

5.4 LATENT IMAGE DATA

Latent image data, as we defined it, includes all data sets that are not initially created for graphical purposes. This is a very large and diverse group of data sets, to say the least. The idea of converting a wide range of data types into images is most often discussed in the field of scientific visualization. A list of possible data structures that scientific visualization software might have to process is included in [Treinish91]. The list is repeated here in unedited form.

- Multiparameter data sets containing fields of different dimensionality, rank, shape, and their access as single blocks, multiple blocks of different structures, hyperplanes, etc.

- Multiple geometries and topologies including rectilinear, tetrahedral, icosahedral, prismatic, etc.

- Multiple coordinate systems, including Cartesian, spherical, cylindrical, polar, nonorthogonal, etc.

- Hierarchical (e.g., groupings, spatial)

- Sparse matrices

- Complex (regular and irregular) meshes, deformed and unstructured grids, etc.

- Graphical geometries (e.g., point, vector, polygon, raster surface, voxel) and object types

As you can see, the range of possible data types and organization schemes is large. The goal of scientific visualization is to develop generic tools that facilitate the creation of images from scientific data and other types of data as well. We do not want to develop new imaging software every time a new data set comes along. Therefore we need a standard set of graphical data formats into which most other data sets could be easily converted. It is still an open question as to what this set of standard graphical data formats should be.

5.5 SUMMARY AND CONCLUSIONS

The main problem with data types is that there are so many different types to choose from. Hopefully, after having read this chapter, you are not more confused than when you started. Let's review the main ideas. Graphical data comes in two basic types: raster data and geometric data. Beyond these two basic types of data, any set of data can be used to create an image given an appropriate transformation. We called this *latent image data*. These data types are summarized in Figure 5.8, along with some *procedural data streams*. A procedural data stream is not a static set of data values but the definition of a process that, when executed, creates graphical images. It is beyond the scope of this book to discuss them further, but they are included in the chart for completeness.

In general, a graphical data stream contains "raw" graphical data in combination with interpretation data, attribute data, documentation data, associated data, and other, possibly unrelated, data.

If you have a choice between storing information in raster or geometric form, which should you choose? This is a very hotly debated topic, especially in applications that involve 3D volume data. Both forms of data have advantages and disadvantages. We list these in the following table which was taken from [Kaufman92] and revised slightly. The table entries shown in italic type are considered advantages while those in normal type are considered disadvantages.

If we ignore the cost of computer hardware required to efficiently process graphical data, the choice between raster and geometry data is predominantly based on how the data needs to be manipulated and processed. Raster data must be manipulated at a sample level,

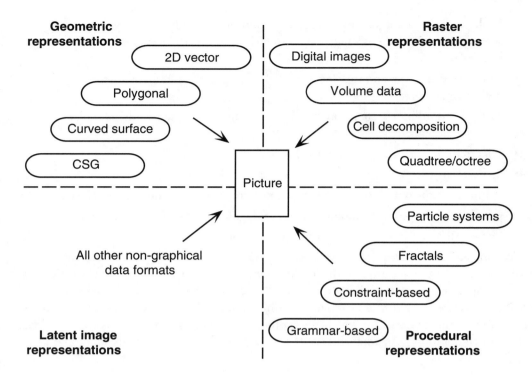

Figure 5.8   Different representations for graphic data

COMPARISON OF GEOMETRIC AND RASTER DATA

	Geometric Data	Raster Data
Space (memory required)	*Less*	More
Aliasing (jaggy edges)	*Less*	More
Transform (move, rotate, etc.)	*Easier*	Harder
Objects are defined	*Yes*	No
Scene complexity (as it relates to data stream size) (without compression)	The data stream grows in size with added complexity	The data stream is a *constant size*, regardless of complexity
Block operations	No	*Yes*
Sampled data	No	*Yes*
Interior (fill an object)	Harder	*Easier*

sample by sample. Geometric data can be manipulated at the object level and then converted to a digital image. The best choice is application dependent.

Of the raster-based data formats we survey in this book, TIFF and PostScript offer the most data type options for 2D image data. Of these two, TIFF is more easily modified to include new data types. Of the 3D raster formats we surveyed, the AVS field format was the only one that dealt explicitly with nonuniform sample spacings. The new ISO Image Interchange Facility (IIF) is perhaps the most comprehensive data specification for multidimensional raster data.

As for geometry-based data streams, there are many variations. They differ according to *what kind* of object primitives they define, *how many* objects they define, how these primitives are *specified*, what types of *attributes* an object can have, and the richness of their *text* layout model. The simpler 2D geometric data streams are compatible mostly with each other. (By *simpler* we mean geometric points, lines, and arcs, but no curves or higher-level objects. By *compatible* we mean they can be converted from one data stream definition to another easily.) When curves and other higher-level primitives are added to a data stream, they become much more complex. Of the data formats we survey in this book, CGM and PostScript offer the widest range of data types for 2D geometric data.

Moving from 2D geometric data to 3D data compounds the problem greatly. Currently only two data formats are commonly used for exchanging 3D geometry data: DXF and IGES. For some applications, capturing static geometry information is not sufficient. These applications need a data format that specifies not only 3D geometry but also the rules or constraints on distortions of this geometry in response to external stresses and other forces. The IGES data format was designed to include some types of manufacturing data along with the geometry data.

Hopefully this explanation will guide you in selecting a data stream that supports the data types your particular application needs. However, data types are only one of many considerations that can impact the use of a data format. After making a list of data formats that support the data types your application requires, continue to investigate the other important aspects of data streams that are discussed in the next several chapters.

CONTENTS

6.1 INTRODUCTION TO COLOR THEORY

Humans perceive color when certain wavelengths[*] of visible light[†] strike the retina of their eyes. An observer can perceive the same color from many different combinations of wavelengths. The number of possible wavelength combinations is infinite, but only a finite number of distinguishable colors can be perceived by humans. A "color model" is needed that assigns a unique code to each humanly perceivable color. Many such color models exist, but only three are commonly used to *physically* create color images. These include:

- The RGB (red-green-blue) color model, used predominantly for light emitting systems (e.g., televisions and computer monitors).
- The CMY (cyan-magenta-yellow) color model, used for light-absorbing systems (e.g., printing).
- The RYB (red-yellow-blue) color model for visual paint mixing in art.

---

[*] The wavelength is the distance a wave travels during one complete cycle of its vibration.

[†] Visible light has wavelengths between approximately 400 and 700 nm (nanometers, 10^{-9} meters). Lasers produce light with a single wavelength; all other light sources produce light that contains varying proportions of all wavelengths.

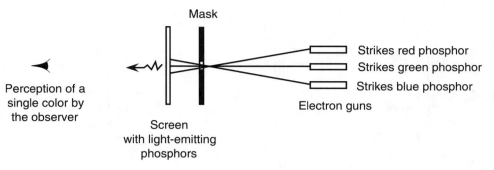

Figure 6.1 The concept behind color production on a CRT display

For a thorough discussion of general color theory see [Durrett87], [Foley90], and [Hill90]. Although *black* and *white* are sometimes not associated with the term *color*, they are indeed colors. White is the color associated with pure illumination without the presence of hue. The term *hue* is used to distinguish between colors such as red, dark olive green, or sky blue. The color black is associated with the absence of illumination. Varying intensities of light that contain only illumination and no hue are said to be grayscale colors. Grayscale colors can be described by a single value that represents the intensity of the light. The physics term *luminance* is often used to describe a light's intensity, as is the psychological term *brightness*. Luminance and brightness are not equivalent terms, but from a data representation standpoint they are typically stored as a single numerical value.

If we want to represent the hue, or color, of light, we need to store more than a single data value. Physically, light is made up of a continuous spectrum of frequencies, but fortunately we do not have to store such a continuous representation. It has been proven that given any four colors, one of them can be represented as a linear combination of the other three. This amazing fact forms the basis for all representations of color. All color models use a minimum of three values to represent each distinct color. The meaning associated with each of the three values varies depending on the color model used.

6.1.1 Additive Color Space

Hardware systems that create colors by the emission of light are based on an *additive* color model; light combines to form various colors. *By convention,* red, green, and blue are the standard basis colors used to form all other colors in an additive color model. These specific colors are used because the human eye is particularly sensitive to them and because they are widely separated in the color space. Figure 6.1 shows the typical method used to create colors on a CRT screen. Three separate electron guns excite phosphors on the screen, and the combined light is viewed by an observer as a single color.

The combination of red, green, and blue light at full intensity produces white light. Black is the absence of light, where each of the three primary colors has zero intensity. All other colors are created by combining different percentages of red, green, and blue light. One common representation of these percentages is to use fractions in the range of 0.0 to 1.0, where the value 1.0 represents full intensity.

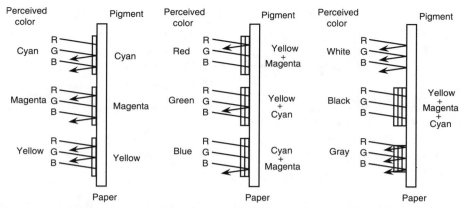

Figure 6.2   How subtractive colors are generated

6.1.2   Subtractive Color Space

Hardware systems that create colors by printing pigments that absorb certain types of light are based on a *subtractive* color model; certain colors are removed from the light reflected off an object. *By convention*, cyan, magenta, and yellow typically form the standard basic colors for a subtractive color system. These are used because cyan removes red light, magenta removes green light, and yellow removes blue light. The color perceived by an observer is the result of the light reflected off the paper and not absorbed by the pigments [Southworth79]. The RGB and CMY systems are closely related by convention. Figure 6.2 and the equations below show how combinations of pigments absorb light to create different colors.

**RELATIONSHIP BETWEEN ADDITIVE AND
SUBTRACTIVE PRIMARY COLORS**

cyan = green + blue   white = red + green + blue
magenta = red + blue   red = white – green – blue
yellow = red + green   green = white – red – blue
                                  blue = white – red – green

A single color value can be represented using a subtractive color model by storing the percentage of pigment for each of the basis colors (i.e., cyan, magenta, and yellow). This is typically done with fractional values in the range from 0.0 to 1.0. Zero represents the absence of pigments, which results in the color of the paper. A value of 1.0 for all pigments represents black. Notice that this is the exact opposite of the typical RGB representation.

File formats generally use the color model associated with their intended output device (i.e., RGB for monitors or CMY for printers). Converting between the two models is *theoretically* simple using the following formulas:

**SIMPLISTIC RELATIONSHIP BETWEEN ADDITIVE AND
SUBTRACTIVE COLOR SYSTEM PRIMARY COLORS**

red = 1.0 – cyan   cyan = 1.0 – red
green = 1.0 – magenta   magenta = 1.0 – green
blue = 1.0 – yellow   yellow = 1.0 – blue

These equations are accurate in theory, but in practice they produce such poor color matching that more sophisticated conversions are usually required. (Refer to Section 6.3).

When using a subtractive color model, black will be produced, in theory, by overprinting cyan, magenta, and yellow. However, in practice not all of the light is absorbed by the pigments, and a dark brown color is typically produced. Greater picture contrast can be achieved if black is printed along with the other three pigments. Consequently, printing processes often use a four-color model—CMYK (cyan, magenta, yellow, and black). The need for this extra color value increases the storage requirements for color values by 33%.

Determining when to print black in place of the three other colors is device dependent; it depends on how the pigments on a particular device mix. A simple generic scheme uses the minimum of the cyan, magenta, and yellow values as the amount of black to print. This amount of black must then be removed from the other colors to compensate for the black ink. This is summarized by the following equations:

**IMPROVED MAPPING BETWEEN ADDITIVE AND
SUBTRACTIVE PRIMARY COLORS**

k (black) = minimum (cyan, magenta, yellow)
cyan = cyan − k
magenta = magenta − k
yellow = yellow − k

These simple, general equations often require modifications to produce the desired results on any particular output device.

6.2   COLOR REPRESENTATION

We have established that color representation requires one, three, and sometimes four discrete values. Each value represents a proportional intensity, ranging from zero to full intensity. How these intensities are represented is quite varied.

6.2.1   Color Precision

Some data formats do not limit the precision of their color-intensity values. Some examples include:

DATA FORMATS THAT DO NOT LIMIT COLOR PRECISION

Data Format	Name of Data Used in Implementation	Comments
IGES	Color Definition Entity	Real numbers in the range of 0.0 to 100.0 that represent a percentage of intensity
IIF		Real numbers can be used to specify pixel intensity values

DATA FORMATS THAT DO NOT LIMIT COLOR PRECISION   *(Continued)*

Data Format	Name of Data Used in Implementation	Comments
PostScript	setcolor	Fractions in the range of 0.0 to 1.0 (ASCII text encoded)
RIB	Color	Fractions in the range of 0.0 to 1.0 (ASCII text encoded)

Most data formats limit the precision of their color-intensity values. The range of precision is usually some power of 2 (since nearly all digital computer data is stored as binary numbers). The following table gives the number of bits[*] commonly used to represent color-intensity values. In general, given n bits, it is possible to represent 2^n discrete values. For monochrome images, this allows 2^n intensity values per pixel. However, for color images, with three intensity values, this allows $(2^n)^3$ shades of color.

NUMBER OF VALUES PER COLOR COMPONENT, FOR VARIOUS APPLICATIONS

# of bits	Range of Intensity Values	Applications
1	2	Fax images (monochrome)
2	4	
4	16	Engineering-type line drawings
8	256	"Natural" image scenes
12	4,096	Medical imaging systems (e.g., digital X rays)
14	16,384	Digital photography systems for "film quality" images
16	65,536	Photo-realistic images created from synthetic data[‡]

[‡]The precision required for certain applications is not always agreed upon by professionals (and is sometimes hotly debated).

How many discrete levels of intensity are needed to produce "nice" images? The answer is: It depends on the resolution of the device (i.e., the number of dots per inch), the characteristic of each dot, how the colors mix to form each dot, and other device characteristics. The bottom-line question is: Does it look good to the human observer? Practical experience has produced a whole range of color precisions that work well in certain situations. Because of this, many data formats support not just one color precision but a range of color precisions. The following chart gives some examples.

---

[*]A bit is one binary digit; a single 0 or 1 in a binary number.

COLOR PRECISIONS SUPPORTED BY VARIOUS DATA FORMATS

Data Format‡	Bits per Intensity Value (3 values per pixel)											
	1	2	3	4	5	6	7	8	10	12	14	16
AVS Image								•				
BMP	•			•				•				
CCITT Fax group 3	•											
CGM†	•	•	•	•	•	•	•	•	•	•	•	•
CUR	•		•	•								
DDES suite	•							•				
EPSI	•	•		•				•				
GEM/IMG	•	•	•	•	•	•	•	•				•
GIF	•	•	•	•	•	•		•				
HDF								•				
ICO	•		•	•								
JBIG	•	•	•	•	•	•	•	•	•	•		•
JPEG (lossless)		•	•	•	•	•	•	•	•	•		•
JPEG (lossY)								•		•		
MacPaint	•											
PCX	•			•				•				
PostScript (image)	•	•		•				•		•		
RLE								•				
SunRaster	•							•				
TGA								•				
TIFF	•	•	•	•	•	•	•	•	•	•		•
X Bitmap	•											
X Pixmap								•				•
xim*	•							•				
X Window Dump	•	•	•	•	•	•	•	•	•	•		•

‡While the definition of a data format might allow for a range of intensity values, individual implementations of the format sometimes support only a limited subset of these ranges.

† The precision of CGM values is not limited to powers of 2.

*The xim definition supports 1 through 8 bits per pixel, but most readers only support 1 and 8 bits per pixel.

Do not be deceived into thinking that the number of bits per intensity value determines the total number of intensities discernible by the human eye. It is common for a high-resolution black and white raster image (1 bit per pixel) to appear to the human eye as a grayscale image with many levels of intensity. If the resolution of a raster image is large enough, groups of local dots appear as single units, and these groups create varying levels of intensity. The technical name for this is *spatial fusion*. Trade-offs between the resolution of a raster data set and the color precision of its pixels are common. These trade-offs allow for varying levels of memory requirements and achieve varying levels of image quality. A general-purpose data format should allow for these trade-offs and therefore accommodate a variety of bits per pixel at different image resolutions.

Currently, 8 bits per pixel has become a widely-used representation for color intensities. The memory of most computers is organized into groups of 8 bits called *bytes*. Storing intensity values, one per byte, typically increases the speed at which data can be accessed. It also makes the software that processes the data less complex. Eight bits of precision provides 256 shades of intensity for each of the three primaries, which is sufficient for many applications. Notice, however, that if an application needs only 6 bits per primary per pixel to represent color, it can save 25% of the memory used in comparison to the 8 bit per pixel representation. There is, however, a computational cost to pack three 6-bit quantities into two and one-quarter 8-bit bytes, and to recover them when needed. Data compression is an important issue for data formats, and one way to compress data is to use no more precision for color values than you really need.

6.2.2   Color Intensities

When we use *n* number of bits to represent each color intensity, we are restricted to a certain range of values. For example, given 2 bits per color value, we can represent the four binary numbers 00, 01, 10, and 11. One way to interpret these values is as equally spaced intensities. This results in intensity values of 0.0, 0.33333, 0.66667, and 1.0. This is called a *linear scale* because the difference between each successive value is the same—in this case one third. When a color value is used directly as an intensity, it is sometimes referred to as *true color*. The name might be a little misleading because it does not mean that the color values are exact. It simply means the color values are indeed color values (and not indexes into lookup tables). True color is used widely in data formats even though it is a poor scheme for color matching between devices.

Data formats that store color values *only* as direct intensities are listed below. In other words, these data formats do not support lookup tables (See Section 6.2.3 for a description of lookup tables).

DATA FORMATS THAT SUPPORT ONLY DIRECT COLOR

Data Format	Name of Data Used in Implementation	Comments
AVS Image	Pixels	ARGB values; each 8 bits
CCITT Fax G3	Picture elements	1 bit per pixel (black or white)
DDES UEF00	Pixels	CMYK (8 bits per value)
EPSI	Samples	Monochrome; grayscale
IGES	Color	RGB values
JBIG	Pixels	Up to 256 bits per pixel
JFIF	Samples	YC_rC_b values
JPEG	Samples	Up to 256 samples/pixel; 8 bits/sample
MacPaint	Pixels	1 bit per pixel (black or white)
MPEG	Pixels	YC_rC_b values

DATA FORMATS THAT SUPPORT ONLY DIRECT COLOR   *(Continued)*

Data Format	Name of Data Used in Implementation	Comments
PICT	Pixels	Grayscale and RGB
X Bitmap	Pixels	1 bit per pixel (black or white)

6.2.3   Color Indexes

A linear mapping between color values and color intensities will not always produce the desired results on a particular output device. Consider the example given previously of 2 bits per color value. Instead of equally spaced intensities, a range of four intensities such as 0.03, 0.25, 0.55, and 1.0 might be needed. In this example the differences between consecutive intensity values are not equal. These intensities are said to be nonlinear. (If you plot the values on a graph, they will not produce a straight line). The typical method of allowing for nonlinear intensity values is through lookup tables. In this scheme a color value represents an index into a table, not an actual intensity. The table holds the actual intensity values. A color lookup table goes by many names, including lookup table, color table, LUT, color map, and palette. All these names refer to exactly the same idea. The color value is usually referred to as a color index.

The use of a lookup table in this way is sometimes referred to as *Direct Color.*[*] Grayscale images use a single lookup table (since they have only one intensity value per pixel). Full-color images often use separate lookup tables for each intensity component per pixel (e.g., one for red, one for green, and one for blue). The following data formats support color tables that define nonlinear ranges of intensity values.

DATA FORMATS THAT SUPPORT NONLINEAR INTENSITY VALUES

Data Format	Name of Data Used in Implementation	Comments
PostScript	settransfer	Can be implemented as a lookup table or as a function calculation; it establishes a single mapping that can be used for grayscale or color pixels
	setcolortransfer	(Same as settransfer) except that it establishes separate functions for each color component; 3 for RGB and 4 for CMYK
TIFF	GrayResponseCurve	One table for grayscale images
	GrayResponseUnit	Specifies the precision of the values in the GrayResponseCurve table
	ColorResponseCurves	Three separate tables; one for red, one for green, and one for blue

---

[*]The term Direct Color comes from the XLib windowing system.

DATA FORMATS THAT SUPPORT NONLINEAR INTENSITY VALUES *(Continued)*

Data Format	Name of Data Used in Implementation	Comments
TGA	Direct-Color	Three independent color tables; one each for red, green, and blue
	Color Correction Table	A block of 256 × 4 two-byte integers, one value each for A:R:G:B (alpha, red, green, blue) components
CGM	Color Calibration	Three independent correction tables; one each for red, green, and blue. They establish the mapping from nonlinear to linear intensities
IIF	Gamma correction	Parameters must be supplied for formulas for gamma addition or removal

A different reason for using color lookup tables is to lower the memory requirements for a raster image. As the number of bits used to represent each color grows, so do the memory requirements. The following chart shows the memory requirements for a raster image that is 512 × 512 pixels, given different numbers of bits per intensity value and different numbers of intensity values per pixel. Provided the data bits are tightly packed (there are no padding bits), the number of bytes of memory required to store a raster image can be calculated by

$$\frac{(\text{image width}) \times (\text{image height}) \times (\text{bits/intensitYy}) \times (\text{intensities/pixel})}{(8 \text{ bits per byte})}$$

As you can see in the following table, the memory requirements for a single "full color" raster image is quite large.

STORAGE NEEDED FOR AN IMAGE AS A FUNCTION OF COLOR PRECISION

# of bits per intensity	Intensities per pixel	# of bytes needed for a 512 × 512 image	Comments
1	1	32,768 = 32 KB	Black and white
4	1	131,072 = 128 KB	
8	1	262,144 = 256 KB	Grayscale
12	1	393,216 = 384 KB	
8	3	786,432 = 768 KB	Full color
12	3	1,048,576 = 1152 KB	

An ideal color scheme would allow for a large range of colors while reducing the number of bits needed to represent each pixel's color. Color lookup tables provide such a scheme. The lookup table uses a precision that allows for a wide range of color intensities. The color of each individual pixel is then represented as an index into the color table. Given a scheme that uses n bits to represent its color indexes, its color table size, N, will be equal to 2^n. Given that the number of bits used to represent the intensity of each color is m bits, the number of possible number of colors, M, will be equal to 2^m. A common phrase in this regard is, "This scheme allows N simultaneous colors out of a possible palette of M colors," where N and M are substituted with their appropriate values.

SOME TYPICAL CONFIGURATIONS FOR COLOR LOOKUP TABLES

# of bits per index	Table size	# of bits per color	Possible colors	Comments
2	4	5	32	4 colors out of a possible 32
4	16	12	4,096	16 colors out of a possible 4,000
8	256	24	16,777,216	256 colors out of a possible 16,000,000

DATA FORMATS THAT REQUIRE THE USE OF COLOR LOOKUP TABLES

Data Format	Name of Data Used in Implementation	Comments
CUR	Color table	Limited to 2, 8, or 16 entries
DDES UEF01	Color table	From 1 to 256 entries allowed
DXF	Indexed	256 entries (0–7 are predefined)
FLI	Color table	Either 64 or 256 entries
GIF	Color table	1, 2, 4, 8, 16, 32, 64, 128, or 256 entries
GRASP	Color table	
HP-GL	Indexed	Selects a pen on a plotter
ICO	Color table	Limited to 2, 8, or 16 entries
X Pixmap	Color table	No limits on the table size

DATA FORMATS THAT SUPPORT BOTH COLOR LOOKUP TABLES AND TRUE COLOR

Data Format	Name of Data Used in Implementation	Comments
BMP	Color palette	Size is 2, 16, or 256 entries
CGM	Color table	Size arbitrary
DDES UEF02	Color table	9 predefined entries (CAD-type data)
HDF	RIS8-color table RIS24	Always 256 entries RGB true color values
IIF	Lookup table	No size restrictions

**DATA FORMATS THAT SUPPORT BOTH COLOR
LOOKUP TABLES AND TRUE COLOR** *(Continued)*

Data Format	Name of Data Used in Implementation	Comments
PCX	Color table	16 or 256 entries
	Grayscale	Does not support RGB
PICT	Color table	
PostScript	DeviceGray	True color monochrome
	DeviceRGB	True color RGB
	DeviceCMYK	True color CMYK
	CIEBasedABC	True color
	CIEBasedA	True color
	Indexed color space	Color table; up to 4,096 entries
RLE	Color map	Size limited to powers of 2
SunRaster	Color map	Limited to 256 entries
TGA	Pseudo-Color	No limit on color table size
	True-Color	4 values per pixel; ARGB
TIFF	ColorMap	3 values per entry; size of the table is a power of 2
xim	Color map	Exactly 256 entries
X Window Dump	Colormap	No limit on the color table size

6.2.4   Color Samples per Pixel

As we have discussed previously, color representations typically use one sample per pixel for grayscale images, three samples per pixel for RGB color values, and four samples per pixel for CMYK color values. In some cases, samples other than one, three, or four are required. For example, duotone printing[*] needs only two samples per pixel. Data formats that allow samples other than the traditional one, three, and four samples per pixel include the following:

**DATA FORMATS THAT PERMIT OTHER THAN 1, 3, OR 4
SAMPLES PER PIXEL**

Data Format	Name of Data Used in Implementation	Comments
DDES UEF01	"Extended definition"	Up to 16 allowed
IIF	Color bands	No limit specified
JBIG	Pixel planes	Up to 256, 1-bit pixel planes allowed
JPEG	Components	Up to 255 allowed; 8 bits per value
RLE	Channels	Up to 255 allowed; 8 bits per value

---

[*] Duotone printing is done typically with red and black inks, but it is not limited to these colors.

To summarize, color values represent percentages of either light intensity or pigment. Three general approaches exist for specifying these values:

- Use real numbers that have basically unlimited precision.
- Use limited precision values that are mapped onto a linear scale.
- Use limited precision values that are mapped onto a nonlinear scale, often through the use of lookup tables.

Of the data formats discussed in the appendices of this book, PostScript is the only format that supports all of these options. TIFF comes close, but it does not allow unlimited precision color values.

A large amount of software is required to support all of the color representations we have just discussed. To reduce software complexity, data formats often only support one or two of these representations.

6.3 MATCHING COLORS

The representation of a color that produces a particular color on one system will, more than likely, not produce the same color on any other system. This is sometimes true even of similar systems made by the same manufacturer. Some of the reasons for this are:

- The type of phosphors used on the surface of CRT varies from one manufacturer to another. Each phosphor generates unique light spectra[*] when voltage is applied to it, therefore producing different colors.
- The type of ink, toner, wax, and other color mediums used for printing varies from one manufacturer to another. These substances have different color qualities, produce different shades of color, and combine differently to form other colors.
- Printing inks and mediums have complex reflective spectra and therefore rarely produce "pure" colors.
- Printing inks and mediums can become contaminated with other inks and substances in the process of making them or through the process of applying them to paper.

It is difficult to reproduce identical colors on different system, and in some cases it is impossible. Two major problems exist. One concerns the rate at which color intensities change with respect to changes in the corresponding color values. The other has to do with the fact that different devices form different ranges of colors. The data needed to correct each problem is examined next.

6.3.1 Gamma Correction

The human eye is not sensitive to the exact amount of change between two intensities of light, only the ratio of change. For example, a change in intensity from 0.1 to 0.2 and from

---

[*] Spectra are the ranges of wavelengths in a light source.

0.2 to 0.4 will be perceived as an equal amount of intensity change because both have a ratio of 2. When a set of intensities do not vary by a constant amount, they are said to be nonlinear. Most graphical systems are nonlinear, including the human eye, the phosphors on CRT screens, the halide emulsions of photographic films, and the pigments used for printing. The critical factor in matching colors between systems is to know the ratio at which changes in intensity produce changes in perceived color.

The equation $I = I_0 + cv\gamma$ is commonly used to approximate nonlinear intensity values in graphical systems.* The value of γ in the equation characterizes the rate of intensity growth. The value of γ varies between systems. For most graphical systems γ lies somewhere in the range from 1.0 to 3.0. A γ of approximately 1.7 is typical for vidicon camera tubes; a γ of approximately 2.5 is typical for standard televisions. When two different systems have different γ values, they will produce drastically different images from the same data. If we know what the γ value is on the system that captured the original image, and the γ value for the output device, we can modify the light intensities to compensate for the differences. Any system that uses the γ information to correct for color intensity is said to use *gamma correction*.

Consider the following four lists of intensity values. Each list contains eight levels of intensity. These are typically represented as simple integers over a certain range. In this case a 3-bit binary index value is sufficient, as shown in the far left column. The first list of intensities has a constant difference of 0.125 between each pair of consecutive values. This constant difference causes the intensity values to have a linear relationship. This is the type of relationship many graphics systems assume for their color values, ignoring totally the nonlinearity of their particular hardware devices.

RELATIONSHIP BETWEEN INDEX AND OUTPUT FOR DIFFERENT VALUES OF GAMMA

Index	Binary value	(1) Linear $\gamma = 1.0$	(2) Nonlinear $\gamma = 2.0$	(3) Nonlinear $\gamma = 3.0$	(4) Nonlinear ratio = 1.6003
0	000	0.125	0.015625	0.00195	0.0372
1	001	**0.250**	0.062500	0.015625	0.059536
2	010	0.375	0.140625	0.0527	0.095276
3	011	0.500	**0.25**	0.125	0.152471
4	100	0.625	0.390625	**0.244**	**0.2440**
5	101	0.750	0.562500	0.42185	0.3904
6	110	0.875	0.765625	0.66992	0.62488
7	111	1.000	1.000000	1.00000	1.00000

The second and third lists include values generated from the nonlinear intensity equation with a γ of 2.0 and 3.0, respectively. Notice how the intensity values vary. The fourth

---

* The I_0 value is the lowest possible intensity value for the device, which is typically not exactly zero. c is some constant factor, and v is the amount of energy for a given intensity.

list is the ideal case, where the ratio between consecutive intensity values is a constant ratio—in this example the ratio is approximately 1.6. Notice that lists three and four are similar but not identical. List four is a theoretical ideal while list three is a close approximation. We say again, the equation $I = I_0 + cv\gamma$ is an approximation. It gives good results in many cases, but it is not exact for any particular device.

Four values in the above lists are shown in bold font for comparison. Notice that if we were using an output device that had linear characteristics (List 1), we would have stored a value of (001) as the color intensity for 0.25. If we use this same value on a system with a γ of 2.0, the resulting intensity will be only 0.0625. This produces a totally different color (and probably not the color intensity we wanted). To get the same intensity on a different device requires a modification of the intensity indexes.

Gamma value recommendations differ between standards and between devices. Some examples include:

GAMMA VALUES FOR STANDARD VIDEO FORMATS

Description	Recommended Gamma Value
NTSC	2.2
EBU (European Broadcast Union)	2.8
CCIR 709	2.22222 (1/0.45)

DATA FORMATS THAT ALLOW THE SPECIFICATION OF A SINGLE GAMMA CORRECTION VALUE

Data Format	Name of Data Used in Implementation	Comments
PostScript[‡]	settransfer	Establishes a function appropriate for the calculations; this function is used for all intensity values of each pixel
	setcolortransfer	Same as settransfer except that a separate function is established for each separate value of the pixel
TGA	Gamma Value	A single γ value (range of 0.0 to 10.0)

[‡]The PostScript "transfer function" is a general purpose mechanism. There is no restriction on the type of function that can be defined. It could define a gamma equation, any other suitable equation, or a lookup table.

In applications where the γ equation is not accurate enough to produce a desired level of color matching, lookup tables are used. (Refer to Section 6.2.3 for a list of data formats that are able to support gamma correction through lookup tables.)

6.3.2   Agreeing on Color Hue

Another requirement for matching colors is the ability to agree on a common precise specification for colors. To say, "I want this object to be red," is not sufficient for color matching. We do not need to store every color in a single precise specification. What we need to know

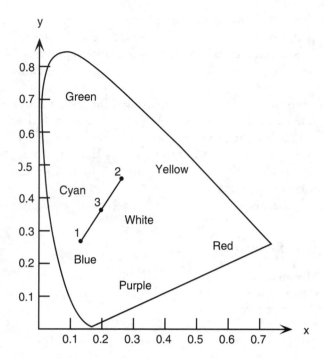

Figure 6.3   CIE 1931 *xyz* color gamut

is how the representation being used relates to a common, agreed-upon standard. In most cases a mathematical conversion is possible between different systems of representation.

An international organization called the Commission Internationale de l'Eclairage (CIE—the International Commission on Illumination) produced a standard for color matching in 1931. The standard defines the CIE chromaticity diagram, which is based on three primary basis values it calls *x*, *y*, and *z*. It is beyond our scope here to explain the CIE 1931 standard in detail, but an in-depth discussion can be found in [Foley90], [Hill90], and [Netravali88]. We will describe enough of the standard to explain the data needed to match colors.

The CIE 1931 *xyz* chromaticity diagram is shown in Figure 6.3. Each point located within the curve on the diagram represents a color at full intensity. For example, black and shades of gray cannot be located in the diagram because they are not full intensity colors. The general locations of typical basis colors are marked within the curve on the diagram. The diagram defines a linear additive color specification system. To explain what that means, pick any two points within the curve of the diagram. If you were to combine equal portions of both colors, you would get the color location exactly on the midpoint of a line connecting the two original locations. An example of this idea is displayed in the diagram as points 1, 2, and 3. All proportional combinations of the colors specified by points 1 and 2 are located along the line segment connecting them.

6.3.3 Color Gamuts

If we specify the locations within the CIE chromaticity diagram of the three basis colors for an additive color system, they define a triangle. This triangle includes all of the displayable colors that can be created by proportional combinations of the three basis colors. The range of colors that can be reproduced by a device is called its color *gamut*. An example of a color gamut specified in terms of the CIE diagram is shown in Figure 6.4. (This particular gamut is the SMPTE recommendation for color television receivers.) Color gamuts vary from one device to the next, and are rarely exactly equal, even between similar devices (e.g., two CRTs). The amount of variance between dissimilar devices, like a CRT and a color printer, is typically quite large. If the color gamuts are known for two different devices, then it is possible to make some adjustments to compensate for their differences. Notice, however, that when two triangles do not lie exactly on top of each other, there will always be colors that are inside one triangle and outside the other. It is impossible to reproduce such colors to match exactly on both devices. (Besides this, due to the nonlinear way in which printer pigments mix, the color gamut of most printers cannot be defined by a triangle on the CIE diagram.)

To make corrections for different gamuts data is needed that specifies exactly the gamut of a device. One standard method for doing this specifies the locations of the basis colors within the CIE chromaticity diagram. Standard values for red, green, and blue have been defined by several standards organizations. Some samples are listed below, including the original values specified by the NTSC for color television, the more recent recommendations for televisions by the Society of Motion Picture and Television Engineers (SMPTE),

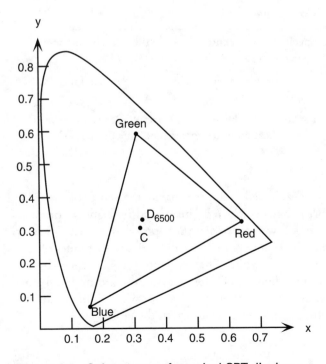

Figure 6.4 Color gamut of a typical CRT display

and the recommendations for the PAL television standard. The original NTSC primary values have been largely abandoned by manufacturers who now use phosphors that have higher color saturation and higher luminance. In any event, these standards are only targets for manufacturers. In practice, the actual values are device dependent and can change over time for a particular device. For example, as a CRT ages, its phosphors become duller. Not only that, the three phosphors age at different rates. The only foolproof method of color matching is to actually measure the values of the primary colors with a colorimeter on a regular basis and use this data to calibrate the device.

**SPECIFICATION OF PRIMARY COLORS FOR SELECTED
VIDEO STANDARDS**

	Original NTSC		SMPTE		PAL	
	x	y	x	y	x	y
Red	0.67	0.33	0.635	0.340	0.64	0.33
Green	0.21	0.71	0.305	0.595	0.29	0.60
Blue	0.14	0.08	0.155	0.070	0.15	0.06

**DATA FORMATS THAT SUPPORT THE SPECIFICATION OF
COLOR GAMUTS USING THE CIE DIAGRAM**

Data Format	Name of Data Used in Implementation	Comments
TIFF	Primary chromaticities	Specifies as the x and y values in the CIE chromaticity diagram for red, green, and blue
CGM:1992	Color calibration	Allows the CIE x and y values to be specified for the primary colors
IIF	Color conversion	For conversion between XYZ and RGB, matrix permits specification of red, green, and blue primary XY values

6.3.4   White Point

In the CIE chromaticity diagram, white is located in approximately the center of the color curve. Some proportional amount of the basis colors red, green, and blue add to produce white. To match colors it is important to know exactly what those proportions are. One way to specify these proportions is to locate the "white point" exactly. This allows shades of colors to be created correctly as they move toward white. The white point is influenced by the viewing conditions, specifically the ambient lighting. Different systems use different definitions of white. In the CIE color standard, several different values for white light are identified. These are designated with the letter *A*, *B*, *C*, etc., as shown in the table.

SPECIFICATION OF VARIOUS WHITE POINT VALUES

Name	Degrees[‡]	x	y	Comments
A	2,854K	0.4476	0.4075	Light from a tungsten lamp
B	4,874K	0.3840	0.3516	Direct sunlight
C	6,774K	0.3101	0.3162	Average sunlight
D5000	5,000K	0.3457	0.3586	Bright tungsten illumination
D6500	6,504K	0.3127	0.3297	"Natural" daylight
E	5,500K	0.3333	0.3333	Normalized reference source

‡ The measurement of white light comes from the light generated by a black body as it is raised in temperature from 1,000 °K to 10,000 °K. The color of the light varies in relation to the temperature applied.

The two most commonly used specifications for white light are C and D6500. These values are marked on the CIE chromaticity diagram (Figure 6.4). Hard copy output is often viewed under D5000 as a standard illumination. Computer displays often have a white point of approximately 9,300 °K. This is a very blue-shifted white value that increases brightness but adds to the difficulty of matching hard copy output to a display image.

DATA FORMATS THAT SUPPORT THE SPECIFICATION OF THE "WHITE POINT"

Data Format	Name of Data Used in Implementation	Comments
PostScript	WhitePoint	Part of the CIE Based ABC color space definition; specified in CIE 1931 XYZ coordinates with Y always 1
TIFF	White Point	Specified as the x and y values in the CIE chromaticity diagram
CGM:1992	White Point	Specified as the x and y values in the CIE chromaticity diagram
IIF	Color conversion	X, Y, and Z tri-stimulus values of white nonlinear point

If the appropriate gamma, color gamut, and white point information is included in a data set, color values can be calibrated to reproduce consistent colors on a wide variety of devices (within the physical limitations of each device). Very few data formats store color calibration information (with the exception of CGM:1992 and the desktop publishing formats, PostScript, and TIFF). As you might infer, color calibration is critical to printing systems. Color calibration between CRTs is not a critical issue for many applications. On CRTs, simple gamma correction often produces satisfactory results.

6.4 OTHER COLOR MODELS

Until recently, nearly all data formats associated with computers have used either RGB or CMYK color models for data storage. This could very well change in the near future because data-compression techniques are using other color models to achieve larger compression ratios. In particular, the YC_rC_b color representation is being increasingly used.

6.4.1 "Color Difference" Representation

In the early 1950s, a color encoding was standardized for the transmission of color television by the United States National Television Systems Committee (NTSC). The NTSC mandated that any new color encoding allow existing black and white televisions to continue functioning without modification. A standard black and white television signal contains a single luminance, or brightness value for each pixel on the screen. The new color signal had to keep this luminance signal unchanged while adding color. A "color difference" encoding resulted.

A television camera receives light from a scene and divides the light into its red, green, and blue components. The luminance Y of the light is calculated with the equation

$Y = 0.299 \times \text{Red} + 0.587 \times \text{Green} + 0.114 \times \text{Blue}^{*}$

Using this calculated luminance value, two "color difference signals" are then calculated that contain the chrominance, or color information. These are the $(R - Y)$ and $(B - Y)$ signals. The $(R - Y)$ value is an orange-cyan hue, which is very important for creating flesh tones. The $(B - Y)$ value is a green-magenta hue. These three values, Y, $(R - Y)$, and $(B - Y)$, form the basic color representation for all current television data encodings.[†]

Using some straightforward mathematics and rewriting these equations in matrix notation produces the following:

$$\begin{bmatrix} 0.299 & 0.587 & 0.117 \\ 0.701 & -0.587 & -0.194 \\ -0.299 & -0.587 & 0.886 \end{bmatrix} \begin{bmatrix} \text{Red} \\ \text{Green} \\ \text{Blue} \end{bmatrix} = \begin{bmatrix} Y \\ (R-Y) \\ (B-Y) \end{bmatrix}$$

The red, green, and blue color values can be regained from the Y, $(R - Y)$, and $(B - Y)$ values without loss of information by using the inverse of the matrix above. This gives:

$$\begin{bmatrix} 1.000 & 1.000 & 0.000 \\ 1.000 & -0.509 & -0.194 \\ 1.000 & 0.000 & 1.000 \end{bmatrix} \begin{bmatrix} Y \\ (R-Y) \\ (B-Y) \end{bmatrix} = \begin{bmatrix} \text{Red} \\ \text{Green} \\ \text{Blue} \end{bmatrix}$$

---

[*] The notation Red, Green, and Blue in a typical analog television specification would read E'_r, E'_g, E'_b respectively. The E stands for energy, and the prime (') means the values are gamma corrected.

[†] There are slight variations between the NTSC, PAL, and SECAM systems relating to the percentage of $(R - Y)$ and $(B - Y)$ that is actually transmitted. Refer to [Netravali88] for details.

   This color representation has two major advantages over an RGB representation. First, the luminance value provides backward compatibility with black and white televisions. Second, the chrominance values can be encoded at a lower precision and resolution than the luminance values while still maintaining reasonable image quality. This is possible because the human eye is more sensitive to small-area changes in luminance than it is to small-area changes in hue and saturation. The human eye perceives fine detail only through the luminance of an image. It can be argued that it is a waste of resources to send luminance and color information at the same level of detail because the human eye cannot discern fine detail from the color values. This lower detail required for the $(R - Y)$ and $(B - Y)$ values is beneficial for data compression.

6.4.2 YIQ and YUV Color Encodings

Three different analog *encodings* of the Y, $(R - Y)$, and $(B - Y)$ signals are currently used around the world for television broadcasting. The differences are due mainly to technological advances between the time each system was introduced, and also due to some political considerations.

   To create an analog NTSC color signal that fits within the 6 MHz bandwidth allowed for a black and white signal, the following encoding was developed. The Y value is carried on an amplitude-modulated (AM) signal with a bandwidth of approximately 4.2 MHz. The $(R - Y)$ value and the $(B - Y)$ value are encoded together on a different signal with a bandwidth of approximately 1.8 MHz. The $(R - Y)$ value is the "in-phase signal" (amplitude modulated) and is designated by the letter I. It uses approximately 1.3 MHz of the bandwidth. The $(B - Y)$ value is the "quadrature signal" (phase modulated) and is designated by the letter Q. The $(B - Y)$ value uses approximately 0.5 MHz of the bandwidth. The acronym *YIQ* comes from this encoding scheme. The remaining details of the *YIQ* encoding are beyond the scope of this text. Refer to [Netravali88] for a thorough discussion.

   When all of the color signals of a television broadcast (i.e., Y, I, and Q) are encoded simultaneously into a single 6-MHz frequency band, the signal is called a *composite* color video signal.

   The color quality of an NTSC encoded image is often criticized, but its quality has nothing to do with the Y, $(R - Y)$, $(B - Y)$ color representation. The poor color quality comes from the low amounts of information encoded for the chrominance values due to the limited bandwidth available.

   The PAL and SECAM color television signals were defined in the mid-1960s, and they created new, "improved" encodings based on the experience gained from the use of the NTSC encoding. The symbols U and V are used to designate the encodings of $(R - Y)$ and $(B - Y)$; thus the acronym *YUV*. For more details on these analog encodings refer to [Netravali88].

6.4.3 YC$_r$C$_b$ Color Representation

A digital encoding of the Y, $(R - Y)$, and $(B - Y)$ values has been standardized as the CCIR Recommendation 601-1, drafted in 1981. The following equations use the same symbols and nomenclature as the 601 specification:

$$E'_Y = 0.299 \times E'_R + 0.587 \times E'_G + 0.114 \times E'_B$$

$$(E'_R - E'_Y) = E'_R - (0.299 \times E'_R + 0.587 \times E'_G + 0.114 \times E'_B)$$

$$= 0.701 \times E'_R - 0.587 \times E'_G - 0.114 \times E'_B$$

$$(E'_B - E'_Y) = E'_B - (0.299 \times E'_R + 0.587 \times E'_G + 0.114 \times E'_B)$$

$$= -0.299 \times E'_R - 0.587 \times E'_G + 0.886 \times E'_B$$

Note that these equations are identical to ones presented in Section 6.4.1. The Red, Green, and Blue values (i.e., E'_R, E'_G, and E'_B) are assumed to be fractions in the range of 0.0 to 1.0. Notice that the luminance equation will always produce a value for Y in the range of 0.0 to 1.0. However, the color difference equation for $(E'_R - E'_Y)$ produces values in the range from -0.701 to $+0.701$, and the color difference equation for $(E'_B - E'_Y)$ produces values in the range from -0.886 to $+0.886$. These ranges are not ideal for digital representations, so they are both remapped into the range of values -0.5 to $+0.5$. This gives

$$E'_{C_R} = 0.713 \, (E'_R - E'_Y) = 0.500 \times E'_R - 0.419 \times E'_G - 0.081 \times E'_B$$

$$E'_{C_B} = 0.564 \, (E'_B - E'_Y) = -0.169 \times E'_R - 0.331 \times E'_G - 0.500 \times E'_B$$

These values are converted to an 8-bit binary encoding using the equations:

$Y = \text{round}\,(219 \times E'_Y + 16)$
$C_R = \text{round}\,(224 \times 0.713 \times (E'_R - E'_Y) + 128)$
$C_B = \text{round}\,(224 \times 0.564 \times (E'_B - E'_Y) + 128)$

To understand these equations we need to explain the idea of "headroom" and "footroom." In printing, film, and video it is common practice to leave some of the possible coding values below "reference black" (called the footroom) and some values above "reference white" (called the headroom). This is done because the original analog signals can sometimes be outside of the legal range. To allow for footroom and headroom, the CCIR 601-1 recommendation specifies a range of 220 values for the luminance value (Y) and 225 values for the chrominance values. This range of values is indicated in Figure 6.5.

Combining all of the above into a single equation and converting it to a matrix notation gives the following equations:

$$\begin{bmatrix} 65.48 & 128.55 & 24.97 \\ 111.96 & -93.75 & -18.21 \\ -37.77 & -74.16 & 111.93 \end{bmatrix} \begin{bmatrix} E'_Y \\ E'_R \\ E'_B \end{bmatrix} + \begin{bmatrix} 16 \\ 128 \\ 128 \end{bmatrix} = \begin{bmatrix} Y \\ C_R \\ C_B \end{bmatrix}$$

$$\begin{bmatrix} 0.004566 & 0.006261 & 0.000000 \\ 0.004566 & -0.003189 & -0.001537 \\ 0.004566 & 0.000000 & 0.007915 \end{bmatrix} \begin{bmatrix} Y \\ C_R \\ C_B \end{bmatrix} + \begin{bmatrix} -0.8745 \\ 0.5319 \\ -1.0862 \end{bmatrix} = \begin{bmatrix} E'_Y \\ E'_R \\ E'_B \end{bmatrix}$$

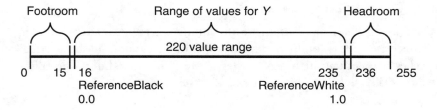

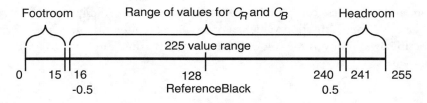

Figure 6.5 Headroom and footroom in digital coding of CCIR 601 video

DATA FORMATS THAT USE THE YC_RC_B COLOR ENCODING

Data Format	Name of Data Used in Implementation	Comments
CGM:1992	RGB related	Matrix and lookup table parameters can be set up to specify the YC_rC_b encoding
IIF	YC_rC_b	
JFIF	YC_bC_r	Uses the entire 256 value range to code each value (i.e., it does not allow for footroom and headroom codes)
JPEG	none	JPEG does not specify a color model, but most implementations of the encoding use a YC_rC_b color representation
MPEG	YC_rC_b	
PostScript	CIEBasedABC	Parameters can be set up to specify the YC_rC_b encoding
TIFF (JPEG)	YC_rC_b Coefficients	Allows either the CCIR 601 or CCIR 709 encoding

6.4.4 CCIR Recommendation 709

The "color difference representation" calculation for luminance works well in general, but other luminance calculations are possible and produce better visual results under specific lighting and color conditions. (This assumes that the color signals are sampled at a lower resolution than the luminance signal and that there is some information loss during encoding). CCIR recommendation 709 specifies another color model that is very similar to 601-1 with the exception that it calculates the luminance value with the following equation:

$$Y = 0.2125 \times \text{Red} + 0.7154 \times \text{Green} + 0.0721 \times \text{Blue}$$

Notice that the green and blue contributions to the luminance are increased while the red contribution is decreased. This luminance calculation produces more pleasing visual results in natural scenes that contain high percentages of green and blue hues. The JPEG encoding supported by TIFF allows for this color encoding scheme.

6.4.5 HSB Color Space

The hue, saturation, and brightness color model (HSB) is allowed in PostScript files. It is also referred to as the HSV (hue saturation value) color space in the literature. Interpreters that translate PostScript always convert the colors specified as HSB values directly into RGB colors before using them.

6.5 SAMPLE COLOR SPECIFICATION SYSTEMS

There are many other color specification systems defined, and each system has its own particular virtues and shortcomings. Only three data formats described in this book allow for color specifications other than the ones we have previously discussed: IIF, ODA, and PostScript.

IIF supports the color specifications listed in the following list. As a side note, the IPI DIS 12087-2 Annex G.3 lists 59 different transformation matrixes that transform values between different color systems. Assuming that these specifications are included in the final International Standard (IS) version of the IPI standard, they will be a good reference to color space conversions.

COLOR SPACES SUPPORTED BY THE SC24 IMAGE PROCESSING AND INTERCHANGE STANDARD

Data Format	Name of Data Used in Implementation	Comments
IIF	Cie1931Space	
	cie-repr	
	subtractive-repr	
	additive-repr	
	video-repr	
	CieRepresentation	
	cie-xyz	
	cie-lab	
	cie-luv	
	cie-uvw	
	cie-yxy	

**COLOR SPACES SUPPORTED BY THE SC24 IMAGE
PROCESSING AND INTERCHANGE STANDARD** *(Continued)*

Data Format	Name of Data Used in Implementation	Comments
IIF	SubtractiveRepresentation	
	cmy	
	cmyk	
	AdditiveRepresentation	
	ntsc-rgb	Linear or gamma
	ebu-rbg	Linear or gamma
	smpte-rgb	Linear or gamma
	ccir-rgb	Linear or gamma
	VideoRepresentation	
	yiq	
	yuv	
	ycrcb	
	Cie1964Space x10y10z10	
	UncalibratedSpace	
	additive-rgb	
	subtractive-cmyk	

ODA Amendment 2 recognizes the color specifications listed next. All conversions between the different color specifications are defined in reference to CIE 1931 *XYZ* color space. A unique feature in the ODA specification is a "color tolerance" factor that specifies the amount of variance colors can tolerate during processing and still satisfy the intent of the document originator.

**COLOR SPACES SUPPORTED BY THE OPEN DOCUMENT
ARCHITECTURE STANDARD**

Data Format	Name of Data Used in Implementation	Comments
ODA	Linear RGB	Nongamma corrected
	Nonlinear RGB	Gamma corrected
	CMY	
	CMYK	
	CIE L*u*v*	
	CIE L*a*b*	

PostScript implements a general-purpose color scheme. It allows for the specification of a set of functions and matrix multiplications that can be applied to the components of a color representation. Assuming these functions are established correctly, any number of color space transformations can be specified. According to the PostScript "red book" (level 2), these transformations can handle the color models listed below (among others).

COLOR SPACE TRANSFORMATIONS PROVIDED BY POSTSCRIPT

Data Format	Name of Data Used in Implementation	Comments
PostScript	DeviceGray	Grayscale
	DeviceRGB	Red, green, blue
	HSB	Hue, saturation, brightness
	DeviceCMYK	Cyan, magenta, yellow, black
	CIEBasedABC	(Some examples include the following)
		CIE 1931 XYZ-space
		Calibrated RGB space
		CIE 1976 L*a*b*-space
		YIQ
		YUV
	CIEBasedA	(Some examples include the following)
		Luminance Y component of CIE 1931 XYZ-space
		Gray component of a calibrated gray space
		L* component of the CIE 1976 L*a*b*-space
		Luminance Y component of NTSC, SECAM, and PAL
	Indexed color space	Color lookup table
	Pattern color space	Painting with patterns
	Separation color space	Color separation for a single color print, apart from the CMYK separations

COLOR SPACES SUPPORTED BY THE COMPUTER GRAPHICS METAFILE STANDARD

Data Format	Name of Data Used in Implementation	Comments
CGM	RGB related	This includes gamma corrected YC_RC_B, YUV, and YIA
	CMYK	
	CIE LUV	
	CIE LAB	

6.6 SUMMARY

Specification of color is a problem with many different dimensions. Data streams vary greatly in their ability to carry the wishes (and knowledge) of the originator about color information. Even if the data stream carries full information, there is no guarantee that the receiver will have the knowledge, hardware capability, or interest to accurately reproduce the received information.

Color information can be expressed in an additive color space, such as used by computer and video displays, or in a subtractive color space suitable for printers. Subtractive color spaces are very complex, since the pigments (inks) have complex nonstandardized absorption spectra, and interactions between the inks are difficult to quantify. Also, black is often added as a fourth "primary" component, replacing some amount of the other inks in dark areas. This means that there is no unique transformation in either direction between additive and subtractive color spaces.

The human visual system is nonlinear in its response to linear increases in light intensity. By chance, this nonlinearity is closely matched by nonlinearity in display monitors, and an inverse nonlinearity in the original video camera tubes. This nonlinearity must be taken into account (but only once) in order to efficiently encode information across a range of brightness levels. Lookup tables can be used to provide the required correction in intensity, known as *gamma correction*. Lookup tables can also be used to specify a small palette of colors needed to present an image. The color index values into the lookup table can be specified with fewer bits than are used to specify the colors in the selected palette, thus providing a form of data compression.

There are two additive color spaces that were standardized by the CIE, based on experimental color, matching studies of human participants. There are also some mathematical transformations of those spaces. One goal is to separate luminance (brightness) information from chrominance (color) information, since the human visual system is more sensitive to fine spatial detail changes in intensity than in color. The color information can thus be spatially subsampled. There are several different ways to encode the three-component chrominance information into two signals. There are several different standards for these color encodings.

The bottom line is that different data formats provide different levels of support for specifying the color of objects and viewing conditions under which the data is displayed. It is up to the receiver of this information to use it appropriately. For some applications, a reddish, greenish, bluish color space may be sufficient, but others require more precise color matching. Information in the data stream related to color can be ignored by a receiver, but a receiver who wants color calibration information not present in the data stream is out of luck.

DATA ORGANIZATION

CONTENTS

7.1 INTRODUCTION

A data set can be conceptualized as a sequential list of individual data values. Such a sequential list is often referred to as a *data stream*. Graphical hardware devices are designed to operate on data streams organized in a particular way. If the organization of a data stream is incompatible with the requirements of a particular graphical device, the data must be restructured to a suitable organization. This restructuring always requires memory (either main memory or secondary memory), and often requires some amount of computational manipulation. A data stream is unusable on any incompatible device if there is either insufficient memory or computational resources to restructure it.

The organization of a data stream has a direct impact on the amount of memory required to use the data and the speed at which the data can be accessed. Memory and computational resources can be minimized if a data stream satisfies the "Structure Principle"— that is, the static structure of a data stream should correspond in a simple way to the dynamic use of the data. Regrettably, the structure principle is generally unattainable because of the vast number of diverse graphical hardware devices that use graphical data streams. Fortunately, however, memory and CPUs have become inexpensive enough to allow data restructuring on many devices.

This chapter discusses data stream organization. It is divided into two major sections. Section 7.2 discusses how individual data values are recognized within a data stream. We call this *low-level* data stream organization. The issues pertaining to how values are recognized have an important impact on the *extendibility* of a data stream's definition. Section 7.3 discusses how data is organized at a conceptual level. This includes topics such as interleaving scan lines in a raster data stream and the ordering vectors in a geometry data stream to minimize plotting time. Data organization has a direct impact on the *efficient* use of the data and on the difficulty of restructuring the data for any particular device.

7.2 LOW-LEVEL DATA STREAM ORGANIZATION[*]

Each data value within a data stream has a meaning, a conceptual representation, and a physical representation. Technically, these are referred to as a data value's semantics, data type, and encoding. This is summarized in the following table:

DISTINCTION BETWEEN SEMANTICS, DATA TYPE, AND ENCODING

Technical Name	Common Name	Example
Semantics	Meaning	Number of pixels (horizontally)
Data type	Conceptual representation	2-byte integer (unsigned)
Encoding	Actual (physical) representation	Huffman encoded (Chapter 9)

To correctly interpret a data stream, the semantics, data type, and encoding associated with each individual data value must be known.

7.2.1 Recognizing Individual Data Values

The simplest data stream organization *predefines* the semantics and data type for each relative location within a data stream. Actual data values are the only information stored in the data stream. The major problem with this scheme is that it is not extendible; new data cannot be added to the data stream.[†] Any variance from the predefined specification causes the data stream to be misinterpreted. This data organization can be visualized as in Figure 7.1.

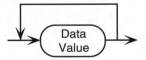

Figure 7.1 Schematic representation of a totally defined data stream

---

[*] It is sometimes difficult to separate organization issues from encoding issues because they are interrelated. This section touches on encoding issues, but the major details on data encoding can be found in Chapter 8.

[†] It is possible to append new data values to the end of the data set, but this is an insufficient solution in most cases.

An alternative data stream organization stores the data type and semantics along with each data value. The order of the data values does not have to be predefined, providing more flexibility as compared to the previous scheme. However, it can significantly increase the storage requirements for a data stream, possibly by a factor of 3. See Figure 7.2.

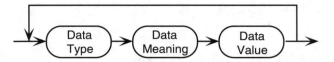

Figure 7.2   Representation of a data stream with type, semantic, and value information

This alternative is still not extendible. To make a data stream extendible, any process that reads the data stream must be able to ignore data it cannot recognize or understand. For a sequential list of data values, this means knowing how to jump to the next value in the list. If a data reader does not recognize a data type, it does not know how the value is represented (i.e., the number of bytes it uses). Therefore, it does not know how far to jump ahead. To accommodate this, the data stream can include an additional data-length value as shown below. In this and the two following examples, the length information can precede or follow the data type information. The data length is usually redundant information for any process that recognizes the data type, but it is not redundant to those processes that are unable to recognize the data type. Adding the length descriptor, we get the scheme shown in Figure 7.3.

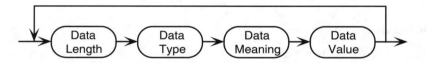

Figure 7.3   Adding length field for each data occurrence, for extendibility

The overhead cost required to make a data stream flexible and extendible can become large. One scheme for minimizing the descriptors is to include a repetition factor that allows one triplet (data type, data length, data meaning) to be associated with more than one data value. This scheme is represented in Figure 7.4.

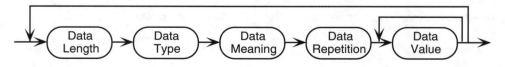

Figure 7.4   Adding a repetition value to create a self-defining data stream

Data formats that store data type and semantic information are often referred to as *self-documenting* data streams. Self-documenting data streams satisfy our extendibility design goal at the sacrifice of simplicity. Comparing the efficiency of self-documenting and predefined organizations is difficult. The self-documenting scheme satisfies our localized cost goal by allowing for the inclusion of only relevant data. If a typical application were always to include all predefined data values, then the self-documenting scheme would waste memory. The predefined scheme stores much less information per individual data value but it requires all predefined data values to be present in the data stream, even if they are not needed. The efficiency of both the self-documenting and predefined data schemes is application and data dependent.

Note that nothing precludes using both schemes within a single data stream. Blocks of data can be predefined and preceded by an identifier and length value. The identifier allows a block definition to be recognized, and the length value allows a block to be skipped if it is not recognized (or not desired by a particular application). This scheme, as shown in Figure 7.5, has become the predominant method for defining data streams. It allows for efficient data storage and for future extensions to the data stream definition.

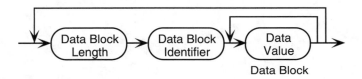

Figure 7.5   Adding length field to a blocked data stream

In summary, there are many ways to structure the low-level organization of a data stream. In the following sections we discuss specific examples of various organization schemes. Each section includes a list of other graphical data formats that use the same general scheme. Note that the data organization scheme used by a data stream is interrelated with its data encoding and compression schemes. Data encodings are discussed in detail in Chapter 8, and compression schemes are covered in detail in Chapters 9 and 10.

Totally Predefined Data Stream (MacPaint)

The MacPaint data format is a good example of a totally predefined data stream. It contains a header of exactly 128 bytes, a set of pattern descriptions of exactly 512 bytes, and a sequence containing the raster data values. The pattern data is required, even if the raster data contains no patterns. This is a highly rigid organization with little room for extension or modification. MacPaint's data format does define several empty data slots in its header to allow for the inclusion of new data items, but this is a very restrictive scheme for extending the data format. Leaving empty slots in a data block for future extensions is common in many data formats. Though this is not a bad idea, it's not very flexible. See Figure 7.6.

"Older" data formats often concerned themselves with device issues such as blocking factors on a disk drive. Notice the 128 byte records defined by MacPaint ($512 = 4 \times 128$). Data partitioned into blocks consistent with a particular hardware device allows for faster

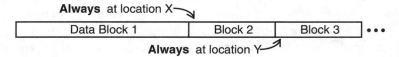

Figure 7.6   Address calculation in a totally predefined data stream

access to the data. Most "newer" data formats do not concern themselves with blocking factors because there is sufficient memory on devices to buffer the data, and any gains in speed by aligning to block boundaries is typically negligible.

DATA FORMATS THAT HAVE TOTALLY PREDEFINED ORGANIZATIONS

Data Format

AVS Image	MacPaint
BMP	SunRaster
CUR	TGA
DDES UEF00	xim
DDES UEF01	
DDES UEF02	

Data Blocks with Lengths

The simple inclusion of a block length with a set of predefined data values allows for easy extension of the data stream. The purpose of the length value is to know the location of the next data block. Assuming that the length value is always used to access the next data block,[*] new data values can be defined and added to the end of the data block without consequence. Older readers will simply skip over and ignore any new data. Newer ones will understand the meaning of new data values and use them accordingly. (This assumes that new data values do not fundamentally alter the structure of the data stream. If they did, older readers would get confused.) See Figure 7.7.

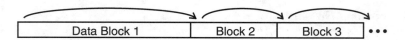

Figure 7.7   Address calculation for data blocks which include length

Data formats that include data block sizes are listed in the following table. These formats implement data block lengths only in certain data sections and not consistently throughout their entire definition. This is a violation of our consistency design principle. If a data format uses block lengths, why not use them consistently throughout the data stream?

---

[*] Software systems that access data streams sometimes cheat to simplify the task of reading the data. Typically, these shortcuts do not become apparent until the specification of a data stream becomes extended.

DATA FORMATS THAT INCLUDE DATA BLOCK SIZE

Data Format	Comments
GIF	Used only for extension blocks and raster data blocks; not used for main header blocks
X Window Dump	

Data Blocks with Lengths and Tags (IFF)

A natural extension to data blocks with lengths is to include an identifier, or "tag," for each distinct data block of a data stream. The tag identifies the format and information content of the block. The data block can be interpreted by any processor that recognizes the tag; otherwise it is skipped and ignored. Now we have two schemes for extending the definition of a data stream: 1) define entire new blocks with new tags, or 2) include additional data values at the end of existing data blocks. See Figure 7.8.

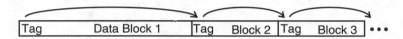

Figure 7.8   Address calculation for data block with tags and lengths

Let's combine the tag and block length values and call them a *header* for the data block. For simplicity and consistency we can divide the entire data stream into logical data blocks, each with a beginning header. The overhead cost for this scheme is minimal if the data blocks are sufficiently large. An example of this scheme is the IFF data format. It refers to each block of data as a *chunk*. Each chunk has a header of 8 bytes. The first 4 bytes define an integer that specifies the size of the chunk. The second 4 bytes give an ASCII character string that identifies the chunk.

The use of headers also facilitates the nesting of smaller data blocks within larger data blocks to any arbitrary depth required by an application. One example of nested data blocks comes from the CCITT Recommendation H.261. The organization of its data stream is shown in Figure 7.9. A "picture" is made up of a group of data blocks, labeled GOB data in the diagram. Each of these data blocks is composed of a header and other data blocks. A nice feature of header-labeled data blocks is the ability to leave out data that a particular application does not need. This is crucial to the H.261 data stream applications that are compressing real-time video data. The portions of a picture that do not change from one video frame to the next can be simply left out of the data stream. The headers ensure that each included block is interpreted appropriately.

Some professionals have proposed the definition of a standard universal header for chunks (clips) of video information. The SMPTE Header/Descriptor Task Force has proposed two possible header definitions as of June 1992.

One final word on headers: for continuous data streams in real-time applications the data stream is incoming at a fixed rate. The idea of skipping over data might be more appropriately termed *waiting*. Instead of counting bytes until the next data block appears, we must scan for a unique identifier that marks the beginning of a new data block. The

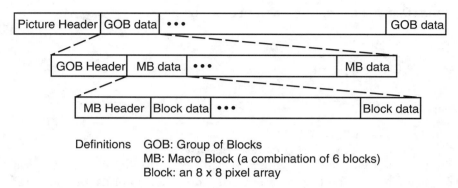

Definitions   GOB: Group of Blocks
              MB: Macro Block (a combination of 6 blocks)
              Block: an 8 x 8 pixel array

Figure 7.9   Data stream structure for CCITT recommendation H.261

ability to recognize the beginning of a new data block is important for two reasons: 1) it allows a device to jump into the "middle" of a data stream and synchronize with it (such as with a real-time digital television signal), and 2) it allows for recovery from errors in the data stream.

Specifying unique identifiers within a data stream is more difficult than simply tagging each data block at its beginning. In the latter case all you have to do is read the tag. You know where it is because you just finished reading the previous block. Searching for a unique tag identifier requires that no other sequence of bits in the data stream match the tag except the actual tag itself. As an example, let's examine the JPEG scheme for tags.

JPEG calls its tags *markers*. A JPEG marker is always 2 bytes long. The first byte is always set to 255 (i.e., the hexadecimal value FF). The second byte can be any number except 0 or 255. The value of the second byte determines the marker's meaning. For example, the sequence of bytes 255, 216 (hexadecimal FFD8) is the Start of Image (SOI) marker. There is a possibility that actual data values within the data steam can contain a byte equal to 255. Such data values could be interpreted as markers if something is not done. To eliminate this possibility, any data value equal to 255 is immediately followed by a "stuffed" zero byte. If a 255 byte is found while scanning the data stream and a zero byte immediately follows it, the 255 byte is treated as data and the zero byte is ignored. (Sequences of more than 1 byte equal to 255 are allowed as "filler bytes" in front of markers.)

The JPEG scheme works well for the uniquely labeling of each data block of the data stream. It requires only 2 bytes per tag. Given the uniqueness of the tags, no data-length values are stored in each header. Each block is found by scanning for the next marker.

Data Blocks With Repetition (TIFF)

The TIFF file structure is unique among the data organizations discussed in this book because it is the only file structure that requires random access support for processing. The essence of this idea is that a "data dictionary" stores a listing of the "types of information" contained in the data stream. Each entry in the data dictionary describes a particular type of data and includes a pointer to the location of the actual data values. The location is represented as an offset, in bytes, from the beginning of the file. This structure is shown in Figure

7.10. There is a fixed-length header at the beginning of the file that, among other things, points to an initial directory. There is one directory per raster image. A TIFF data stream can contain more than one raster image by including more than one data directory.

Information in a TIFF data stream is labeled by both its semantics (tag) and its data type. These are not combined into a single value as other formats often do, for two reasons. First, not combining them allows the same information to be represented by more than one type of data. This allows the data to be represented in the most efficient data type for the particular image. For example, a set of pointers can be shorts (2 bytes) or longs (4 bytes), depending on the size needed to represent locations in the data stream. It also makes the format a little more extendible. Second, when a TIFF reader encounters a tag that it does not recognize, it can still print out the information in a correct and readable format for a user to examine.

The overhead cost for storing the data dictionary information is minimal for large blocks of data but becomes significant when single data values are stored. To reduce this cost, TIFF stores actual data values within the data dictionary if they will fit within the 4 bytes normally used to store the location pointer (i.e., the "offset to values" field). This saves memory in the data stream and speeds access to the data.

A directory can be positioned anywhere within a TIFF data stream, even at the end. In fact, placing the directory at the end simplifies the creation of a TIFF data stream. The directory entries contain pointers to the data values. The value of each pointer is not always

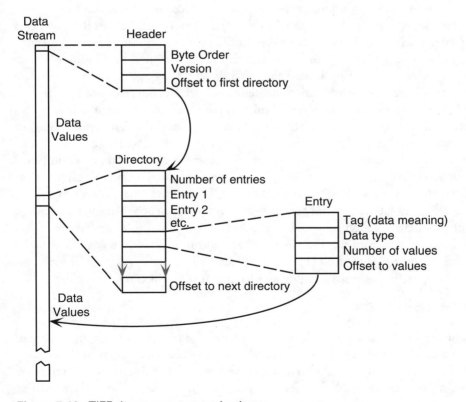

Figure 7.10 TIFF data stream organization

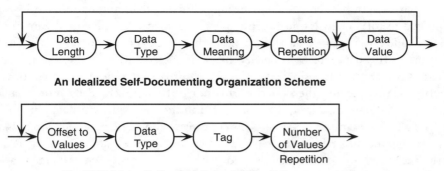

An Idealized Self-Documenting Organization Scheme

The TIFF "data dictionary" Organization Scheme

Figure 7.11   Comparison of self-defining data stream and TIFF data dictionary organization

known until the data values have been positioned in the data stream. Placing the directory in front of the actual data requires preprocessing to calculate the required space for each data item. This is time consuming in some cases, such as when data compression is used to reduce the size of the data. (The size of the data is unknown until after the compression operation has been performed.)

A TIFF-compliant reader is expected to follow the offset pointers to each data item in the data stream. The reader should not assume anything about the order of the data, except that the directory entries are contiguous. In the worst-case scenario, there can be a significant number of "seeks" back and forth through the data stream, which slows the process of reading the data. This is a good example of the conflicts that can occur between creating a data stream and accessing a data stream. TIFF is organized to simplify the creation of a data stream. The organization is not optimized for speed of access, though it can be if the data stream is structured properly—something the definition permits but does not require.

The TIFF organization structure is very similar to the idealized self-documenting structure we described earlier. Both structures are shown in Figure 7.11. The only difference between the schemes is that TIFF uses a data-pointer in place of a data-length. This is possible (and necessary) because the data values are stored separately from their "definition." One advantage to this scheme is the ability of a data reader to determine quickly the contents of a data stream without having to read all of it. This allows a data reader to request and allocate resources needed to process the data more efficiently. Another advantage relates to our Modularity design principle. If the data stream contains more than one raster image, the directory structure has the effect of segmenting the file into logical modular divisions. One disadvantage to the TIFF format is that, while it allows for good modularity, it does not require it. Potentially highly inefficient data streams can be created.

Predefined Data Blocks (IGES)

All data within an IGES data stream is represented by an entity record and an associated parameter record. These two records are stored separately in the data stream and are associated by a unique index value. In the first several versions of IGES, all entity records are defined using a fixed-length, fixed-field format that predefines two 80-character text lines. The entity records are stored sequentially in a "Directory Entry Section." The unique value assigned to each entity is equal to the line number of its first text line (relative to the beginning of the section). Figure 7.12 shows the definition of an entity record, where each predefined field is labeled and delimited by column numbers.

It is beyond our purpose to specifically define each field. You can correctly infer most of their meanings by their labels. This record definition is logical for many primitive graphical entities, such as line segments and arcs. Such graphical primitives must typically have associated attributes like line weight, color, and level. These data values are associated with the graphical primitive by being stored together contiguously within a single record. The semantics of each data value is predefined according to its location in the record. The IGES format is consistent: *all* data entities use this record structure for their definition. For example, consider the following sample definition of a Transformation Matrix Entity (type number 124).[*]

```
{ other lines above }
     124        2        1        0        0        0        0        0      10300D  3
     124        0        0        2        0                                     0D  4
{ other lines }
124,-0.67499,-0.171,0.71774,1.00728,-0.24401,0.96977,                           3P  2
0.00157,-0.821391,-0.69631,-0.17408,-0.69631,4.613057,0.0;                      3P  3
```

Perhaps it is not obvious, but there is a tremendous amount of wasted storage in using this scheme. A transformation matrix does not typically have an associated color! The consistency of the IGES format makes it complex instead of simple. Each type of entity requires the inclusion of different fields within the entity record, and the fields default to various values depending on the entity type. Having one predefined record for all the representations of all data types is not a good idea when you have dissimilar types of data. The initial versions of the IGES format used storage inefficiently and were confusing. The latest version of IGES addresses this problem somewhat by defining variable-length records.

Associating data values by organizing them contiguously is a good idea but not by using the single fixed-length entity records defined in the initial IGES format. Graphical entities that are dissimilar in structure should each have their own unique data structures.

1–8	9–16	17–24	25–32	33–40	41–48	49–56	57–64	64–72	73–80
Entity Type Number	Parameter Data	Structure	Line Font Pattern	Level	View	Transformation Matrix	Label Display Assoc.	Status Number	Sequence Number
Entity Type Number	Line Weight Number	Color Number	Parameter Line Count	Form Number	Reserved	Reserved	Entity Label	Entity Subscript Number	Sequence Number

Figure 7.12 Fields in an IGES entity record

---

[*] *Initial Graphics Exchange Specification (IGES) Version 4.0,* U.S. Department of Commerce, June 1988, pp. 363, 367.

Self-documenting—ASCII-encoded (DXF)

A DXF data stream is encoded as ASCII text and is organized as a set of *groups*. A group is composed of two lines of text. The first line contains a *group code*, and the second line contains a *group value*. The group code specifies both the data type and semantics of the group value. Ranges of code values are associated with a particular data type. Using this scheme, even if a decoder does not recognize the meaning of a particular value, it always knows the data type.

**DATA TYPES ASSOCIATED WITH
RANGES OF DXF GROUP CODES**

Group Code Range	Type of Data that Follows Code
0–9	String
20–59	Floating-point
60–79	Integer
210–239	Floating-point
999	Comment (string)

An example of a DXF encoding of a line segment going from the *x-y-z* point (23.34, 34.2, 45.3) to the point (12.5, 13.4, 23.4) is shown below. A data group is always stored on two consecutive lines of text; the group code comes first followed by the group value. Each line is terminated by an end-of-line marker (typically a carriage-return character). The 0 group identifies the start of a new entity. The 8 group defines an entity's "layer." Codes 10–18 are used to specify *x* coordinate values; codes 20–28 are used to specify *y* coordinate values; and codes 30–37 are used to specify *z* coordinate values. The order of the *x-y-z* values in the data stream is not specified, and a DXF reader should accept the point values in any order.

```
0
Line
8
0
10
23.34
20
34.2
30
45.3
11
12.5
21
13.4
31
23.4
```

Only those values related to the line segment that are different from normal default values need to be included with the entity definition. For example, groups can be included to specify line type, line thickness, line color, etc. Two-dimensional data is easily represented by simply leaving out the z coordinate group codes. This scheme satisfies the localized cost principle because only the needed data is stored. This ability comes at the cost of requiring the storage of the data type and semantics of each and every data value. The overhead is minimized by combining the type and semantics into a single value.

The DXF format is totally consistent throughout its definition. The overall organization of a DXF data stream is divided into four major sections: HEADER, TABLES, BLOCKS, and ENTITIES. Each of these sections is delimited with appropriate groups. For example, the HEADER section would look like the following:

```
0
SECTION
2
HEADER
{data groups that define header data go here}
0
ENDSEC
```

The structure of a DXF file is simple, straightforward, and consistent. It also can create very large data streams because every *single* data item must be tagged. The size of the file depends on the number of nonstandard entities in the data stream. Perhaps this is an extreme use of data tags. A compromise between the rigid records of IGES and the free format of DXF seems appropriate.

Data Tags in General

The tags employed by DXF have predefined meanings, at least by ranges of numbers. ISO has defined a Standard Generalized Markup Language, known as *SGML*, which can be used to tag any type of information. The power of SGML is that a community of users can define a set of tags that satisfies its needs. The rules for what combinations of tags are legal and where they can appear in a data stream can be set by the community of users as well.

Because SGML has no semantic biases of its own, it can be used with any type of information. Its initial use was to demark logical units in documents. However, it has also been used to encode a subset of the Computer Graphics Metafile (CGM), although this work has not yet been adopted as an ISO-approved encoding. SGML tags are expressed in text characters, so they can be read by humans.

There is one problem with SGML. Although anyone receiving a document encoded in SGML can determine the presence and location of start and end tags, the meaning of the tags is not predefined. The semantics of a tag are contained in the "tag expansions," or backing functions. However, there is no standardized language for writing (or transmitting) backing functions. Thus, it is easy for users to add new tags and extend an SGML-based encoding. The problem is that old processors may not be able to do anything with the data. However, the requirement that every start tag have an associated end tag means that an interpreter can at least skip over information it does not understand.

Data Organizations for ASCII Encodings

Data that is ASCII-encoded (i.e., text) follows different schemes from those we have discussed so far. The data type of each data item can be inferred. For example, consider the following line of text from a GRASP file:

```
waitkey    500
```

The first data item is a character string, whereas the second is an integer. In addition, the length of each data item is inferred from the "white space" that separates the data items. The data type and length are easily discernible without their explicit inclusion in the data stream. The data semantics can be inferred by the location of the data item within the data stream. In the previous example the value 500 is a parameter to the waitkey function.

7.2.2 Connecting Data Values

Up to this point in our discussion we have been talking about a set of data values without any reference to the relationships between values. In most cases there are important relationships that must be represented. The following table summarizes four possible methods for representing relationships between data values. The first two schemes use data organization to imply association; the last two schemes use extra data values. It is possible to use all four schemes within a single data stream. The first two schemes are more efficient with respect to storage because they do not require extra data values. However, there is a limit to the kinds of associations that can be represented by physical organization alone.

DIFFERENT WAYS TO ESTABLISH RELATIONSHIPS AMONG DATA VALUES

Method Used	Advantages	Disadvantages
Store associated data contiguously within a data stream	Simple	Does not allow for complex relationships between data values to be defined
Construct the data stream according to a predefined strategy that associates the data values correctly	Minimizes the repetition of data values	The association of data values is not always clear
Store a pointer to the exact location of the associated data values	The associated data can be retrieved without searching Can allow for multiple pointers for complex data relationships	Difficult to modify the locations of the data while maintaining the associations
Label a data value with a unique identifier that allows other associated data to reference it	The locations of the associated data does not have to be known	Requires searching to find associated data values

We want data formats to be both "information preserving" and to satisfy the principle of "localized cost." The organization scheme should allow for the representation of all data relationships that exist without overhead cost for the storage of relationships that do not exist.

7.3 RASTER DATA ORGANIZATION

This section surveys the typical organizations used to order raster data. A raster data stream is a group of sampled values. The organization of these sampled values is based on one or more of the following dimensions:

- *Spatial (i.e., geometric space)*   The location of the sample values within space.
- *Spectral*   Multiple values per sample location, typically to represent color, but other values are possible, such as scientific instruments that sense invisible infrared light, or vector components of a flow field.
- *Temporal*   Relationships according to time, usually relating to a series of raster data streams played back in sequence to create moving pictures.

Several factors determine how data is organized within these dimensions. These include:

- The ordering required for specific output devices
- The data processing performed by specific applications
- Bandwidth limitations on communication channels
- Data compression schemes

7.3.1 Spatial Organization for Two-Dimensional Data

The most common scheme for ordering 2D raster samples is by horizontal rows referred to as *scan lines*. Most raster hardware devices display data in scan-line order from top to bottom. They define their Cartesian coordinate system with the origin in the upper-left-hand corner and the *Y* vertical axis going down. This is a "natural" orientation for hardware devices. For example, it is natural for a printer to print the top of a page first and then proceed down the page. In contrast, the typical orientation used to define 2D space in mathematics will position the origin in the lower-left corner with the *Y* vertical axis going up. People typically like to think about and process data in this coordinate system. These two scan-line orderings are shown in Figure 7.13.

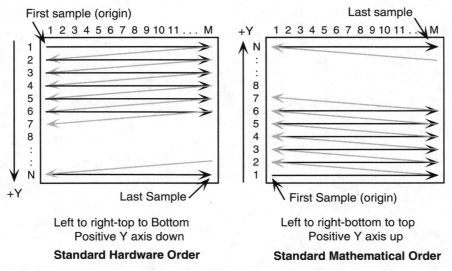

Figure 7.13 Natural raster ordering for hardware and in mathematics

To be compatible with hardware devices, most raster data formats order their scan-lines from top to bottom. Some data formats use the standard mathematical ordering; these are listed in the following table. Note that these data formats must reorder their data for display and that the reorganization requires memory. Also note that HP-GL/2 is included in the list, but HP-GL is not. Probably the most dramatic change that occurred between HP-GL and HP-GL/2 was the flip in axis orientation.

DATA FORMATS THAT USE MATHEMATICAL RASTER ORDERING

Data Format	Name Used in Implementation	Comments
BMP		
CGM	VDC EXTENT	The default is $+Y$ axis up, but it can be redefined to go down; $+X$ axis can also be redefined to go left
CUR		
DDES	picture orientation	9 different orderings are defined (see appendices)
HP-GL/2		
ICO		
PostScript		The "scale" command can flip either orientation axis

Some raster data streams alter the purely sequential ordering of scan-lines to meet application-specific needs and constraints. Raster data streams for television are *interlaced* into even and odd rows to reduce the perception of flicker during viewing. By interlacing the scan lines, all of the even (or odd) scan lines can be updated on the screen in one-half the time of the full refresh rate. The entire screen is updated in two separate passes down the screen. Even/odd interlacing is shown in Figure 7.14. It is universally agreed that interlacing scan lines is not ideal for image quality [Amanatides90]. It is used only because of the bandwidth restrictions on a broadcast television signal. Most televisions today do not have memory; instead they display the incoming data directly onto the screen. If current trends

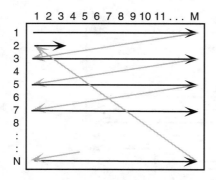

(Only the odd scan-lines are shown)

Figure 7.14 Odd-even scan line interlacing

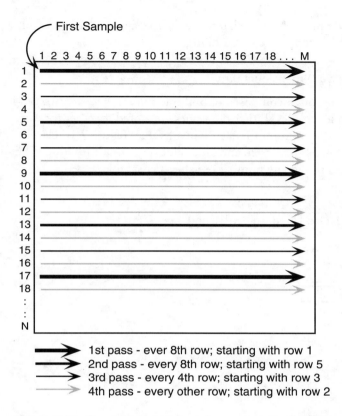

1st pass - ever 8th row; starting with row 1
2nd pass - every 8th row; starting with row 5
3rd pass - every 4th row; starting with row 3
4th pass - every other row; starting with row 2

Figure 7.15 Four phase interlaced sample order for GIF raster data

continue, however, newer televisions will have memory and the need for interlacing will vanish. (More than likely the new HDTV data format will not be interlaced.)

Another use for interlacing is to allow users to terminate the transmission of data over slow communication channels if they determine that the data is not wanted. This allows for savings of both time and money. The GIF data format defines an optional interlaced ordering that requires four passes to process all of the scan lines of a raster data stream. Refer to Figure 7.15. The first pass contains one-eighth of the image scan-lines (every 8th row). The second pass contains another one-eighth of the scan lines, the third pass contains another fourth, and the last pass contains the remaining scan lines (i.e., one-half). This scheme presents a quick overview of the image data while gradually filling in the fine details on the final pass.

Some data schemes do not define an ordering of the scan lines at all, and the data stream is required to label the position of each row. The RLE data format uses this scheme with its "SkipLines" operator.

In summary, the selection of an ordering of scan lines within a raster data stream is influenced by the orientation of the coordinate system and the communication-channel bandwidth. These issues become less critical for devices that have memory. Given sufficient memory (and processing) capacity, the organization of incoming raster data is less critical to a hardware device. With cheaper memory, more hardware devices are becoming capable of accepting any data stream and reordering it to their liking.

7.3.2 Spectral Organization for Two-Dimensional Data

Each sample of a raster data stream is often composed of multiple values; there are two typical organizations for these multiple samples. Either the values are stored together for each sample or they are stored as separate structures for each type of value. Figure 7.16 clarifies these two schemes using a typical case of red, green, and blue values per sample location. The general idea holds for any type of data and any number of values per sample.

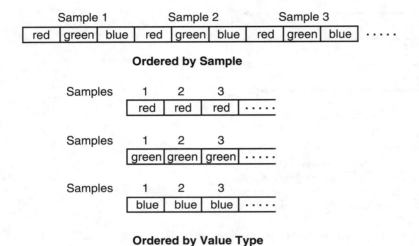

Figure 7.16 Ordering multiple value per sample raster data by sample, and by value type

Different disciplines use different terminology to express the separation of raster data according to value types. Computer graphics uses the term *color planes*. Prepress creation for the printing industry uses the term *color separation*. Scientists sometimes use the term *vector field*. All of these terms add meaning to the data values used in particular applications, but the structure of the values remains identical.

**DATA FORMATS THAT ALLOW MULTIPLE DATA VALUES PER SAMPLE
AND THAT SUPPORT ONLY ORDERING BY SAMPLE**

Data Format	Name of Data Used in Implementation	Comments
AVS Image		Always 4 values per sample: ARGB
AVS Field		
BMP		RGB if 24 bits per pixel
CGM		RGB
CUR		

**DATA FORMATS THAT ALLOW MULTIPLE DATA VALUES PER SAMPLE
AND THAT SUPPORT ONLY ORDERING BY SAMPLE**   *(Continued)*

Data Format	Name of Data Used in Implementation	Comments
FITS		
Flux	pixel3, pixel4	
GEM/IMG		
ICO		
SunRaster		
TGA		
X Pixmap		

The XIM data format supports only ordering by value type.

DATA FORMATS THAT SUPPORT ORDERING BOTH BY SAMPLE AND BY DATA TYPE

Data Format	Name of Data Used in Implementation	Comments
DDES—UEF00		Allows color separation by both individual scan line and by page
HDF	RIS24	Allows color separation by both individual scan line and by page
IIF		
JBIG	ILEAVE flag	Organized as interleaved or noninterleaved bit-planes
JPEG	(See Section 7.3.3)	
netCDF		
PostScript	"multi" parameter to the "colorimage" command	Stands for multiple data sources
RLE	SetColor operand	Allows ordering "by sample" as scan lines (not sample by sample)
TIFF	PlanarConfiguration	
X Window Dump	XYBitmap XYPixmap ZPixmap	

7.3.3   Block Organization for Data Compression

Data compression is often performed on raster data organized in scan-line order, but other data organizations can greatly enhance the efficiency of compression schemes. Currently, the

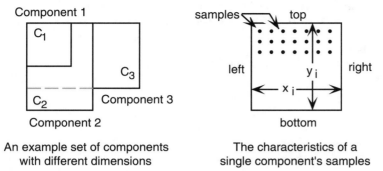

Figure 7.17   Block organized data examples

most widely used compression scheme for non–scan-line organized data is the discrete cosine transform (DCT). The DCT uses blocks of values instead of strips (i.e., scan-lines). Consequently, the source image data is organized by blocks. The standard block size used in most implementations is an 8×8 array of samples.[*] Data formats that use the DCT include JPEG, MPEG, and CCITT H.261. Let's examine the JPEG data organization first.

JPEG's data is organized as a set of 2-dimensional sample arrays. Each array of samples is called a *component*. The sample arrays are not required to have the same dimensions. Some of the samples can be taken at higher resolutions than other samples. This is different from the previous schemes discussed, where all of the samples are assumed to be at the same resolution. Typically, there are three components: one luminance component, and two chrominance components that are sampled at half the spatial resolution of the luminance data. Each component has its own dimensions, as shown in Figure 7.17. The number of samples in the horizontal direction for component C_i is called x_i. The number of samples in the vertical direction is called y_i.

Figure 7.17 is drawn to indicate that each component can contain a different number of samples in either spatial direction. In actuality, each component covers the same physical area, but it is just sampled at a different resolution.

Each component is divided into blocks of 8×8 samples, starting from the upper-left corner. In a noninterleaved scheme, the blocks from each component are ordered left to right and top to bottom. These groups of blocks are then concatenated starting with component one, and proceeding sequentially. Figure 7.18 gives an example of this scheme. Each labeled square is an 8×8 block of samples.

The JPEG standard also defines an interleaved scheme where the data blocks from the different components are intermixed in the data stream. If the number of samples is the same for each component, then the interleaved scheme is straightforward—it takes a block from each component in sequence. For example, given three components A, B, and D, the ordering would be A_1, B_1, D_1, A_2, B_2, D_2, etc.

Interleaving data blocks from components sampled at different resolutions requires intermixing a different number of blocks from each component. To accomplish this, a horizontal scaling factor H_i and a vertical scaling factor V_i is defined for each component C_i.

[*] Other block sizes are possible. Our discussion is limited to the 8×8 block, but it can be easily generalized to other block sizes.

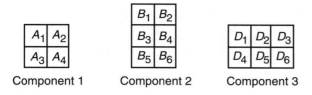

Order: A_1 A_2 A_3 A_4 B_1 B_2 B_3 B_4 B_5 B_6 D_1 D_2 D_3 D_4 D_5 D_6

Figure 7.18   Noninterlaced ordering of multiple component data blocks

The maximum horizontal and vertical scaling factors for all of the components are designated H_{max} and V_{max}. H_i and V_i are not unique for a given set of components, but they must satisfy the following equations such that the number of samples for each component can be calculated correctly. In the equations, X is the maximum of all x_i and Y is the maximum of all y_i.

$$x_i = \left\lceil X \frac{H_i}{H_{max}} \right\rceil \qquad \text{and} \qquad y_i = \left\lceil Y \frac{V_i}{V_{max}} \right\rceil$$

These equations illustrate that the size of each smaller component is a fractional proportion of the size of the largest component. The H_i and V_i values define a partitioning of each component. Within each partition, the blocks are ordered from left to right and top to bottom. Refer to Figure 7.19. Component 2 has samples at twice the resolution compared to Component 1. Therefore, four blocks of samples from Component 2 cover the same area as a single block from Component 1. When these blocks are interleaved, they need to be grouped accordingly. For example, the A_1 block from Component 1 is grouped with the B_1 B_2 B_5 B_6 blocks from Component 2, and the D_1 D_2 blocks from Component 3.

The JPEG scheme for interlacing components of various resolutions is very general, but the interlacing schemes for MPEG and CCITT H.261 are more rigid. They specify that an image is always composed of pixels representing the YC_rC_b color model and that the C_rC_b values are always subsampled at half the resolution of the Y values. The location of these samples is shown in Figure 7.20.

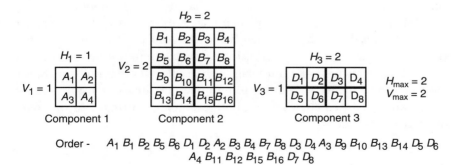

Order - A_1 B_1 B_2 B_5 B_6 D_1 D_2 A_2 B_3 B_4 B_7 B_8 D_3 D_4 A_3 B_9 B_{10} B_{13} B_{14} D_5 D_6
A_4 B_{11} B_{12} B_{15} B_{16} D_7 D_8

Figure 7.19   Interleaved ordering of data blocks from nonuniformly sampled components

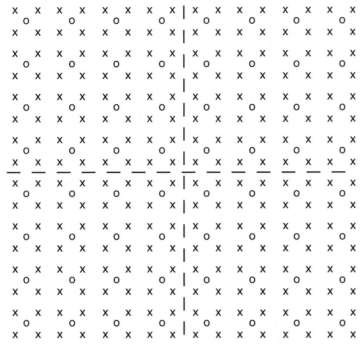

x: Position of luminance samples (Y)
o: Position of chrominance samples (C_R C_B)

Figure 7.20   Sample locations used by MPEG and CCITT H.261

7.3.4   Precision Organization for Two-Dimensional Data

All three organization schemes we have just discussed for raster data can store (or transmit) each sample value at full precision. For real-time or near real-time applications we would want it no other way. However, in some situations it is beneficial to initially send data at less than full precision. Over time, precision is added to the initial image until either the precision matches the maximum precision capacity of a receiving device or a user terminates the data stream because they determine the image is not wanted.

Let's consider an example of both cases. Suppose we have an image sampled at a resolution of 1024×1024 pixels. If we transmit such an image to a receiving device that can display only 640×480 pixels, we have wasted 75 percent[*] of the transmission time. Consider another example: a deep space probe using a slow communication channel. We do not want to wait for the retrieval of a full image only to discover that our camera was pointed in the wrong direction. We would like to terminate the image transmission and try again with the camera pointed elsewhere. In both examples, starting with the transmission of a low-precision image is beneficial.

---

[*] Assuming that we display the 1024×1024 image at half its resolution, the resulting image will be 512×512, which has only one-fourth as many pixels as the larger image.

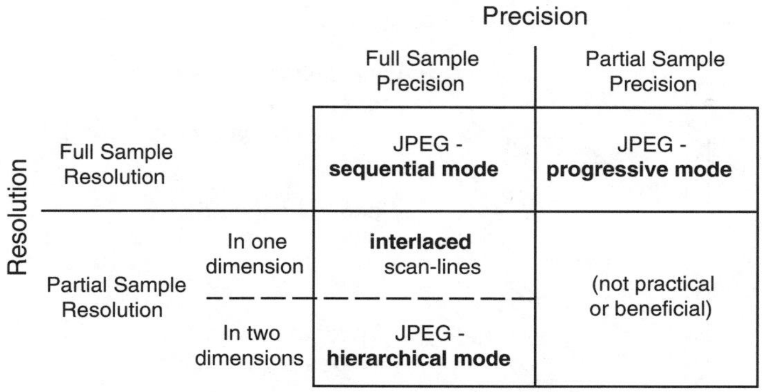

Precision

	Full Sample Precision	Partial Sample Precision
Full Sample Resolution	JPEG - **sequential mode**	JPEG - **progressive mode**
Partial Sample Resolution — In one dimension	**interlaced** scan-lines	(not practical or beneficial)
Partial Sample Resolution — In two dimensions	JPEG - **hierarchical mode**	(not practical or beneficial)

(Resolution — left axis label)

Figure 7.21 Possible schemes for image precision reduction

The precision of an image can be lowered either by lowering the precision of each sample or by lowering the resolution of the samples. Doing both at the same time is not practical. Figure 7.21 summarizes these possible schemes. JPEG is the only data stream definition that actually defines and supports all three options.

In JPEG progressive mode the entire image is stored at full resolution but each block of 8×8 pixels has a reduced precision. To fully understand this mode, you need to understand JPEG's compression scheme, which is described in detail in Chapter 10. For now, just recognize that JPEG divides a raster image into 8×8 blocks of samples and then orders the resulting 64 values into a sequential list. The beginning values in the list are more significant to the precision of the image than the later values in the list. By sending only the first couple of values from each data block, we can get an idea of what the image looks like. We follow the first image with another image that contains another group of values from each data block and these progressively add more detail to the image. JPEG calls this scheme *spectral selection progressive encoding*. A visual representation of this is shown in Figure 7.22. Note that this scheme requires a decoder to work harder than normal to create an image. Each time new data comes in, it must recompute the entire image. This is acceptable if we have plenty of computational power but limited transmission bandwidth.

Figure 7.22 shows a list of 64 values broken into groupings of 1, 4, and 6. The JPEG standard does not limit the number of groups or how many values are included in each group. In the extreme case an image could be broken into 64 separate groups. In the typical case an image might have 3 to 6 groups. The only restriction is that the first value must be sent separately from the others. (This is the DC term, which is described in Chapter 9.) Note that the groups do not have to be sent in numerical order. For example, we could send values 5–10 as a first scan, values 1–4 as a second scan, values 20–45 as a third scan, etc.

Another way of reducing the precision of an image and transmitting it as a series of images is to reduce the precision of each individual value. For a JPEG image this means reducing the precision of each value within an 8×8 data block. This scheme is shown in Figure 7.23. The first value in each data block (i.e., the DC term) is always treated separately. The first "image" is always made up of these values. The remaining 63 values per block are sliced into groupings of bits. The number of bits grouped together in each group is controlled by an encoder. Typically only 3 to 6 groups would be used. JPEG calls this mode its *successive approximation progressive encoding*.

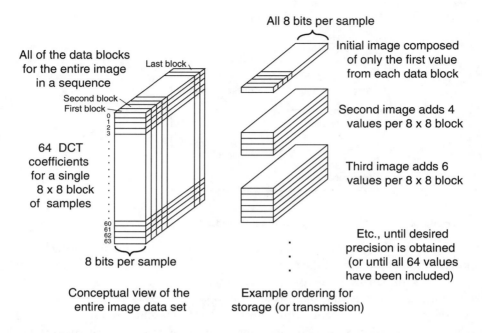

Figure 7.22 Reduced precision of an image by subsampling data blocks

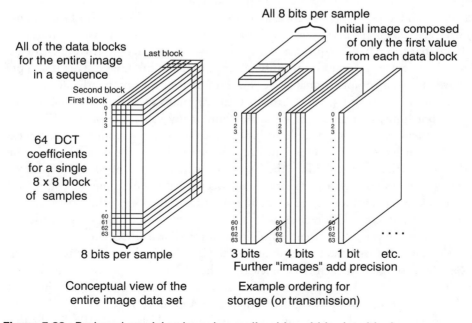

Figure 7.23 Reduced precision by subsampling bits within data blocks

The third and last scheme for reducing the precision of an image is called *hierarchical encoding*. In this scheme the precision of the samples is maintained but the number of samples is reduced. We discussed this idea earlier in Section 2.3.2. Interlacing skips scan-lines to reduce the amount of time it takes to get an image onto a screen. Hierarchical encoding is a similar idea but it reduces the number of pixels in both horizontal and vertical directions. The result is a series of images, each at one-half the resolution of the previous image. Examine the table that follows.

EXAMPLE RESOLUTION REDUCTION OF A RASTER IMAGE

Image Resolution	Total pixels	Percentage of Total Image	Percentage of Original Image
1024×1024	1,048,576	75.02%	100.00%
512×512	262,144	18.75%	25.00%
256×256	65,536	4.68%	6.25%
128×128	16,384	1.17%	1.56%
64×64	4,096	0.29%	0.39%
32×32	1,024	0.07%	0.10%
Total		100.00%	133.30%

At first glance this scheme might seem to greatly increase the total number of pixels within an image. In actuality, the amount of additional pixels is relatively small. The table shows that we made five reductions in an image and increased the data set by only 33 percent above its original size, and this was without taking advantage of the relationships between images that facilitate compression. The JPEG standard defines two compression schemes for data organized as a hierarchy: one is lossy and the other is lossless. JBIG defines a different lossless compression scheme based on a hierarchical encoding.

JPEG defines the ordering of a hierarchical data stream to be from smallest resolution image to largest resolution image. This ordering matches our criteria for terminating a transmission before full precision of an image is received. JBIG, on the other hand, allows a hierarchical data stream to be ordered in either order. Why would we want to receive the highest resolution image first? The answer lies in memory resources. If a data transmitter is going to send a series of reduced resolution images and it wants to send the lowest resolution image first, it must calculate all the reduced images before it sends the first image.[*] This requires enough memory to store all the images. Either the transmitting device or the receiving device must have sufficient memory to store all the images at once. Which device has sufficient memory determines which ordering the data set must use. If both devices have sufficient memory, either ordering is acceptable.

---

[*] Or it is required that the images be recalculated each time a new image is needed.

7.3.5   Summary and Conclusions on 2D Raster Data Organizations

Each of the above organization schemes were designed to satisfy one of the following goals:

- Minimize the amount of memory required to decode the data stream and therefore the cost of devices (e.g., TIFF)
- Minimize the cost of communications (e.g., GIF)
- Minimize visible flicker (e.g., NTSC, PAL, SECAM)
- Maximize data compression (e.g., JPEG, MPEG, H.261)

No one data organization will satisfy all of the above design goals. All the goals come down to two issues: the cost of memory and the cost and amount of available bandwidth for communication channels. The cost of memory continues to drop, but in many instances the bandwidth of communication channels remains constant. (In terms of broadcast frequencies, there is a physical limit to the frequency spectrum, and what we have now is what we will always have). In the future, data organizations that facilitate data compression will dominate data formats.

7.4   GEOMETRY DATA ORGANIZATION

In general, geometry data does not need to be organized to nearly the extent required by raster data. This is primarily because the coordinate information in geometry data is explicit, whereas in the case of raster information it is largely implied (except for the origin and dimensions of the raster image). One notable exception is the case of a data stream specifically intended to drive a pen-type plotter or a similar device.

Pen plotters employ the concept of a "Current Position," which is the coordinates of the end (concluding) point of the preceding output primitive. The next output primitive to be processed can start at the current position or at some offset relative to the current position. The current position can also be moved by some relative amount or set to some absolute value. Modern systems and graphics standards have generally dropped the concept of current position for various reasons. One result is that future hardware implementations will be able to process parts of a graphical data stream in parallel, since elimination of the concept of current position eases the requirement for sequential processing.

Graphic data stream organization is sensitive to how attributes that control the appearance of graphics primitives are handled. The two primary schemes can be characterized by whether or not they are *modal*. A nonmodal attribute—for example, the color of an output primitive—must be expressed as part of each primitive. Thus the data is replicated. However, the graphical primitives are now self-contained and can be transmitted (and interpreted) in any order. The modal approach to attributes establishes the value of an attribute, such as color or line style, which applies to all subsequent primitives of that type until the value is changed by a new "set attribute" command. This factors out common information from the data stream, reducing its size, but requires sequential processing of the data stream.

Geometry data often includes the use of what are sometimes called *graphic subroutines*. These are groups of primitives (and their associated attribute information) that can be referenced or invoked by name. The invocation process normally includes the ability to define the location of some reference point in the subroutine, typically the origin of the coordinate space in which the subroutine primitives are defined. Additionally, the orientation and scale of the subroutine can usually be specified, as can replacement values for some or all of the attributes. This subject is raised here because, for direct execution of a graphic data stream containing subroutines without using temporary storage, the subroutines must be transmitted before they are referenced. This is yet another constraint on the ordering of some geometry data streams, at least for some environments.

Model Data Organization

About the only thing that can be said about the organization of model data is that it is dependent on the model employed. The only standardized model is IGES, and the STEP follow-on work in ISO.

7.5   OVERALL DATA STREAM ORGANIZATION

In Chapter 5 we distinguished five different types of data stored in a typical graphical data stream: graphical data, interpretation data, documentation data, associated data, and unassociated data. Let's drop unassociated data from consideration for now, which leaves us with four basic categories of data. If we assume that each category is stored as a unit within the data stream, there are 24 possible orderings of such data. This is the number of permutations of four things taken four at a time, which is four factorial. If we intermix the data, there are an infinite number of possible orderings. How should the data be ordered?

Let's assume that we have a single stream data stream that is to be accessed sequentially. The *documentation data* is often not critical to the actual use of the data, but in some situations it *must* be accessed first—say, when there is a possible copyright notice that effects the use of the entire data stream. It makes sense to place the documentation data first in the data stream, even though in many situations it could go elsewhere. The *graphical data* cannot be interpreted correctly in most cases without the *interpretation data*. Access to the interpretation data must precede the graphical data access. This leaves the *associated data*. This data could precede the interpretation data or be placed after the graphical data. We have arbitrarily positioned the associated data after the graphical data in Figure 7.24.

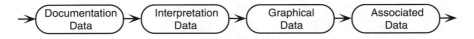

Figure 7.24 A logical order for the different types of data in a data stream

For a variety of reasons, this simple organization of data is rarely used. The more typical approach intermixes the data types, as shown in Figure 7.25. Graphical data is being shared more and more between applications, and for this reason, one goal of data stream organization should be to minimize the effort required to extract subsets of graphical data from

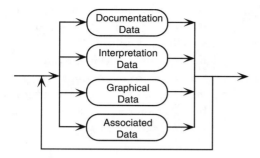

Figure 7.25 Typical unconstrained order of data types in real data streams

large complex data streams. The tagged block organization scheme we discussed earlier in this chapter is the current best method for facilitating such data extraction.

7.6 MULTIPLE DATA STREAMS

We use the term *data stream* to mean a group of related data. The data is not required to be in a single file, as is the typical case on many computer systems. The related data can be viewed as either a single stream (linear list) of data values or as a set of multiple streams. In the single stream case, it may be possible for the data to be accessed in either a sequential or random order. This is usually controlled by the hardware device used to store the data. In the multiple stream case, the data is separated into separate but related groups. The data groups can be accessed simultaneously (typically synchronized) or they can be accessed disjointly. These possible organizations are shown in Figure 7.26.

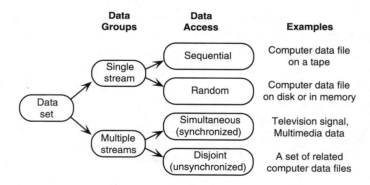

Figure 7.26 Classification of data sets by type of access and grouping

7.7 SUMMARY

The way a data stream is organized impacts the efficiency with which it can be accessed by an application. Ideally, the organization will match the needs of the application. If two or more different applications with different access patterns need to use a single data stream, it is unlikely that a single organization scheme will be optimal for both applications.

The second major consideration of data organization is the need to permit extendibility, that is: How can new data types be added to a data stream in a way that does not "break" existing data stream interpreters? The usual solution is to include a tag for each type of data in the stream, with a length field that can be used by interpreters to skip over the data associated with tags that they cannot process. The use of length fields can occur at several levels in a hierarchical data stream organization.

Data streams are often thought of as being accessed sequentially, with all data present "in line." A data dictionary, based on the use of pointers, can provide flexibility in addition of new data and new data field types but does require random access capability for its processing. This concept is related to general tag-based approaches such as SGML, where pieces of a data stream are delimited by tags, but the semantics to be associated with a tag are stored separately, and can even be changed.

There are several different techniques available to record the relationships between pieces of information in a data stream. Adjacency is efficient for a single application but cannot be used when different applications wish to associate different sets of information. The use of indirection (pointers) provides a general solution at the expense of address processing time for all applications. Application usage will determine the correct trade-off between these two schemes.

Raster data is unique in that its order is normally defined by the creation process (if it was scanned) or by the anticipated presentation device. Video cameras and some displays typically use two interleaved fields to create a full display frame. This provides a higher refresh rate but produces some visual artifacts. Noninterlaced displays (and raster printers) provide better quality but require greater bandwidth, thus costing more.

Raster data often employs multiple data values per sample point (typically three for color). There are three common ways for this data to be organized: all data values interleaved for each sample point, separate groups of each data type on a scan-line basis, or separate images of each data type. Once again, the natural format is determined by characteristics of the source or destination hardware. Some compression schemes group multiple samples of raster data together for further processing. Also, compression schemes sometimes transmit an image in blocks or builds up detail in successive passes over an entire image.

Graphical data streams sometimes make use of subroutines, which are common blocks of information that can be replicated or "invoked" multiple times. The subroutine definition must appear in the data stream before it is referenced or "used," or the entire data stream must be read before it is processed and subroutines extracted. If modal attributes are used, they must appear before the primitives that use them.

There may be logical data stream organizations, but they always need to be checked against the needs of a particular application. Flexibility, extendibility, and efficiency must be balanced, and there is no universally correct answer. All we can do is provide you with information to help you make the decision that is optimal for your environment.

CHAPTER

8

DATA ENCODING

CONTENTS

8.1 INTRODUCTION

All desired data must be assigned some representation. Nearly all digital data used today is stored as binary numbers. Binary numbers are represented using only two digits—ones and zeros. Each digit is called a *bit*. A set of 8 bits is called a *byte*. Any number of bits can be combined to represent a set of values. Using n bits, it is possible to represent 2^n distinct values. There are a variety of schemes for assigning binary numbers to data values. These schemes fit into one of three general categories:

- Text encoding
- Character encoding
- Binary encoding

The next three sections describe these encodings and the situations where they are required.

8.2 TEXT ENCODING

8.2.1 Description of ASCII

A text encoding assigns a set of binary numbers to represent letters of a language alphabet. There are standard code assignments for many of the world's languages. There is a new ISO standard for character codes for all of the world's languages, known as ISO 10646, which is based on an industry standard known as Unicode[Unicode90]. Let's look at the standard English code assignments used in North America called ASCII, the American Standard Code for Information Interchange. ASCII is a 7-bit code that associates 128 distinct values to distinct symbols, as shown in Figure 8.1.

Notice in the figure that the first two columns contain what is referred to as the *C0 set of assignments*. These are the *control values*, which include functions such as CR—Carriage Return, DLE—Data Link Escape, and ESC—escape. These control values are nonprinting characters that are used to control the communication between hardware devices. Most text encodings limit the inclusion of these characters in the data set to the HT (Horizontal Tab), the LF (Line Feed), and the CR (Carriage Return). Inclusion of other control characters typically makes the data set device dependent.

0 NUL	16 DLE	32 SP	48 0	64 @	80 P	96 `	112 p
1 SOH	17 DC1	33 !	49 1	65 A	81 Q	97 a	113 q
2 STX	18 DC2	34 "	50 2	66 B	82 R	98 b	114 r
3 ETX	19 DC3	35 #	51 3	67 C	83 S	99 c	115 s
4 EOT	20 DC4	36 $	52 4	68 D	84 T	100 d	116 t
5 ENQ	21 NAK	37 %	53 5	69 E	85 U	101 e	117 u
6 ACK	22 SYN	38 &	54 6	70 F	86 V	102 f	118 v
7 BEL	23 ETB	39 '	55 7	71 G	87 W	103 g	119 w
8 BS	24 CAN	40 (	56 8	72 H	88 X	104 h	120 x
9 HT	25 EM	41)	57 9	73 I	89 Y	105 i	121 y
10 LF	26 SUB	42 *	58 :	74 J	90 Z	106 j	122 z
11 VT	27 ESC	43 +	59 ;	75 K	91 [	107 k	123 {
12 FF	28 FS	44 ,	60 <	76 L	92 \	108 l	124	
13 CR	29 GS	45 -	61 =	77 M	93]	109 m	125 }
14 SO	30 RS	46 .	62 >	78 N	94 ^	110 n	126 ~
15 SI	31 US	47 /	63 ?	79 O	95 _	111 o	127 DEL

The C0 Set   The G0 set

Figure 8.1 ASCII 7-bit code point assignments

Data values are represented by assigning a set of characters (words) to each command or value that needs to be represented. These words must be separated to distinguish one word from the next. Two common methods are used to separate words: commas or *white space*, which can be a space, a tab, or a carriage return.

8.2.2   Text Encoding Example

An example of text encoding will help explain how code assignments work. A text-encoded PostScript file might contain the following data to draw a line:

```
210 200 moveto 100 80 lineto
```

This data, stored as text, requires 1 byte of memory for each character. The entire line of text uses 29 bytes, which includes spaces and a carriage return at the end of the line. Figure 8.2 shows the set of bytes that would represent this set of data. Each rectangle represents a single byte. The code values are shown in decimal notation to simplify a comparison with the ASCII chart in Figure 8.1.

```
 2   1   0       2   0   0           m   o   v   e   t   o
| 50 | 49 | 48 | 32 | 50 | 48 | 48 | 32 |109|111|118|101|116|111| 32 |

 1   0   0       8   0           l   i   n   e   t   o
| 49 | 48 | 48 | 32 | 56 | 48 | 32 |108|105|110|101|116|111| 13 |
```

Figure 8.2   ASCII values for a move command

Initially, the standard encoding for IGES files used a fixed field-length record, 80 characters per line, and textual encoding. (This was a holdover from the punched-card days). A simple method of reducing the file size of this format is to allow variable length records when full records are not needed. This "compressed ASCII" format was introduced with release 3 of IGES in 1986. Thankfully, the days of fixed field records (in the form of 80-character "virtual cards") are quickly fading away.

8.2.3   Advantages of Text Encodings

There are three major advantages of text encoding. One advantage is that text encodings are free from *control sequences*. Some (but not all) communication channels interpret certain sequences of bytes as messages to the channel and not as data. These control sequences are typically made of *control characters*—characters from the C0 character set shown in Figure 8.1. Data in a binary format can contain such sequences by accident. A text encoding does not contain these control characters and therefore cannot contain any of the control sequences. Textual encodings are much more device independent and can be transferred from device to device with minimal problems. This is not always true of other encodings.

Another advantage of text encodings is their representation of numbers. The encoding can ignore concerns about byte order, the representation of negative numbers, the representation of exponents and mantissas, and the maximum digits of accuracy. A processor on any given system can convert a textual encoding into the binary representations used for that machine. The accuracy maintained by the conversion is machine dependent. Again, the textual encoding is much more device independent. Take for example the encoding of the following PostScript instruction that specifies an RGB color value:

```
0.543245 0.123 0.8 setcolor
```

The specification can be as accurate as the originator of the data desires, without worrying about the type of representation a particular machine might use to store real numbers, or about the accuracy of the values. Those issues are dealt with when the data is used, not when it is initially stored.

A third advantage of text encodings is the ease with which they can be viewed, edited, and modified. They are "human readable." All you need is a text editor.

8.2.4 Disadvantages of Text Encodings

The major disadvantage of text encodings is that they produce large files. A text encoding can produce data sets three to ten times larger than other encoding schemes. Their large size makes them expensive to transport over communication channels and requires large amounts of disk space to store. The choice between text encoding and other encodings is a choice between device independence and file size. The choice also effects the speed of processing. The sheer volume of data in a text-encoded data set increases the time needed to access it, and the translation of the data into a machine's native data representations can be time-consuming.

DATA FORMATS THAT USE A TEXT ENCODING

Data Format	Name of Data Used in Implementation	Comments
CGM	Clear text encoding	
DXF	ASCII text file	Uses "group codes," i.e., tags
IGES	ASCII	Fixed length, 80-character records; fixed-format records
	Compressed ASCII	Allows variable length lines of text
PostScript	ASCII encoding	Tokens separated by white space; postfix notation
RIB	ASCII text	Tokens separated by white space

8.3 CHARACTER ENCODING

A character encoding uses a character set, much like the ASCII code assignments. But instead of each code being assigned a specific letter or symbol, each code is assigned to a specific command or data item. By having a single code value represent a command instead of a group of codes, the size of the file can be greatly reduced. And if the control codes (code values 0–31) are not used, then the encoding can avoid the problems associated with transmitting data over some communication channels.

Unlike the standard ASCII table, there is not one single set of standard character code assignments in character encoding; each data format defines its own unique set. Therefore, you must refer to the documentation on each data format for specific details. In place of a comprehensive discussion on the myriad of details related to character encoding, two examples from specific data formats are provided—CGM Character Encoding and the PLPS Protocol.

8.3.1   The CGM Character Encoding

The character encoding of the CGM format is used to minimize the size of the file for storage and to allow for transmission over character-oriented communication channels. There are both a 7-bit and an 8-bit code assignment.[*] The file is structured as a sequence of data pairs, where the first data value is an operation code (opcode) and the following data is any related parameters needed by the opcode. The most frequently used commands, which are the graphical primitive commands, are coded with a single byte. The remaining commands are coded with 2 bytes. The allocation of codes is shown in Figure 8.3. Sixteen codes are

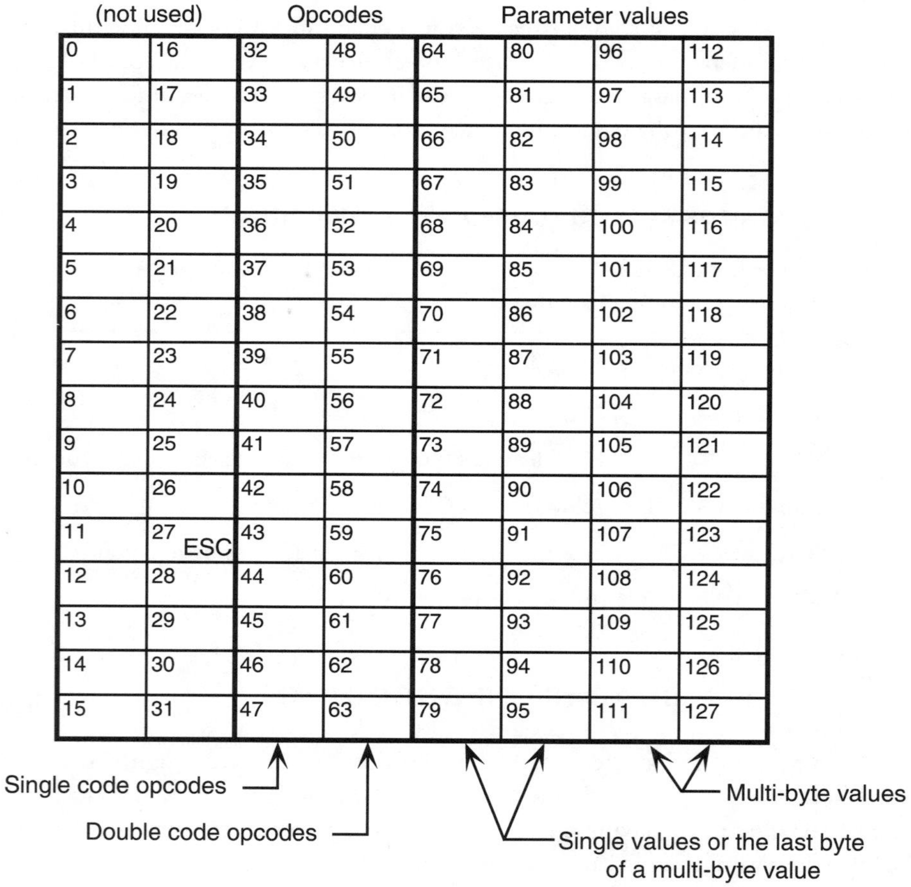

(not used)		Opcodes		Parameter values			
0	16	32	48	64	80	96	112
1	17	33	49	65	81	97	113
2	18	34	50	66	82	98	114
3	19	35	51	67	83	99	115
4	20	36	52	68	84	100	116
5	21	37	53	69	85	101	117
6	22	38	54	70	86	102	118
7	23	39	55	71	87	103	119
8	24	40	56	72	88	104	120
9	25	41	57	73	89	105	121
10	26	42	58	74	90	106	122
11	27 ESC	43	59	75	91	107	123
12	28	44	60	76	92	108	124
13	29	45	61	77	93	109	125
14	30	46	62	78	94	110	126
15	31	47	63	79	95	111	127

Single code opcodes

Double code opcodes

Single values or the last byte of a multi-byte value

Multi-byte values

Figure 8.3   CGM character encoding code point assignments

[*]The same code assignments are used for both the 7-bit and 8-bit assignments. The 7-bit code allows a parity bit if desired. The 8-bit code always has its high-order bit set to zero.

bit order   7 6 5 4 3 2 1 0
byte format | X 1 e s b b b b | first byte in the sequence

bit order   7 6 5 4 3 2 1 0
byte format | X 1 e b b b b b | remaining bytes in the sequence

where   "X" is a parity bit (or omitted) for 7-bit coding and is always 0 for 8-bit coding,
             "e" is the extension flag; it is 1 in all bytes except the last byte, where it is 0,
             "s" is the sign bit; it is 0 for nonnegative numbers and 1 for negative numbers,
             "b" is the data bits.

Figure 8.4   CGM character encoding of integers

designated as single-byte opcodes. Another fifteen are designated as 2-byte opcodes (code value 63 is not included). The second byte of a 2-byte opcode can be any of 32 different values (i.e., 32–63). This scheme allows 496 different opcode assignments (16 + 15*32).

The number of parameters following an opcode is dependent on the opcode. The parameter values can be of several different data types, including integers, reals, points (two numbers), point lists, color specifiers, color lists, or character text strings. Because there are too many details to include here on all of the encodings for each data types let's just look at the integer encoding to get an idea of how these encodings work.

Integers are coded as a sequence of one or more bytes. The first byte of the sequence is slightly different from the remaining bytes in the sequence. The format for the bytes is shown in Figure 8.4.

The first byte contains the high-order bits of the integer value, and the remaining bytes contain the low-order bits. Only the significant bits need to be encoded. An example will help clarify this encoding scheme. This example uses 8-bit coding, where the high bit of each byte is 0.

EXAMPLES OF ENCODING INTEGERS IN CGM

Decimal Integer Value	In Binary	Encoded Byte Sequence (In Binary)
+3	11	01000011
+3	11	01100000, 01100000, 01000011
−17	−10001	01110001, 01000001

Notice three things about this encoding. First, none of the bytes in the sequence can ever be control characters because all control characters have a value less than 32. The 1 bit in position 6 makes all of the bytes larger than 32. Second, the encodings are not unique, as shown by the two encodings of +3. However, the meaning of any encoded data is unambiguous. The single-byte encoding requires less memory and is therefore the preferred encoding. And third, the number of bytes required to code a particular integer value depends on the magnitude of the integer. Small integers require fewer bytes than larger integers.

8.3.2   The PLPS Protocol

The (North American) Presentation Level Protocol Specification, or (NA)PLPS, is a protocol for transmitting a mixture of graphical and textual data. It is a character encoding that defines four distinct character-coding tables. Certain code sequences are used to make one of the tables the "active table." Character codes received thereafter are interpreted as indexes into the active table. There are three predefined character-coding tables and one user-definable table. Figure 8.5 shows the Mosaic character set defined to draw low-resolution graphics. The symbols represent all possible combinations of bitmaps using a grid size of 2 pixels across and 3 pixels down. There are 64 such predefined symbols.

High-resolution graphics are drawn by issuing commands using the Picture Description Instructions (PDI) character set. When a code for a graphical primitive is used with this character set, the bytes following the code represent parameters to the command. Figure 8.6 shows the structure for bytes used to represent a high-resolution graphical line.

Each byte contains a portion of the data for both the x and y coordinates of the line endpoint. (The command draws a line segment from the last referenced point to this x, y position). Only 6 bits of each byte is actual data; 3 bits per byte for the x and y coordinates, respectively. Notice that the data uses as many bytes as needed to achieve the desired

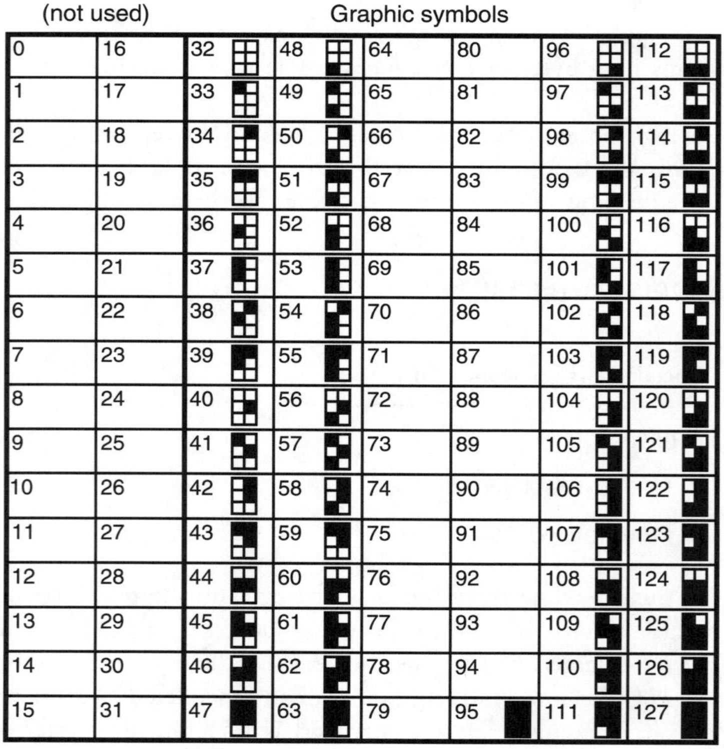

Figure 8.5   PLPS mosaic character set assignments. The grid shown with each character is shown for comparison only and is not part of the actual symbol

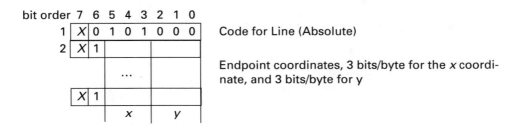

Figure 8.6   Data structure for a line in (NA)PLPS PDI character set

precision of the values. The most significant bits of the values are in the initial bytes, and the least significant bits are in the final bytes. The absence of a 1 value in bit position 6 indicates the end of the coordinate data.

8.3.3 Advantages and Disadvantages of Character Encoding

Character-based encoding provides a device-independent, but efficient, coding scheme for data. It typically excludes control characters from the data set to allow the data set to be sent over any communication channel without misinterpretation or an abnormal termination of the data stream.

Because data values often span byte boundaries and are intermixed with flag and type bits, a significant amount of software to decode the data sets is required. The time needed to accomplish the decoding slows access to the data set.

DATA FORMATS THAT USE SOME FORM OF CHARACTER ENCODING

Data Format	Name of Specific Implementation	Comments
CGM	Character Encoding	Defines on character table
PLPS	Picture Description Instructions (PDIs)	Character encoded, graphical Commands to draw lines, arcs, rectangles, etc.
	Mosaic Set	Character encoded, low resolution, bitmap graphical primitives
	Dynamically Redefinable Character Set (DRCS)	Character encoded, custom defined Patterns for creating graphics

8.4 BINARY ENCODING

The term *binary encoding* refers to a broad range of encoding schemes that are machine dependent, that is, they encode data in the same way a particular machine encodes that data. The data can be used immediately without any translation or manipulation (on compatible hardware) which speeds the user access to the data. The details of each binary encoding are machine dependent and too numerous to include in this book, but the following discussion includes several examples of binary encodings to help explain the similarities and differences between them. These examples show how integer data is represented in several different encodings. Integer representations are the simplest encodings to compare.

8.4.1   The Binary Token PostScript Encoding

Binary token PostScript encoding emphasizes compactness to minimize the size of the data set. Each data item is preceded by a single byte that specifies the type of data that follows. These codes can represent 32 possible data types using the integer values 128 through 159, which is important because these values are outside the range of the 7-bit ASCII codes used to represent the standard text coding of PostScript files. This allows a single PostScript data set to contain both text and binary encodings mixed in any order desired. In fact, the binary encoding only specifies codes for the most-often used primitives, and, in most cases, a Post-Script binary data set will always contain some text encoding.

LEGAL TYPES OF INTEGERS FOR BINARY TOKEN DATA TYPES

Token Data Type Code	Number of Bytes Following Token	Interpretation
132	4	32-bit integer, high-order byte first
133	4	32-bit integer, low-order byte first
134	2	16-bit integer, high-order byte first
135	2	16-bit integer, low-order byte first
136	1	8-bit signed integer in the range from $-128 \leq n < 127$

Suppose that we assign a unique code to each valid operation that could be included in a PostScript file. Let's assume that there are less than 256 such operations, and therefore the codes require only one byte of memory. Now the operation *moveto* requires only one byte of memory instead of the 6 bytes it used in the text encoding. Similar assignments can be made for other types of data, such as integer numbers, real numbers, and character data.

You can probably recognize a problem with this scheme. A typical data set contains many different types of data such as commands, data points, flag settings, etc. The different data types must be distinguished from each other. One technique would be to use a unique code for each possible data item in the set, but this makes the code values too large. Another approach is to include a *type code* in front of each data item to distinguish it from other types of data. Now the moveto operation requires 2 bytes. The first byte is used to specify that the next byte in the data stream is a command. The second byte is used to specify that this is the moveto command.

Let's examine the same sample PostScript data we used in the text encoding example, Figure 8.2. Each of the numerical values is less than 256 and each one can be coded using only 1 byte of memory. The total encoding requires 2 bytes per token, or 12 bytes. The binary encoding uses only 30% of the memory required by the text encoding.

bit order	15 14 13 12 11 10 9 8 7 6 5 4 3 2 1 0
8-bit integer(s)	S msb lsb S msb lsb

bit order	15 14 13 12 11 10 9 8 7 6 5 4 3 2 1 0
16-bit integer	S msb lsb

bit order	15 14 13 12 11 10 9 8 7 6 5 4 3 2 1 0
24-bit integer(s)	S msb
	lsb S msb
	lsb

bit order	15 14 13 12 11 10 9 8 7 6 5 4 3 2 1 0
32-bit integer	S msb
	lsb

Figure 8.7 CGM binary encoding of integers

8.4.2 The CGM Binary Encoding

The binary encoding of the CGM format is optimized for speed of generation and interpretation. The data values are stored in formats that are typical of many computer systems. In some cases the data can be read in without any translation. Another nice feature of this encoding is that all elements include an associated parameter length value. Elements that are not desired (or recognized) by an application can be easily skipped using this length value. This also makes the format easily extendible, since an "old" decoder can recognize "new" control codes, and skip over their associated data.

Integers are stored as normal binary numbers using two's complement representation for negative values. The format specifies eight different types of integers. These types provide precisions of 8, 16, 24, and 32 bits, each in signed and unsigned formats. All data in the binary encoding is aligned on word boundaries. A word is defined to be 2 bytes. The 8-bit and 24-bit precision values do not fit neatly into words, and therefore they are either combined into multiples of two, or extra unused bits are filled with zeros. The signed formats are shown in Figure 8.7 as examples, where "S" is the sign bit, "msb" is the most significant bit, and "lsb" is the least significant bit.

8.4.3 The Binary Form of IGES Data Set

The binary form of the IGES format decreases the size of the data files by using binary instead of text encodings. When encoding data, the scheme includes a *control byte* in front of each data item. The control byte specifies the type and number of data items that follow it. The structure of the control byte is shown in Figure 8.8.

The format used to represent integer data is presented in Figure 8.9. The precision of the values is controlled by a global precision value I_s specified at the beginning of the data set. If the precision value I_s is not a multiple of eight, then a pad of zeros is appended to the data items to align them to 8-bit byte boundaries.

bit order   7 6 5 4 3 2 1 0
control byte | P | Repetition | Format |

Where   "P" is the "presence" flag. If P = 0 then only one value follows the control byte and it
        is repeated "repetition" number of times. If P = 1, then there are "repetition" number
        of data values following the control byte

        "Repetition" +1 equals the number of data values following the control byte

        "Format" specifies the data type; 0 for default value, 1 for single-length integer, 2 for
        double-length integer, 3 for single- precision floating point, 4 for double-precision
        floating point, 5 for a pointer, and 6 for a text string

Figure 8.8   IGES binary encoding control byte

8 bits	1 bit	$I_s - 1$ bits	$8N - I_s$ bits
Control byte	Sign	Integer value	Pad

Figure 8.9   IGES binary format integer data

8.4.4   The Binary Object Sequence PostScript Encoding

This PostScript encoding emphasizes efficient execution. It encodes a sequence of data and
operations that are to be executed immediately when they are encountered in a PostScript
data stream. This scheme is a departure from the normal processing of a PostScript data set
that places data on a stack to be executed later. The details for this encoding can be found in
the PostScript "red book." This encoding scheme is mentioned here because most binary
encodings define only the representation of the data, but not its structure, organization, or
interpretation. This PostScript encoding modifies not only the data representation but also
its structure, organization, and interpretation. A BinaryObject Sequence can be embedded
within an otherwise normal PostScript encoding. This attempt to preserve the best features
of each encoding scheme keeps part of the PostScript data set as ASCII for readability while
it optimizes parts of the data for speed.

8.4.5   XDR Binary Encoding

A binary format for the exchange of binary data between computer systems has been defined
by Sun Microsystems called *XDR*, an abbreviation for external data representation. The
XDR encoding scheme is essentially 32-bit big endian integers and IEEE standard floating
point format numbers. Several data formats such as AVS Field, Flux, and netCDF use this
scheme to increase the device independence of their binary data.

8.4.6   Advantages and Disadvantage of Binary Encoding

A binary encoding reduces the size of a data set, which reduces the memory requirements of
mass storage. It also reduces the amount of data translation and manipulation required to
make the data accessible to a user.

Binary representations are device dependent, and it is therefore difficult to transport
data between systems without translation.

Except for the (NA)PLPS Character Encoded data format, all of the data formats discussed in the appendices of this book have a binary encoding defined for them. For many of the formats, their only encoding is binary. Therefore, we have omitted a listing of all of the data formats that use binary encoding.

8.5 SUMMARY

Some of the issues discussed in this chapter would go away if we lived in an ideal world where machines agreed on binary representations for data values and on the control-character sequences that send messages between devices. But we do not live in an ideal world. Even if we did, not all of these issues would be resolved. It is very beneficial in some situations to edit your data with a simple text editor. In other situations, the speed of access mandates a binary encoding. Figure 8.10 summarizes the three main issues related to data encodings: device independence, file size, and decoding time. In an ideal situation, a data format could be easily edited, have minimum size, and be used as easily on one system as on another. It is nearly impossible to satisfy all three issues with one encoding scheme.

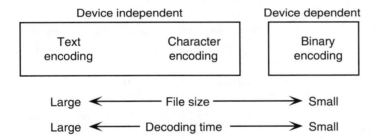

Figure 8.10 Relative device independence, file size, and decoding time for three classes of encodings

Because of the conflicting issues, many data formats have defined more than one type of encoding. This is beneficial in some ways, yet it adds a level of complexity to the use of the data formats. The conversion of data between encodings is nontrivial, even when the data is defined within the same conceptual data model. In addition, it is common for software systems to support only one of the encodings while ignoring the others. This further complicates the task of transporting and sharing data between systems.

DATA FORMATS THAT DEFINE MORE THAN ONE ENCODING

Data Format	Text	Char	Binary	Comments
CGM	•	•	•	Two types of binary encodings
DXF	•		•	
EPS	•		•	
Flux	•		•	
IGES	•		•	
PostScript	•		•	

8.6 CONCLUSIONS

To conclude this chapter, we present an idealized model for data encoding. Figure 8.11 summarizes this ideal scheme. The "normal" encoding for a data set would be a machine-dependent binary encoding that minimizes the physical size of the data set and optimizes the speed of access to the data set. When direct manipulation of the data set is desired (outside of an application that uses the data), the data would be converted to a text encoding that could be edited by a standard text editor. After completion of the editing, the data set would be converted back into its native binary format. When the transport of the data is desired on any character-oriented communications channel, the data set would be converted to a character encoding and sent over the channel. After receiving the data on the other end of the channel, the other system could transport the data into its own native binary format. This idealized design requires the definition of three separate encodings for each data format and four procedures for the conversions between encodings.

To carry this idealized scheme further, any software that used these encodings would know how to automatically invoke the appropriate conversion procedure to modify the data into the needed encoding. For example, if a text editor opened a data set defined in a binary encoding, then the data would automatically be converted to a text encoding and brought into the editor. When the editing was finished, the data would be converted automatically back into its native binary format. These issues can be classified as functions of operating systems. In any case, the goal would be to shield the user from the details of these underlying encodings.

Even in this idealized scheme, there are three major problems. Two of the problems deal with data accuracy and data correctness. If a user modifies a data set in a text encoding, it is quite easy to create invalid data. The text-to-binary-conversion program must include a significant amount of error checking if it is to create a correct binary encoding. This makes the conversion process less than straightforward, especially if the software is to give any

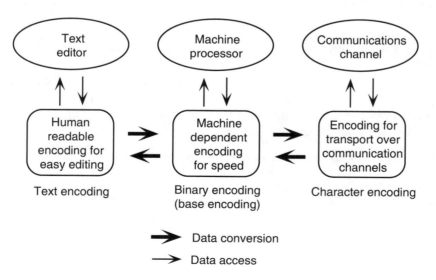

Figure 8.11 Usage environments of various data encodings

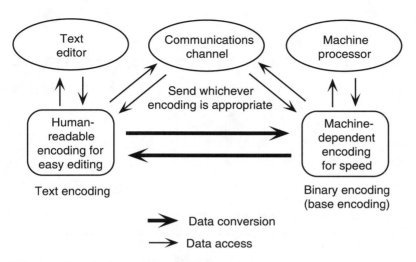

Figure 8.12 A minimal set of data encodings

helpful hints on how to correct errors that are found. An alternative approach is to use an intelligent editing environment, which can prevent the entry of invalid information in a binary encoding.

The third problem, data accuracy, also is related to the conversion process. Most binary encodings use fixed-length numerical values that have a limited range of precision. Text encodings typically have no such limits. A user editing a text encoding must understand the limitations of the binary encoding—or be surprised by the "different" values that appear in their data. (These issues are discussed further in Chapter 12.)

Many of the data channels in use today have a binary mode of operation that allows for "raw data" to be transported without the worry of misinterpreted data-control sequences. In these cases the character encoding is really not needed, assuming that the sending and receiving system use the same binary representations for data. However, when the binary representations differ between systems, the character encoding serves the additional purpose of converting between the different binary encodings. If the character encoding could be done away with, we would eliminate the work required to define the encoding, and the need for two conversion programs—a significant savings.

How can we simplify data encodings as much as possible? We should push for the standardization of the binary encoding of standard data objects, such as integer and real numbers, and for the ability to transport binary data over communication channels in raw, binary mode. Standard encoding definitions exist, but they are just not universally used. This situation may change with the development of "common language independent data types," by JTC1 SC22, for use in all programming languages. This would eliminate the need for the character encodings, which most data formats ignore anyway. The ideal data encoding structure is shown in Figure 8.12.

DATA COMPRESSION — THE BASICS

CONTENTS

9.1 PURPOSE AND RATIONALE

Data compression reduces the number of bytes required to represent a data set. As we have discussed in previous chapters, graphical data sets are often large in their raw form. This is especially true of raster data sets. Compression *reduces the amount of memory* (disk or tape space) required to store a data set. Consequently, it also *reduces the amount of time* required to transmit a data set over a communications link at a given rate.

9.2 GENERAL TERMINOLOGY

The terms presented in this section are used to describe compression schemes.

Compression ratio   The ratio of the size of the original data set to the size of the compressed data set. That is:

$$\text{Compression ratio} = \frac{\text{Number of bytes in the original data set}}{\text{Number of bytes in the compressed data set}}$$

The compression ratio is expressed as a single number or as two numbers, with the second number typically being 1. For example, 10:1 means 10 bytes of the original data are represented by one byte in the compressed data. Larger compression ratios imply smaller compressed data sets.

Bits/Pixel   The average number of bits required to represent the data value for a single pixel of an image. This is another standard method of specifying a compression ratio and is typically used when discussing the compression of full-color raster images.

Lossless Compression   Compression that results in no loss of data or information.

Lossy Compression   Compression that may lose portions of the original data set. Lossy compression schemes can obtain higher compression ratios when compared to lossless schemes, at the price of lost data.

Encoder   A process that takes as input a data set and produces as output a compressed data set (a data set requiring less memory).

Decoder   A process that takes as input a compressed data set and produces as output the original data set (or a close approximation to the data set if lossy compression is used).

Real-time Encoding   A process that compresses a data set fast enough to satisfy the needs of its intended application. For example, a real-time encoder for picture telephones must be able to encode the image data it transmits within the refresh rate of the telephone display unit.

Real-time Decoding   A process that can decompress a data sets fast enough to satisfy the needs of its intended application. For example, a real-time decoder for video applications must be able to decompress data sets within the update rate of the video device.

Codec   Refers to either an encoder or a decoder or both. It is an abbreviation of *coder/ decoder.*

Entropy   A measure of the randomness in a set of data. A totally random data set *cannot* be compressed. The more order in a data set, the more a data set can be compressed. If a data stream contains some type of order, we can "exploit" this order and remove any redundant information that the data stream contained originally.

9.3 DESIGN CRITERIA

The compression of graphical data is useful for a variety of applications, and each application imposes different design criteria and constraints on the compression schemes. As with almost any design task, tradeoffs must be made between design constraints to meet cost and performance criteria. Consider the following design constraints and the range of options that exist to satisfy the specific constraint:

COMPRESSION DESIGN CONSTRAINTS AND POSSIBLE OPTIONS

Design Constraint	Options
Time	• Both real-time encoding and decoding required • Only real-time decoding required • Slower than real-time processing acceptable

COMPRESSION DESIGN CONSTRAINTS AND POSSIBLE OPTIONS *(Continued)*

Design Constraint	Options
Cost	• Requires only software (low cost) • Requires a floating point coprocessor (additional cost) • Requires special purpose hardware (more expensive)
Information loss	• No information loss; all data is recoverable to its original precision • Some data is lost, but the loss is not discernible by the human eye • Large amounts of the original data are lost, but the information required by the application is retained
Compression ratios	• Low compression satisfactory (2:1 or 3:1) • Medium compression satisfactory (5:1 or 10:1) • High compression required (20:1 to 100:1, or higher)

Many applications need compressed graphical data. Some examples follow.

APPLICATIONS THAT NEED DATA COMPRESSION

Application	Device Characteristic	Design Constraints
Videodisc (digitally encoded movies)	Read-only storage device	• No time constraints on encoding, but decoding must be in real time
Desktop publishing	Read-write storage devices	• Near real-time encoding and decoding • Minimize hardware assistance to minimize cost
Video telephones	Low bandwidth communication channel	• High compression ratios because of low bandwidth • Near real-time decoding and encoding that require approximately equal amounts of time
Teleconferencing	High bandwidth communication channel	• High compression ratios for high resolution images (to display on large screens) • Real-time encoding and decoding
Remote medical consultation	Low and high bandwidth communication channels	• Minimal loss of information to avoid misdiagnosis
Earth satellite surveys	Satellite links	• Loss of data acceptable sometimes (e.g., searching for deforestation requires only the distinction between forest and nonforest, not details)

9.4 COMPRESSION METHODOLOGIES

There are three basic methods involved in any data compression scheme: 1) transformation, 2) reduced precision, and 3) minimization of number of bits.

Method 1 Transforms a data set into another equivalent data set that is in some way smaller than the original. Some transformations reduce the number of data items in the set. Other transformations reduce the numerical size of data items that allow them to be represented with fewer binary digits.

Method 2 Reduces the precision of individual data values within a data set which reduces the number of binary digits required to represent each item. Method 2 can also reduce randomness in a data stream.

Method 3 Represents (encodes) each data item to minimize the total number of binary digits required to represent the entire data stream.

Figure 9.1. summarizes the main idea, the methodology, and the technical names given to each compression technique, along with the general schemes used to implement these ideas.

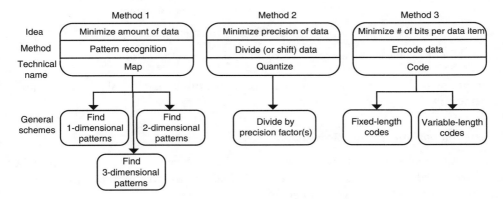

Figure 9.1 General schemes for the three major compression techniques

This chapter discusses each method independently. In Chapter 10, we will consider how the methods can be combined in interesting ways to produce more efficient (and complex) compression schemes.

9.5 METHOD 1 — TRANSFORMATION

A data set can be reduced in size by exploiting patterns (or order) that exist in the data. A pattern is any form of repetition or redundancy that exists among the data values. If a data set contains no patterns, then it is totally random. Totally random data sets cannot be compressed. Applying a compression scheme to totally random data can potentially *increase* the size of such a data set!

There are three major techniques used to exploit patterns in a data set:

- *Reduce the number of data values* in the data set by removing redundant information. There are many possible schemes for doing so, including recognizing repetition of value sequences and recognizing general patterns in the data. A list of patterns can be created, thus reducing the data set to indexes into the pattern list.

- *Reduce some of the data's significance* by finding patterns that capture the "essence" of a set of values. We can compress the data by keeping only the most significant values.

- *Reduce the magnitude of data values* in the data set. This allows for more efficient encoding of the data due to the smaller range of values that must be encoded.

The technical name given to these processes is *mapping,* in that they *map* patterns in the original data to codes for those patterns in the transformed data. Patterns can be found in a variety of ways. We have categorized pattern searching into three groups based on how the data stream is processed:

Data stream is processed as:	Category
Sequential list	One-dimensional pattern searching
2-dimensional array	Two-dimensional pattern searching
A sequential list of 2-dimensional arrays	Three-dimensional pattern searching

Let's examine the simplest schemes first. These are the one-dimensional pattern recognition schemes.

9.5.1   One-Dimensional Pattern Recognition

If a data set is treated as a single one-dimensional list of values, then patterns can be exploited among adjacent values in the list. Figure 9.2 summarizes the most commonly-used schemes that exploit redundancy in sequential lists.

Note that it is impractical to search for *all* patterns of *any* length in a sequential list, because the number of potential patterns is too enormous. Therefore, simpler schemes are used.

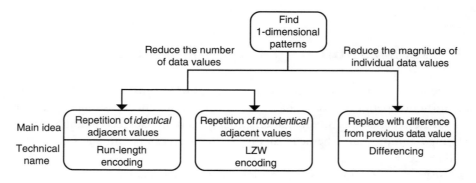

Figure 9.2   Classification of 1-dimensional pattern recognition schemes

Run-Length Encoding

Run-length encoding is a pattern-recognition scheme that searches for the repetition of identical data values in a list. The data set can be compressed by replacing the repetitive sequence with a *single data value* and a *length value*. For example, consider the data set in Figure 9.3 and its resulting run-length encoding.

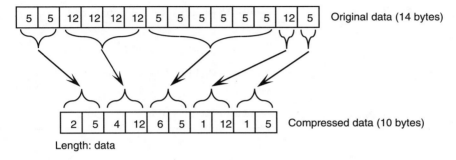

Figure 9.3 Example of run-length encoding

Notice that the last 2 bytes in the original data set require 4 bytes in the compressed data set. This is due to the lack of repetition in this section of the data stream. Most run-length implementations, however, include schemes to handle such cases efficiently.

DATA ENCODINGS THAT SUPPORT RUN-LENGTH ENCODING

Data Format	Name of Specific Implementation	Comments
CCITT Fax	Group 3	Run-length plus Huffman encoding, only for bilevel images
CGM	None	Four-cell array element
DDES-UEF01	None	All codes are run lengths; no allowance for raw data
DDES-UEF03	None	All codes are run lengths; no allowance for raw data
GEM/IMG	None	Exploits the repetition of identical lines
HDF	DFTAG_RLE	Similar to PackBits
MacPaint	PackBits	Run lengths and literal data
PCX	None	Not a general-purpose method; good for line drawings
PostScript	RunLengthEncode RunLengthDecode	Similar to PackBits
RLE	RLE	Used for color raster data, not for monochrome data

DATA ENCODINGS THAT SUPPORT RUN-LENGTH ENCODING *(Continued)*

Data Format	Name of Specific Implementation	Comments
SunRaster		Uses a value of 128 to signal the presence of a run length
TARGA	Type 9	Similar to PackBits (for color-mapped images)
	Type 10	Similar to PackBits (for RGB images)
	Type 11	Similar to PackBits (for black and white images)
	Type 32	Similar to PackBits (for color-mapped images) plus Huffman and Delta encoding
	Type 33	Similar to PackBits (for RGB images) plus Huffman and Delta encoding
TIFF	Type 2	Identical to CCITT Fax
	Type 32773	Identical to PackBits

The next section discusses the details related to five different run-length encoding schemes.

PackBits

PackBits is a run-length encoding scheme created for Macintosh users. It is the simplest implementation of all the run-length encoding schemes because it allows for both run lengths and literal data. An example set of data compressed by PackBits is shown in Figure 9.4.

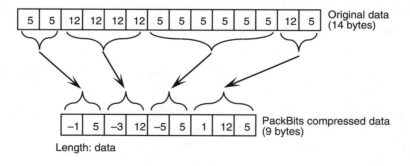

Figure 9.4   An example set of data compressed by PackBits

Algorithm for PackBits Decoding

```
repeat
    Count = the next byte from the data stream
    if 0 ≤ Count ≤ 127
        then output the next (Count+1) bytes as literal data
    if -127 ≤ Count ≤ -1
        then output the next byte (-Count+1) times
    if Count = -128 then do nothing
until all of the data stream has been read.
```

SunRaster

The SunRaster run-length encoding scheme uses a special byte value to signal the presence of a run length. A byte value of 128 is followed by a pair of values: a count value and a data value. The data value is replicated "count" number of times. If a data value of 128 needs to be included in the data stream, it is followed by a zero byte to distinguish it from a run-length code.

Algorithm for SunRaster Decoding

```
While the raster data stream is not empty do the following
    {
        c = next byte in data stream
        if c is not equal to 128 (hex 80) then output c
        else
            {   c = next byte in data stream
                if c = 0 then output a single byte value 128
                else
                {   value = next byte from data stream
                    output value (c+1) times
                }
            }
    }
```

PCX

The PCX run-length scheme uses the first 2 bits of each byte to distinguish length values from data values. If a data value already has its first 2 bits set, then a length value must be inserted in front of the data, even if there is no repetition of the value. In the worst-case scenario, this scheme will double the size of the data set! This scheme is highly data dependent, and it functions best on raster images that contain monochrome line drawings where the solid background is very repetitive.

Algorithm for PCX Run-length Decoding

```
repeat
    Byte = next byte in the compressed data stream
    if Byte < 192             (the high order 2 bits of Byte are zero)
        then output Byte
        else {(strip off the high order 2 bits of the Byte)
            Count = Byte - 192
            Byte = next byte in the compressed data stream
            output the Byte, Count number of times
            }
until all compressed data bytes have been decompressed
```

GEM/IMG

The GEM/IMG run-length encoding scheme is the most complex run-length scheme in this review. It recognizes the repetition of the following types of data:

DIFFERENT CLASSES OF REPETITION DATA IN GEM/IMG ENCODING

Type of Data	Byte Sequence (in Hexadecimal) in the Data Stream
duplicate lines	00 00 FF XX, where XX equals the number of lines to repeat
duplicate 'patterns'	00 XX, where XX equals the number of patterns to repeat
raw data (no repetition)	80 XX, where XX equals the number of raw data bytes
'runs' of solid black	< 80, where the value is the number of solid black bytes
'runs' of solid white	> 80, where the value over 80 is the number of solid white bytes

Algorithm for
GEM/IMG
Run-length
Decoding

(All constants for this algorithm are shown in a single-byte hexadecimal format.)

```
repeat
    Byte = next byte from the data stream
    if Byte = 00 then
        {
            Byte = next byte from the data stream
            if Byte = 00 then
                {       (line repetition count)
                    Byte = next byte from data stream (ignore)
                    RepeatLineCount = next byte from data stream
                }
            else {      (pattern repetition)
                Length = next byte from the data stream
                get the next PatternSize number of bytes from the
                                    data stream
                output this pattern Length times
            }
        }
    else (if Byte ≠ 00)
        {
            if Byte = 80 (in hex) then                 (raw data)
                {
                    Length = next byte from the data stream
                    output next Length bytes from data stream
                }
            if Byte > 80 (in hex) then(solid White run)
                {
                    Length = Byte - 80 (in hex)
                    output byte value FF Length number of times
                }
            if Byte < 80 (in hex) then(solid Black run)
                {
                    Length = Byte
                    output byte value 00 Length number of times
                }
        }
until all of the scan-line is processed and decoded
```

RLE

The RLE format is similar to the PackBits scheme. It allows for raw data when there is no repetition, and for run lengths when there is repetition of identical data values. In addition, it allows the file to skip pixel values altogether. The skipped pixel values have no data associated with them in the data file and are assumed to have the background color. A preprocessing step fills the entire image with the background color.

The RLE format is designed on the basis of operators followed by operands. An operator specifies what to do next in the process of filling a raster image. There are six operators defined by the format. Notice that two of the operators are used for skipping pixels. The algorithm manipulates three variables that keep track of where the next data values should be placed in the image data. These variables are:

CurrentChannel	Indicates which color is currently active
ScanLineNumber	The Y position of the scan line in the image
PixelIndex	The X position in the current scan line

Algorithm for RLE Decoding

(Note: the RLE format maintains data on even-byte word boundaries. This algorithm does not include the fill bytes used to maintain word alignment.)

```
fill the image memory with the background color
while not Done do the following
{   Operator = next byte from data stream
    case Operator of
        SetColor:{      Operand = next byte from data stream
                        CurrentChannel = Operand
                        PixelIndex = xpos    (far left of image)
                    }
        SkipLines:{     Operand = next byte from data stream
                        ScanLineNumber = ScanLineNumber + Operand
                        PixelIndex = xpos    (far left of image)
                    }
        SkipPixels:{    Operand = next byte from data stream
                        PixelIndex = PixelIndex + Operand
                    }
        PixelData:{     Operand = next byte from data stream
                        copy the next Operand bytes from the data
                            stream into the current scan-line starting
                            at the PixelIndex
                        PixelIndex = PixelIndex + Operand
                    }
        Run      :{ Length = next byte from data stream
                    DataValue = next byte from data stream
                    Copy the DataValue Length number of times into
                        the current scan-line starting at the
                        PixelIndex
                    PixelIndex = PixelIndex + Length
                }
        EOF      : Done = TRUE
}
```

NUANCES RELATED TO RUN-LENGTH ENCODING

Each scan line is typically encoded separately (with the exception of the SunRaster scheme) to allow the scan lines to be ordered nonsequentially within the data stream. (Refer to Section 7.3.1 for further discussion on this topic.) Separately encoding the scan lines also allows for a greater chance of error recovery if the data stream becomes corrupted.

The ordering of data values within a data stream affects the efficiency of run-length encoding, especially for full-color raster image data. If pixel values are ordered as color planes (i.e., all red, then all blue, then all green), there is a greater chance of repetition between adjacent data values. See Figure 9.5.

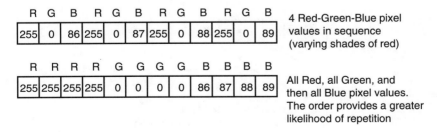

Figure 9.5   Effect of data ordering on compression

The repetition of adjacent pixel values is obviously not restricted to scan lines (i.e., horizontal repetition). Some digital images contain more repetition of vertically adjacent pixel values. While this is a known fact, the advantages of implementing both horizontal and vertical schemes are not enough to offset the added complexity. All run-length encoding schemes are data dependent. The goal is to select a run-length encoding scheme that functions well on the general type of data associated with a particular application and to make sure the scheme's worst-case scenario occurs rarely for this type of data.

The type of data affects the scheme used for run-length encoding. Bilevel images have only two colors (foreground and background), and the data values along a single scan line always alternate between these two colors. Therefore, the actual color values do not need to be stored; only the run length of each color is needed. The CCITT Fax group 3 one-dimensional encoding scheme uses this variation of run-length encoding.

Conclusions

The compression ratios obtainable from run-length encoding schemes vary depending on the type of data to be encoded and the repetition present within any given data set. Some data sets can be highly compressed by run-length encoding whereas other data sets can actually grow larger due to the compression. Compression ratios from 2:1 up to 5:1 are typical.

LZW Encoding

If a sequence of nonidentical data values is repeated more than once in the data stream, not necessarily contiguously, then this repetition can be exploited to compress the data. A unique code can be assigned to the repeated sequence and then stored in the encoded data set. Study Figure 9.6, which contains two sequences that are repeated. Notice that there are other repeated sequences in this data that are not marked and assigned codes. The sequence (12, 5) is repeated twice, but it is not assigned a code because it overlaps the repeated sequences that are coded. The sequence (5, 23, 7, 6, 12) is also repeated twice in the example, but it is not used for the encoding either. These examples highlight the problem of finding the best grouping of data values to obtain the highest data compression.

A best grouping exists for any given data set, but to find it involves examining every possible grouping of data values—a very inefficient and time-consuming task. A more realistic approach simply "remembers" data sequences as the data stream is scanned and recognizes when the sequence is repeated in the remainder of the data stream. In the example above,

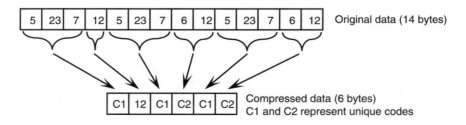

Figure 9.6   Example of assigning repeated patterns to unique code values

the sequence (5, 23, 7) was seen first and therefore used to encode the next occurrence of this sequence. In so doing, it missed the longer repeated sequence (5, 23, 7, 6, 12).

The codes and their associated data sequences constitute a "CodeBook" that must be stored along with the encoded data; otherwise a decoder would have no way of knowing what the codes represent. If the CodeBook is large, the overhead costs of having to store the CodeBook can greatly decrease the efficiency of compression. A compression scheme developed by Lempel-Ziv and Welch, commonly referred to as LZW compression, avoids the need to remember the CodeBook. LZW compression has several beneficial features. It processes data sequentially and therefore has relatively low memory requirements. In addition, the algorithms can be implemented in a reasonably small amount of computer code.

LZW compression is based on a simple idea. The encoder and the decoder build identical CodeBooks as a data stream is processed sequentially. The encoder outputs a pattern code only after it has found the pattern more than once. The first time it processes a sequence of data, it places that sequence in its CodeBook and outputs the sequence without any encoding. The decoder will receive this sequence and place it in its CodeBook. The encoder, when it sees a pattern repeated for a second time, will output the code from its CodeBook for the pattern. The decoder can recognize the code because it has built an identical CodeBook from the previous sequences of data.

The LZW compression technique works well on a variety of data. The Unix *compress* utility and the personal computer *ARC* utility are based on LZW compression.

LZW compression was patented on December 10, 1985, under the United States patent number 4,558,302 by the Sperry Corporation (now the Unisys Corporation). A license to use LZW compression in commercial applications can be purchased from Unisys. For further information, write: Welch Licensing Department, Law Department, M/SC2SW1, Unisys Corporation, Blue Bell, Pennsylvania, 19424-0001.

DATA STREAMS THAT SUPPORT LZW ENCODING

Data Format	Name of Specific Implementation	Comments
GIF	LZW compression	Allows for codes ranging in size from 2 to 12 bits
PostScript	LZWDecoder	Always assumes an initial data size of 8 bits per byte
	LZWEncoder	
TIFF	Scheme 5	Always uses 8 bits per byte for data, despite the number of bits per pixel of the image data

Details | To understand the algorithms for LZW encoding, the concept of a *string of data values* must be defined. A string of data values is a sequential ordered list of data values represented by a prefix and the last data value. For example, given the string of data values (12, 34, 18, 11), the Prefix is (12, 34, 18) and the last value is 11. A string of data values is a pattern of data that the encoder and decoder remember in their respective identical CodeBooks.

The LZW encoding algorithm is shown below. A colon is used to represent *data string concatenation*. For example (2, 8, 4): (3) represents the data string (2, 8, 4, 3). Note the following points as you study the algorithm:

- A string of data values is built until the string is different from any other previously coded string. That is, there is no entry in the CodeBook for this string.

- New data strings are *always* made of some previously known data strings plus one new data value.

- When a new pattern is found, three things happen: 1) the new pattern is immediately added to the encoder's CodeBook, 2) the code for the prefix of the new data string is output, and 3) The data string is re-initialized to begin the search for a new data string.

Algorithm for LZW Encoding

```
initialize the CodeBook (one entry for each possible individual
                                 data value)
Prefix = empty string
repeat
    DataValue = next data value in data stream
    if Prefix + DataValue is already in the CodeBook
        then Prefix = Prefix + DataValue
        else {
                add Prefix + DataValue to the CodeBook
                output the Prefix code from the CodeBook
                Prefix = DataValue}
until all the data values are processed;
output the code from the CodeBook for the last Prefix
```

Simulations of Encoding

Let's take a sample stream of data values and hand simulate the algorithm for LZW encoding. For this example, assume that data values in the uncompressed data can have one of three possible values—0, 1, or 2.

   Sample data stream: 0 1 0 1 1 1 1 2

HAND SIMULATION OF THE LZW ENCODING ALGORITHM

Initialize the CodeBook as follows:

Code	DataValue	(Prefix: DataValue)
0	0	−: 0
1	1	−: 1
2	2	−: 2

Prefix = (empty string)

Begin processing data values from the data stream, one value at a time:

Input DataValue	Prefix: DataValue	New CodeBook Entries		Output	New Prefix
		Code	DataString		
0	–: 0	(already in table, code 0)			0
1	0: 1	3	0, 1	0	1
0	1: 0	4	1, 0	1	0
1	0: 1	(already in table, code 3)			3
1	3: 1	5	0, 1, 1	3	1
1	1: 1	6	1, 1	1	1
1	1: 1	(already in table, code 6)			6
2	6: 2	7	1, 1, 2	6	2
	output the last prefix code			2	

Notice that each time a code value is output, the CodeBook gets a new entry. This corresponds to the decoder creating a CodeBook entry each time it reads a new code. Also notice that only on the *second* occurrence of a data string does the encoder send out the code for that string (i.e., data sequence).

The algorithm for decoding an LZW compressed data set is shown below. Each time a code value is taken from the compressed data, its associated data string is output to the uncompressed data set. Each new code creates a new entry in the decoder's CodeBook. In this way, a decoder builds a CodeBook that is identical to the encoder's original CodeBook. (It is possible to read a code from the compressed data stream that is not yet in the decoder's Codebook. This special case is included in the algorithm and explained in detail below.)

Algorithm for LZW Decoding

```
initialize the CodeBook (one entry for each individual data value)
Code = the first code value in the compressed data
output the "data string" from the CodeBook associated with the
                          Code value
repeat
    OldCode = Code
    Code = the next code value in the compressed data stream
    if the Code already exists in the CodeBook
        then   {   output the data string associated with the Code
                   Prefix = OldCode
                   Suffix = 1st value from the Code data string
               }
        else   {   Prefix = OldCode
                   Suffix = 1st value from the Prefix data string
                   output the (Prefix: Suffix) data string
               }
    add (Prefix: Suffix) to the CodeBook
until all the Code values are processed;
```

Simulation of Decoding

Let's take the compressed data from the above encoding example and hand simulate the decoder algorithm.

Input to decoder (from the previous example):   0 1 3 1 6 2

HAND SIMULATION OF THE LZW DECODING ALGORITHM

Initialize the CodeBook as follows:

Code	DataValue	(Prefix:Suffix)
0	0	–:0
1	1	–:1
2	2	–:2

Code = 0 (first data code)

output 0 (the "data string" from the initialized CodeBook)
repeat for each code in the input data stream:

OldCode	Input Code	Is the Code in the CodeBook	Prefix	Suffix	Output	Code Index	Data Values	Prefix: Suffix
0	1	Yes	0	1	1	3	0, 1	0:1
1	3	Yes	1	0	0, 1	4	1, 0	1:0
3	1	Yes	3	1	1	5	0, 1, 1	3:1
1	6	No	1	1	1, 1	6	1, 1	1:1
6	2	Yes	6	2	2	7	1, 1, 2	6:2

Notice that the decoder adds a new code to its CodeBook *every time* a new code is read from the compressed data stream (except for the first code). Also notice that the decoder is always "one step behind" the encoder in adding code entries to its CodeBook. Compare the two charts above (the encoding and decoding examples). Because the encoder is always one step behind, the next code in the compressed data steam may or may not be in the decoder's CodeBook.

If a Code is already in the decoder's CodeBook, then it is a straightforward process to output the data values associated with the Code. The previous code and the first data value from the new code are entered into the Code Book as a new pattern.

If a Code is not in the CodeBook, there can be only one reason: the immediately preceding data values formed the data string. In this case the first and last data values in the two data strings must be equivalent because the previous (Prefix: Suffix) is equivalent to the data string associated with the new code, and the new data string had to begin with the suffix value. We know what the first data value in the previous prefix is; therefore, we know what the suffix of the new pattern must be. Study Figure 9.7.

Nuances

Each implementation of LZW encoding listed in the "Users" table implements a variable-length Code value to further compress the data. In each case the CodeBook is restricted to 4096 entries (indexes 0 to 4095). The Code values start with the number of bits needed to represent the largest index in the initial CodeBook plus 1 bit. If while building the CodeBook (an index into) the table totally uses the current code length, then the code length is increased by 1 bit. For example, if the initial CodeBook was created to handle 256 different data values, then the code lengths would start with 9 bits. After the 511th entry into the CodeBook table, the data values would automatically increment to 10 bits, and so on.

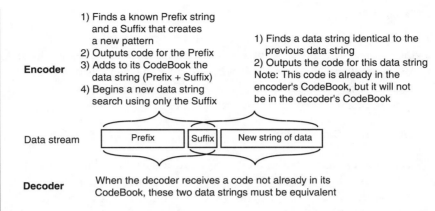

Encoder
1) Finds a known Prefix string and a Suffix that creates a new pattern
2) Outputs code for the Prefix
3) Adds to its CodeBook the data string (Prefix + Suffix)
4) Begins a new data string search using only the Suffix

1) Finds a data string identical to the previous data string
2) Outputs the code for this data string
Note: This code is already in the encoder's CodeBook, but it will not be in the decoder's CodeBook

Data stream

| Prefix | Suffix | New string of data |

Decoder When the decoder receives a code not already in its CodeBook, these two data strings must be equivalent

Figure 9.7 Special case when the decoder receives a code not in its CodeBook. The suffix data value must be equivalent to the first *and* the last data value of the New String of Data

The packing of these bits differs between implementations. The GIF implementation packs the bits in the low-order portion of consecutive bytes. The data can be conceptualized as contiguous data if the data stream bytes are viewed from right to left. See Figure 9.8.

Byte #   3   2   1   0

| ···· | dddddccc | cccccbb | bbbbbba | aaaaaaaa |

9 bits per data value

Figure 9.8 GIF packing of LZW bits into bytes

The other implementations (PostScript and TIFF) pack the bits in the high order portion of consecutive bytes. The data can be conceptualized as contiguous data if the data stream bytes are viewed from left to right. See Figure 9.9.

Byte #   0   1   2   3

| aaaaaaaa | abbbbbbb | bbccccc | cccddddd | ···· |

9 bits per data value

Figure 9.9 PostScript and TIFF packing of LZW bits into bytes

The CodeBook can become full due to the limit of 4,096 entries. Each implementation designates a ClearCode value that re-initializes the CodeBook table when it becomes full (or at any time before becoming full). The ClearCode value is always the value immediately following a fully initialized CodeBook table. For the PostScript and TIFF implementations (which always use an initial data size of 8 bits per byte), the ClearCode value is always 256. The ClearCode value can vary in the GIF implementation, depending on the initial CodeBook size. In addition, each implementation defines an EndOfData marker that always has a value of (ClearCode + 1). The EndOfData marker must be the last code sent by the encoder.

Conclusions

The compression ratio achievable by LZW compression is data dependent. Simple line drawings stored in a raster format can be compressed to 16:1 or higher. On the other extreme, basically no compression is achieved on some data sets that contain raster scanned photographs (e.g., a natural landscape scene). Typical compression ratios for raster scanned photographs lie somewhere in the range of 9:1 to 2:1.

One-Dimensional Differencing

Differencing is a scheme that attempts to reduce the size of individual data values within a data set. The smaller data values can then be encoded using fewer binary digits (i.e., bits).

Data sets that represent raster images often contain data values that are close in value from one pixel to the next. Instead of storing the actual data values for each pixel, we store the difference between the pixel values. In many cases the difference value is much smaller in magnitude than the original data value.

DATA STREAMS THAT SUPPORT DIFFERENCING-BASED SCHEMES

Data Format	Name of Specific Implementation	Comments
JPEG	Predictive	Used for lossless encoding
	Predictive	Used to code the DC coefficients of each DCT block in lossy encoding
LANDSAT*	(None)	
MPEG	(None)	Used to code the DC coefficients of each DCT block
CCITT H.261	(None)	Used to code the DC coefficients of each DCT block

*NASA's LANDSAT (Land Satellite) images are discussed only in this chapter.

Details

Examine the following example data set and its corresponding "differenced" data set.

Original data set   45   47   50   51   53   52   49   ...

Differenced data set   45   −2   −3   −1   −2   1   3   ...

Notice that the values in the differenced data set are "small" in magnitude. These values can be coded more efficiently than the original data due to their smaller size. Typically the *first* data value is coded differently then the other values; it is not a differenced value and it is typically not small.

Conclusions

By combining differencing with a minimizing coding scheme, compression ratios ranging from 1.5 to 3.0 can be achieved. The achievable compression ratios are data dependent. (Minimizing coding schemes are discussed in Section 9.7.)

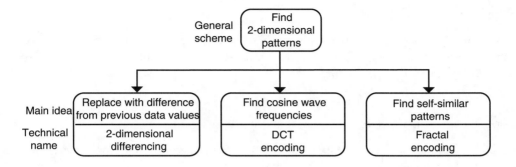

Figure 9.10 Classification of two-dimensional pattern recognition schemes

9.5.2 Two-Dimensional Pattern Recognition

This section discusses more complex schemes that treat a data set as a two-dimensional array of values. Patterns that exist in two-dimensional subsets of this data are exploited. Figure 9.10 summarizes these schemes.

The two-dimensional differencing scheme is a straightforward extension of the one-dimensional scheme discussed above. DCT encoding is a more complex scheme that can produce much higher compression ratios, but is lossy. The DCT transformation can reduce the magnitude of many data values in some data sets. It also reduces the significance of many of the data values, which allows less significant values to be dropped from the data stream. Fractal encoding is based not on a single data transformation but on a series of transformations.

Fractals

A fractal-based compression technique has been developed that recognizes broad patterns contained throughout an entire raster image data set (or subsets of the data set). The main idea is to find a small simple data set that can be changed through repeated transformations into the original data set (or a close approximation to the original). These small data sets are "self-similar" to the original data. Compression is achieved by storing only the small data set and the set of transformations. The encoding process typically requires large amounts of computer time to find the self-similar patterns. Compression ratios as high as 1000:1 have been reported on some data sets. More typical compression ratios vary in the range of 50:1 to 100:1. The amount of compression possible, while maintaining good image quality, is data-set dependent.

Fractal-based compression was developed by Michael Barnsley. Along with his company, Iterated Systems, Barnsley holds the U.S patent number 5,065,447 on fractal-based compression. For information concerning licensing this technology write: Licensing Department, Iterated System, Inc., 5550-A Peachtree Parkway, Suite 650, Norcross, GA 30092. For a thorough explanation of fractal compression, including some C programs to implement the techniques, see [Barnsley93].

Two-Dimensional Differencing

This section is divided into two parts: one on black and white images (i.e., bilevel images) and the other on color images. The two-dimensional differencing schemes used for both of these types of data are quite different.

TWO-DIMENSIONAL DIFFERENCING FOR BLACK AND WHITE IMAGES

The CCITT Fax standards for Group 3 and Group 4 define a two-dimensional differencing scheme for bilevel images. The main idea is this: most "black" pixels are grouped together on a page. Given that we are at the end of a set of "black" pixels, we would like to efficiently "jump over" the following "white" pixels to get to the next group of "black" pixels.[*] In the typical case the previous scan line gives us a good reference on where to jump to on the current scan line. Skipping over large runs of pixels by using the previous scan line as a reference guide can provide good lossless compression on certain classes of images, such as images of text.

The scheme standardized by CCITT Group 4 Fax is shown below. There are 9 possible cases that are recognized by this scheme. They are based on the relationship between certain key points on a current *coding line* and on a previous *reference line* (that has already been encoded). Given that a *changing pixel* is defined as a pixel whose previous pixel on the same scan line is a different color, the key points are defined as follows:

a_0 is the reference or starting pixel on the coding line

a_1 is the next changing pixel to the right of a_0 on the coding line

a_2 is the next changing pixel to the right of a_1 on the coding line

b_1 is the first changing pixel on the reference line to the right of a_0 and of the opposite color to a_0

b_2 is the next changing pixel on the reference line to the right of b_1

Notice that points a_1 and b_1 are guaranteed to have the same color. In many cases the offset (or difference) between points a_1 and b_1 will be small, because "colors" on a page are typically grouped together. Therefore, the difference between a_1 and b_1 is coded instead of the actual index of a_1. The coding assignments shown in the following table come from studying large samples of "typical" documents and discovering which differences occurred most often. These are Huffman codes based on the discovered occurrences. (Refer to Section 9.7.2 on Huffman codes later in this chapter). The table illustrates vertical edges (code = 1), edges that slope right or left at large or small angles, and features that start or stop on the line being encoded.

---

[*] The colors "white" and "black" are enclosed in quotes to indicate that their meaning could be reversed and the idea still holds true (i.e., change "white" to "black" and vise versa).

THE NINE CASES ENCODED BY THE CCITT GROUP 4 2D ENCODING SCHEME

Case Found	Code Assigned	Example Diagrams	Reset After As
$a_1 - b_1 = 0$	1		$a_0 = a_1$
$a_1 - b_1 = 1$	011		$a_0 = a_1$
$a_1 - b_1 = -1$	010		$a_0 = a_1$
$a_1 - b_1 = 2$	000011		$a_0 = a_1$
$a_1 - b_1 = -2$	000010		$a_0 = a_1$
$a_1 - b_1 = 3$	0000011		$a_0 = a_1$
$a_1 - b_1 = -3$	0000010		$a_0 = a_1$
$\lvert a_1 - b_1 \rvert > 3$	001 + $\mathrm{code}(a_0 a_1)$ + $\mathrm{code}(a_1 a_2)^{*}$		$a_0 = a_2$
$a_1 - b_2 > 0$	0001		$a_0 = b_2$

*The code values used to encode these run lengths of pixels are identical to the Huffman codes used in the one-dimensional Fax encoding scheme defined by the CITT group 3 standard. Refer to the original documentation for full details.

Encoding proceeds as follows. Given the position of a_0, find the location of the other key points a_1, a_2, b_1, and b_2. The last condition in the table above (i.e., $b_2 - a_1 > 0$) is checked first. If it is true, a code of 0001 is output to the compressed data stream. If it is not true, the code for one of the other appropriate cases is output to the data stream. a_0 is reset as shown in the table, and the process is repeated until the entire scan line is coded. The last pixel to be encoded is an imaginary changing pixel located just past the end of the scan line. (The first pixel to be coded on a scan line is also an imaginary pixel just before the actual first pixel. It is always assumed to be white.)

This scheme is designed for bilevel images. It would not be very efficient for color images unless there were very large areas of background color within the image.

TWO-DIMENSIONAL DIFFERENCING FOR COLOR IMAGES

The idea of two-dimensional differencing on color images is identical to one-dimensional differencing, except that the difference value is not necessarily calculated from the previous data value on the same scan line.

DATA STREAMS THAT SUPPORT 2-DIMENSIONAL DIFFERENCING SCHEMES

Data Format	Name of Specific Implementation	Comments
JPEG	Predictive	Used for lossless encoding
MPEG	None	Used for lossless encoding
CCITT H.261	None	Used for lossless encoding

Details

A variation on the differencing scheme is called *prediction*. This scheme tries to predict what the next value in the data stream should be, and then it stores the difference between the prediction and the actual value. In many cases this will result in even smaller values than in a straightforward differencing scheme.

The JPEG standard incorporates eight different prediction schemes. The particular scheme used can vary from scan line to scan line so that the best scheme can be used depending on the current data stream. Consider Figure 9.11.

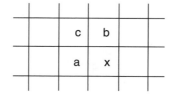

Figure 9.11 Identification of sample points for JPEG prediction scheme

Let's assume that we want to predict the value for position x, and that the values for a, b, and c are known. The schemes defined in the JPEG standard to predict x (i.e., Px) are:

PREDICTION SCHEMES USED IN JPEG

Option	Prediction	Comments
0	No Prediction	Used only for hierarchical mode of operation
1	P$x = a$	One-dimensional predictor
2	P$x = b$	One-dimensional predictor
3	P$x = c$	One-dimensional predictor
4	P$x = a + b - c$	Two-dimensional predictor
5	P$x = a + (b - c)/2$	Two-dimensional predictor
6	P$x = b + (a - c)/2$	Two-dimensional predictor
7	P$x = (a + b)/2$	Two-dimensional predictor

The coded value for each data item is its difference from the predicted value (i.e., the coded value = $x -$ Px).

Option 1 must be used on the first line of data because no values are known for the "above" line. Option 2 must be used for the first value on each new line of data because there is no a or c values in relation to the first value on the line. Beyond these restrictions, the best predictor can be used for any individual scan line of data. Consider the following stream of data values along with the resulting prediction values and the final coded values.

EFFECT OF PREDICTION TECHNIQUE ON COMPRESSED DATA STREAM

Original data set	(scan line 1)	45	47	50	51	53	52	...
	(scan line 2)	47	49	50	52	53	50	...
Predicted values	(using option 1)	45	45	47	50	51	53	...
	(using option 4)	47	47	52	51	54	52	...
Output values (original – prediction)		45	–2	–3	–1	–2	1	...
		47	–2	2	–1	1	2	...

CONCLUSIONS

By combining 2-dimensional differencing with a minimizing coding scheme, compression ratios ranging from 1.5 to 3.0 can be achieved. The achievable compression ratios are data dependent. (Minimizing coding schemes are discussed in Section 9.7)

DCT Scheme

Many mathematical transformations exist that, in general, transform a set of data values from one system of measurement into another. Sometimes the data represented in the new system has properties that facilitate the data's compression. Some mathematical transformations have been invented for the sole purpose of data compression. Others have been borrowed from various applications and applied to data compression. A partial list includes:

Discrete Fourier Transform (DFT)
Discrete Cosine Transform (DCT)
Hadamard-Haar Transforms (HHT)
Karhunen-Loeve Transforms (KLT)
Slant-Haar Transforms (SHT)
Walsh-Hadamard Transforms (WHT)

It is beyond the scope of this book to explain each of these transformations in detail. Refer to [Gonzalez87] and [Rao90] for more information.

Of the above transformations, the Discrete Cosine Transform (DCT) has become the predominant transformation used for digital raster image compression. Two of the more important reasons for this are:

- The DCT has some nice computational properties, primarily a fast algorithm for implementing the transform.

- Extensive testing has shown that the DCT produces visually better quality images at higher compression ratios than most other transformation schemes.

The forward DCT (FDCT) transforms a block of original data into a new set of values. The inverse DCT (IDCT) reverses this process and restores the original data values. In theory, no information is lost when it is transformed and then restored. However, in practice, there is some information loss due to two factors; 1) the cosine values cannot be calculated exactly because they are transcendental numbers, 2) and repeated calculations using limited precision numbers introduce round-off errors into the final result. The variances between the restored data values and the original data values are typically small, but the amount of error is dependent on the method used to calculate the DCT.

The DCT can be applied to any size block of data, but testing has revealed that selecting an 8×8 block provides good compression ratios while maintaining image quality at the resolutions available on today's displays. Also, at the time the algorithms were first being implemented commercially, an 8×8 block size could be accommodated on a single chip of LSI logic, while a block size of 16×16 could not. The remaining discussion assumes the DCT is applied to an 8×8 block of data.

COMPRESSION SCHEMES THAT USE THE DCT

Data Format	Name of Specific Implementation	Comments
ACATS	(To be announced)	The high-definition TV HDTV digital encoding to be announced in 1994
JPEG	DCT	Still-frame images
MPEG	DCT	Moving-picture images
CCITT H.261	DCT	Visual telephony

Details

For those interested in a formal definition of DCT (as defined in the JPEG standard), it is:

$$\text{FDCT:}\; S_{vu}(v, u) = \frac{1}{4} C_u C_v \sum_{x=0}^{7} s_{yx} \cos\left(\frac{(2x+1)\,u\pi}{16}\right) \cos\left(\frac{(2y+1)\,v\pi}{16}\right)$$

$$\text{IDCT:}\; s_{yx}(x, y) = \frac{1}{4} \sum_{y=0}^{7} C_u C_v S_{vu} \cos\left(\frac{(2x+1)\,u\pi}{16}\right) \cos\left(\frac{(2y+1)\,v\pi}{16}\right)$$

where s_{yx} is the original data value, S_{vu} is the transformed data value, and C_u, $C_v = \frac{1}{2}$ when u = 0 and $v = 0$; C_u, $C_v = 1$ otherwise.

The DCT can be easily implemented using the above formulas, but faster incremental methods exist. Refer to [Rao90] for such algorithms.

It may not be obvious from the above formula, but each value calculated in the transformation process involves a unique 8 × 8 transformation matrix. A visual representation of these 64 unique matrices is shown in Figures 9.12–9.15. The graphs are arranged on the pages in accordance with the terms they derive. For example, the term S_{00} that is calculated in the FDCT process is derived by using the matrix values represented in the graph labeled T_{00}. These graphs were generated by Mathematica using the formulas given above and saved as PostScript files. The 64 graphs were then imported to Adobe Illustrator and sized and arranged on four separate pages.

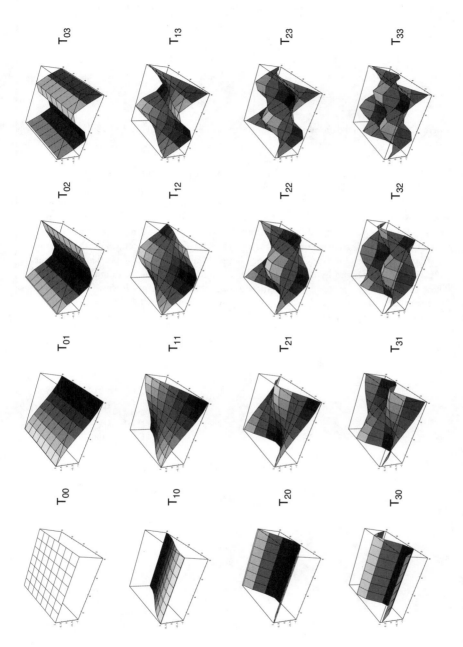

Figure 9.12 Graphs representing the DCT in the upper-left corner of the 8 × 8 block—transformations for terms S_{00} through S_{33}

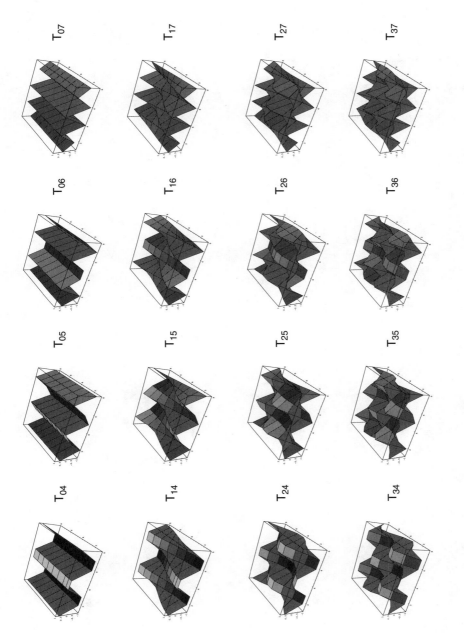

Figure 9.13 Graphs representing the DCT in the upper-right corner of the 8 × 8 block—transformations for terms S_{04} through S_{37}

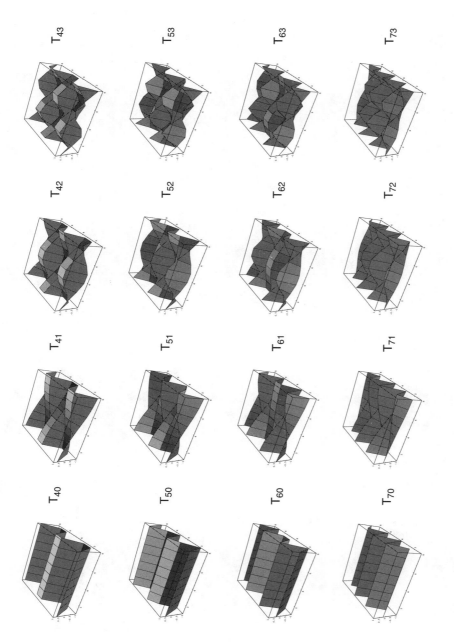

Figure 9.14 Graphs representing the DCT in the lower-left corner of the 8 × 8 block—transformations for terms S_{40} through S_{73}

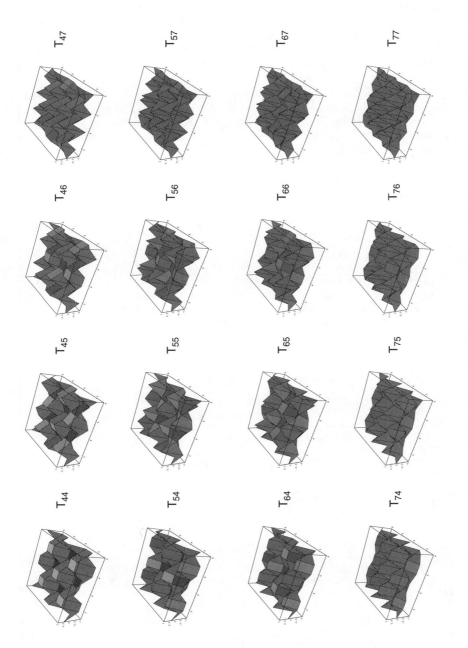

Figure 9.15 Graphs representing the DCT in the loer-right corner of the 8 × 8 block— transformations for terms S_{44} through S_{77}

Each transformation matrix represents a combination of frequencies of the cosine wave form in two dimensions. The idea is to determine how much of each frequency pattern exists in the 8×8 block of data. A measurement of each frequency is calculated in two basic steps. First, each term of a specific transformation matrix is multiplied by its corresponding term in the 8×8 block of data. Second, all of these products are summed together into a single value. This single value is a measurement of the amount of this frequency that is contained in the block of data. In essence, the DCT changes the original values that typically represent color intensity into values that represent cosine frequencies over the 8×8 area.

Several examples will help clarify these ideas. In the following examples, an 8×8 block of data is transformed into discrete cosine space using the forward DCT and then transformed back into its original form using the inverse DCT. Both DCT processes were calculated with a straightforward implementation of the equations shown previously. All of the arithmetic was done using double precision.

In the following examples, the original data values represent color intensities in the range of 0 to 255. The DCT produces better values for compression if the original data is in a range that is centered around the origin. Therefore, the values used in these examples are shown in their shifted form, where 128 was subtracted from each original value to produce values in the range of -128 to 127.

Consider the first example in Figure 9.16, where the data block represents a region of solid color. There are no frequencies in this data and consequently all of the terms except the upper left term are zero. Refer back to the graph of the transformation matrix T_{00} (Figure 9.12). The graph is a flat surface; all of its values are 1.0. This term is special in that it represents the zero-frequency case. The S_{00} term is referred to as the DC coefficient. The name *DC* is borrowed from electrical terminology and stands for Direct Current. (Direct current does not alternate and has no frequencies.) All of the other terms in the 8×8 block are referred to as the AC coefficients. The term *AC* stands for Alternating Current in electrical terminology, and it is borrowed here to indicate terms that represent frequencies.

Original data block

127	127	127	127	127	127	127	127
127	127	127	127	127	127	127	127
127	127	127	127	127	127	127	127
127	127	127	127	127	127	127	127
127	127	127	127	127	127	127	127
127	127	127	127	127	127	127	127
127	127	127	127	127	127	127	127
127	127	127	127	127	127	127	127

Data values after FDCT

1016	0	0	0	0	0	0	0
0	0	0	0	0	0	0	0
0	0	0	0	0	0	0	0
0	0	0	0	0	0	0	0
0	0	0	0	0	0	0	0
0	0	0	0	0	0	0	0
0	0	0	0	0	0	0	0
0	0	0	0	0	0	0	0

Restored values from IDCT

127	127	127	127	127	127	127	127
127	127	127	127	127	127	127	127
127	127	127	127	127	127	127	127
127	127	127	127	127	127	127	127
127	127	127	127	127	127	127	127
127	127	127	127	127	127	127	127
127	127	127	127	127	127	127	127
127	127	127	127	127	127	127	127

Differences (Errors)

0	0	0	0	0	0	0	0
0	0	0	0	0	0	0	0
0	0	0	0	0	0	0	0
0	0	0	0	0	0	0	0
0	0	0	0	0	0	0	0
0	0	0	0	0	0	0	0
0	0	0	0	0	0	0	0
0	0	0	0	0	0	0	0

Figure 9.16 Example of the DCT on a region of solid color

The data in Figure 9.16 resulting from the FDCT can be compressed by storing the single S_{00} value (i.e., 1016) and some special code that indicates that all of the other values are zero. (Chapter 10 explains how this data is actually coded in the various data formats.)

Consider another example in Figure 9.17. This data represents a surface where the color values are smoothly changing through the 8×8 block of data. Notice that all of the nonzero values in resulting from the FDCT are in the upper-left corner (and along the top row and left column). These nonzero terms correspond to the low-order frequencies in the original data. This data can be compressed by storing only the important nonzero terms.

Original data block

60	59	58	57	56	55	54	53
59	58	57	56	55	54	53	52
58	57	56	55	54	53	52	51
57	56	55	54	53	52	51	50
56	55	54	53	52	51	50	49
55	54	53	52	51	50	49	48
54	53	52	51	50	49	48	47
53	52	51	50	49	48	47	46

Data values after FDCT

424	18	0	2	0	1	0	0
18	0	0	0	0	0	0	0
0	0	0	0	0	0	0	0
2	0	0	0	0	0	0	0
0	0	0	0	0	0	0	0
1	0	0	0	0	0	0	0
0	0	0	0	0	0	0	0
0	0	0	0	0	0	0	0

Restored values from IDCT

60	59	58	57	56	55	54	53
59	58	57	56	55	54	53	52
58	57	56	55	54	53	52	51
57	56	55	54	53	52	51	50
56	55	54	53	52	51	50	49
55	54	53	52	51	50	49	48
54	53	52	51	50	49	48	47
53	52	51	50	49	48	47	46

Differences (Errors)

0	0	0	0	0	0	0	0
0	0	0	0	0	0	0	0
0	0	0	0	0	0	0	0
0	0	0	0	0	0	0	0
0	0	0	0	0	0	0	0
0	0	0	0	0	0	0	0
0	0	0	0	0	0	0	0
0	0	0	0	0	0	0	0

Figure 9.17 Example of the DCT on a region of gradual change in color

Consider another example in Figure 9.18. This data comes from a digitized realistic photograph of a Coca-Cola can. The color-intensity values are gradually changing over the surface of the can, but there is some randomness and slight fluctuation throughout the data block.

Original data block	Data values after FDCT

45	45	50	45	58	56	50	48	425	−25	−6	−5	−3	4	−15	13
43	50	43	45	50	56	56	53	−17	−1	0	10	−7	−6	4	−3
43	53	48	50	61	53	63	56	−3	0	−3	9	4	−10	10	−2
48	50	58	53	53	48	68	50	−5	5	−3	−1	3	2	0	−2
45	48	56	56	50	45	68	61	0	0	0	−4	−1	6	6	6
48	53	50	61	61	45	61	50	4	4	−3	2	−2	0	1	4
50	53	56	56	58	53	63	61	1	2	−8	3	5	−3	−4	3
50	48	56	56	63	53	61	61	3	−6	3	−4	1	−3	2	0

Restored values from IDCT	Differences (Errors)

45	45	50	45	58	56	50	48	0	0	0	0	0	0	0	0
43	50	43	45	50	56	56	53	0	0	0	0	0	0	0	0
43	53	48	50	61	53	63	56	0	0	0	0	0	0	0	0
48	50	58	53	53	48	68	50	0	0	0	0	0	0	0	0
45	48	56	56	50	45	67	61	0	0	0	0	0	0	1	0
48	53	50	61	61	45	61	50	0	0	0	0	0	0	0	0
50	54	55	56	58	53	62	61	0	−1	1	0	0	0	1	0
50	48	56	56	63	52	61	61	0	0	0	0	0	1	0	0

Figure 9.18 Example of the DCT on a region of gradually changing solid with some randomness

The randomness in the original data results in a nonzero term for almost every position in the transformed data block. However, now we can eliminate the values in the lower right of the block and still get a reasonable approximation to the original values using the IDCT process. This is because these values are "less important." We'll discuss this in detail after one more example.

Notice that in this last example, the IDCT process does not restore the original data exactly, but the errors are proportionally small. For an image whose color values range from 0 to 255, errors such as these are not distinguishable to the human eye.

Consider one more example in Figure 9.19. This data block comes from a digitized realistic photograph of a forest scene. It represents the color intensities of the vegetation in the background of the picture. The data values are, in essence, random. In this example, the S_{00} (DC) term is 0 "by accident," but it is a good example showing that the S_{00} term is not larger than the other terms in all cases (as might be inferred by the previous examples).

The results of the DCT process for this example do not appear to produce new data in a form that is somehow enhanced for compression; the new data values appear to be as random as the originals. The key is that the importance of each data value has been changed. Re-examine Figures 9.12–9.15. Notice that the transformations in the upper-left corner of the 8×8 block (Figure 9.12) capture lower frequencies, whereas the transformations in the lower-right corner (Figure 9.15) capture the higher frequencies. Higher frequencies capture the "noise" within the data block and the fine detail. The lower frequencies capture the "essence" of the data block, without the fine detail. In some cases the noise contained in the data block can be totally eliminated with no visual loss of information (i.e., the human eye cannot detect any differences).

The amount of noise (high-frequency terms) that we leave out of a compressed data block determines the resulting image quality, and it is the major determining factor in the amount

Original data block	Data values after FDCT
22 22 –128 6 54 –39 38 –55	0 –129 8 8 28 –6 16 –24
–15 –39 22 –128 22 6 –47 71	73 –14 9 15 –43 –53 –72 18
–128 38 6 71 6 54 71 22	–166 68 –38 66 76 –32 –55 53
22 22 54 71 38 87 54 103	–55 35 118 115 40 30 0 18
–31 –15 6 22 –55 22 54 103	66 15 –58 –45 5 32 –86 –29
22 –31 –15 –47 –39 54 22 –31	49 12 18 80 85 32 –30 –34
87 –128 –104 –55 –15 –15 –72 71	10 19 –120 –2 –110 46 –123 –49
–112 –39 6 54 14 –39 –39 –55	–37 –46 7 –34 25 23 –59 –45

Restored values from IDCT	Differences (Errors)
22 22 –129 5 54 –39 39 –55	0 0 1 1 0 0 –1 0
–15 –39 22 –127 22 6 –47 71	0 0 0 –1 0 0 0 0
–128 38 6 71 6 54 71 22	0 0 0 0 0 0 0 0
22 22 54 71 37 87 54 103	0 0 0 0 1 0 0 0
–32 –15 6 22 –55 22 54 103	1 0 0 0 0 0 0 0
22 –31 –15 –47 –39 54 22 –32	0 0 0 0 0 0 0 1
87 –128 –104 –55 –15 –15 –72 71	0 0 0 0 0 0 0 0
–112 –39 6 54 14 –39 –39 –55	0 0 0 0 0 0 0 0

Figure 9.19 Example of the DCT on a region of random color

of available compression. Regrettably, the amount of noise that we can leave out while still retaining good image quality is data-block dependent. In summary, the DCT can potentially, for certain types of data, zero out many of the terms in an 8 × 8 data block, and compression can be achieved by simply leaving out all of the zero terms. However, in the general case, the DCT does not zero out terms, but it does change their importance, with the lower-order frequency terms being the most important. (We will come back to this topic in Section 10.2.3 when we discuss JPEG quantization.)

9.5.3 Three-Dimensional Pattern Recognition

This section discusses schemes that treat a data set as a three-dimensional array of values. The three-dimensional pattern-recognition schemes we will discuss are natural extensions of the one- and two-dimensional differencing and prediction schemes discussed previously. Two natural candidates for three-dimensional differencing include volume data (such as medical CAT and MRI scans) and video data, where a sequence of still images is used to produce "motion pictures." The simple and straight forward application of three-dimensional differencing to volume data is left to the reader. We will concentrate our discussion on video data.

Let's call each still image of a video sequence a *frame*. One method of compressing video sequences is to simply compress each frame separately. However, this is not sufficient in many instances because of the large number of frames in even a short video sequence. We can further compress video sequences by taking advantage of the similarities between frames. In many instances, the differences between one frame and the next is small because of the short time interval between frames. (These schemes are referred to as *inter-frame* compression, as opposed to *intra-frame* compression, which involves only a single frame.)

Frame Differences

One simple scheme of video compression is to store only the pixels that actually change from one frame of the video sequence to the next. Said in a technical way, the scheme is to store only the pixels that produce a nonzero difference when subtracted from their corresponding pixels in the previous frame. The FLI and FLC data formats use such a scheme.

In an FLI video sequence the first frame is encoded by using a run-length encoding scheme similar to PackBits. The next and future frames can be encoded as "frame differences" if the encoder chooses. A frame difference is encoded as a set of "compressed lines." Each compressed line is composed of a set of "run-length packets" that each contain three values: a skip, a count, and a data value. The skip value specifies the number of pixels to skip on the current scan line from the current pixel position. These pixels remain unchanged. The count and data values form a run-length encoding according to the PackBits encoding scheme. An entire scan line can be skipped by including zero run-length packets for it. This scheme is easily implemented in software and is lossless, but it cannot produce high-compression ratios in the general case.

Motion Compensation

Another approach to video compression is to calculate the differences between corresponding pixels in consecutive frames and then encode the differences instead of the original values. We would like the differences to be as small as possible to facilitate compression. Since we are dealing with motion pictures we can assume that the pixel values have shifted in position from one frame to the next. If we can find that shift in position and then calculate the differences between the shifted pixels, we can minimize the difference values. This technique is referred to as *motion compensation*.

Performing motion compensation for each individual pixel will *not* facilitate compression. We would have to store the motion and the difference value for each pixel—an obviously inefficient scheme. However, doing motion compensation on a group of pixels can be very efficient. If we can offset a block of pixels in one frame such that all of the differences are minimized, then higher compression ratios can be achieved, even though the offset must now be stored with the compressed data. An offset is typically represented as a pair of numbers that specifies a shift in the horizontal and vertical directions. Technically the offset is referred to as a *motion vector.*

COMPRESSION SCHEMES THAT USE MOTION COMPENSATION

Data Format	Name of Specific Implementation	Comments
MPEG	Motion compensation Interpolative motion	(also called bidirectional prediction)
CCITT H.261	Prediction Motion compensation	

Details

Motion compensation is often used in combination with other compression schemes—in particular the DCT. Because of this, the typical block size used for motion compensation is either 8×8 or 16×16. Examine Figure 9.20. It shows two corresponding 8×8 data blocks from consecutive frames of a video sequence. If we calculated the difference between corresponding pixels the differences would not all be zero, but if the second data block is differenced with corresponding pixels, in the top data block indicated by the dashed lines, all of the differences would go to zero. This offset that produces the minimum differences is our motion vector (in this case two columns horizontally and one row vertically).

40	42	43	47	51	47	54	53	52	49
39	41	45	45	50	45	58	56	50	48
40	42	43	50	43	45	50	56	56	53
41	43	43	53	48	50	61	53	63	56
42	54	48	50	58	53	53	48	68	50
43	44	45	48	56	56	50	45	68	61
47	46	48	53	50	61	61	45	61	50
48	49	50	53	56	56	58	53	63	61
50	51	50	48	56	56	63	53	61	61

Pixel values from a *reference frame*

45	45	50	45	58	56	50	48
43	50	43	45	50	56	56	53
43	53	48	50	61	53	63	56
48	50	58	53	53	48	68	50
45	48	56	56	50	45	68	61
48	53	50	61	61	45	61	50
50	53	56	56	58	53	63	61
50	48	56	56	63	53	61	61

Coorresponding pixel values from a *"next" frame*

Using a *motion vector* of "2 pixels right," "1 pixel down," the difference between data blocks goes entirely to zero

Figure 9.20 Example of alignment of an 8×8 data block using a motion vector

The goal of differencing and motion compensation is to transform a block of values into another block of values that are somehow "minimal" and therefore easier to compress. In the previous discussion, we considered the case where only two frames were involved in the differencing—a "reference frame" and a "next frame." Consider the case where there are pixel values in the next frame that are not included in the reference frame. This will happen in cases where an object that is hidden in the reference frame moves into view in the next frame. These uncorrelated pixel values hinder our ability to minimize the differences between frames. MPEG provides a way to solve this problem by calculating differences using two reference frames—one *before* and one *after* the frame to be encoded. MPEG calls this *interpolative motion compensation* (or *bidirectional interpolation*). It is nothing more than another way to get the difference values as small as possible.

The technical description of the MPEG prediction scheme is given in the following table. Assume that we have three frames of a video sequence designated in order as frames 0, 1, and 2.[*] We can predict what the pixel value will be in frame 1 by using pixel values from either frame 0 (forward prediction), from frame 2 (backward prediction), or from both frames (average or interpolated prediction). Using this predicted value, we calculate a difference value that is then encoded in our compressed data steam. The differencing is done pixel by pixel, but the same motion vector is used for all of the values within a data block.

PREDICTION SCHEMES USED BY MPEG

Prediction Type	Equation
Forward Prediction	$IP_1(x) = IP_0(x + mv_0)$
Backward Prediction	$IP_1(x) = IP_2(x + mv_2)$
Average Prediction	$IP_1(x) = {}^1\!/2\,(IP_0(x + mv_0) + IP_2(x + mv_2))$

where IP_i is the intensity value predicted at a certain position in frame i, x is the position vector (x and y coordinates) of the pixel, mv_0 is a motion vector with reference to frame 0, and mv_2 is a motion vector with reference to frame 2.

The most difficult part of this scheme is to find the motion vectors in the first place because the MPEG standard does not specify how the motion vectors are to be found. That is left to the specific implementations. The search for the motion vectors will be less time-consuming if a restricted amount of area is compared between frames. However, increasing the search area can produce "better" motion vectors that can likewise produce larger compression ratios. Trade offs must be made between the search time used to find "good" motion vectors, high compression ratios, and image quality. These trade-off decisions are not part of the MPEG standard and are left to individual implementations.

Nuances

It generally takes longer to find good motion vectors than it does to use the motion vectors. In other words, if high compression is the goal, MPEG *encoding* can be quite time-consuming while the *decoding* of the resulting data stream would be comparatively much faster. MPEG can be used in real-time applications, but such applications would typically ignore the more complex features of the standard, such as bidirectional interpolation.

The CCITT H.261 standard is designed for real-time applications *only* and consequently must minimize the amount of searching an encoder would do for good motion vectors. It omits schemes such as bidirectional motion compensation because they require too much searching. In nonreal-time applications, such as video editing, forward and backward predictions make sense because they facilitate tasks such as fast forward and fast reverse. MPEG was designed to allow such operations on compressed data streams. (CCITT H.261 is basically a subset of MPEG but without MPEG's complexity.[†])

---

[*] The frames are ordered but not necessarily adjacent; that is, there can possibly be other frames between frames 0 and 1 and other frames between frames 1 and 2.

[†] The CCITT H.261 standard restricts many of the video parameters that MPEG leaves as variables. For example, H.261 allows only two image sizes (352 × 288 and 176 × 144), whereas MPEG makes no such restriction on image size.

Prediction with Resolution Reduction

Another form of three-dimensional differencing is an integral part of the JBIG standard, which defines a lossless compression scheme for bilevel images (i.e., where each pixel is either 0 or 1). JBIG defines an encoding of a single two-dimensional raster image, but it creates a series of images, each of which is half the resolution of the previous image, to accomplish its encoding. JBIG uses a *resolution-reduction* algorithm to create the images. A JBIG encoder and decoder use the same resolution-reduction algorithm, and in certain situations they can predict what value a certain pixel must have. The encoder does not put data into the compressed data stream for such pixels, and the decoder, when it recognizes such situations, simply fills in the correct pixel value without extracting data from the compressed data stream.

The JBIG document states that on text and line-art images, this scheme allows an encoder to avoid coding over 95% of the pixels. The savings are significantly smaller on bilevel images that come from the dithering of grayscale images. Note that this scheme is only one of five compression schemes used by the JBIG standard. (For more details on this refer to the JBIG documentation.)

9.6 METHOD 2 — REDUCED PRECISION

This section begins a whole new discussion on Method 2 of compressing data—reducing the data's precision. In some instances, graphical data is more precise than it needs to be, as in taking a full-color image and using it in a black and white newspaper article. If the end-use application of a data set is known, then any unnecessary precision of the original data can be removed, and the reduced precision can be exploited to compress the data.

In other instances, the gathering of graphical information produces data that is more precise than the human eye can distinguish. One typical example of this is the electronic scanning of a photograph. Consider the following list of intensity values for pixels along a scan-line read by a scanner. Let's assume they are grayscale intensity values:

```
122   121   123   122   121   122   123
```

There is no repetition in the sequence, but the data values are very similar. In fact, this part of the original image is basically a solid gray level, but the scanner has detected slight variations in intensity. This precision is often not needed to create a "good" reproduction of the original image. Reducing the data's precision is not easily detectable by the human eye. (The technical term used to describe this fact is *noise*. Think of it as the existence of background sounds while trying to listen to music. The background noise is unwanted, and it can corrupt the purity of the music. Hence, it is beneficial to filter out the unwanted sounds, even if it means losing part of the original music.)

Another reason for reducing the precision of graphical data values is a result of the mathematical transformations previously discussed in Method 1. Reducing the magnitude of "less-significant" terms can facilitate compression.

Regardless of the reasons for reducing the precision of data values, doing so creates lossy compression schemes; data is lost that cannot be recovered.

No data formats discussed in this book use Method 2 as their primary compression technique, but several use reduced precision in combination with other schemes. (Refer to the descriptions of the JPEG and MPEG data formats in Chapter 10.)

Details

Consider again the data values given above, this time represented in both decimal and binary formats:

SAMPLE VALUES (IN BOTH DECIMAL AND BINARY REPRESENTATIONS)

Decimal	Binary
122	1111010
121	1111001
123	1111011
122	1111010
121	1111001
122	1111010
123	1111011

Notice that only the low-order bits change while the high-order bits remain constant. The data can be compressed by removing one or more of the low-order bits during encoding. If we do this by shifting the binary digits to the right, this lowers the magnitude of the data values. The decoder must restore the data values to their correct magnitudes by filling in the correct number of zero bits. This stripping off of low-order bits is equivalent to dividing the values by powers of 2; stripping one bit divides by 2, stripping 2 bits divides by 4, stripping 3 bits divides by 8, etc. In some cases division by values other than powers of 2 is desirable, though it usually requires more computational power or computational time.

Reducing data values by a constant division factor has the effect of partitioning the range of data values into "bins," where each bin holds one range of values. Consider Figure 9.21, where the range of original values is 0 through 15 and the precision is reduced from 4 binary bits to 2 binary bits. The result is data being funneled into 4 bins.

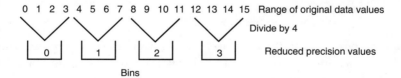

Figure 9.21 How quantization can group data values

The technical name given to this process is *to quantize*. A quantizer captures the quantity or magnitude of each data value while reducing its precision.

Nuances

Using a constant division factor produces uniform bins. Nonuniform division factors can be used to create different-sized bins, as long as both the encoder and decoder use the same factors at the appropriate times.

Reducing data precision works only for full-color and grayscale-type image data. On image data that uses a Color Look Up Table, the loss of precision would result in using the incorrect table entry and, in the general case, totally corrupting an image.

Conclusions

Used in moderation, reducing the precision of data values can facilitate data compression with a minimal loss of information as perceived by the human eye. Used in excess, reducing the precision can create abrupt changes in intensity values from one pixel value to the next when the data is decompressed. These abrupt changes can be very noticeable to the human eye. The technical name used to describe these abrupt changes is *banding*.

9.7 METHOD 3 — MINIMIZE THE NUMBER OF BITS

This section discusses the third major method of data compression, which consists in reducing the overall number of bits needed to represent (code) a data set. The coding process assigns a unique code value to data items in the set. Depending on the scheme used, a code value can represent a single data item or it can represent a unique sequence of data items. Note that a single file can contain more than one set of data, each with its own unique set of codes. The number of possible coding schemes is large. Refer to [Gonzalez87], and [Storer88] for a comprehensive overview. The following discussion is restricted to the coding schemes used by data formats discussed in this book. The following terms must be defined.

Fixed-length Codes (or equal length codes)   Every code value uses the same number of bits in its representation. An example is the normal counting sequence used for binary numbers specified over a set range. The range determines the number of bits used in each code. Fixed-length codes are discussed in Chapter 8.

Variable-length Codes   All code values used for a set of data are not of the same length; some codes may have only a few bits while some may have many bits.

Instantaneous Code   Given an incoming stream of bits (or bytes) that represents a sequential list of code values, each code can be recognized instantaneously when its last bit is received. There is no look-ahead required to recognize that a full code value has been received.

9.7.1 Shift Codes

Given a data set, if only a small subset of its values occur most of the time, then it seems reasonable to select a code length whose range of values can represent this subset. For the occasional value that is outside this typical subset, an "overflow" code can signal the start of another set of codes used to represent these larger values. Compression is achieved because the majority of the data values are coded with a minimal number of bits.

NASA uses shift codes to store LANDSAT (Land Satellite) images produced by its earth-monitoring satellites [Gonzalez87]. When the one-dimensional differencing scheme described previously was used on LANDSAT images, an analysis of the resulting data showed that the majority of difference values were between -7 and $+7$. Values outside of this range occurred very infrequently (i.e., values between -128 and -7 and between $+7$ and $+127$). Therefore, a code size of 4 bits that can represent 16 different values was implemented. Obviously using 4 bits instead of the normal 8 bits facilitates compression.

Details

Figures 9.22 and 9.23 show part of a shift-code assignment to represent values in the range from −128 to +127. A fixed-length code assignment would require 8 bits per data value. This shift code uses only 4 bits for the values that occur most frequently in the data stream. A code of zero (0000) or 15 (1111) indicates a data value that is outside of the specified range (−7, 6). In these cases, other 4-bit codes follow immediately, which indicate an amount above or below this range. An example of the "above" range is shown in Figure 9.23. Given these 4-bit code assignments, Figure 9.24 shows an example encoding.

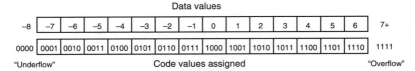

Figure 9.22 Shift-code values for data values ranging from −8 to +7

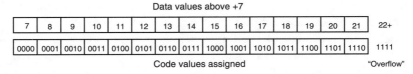

Figure 9.23 Shift-code values for data values greater than +7

Coded data (in binary)	1010	0101	1111	0001	1111	1111	0000
Interpreted data values	2	−3	8			22	

Figure 9.24 Interpretation of a shift-coded data stream example

Nuances

In Figure 9.24's example, all of the codes are multiples of 4 bits. That is, the codes are in lengths of 4 bits, 8 bits, 12 bits, and so on. Shift codes can be of any length. The example could have used an additional 7-bit code to represent all of the values above or below the initial range (−7,6). The probabilities of how often these larger values occur in the data stream determine which scheme produces a more compressed data set. Consider the following possible scenarios.

FREQUENCY OF OCCURRENCE OF DIFFERENT SHIFT-CODE SIZES

Range of Data Values	Code Length	Frequency of Occurrence	Best Scheme
(−127, −23)	12+	2%	Use the bit scheme of 4, 8, 12, 16, etc. because the long codes occur very infrequently (2 + 2 = 4%), and the prevalence of the ranges (−22, −8) and (7, 21) require only an additional 4 bits to code
(−22, −8)	8	13%	
(−7, 6)	4	70%	
(7, 21)	8	13%	
(22, 127)	12+	2%	
(−127, −23)	11	12%	Use the bit scheme of 4, 1 because the "potentially long" codes occur frequently (12 + 14 = 26%). (This avoids codes longer than 12 bits as in the scheme above)
(−22, −8)	11	4%	
(−7, 6)	4	66%	
(7, 21)	11	4%	
(22, 127)	11	14%	

Conclusions

Shift codes are straightforward and easy to implement. They typically produce compression ratios of 2:1 to 3:1. The compression ratio achievable is data-set dependent.

9.7.2 Huffman Codes

Named after its inventor [Huffman52], Huffman codes assign a variable-length code to each possible data item, such that the values that occur most often in the data set have smaller-length codes while the values that occur less frequently have longer-length codes. Given the probability of occurrence of each individual data value, the Huffman algorithm can automatically create an appropriate code assignment for each data value.

DATA STREAMS THAT USE HUFFMAN ENCODING

Data Format	Name of Specific Implementation	Comments
CCITT Fax	Group 3	Huffman encoding used on run-length values
JPEG	Huffman	Used to code the values in a "block" of data—the values are run-length pairs (Run/Size)
MPEG	Huffman	Similar to JPEG, except there is an escape symbol used to terminate the encoding to avoid long code words on very random data
TARGA	Type 32	Similar to PackBits (for color-mapped images) plus Huffman and Delta encoding
	Type 33	Similar to PackBits (for RGB images) plus Huffman and Delta encoding

Details

The algorithm for creating a Huffman code assignment uses the probability of occurrence of each data item to assign the smallest-length codes to the most frequently occurring data items. It creates a tree structure where the leaf nodes are the original probabilities associated with each data value from the data set. Each branch in the tree is labeled with a one or a zero. The Huffman code assigned to each original data value is the set of labels along a path from the root node to the associated leaf node.

The algorithm for assigning Huffman Codes is:

```
Let SetOfOccurances be the set of all occurrence probabilities
While the size of the SetOfOccurances is greater than one do
{
    Small1 = smallest probability in the SetOfOccurances;
    Small2 = next smallest probability in the SetOfOccurances;
    create a parent node of the code tree and let Small1 and Small2 be
                its child nodes
    label the Small1 node 0 (ZERO) and the Small2 node 1 (ONE)
    delete the values Small1 and Small2 from the SetOfOccurances
    add (Small1 + Small2) to the SetOfOccurances;
    }
```

Consider Figures 9.25 and 9.26, which show two examples of data set probabilities and their resulting Huffman Codes. Notice that the larger probabilities are processed last by the procedure, which gives them a shorter path to the root of the tree and therefore a shorter code length.

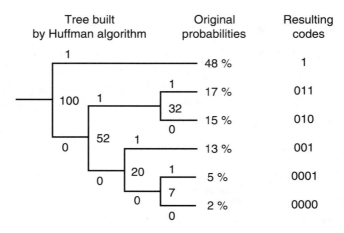

Figure 9.25 Huffman codes for example 1

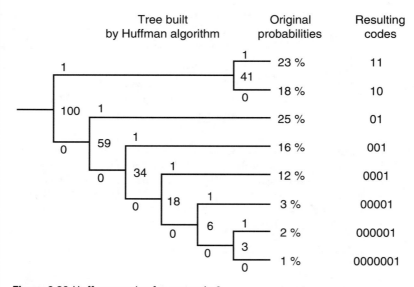

Figure 9.26 Huffman codes for example 2

Conclusions

The Huffman code assignments produce what is called a *minimal code.* This is to say the Huffman code assignments are the "best you can do" when creating a one-to-one coding scheme (i.e., a unique code for each original data value). Huffman codes typically produce compression ratios in the range of 1.5:1 to 2:1, but the exact amount of compression is data-set dependent.

There are two basic options when using Huffman encodings: Create a "generic" Huffman code for a general class of data sets that does well in the "general case," or Create a new Huffman encoding for each new data set used. If we create a new Huffman encoding, we must store it with the compressed data set so that the decoder will know how to interpret the data stream properly. Storing the Huffman codes decreases the efficiency of the compression. If we use a generic Huffman code, then it will not be optimal for any particular data set, but we will not have the overhead cost of storing it with the compressed data. The best scheme to use depends on the size of the data set to be compressed and on the amount of similarity that can be found for a given group of related data sets. Both schemes are used: CCITT Fax formats and MPEG predefine their Huffman codes while JPEG allows both predefined and "new" Huffman codes.

9.7.3   Arithmetic Encoding

Arithmetic codes are based on *sequences* of data values. Instead of assigning a unique code to each individual data value, this scheme outputs a series of values that correspond to unique sequences of data. The probability of occurrence of each individual data value is used to create the output codes.

DATA STREAMS THAT USE ARITHMETIC ENCODING

Data Format	Name of Specific Implementation	Comments
JBIG	Arithmetic encoding	It is the only encoding defined by JBIG
JPEG	Arithmetic encoding	Can be used to code the values in a DCT coded "block" of data—the values are run-length pairs (Run/Size)

Details   This scheme can best be understood by walking through an example. Assume that we have a data set where each item in the set can have one of four possible values with the probabilities of occurrence shown below:

DATA VALUES FOR AN ARITHMETIC CODING EXAMPLE

Data Value	Probability of Occurrence
a	5%
b	15%
c	30%
d	50%

First, map the data values onto a number line between 0 and 1, according to their probabilities. (The order of the ranges is not important.) See Figure 9.27.

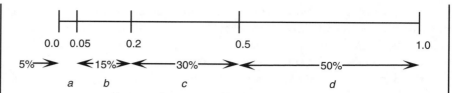

Figure 9.27 First application of arithmetic coding to the unit interval

Now take this same number line and subdivide each region into smaller subregions associated with the probability of a pair of data values. For example, subdividing the region associated with the data value *d* gives Figure 9.28.

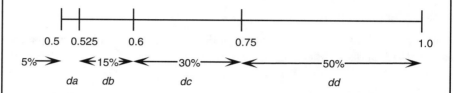

Figure 9.28 Second application of arithmetic coding to a subinterval

And, subdividing the region associated with the data value *dc* gives Figure 9.29.

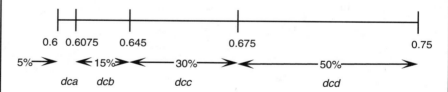

Figure 9.29 Third application of arithmetic coding to a subinterval

Conceptually this subdivision continues forever with the result that each region on the number line between 0 and 1 represents a unique sequence of data values. An encoder could output the upper and lower bounds of a given region, and a decoder could determine the associated sequence of data values corresponding to that region. Obviously, in the general case, infinite precision would be needed for the upper- and lower-bound values, but this is not practical. Instead, when a sequence of data values has been isolated to a range on the number line where the upper and lower bounds have the same high-order digits, then that digits is sent as a code, the number line is renormalized (rescaled to fit between 0 and 1), and the process continues.

For example, given the diagrams in Figures 9.27–9.29, an arithmetic encoder would process the sequence of data values *dcba* as follows:

AN EXAMPLE OF HOW AN ARITHMETIC CODE STRING IS DECODED

Data Value	Lower Bound	Upper Bound	Output	Comments
d	0.5	1.0		No common digit
c	0.6	0.75		No common digit
b	0.6075	0.645	6	
a	0.00	0.05	0	Scale renormalized

Nuances

It is common to implement arithmetic encoding with binary numbers (using digits 0 and 1). The scheme works similar to the example just given, with the exception that the coded sequence is a stream of bits and not a stream of decimal digits. Let 0 represent a restriction to the range 0 to 0.5 and let 1 represent a restriction to the range 0.5 to 1.0. Continue in this same subdivision in each of the subranges. The following output would be generated for the example data given above (i.e., the sequence of values *dcba*):

EXAMPLE OF BINARY-BASED ARITHMETIC ENCODING

Data Value	Lower Bound	Upper Bound	Output
d	0.5	1.0	1
c	0.2	0.5	01
b	0.05	0.02	001
a	0.0	0.05	0000

The assignment of ranges for each probability does not have to be static. The assignment can be assigned to best suited to a particular data set and then stored with the data set to allow for correct decoding. JPEG allows the probability ranges to be included with the data set as an "arithmetic coding table." This makes it possible to use the best arithmetic coding assignments for any given data set.

CONCLUSIONS

Arithmetic coding is more complex to implement and understand than Huffman coding, but it can produce 5% to 10% more compression.

The use of arithmetic coding is covered by patents in both the United States and abroad. In Annex L of the JPEG standard document 10 such patents are identified, one of which is US patent number 4,905,297, "Arithmetic Coding Encoder and Decoder System," February 27, 1990, by G. G. Langdon, Jr., J. L. Mitchell, W. B. Pennebaker, and F. F. Rissanen. Whether one or more patent licenses are required is not yet clear. For the sake of brevity we list only one of the related patents here, but be advised that other patents may apply to the implementation of arithmetic coding.

9.8 SUMMARY AND CONCLUSIONS

This chapter has discussed the three basic methods used by all compression schemes to reduce the size of a data set. These methods include:

- Changing the values somehow to produce more compressible data (a transformation; a mapping)
- Reducing the precision of the values (quantize)
- Assigning codes that minimize the total number of bits needed to represent a data set (code)

These methods can be used as stand-alone compression schemes or they can be combined in interesting ways to produce better (and more complex) compression schemes.

DATA COMPRESSION —
ADVANCED

CONTENTS

10.1 COMBINING COMPRESSION METHODS

Some compression schemes combine two or more of the methods discussed in Chapter 9 to achieve compression ratios larger than any one scheme is capable of producing by itself. The number of scheme combinations is large, but typically compression is accomplished by a sequential process of transformation, precision reduction, and coding. Coding is always the final stage of the process, but there are sometimes several transformation and precision-reduction iterations. This process is summarized in Figure 10.1.

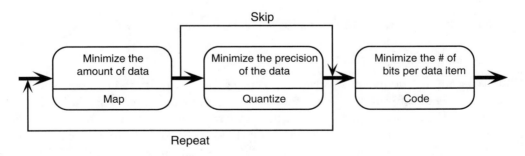

Figure 10.1   Typical combinations of compression methods

In most cases, the distinction between lossless and lossy compression schemes is determined by the exclusion or inclusion of the quantization step. Schemes that include the quantization step are always lossy. Lossless schemes are limited in the amount of compression they can achieve. Many applications, such as video, require larger compression ratios that only lossy schemes can provide. The following sections discuss three lossy compression schemes: JPEG, MPEG, and CCITT H.261.

10.2 JPEG FORMAT

The JPEG standard format defines a suite of data encodings for full-color and continuous-tone raster images. It includes four distinct modes of operation. One of the modes produces limited compression using a lossless encoding technique. This mode was previously discussed in the two-dimensional pattern recognition section. The other three modes provide much higher compression ratios with lossy techniques based on the DCT. The following chart summarizes JPEG's four different modes of operation.

COMPRESSION MODES DEFINED BY JPEG

Mode of Operation	Dominant Compression Scheme	Image Reconstruction
1. Lossless	Predictive (a form of differencing)	Each row (scan line) is decoded and is sequentially displayed in full resolution
2. Sequential	DCT	Each row (blocks of 8 × 8 pixels) is decoded and is sequentially displayed in full accuracy and resolution
3. Progressive	DCT	The entire image is decoded and displayed at a certain accuracy, and further decodings of the entire image add to this accuracy
4. Hierarchical	DCT or predictive	The image is decoded at a certain resolution, and further decodings at higher resolutions are added into the previous decodings to increase the resolution

Refer to the appendix on JPEG for a list of all 29 encoding options allowed by JPEG.

10.2.1 Users

JPEG is becoming a dominant standard in imaging applications. It can be implemented in either hardware or software. JPEG is not a data format but a data-encoding scheme. It was developed with the intention that a JPEG data stream would be embedded within other data formats. Some data formats that allow JPEG encodings are listed in the following list.

The following section further describes JPEG's default encoding called the *baseline sequential scheme.*

DATA FORMATS THAT ALLOW INCLUSION OF JPEG DATA STREAMS

Data Format	Name of Specific Implementation	Comments
IIF	JPEG-intermediate-format	
JFIF	JPEG	An exact JPEG bit stream with one predefined data block included
JTIFF	JPEG	Defines several new TIFF tags to describe the JPEG bit stream (See TIFF appendix)
QuickTime	Photo Compressor	
PostScript		PostScript Level 2 only

10.2.2 Overview

JPEG's baseline sequential scheme is a combination of the Discrete Cosine Transform (DCT), reduced precision of the DCT coefficients (quantization), run-length encoding, and Huffman or arithmetic encoding. (Refer to Chapter 9 for the details on each separate scheme.)

To compress an image, the image data is divided into blocks, where each block is an 8 × 8 array of values. Each block of data is put through three processes: a Forward Discrete Cosine Transform (FDCT), a quantizer, and a coder. To decompress an image, these processes are reversed: an un-coder, a de-quantizer, and an Inverse Discrete Cosine Transform (IDCT). Figure 10.2 summarizes these steps.

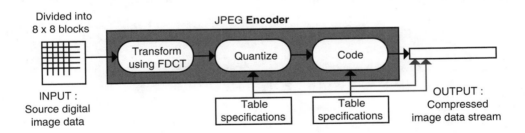

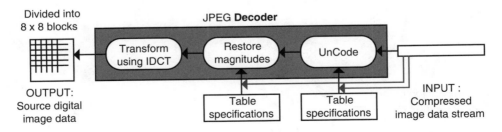

Figure 10.2 Sequence of operations for JPEG encoding and decoding

We remind you that the DCT transforms a data set into the cosine-frequency domain. The values in the upper-left corner of the transformed data represent the lower-order frequencies while the values in the lower-right corner represent the higher-order frequencies. The low-order frequency terms capture the "essence" of the data while the higher-frequency terms capture the fine detail and "noise." The precision of one or more of these terms can be reduced, if desired, to facilitate higher compression ratios. The precision of the higher-frequency terms can often be greatly reduced with minimal loss of image quality in the decompressed image.

10.2.3   Quantization

The precision is reduced during encoding (i.e., the quantization process) by dividing each data value in the 8 × 8 block by a unique divisor that is stored in an 8 × 8 table. Mathematically the quantization step is simply a division operation, but it can be done more efficiently in hardware with a shift operation if the quantization factors are restricted to powers of 2. The decoding process restores the magnitudes of the terms by multiplying by identical quantization factors, but it obviously cannot restore the precision of the original terms. This process is stated mathematically by the following two formulas. Figure 10.3 shows one possible quantization table.

Encoding process: $\text{QuantizedTerm} = \text{round}\left(\dfrac{\text{Original Term}}{\text{Quantization Factor}}\right)$

Decoding process: $\text{Restored term} = \text{QuantizedTerm} * \text{QuantizationFactor}$

The following example shows the effect of increasing quantization on a sample data block. The sample data block comes from a photo-realistic digital image of a Coca-Cola can. Examine the effects that the two quantization tables have on the restored data blocks.

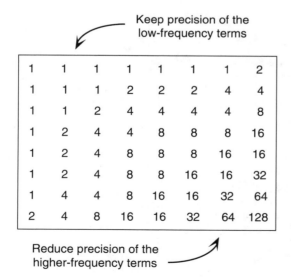

Keep precision of the low-frequency terms

1	1	1	1	1	1	1	2
1	1	1	2	2	2	4	4
1	1	2	4	4	4	4	8
1	2	4	4	8	8	8	16
1	2	4	8	8	8	16	16
1	2	4	8	8	16	16	32
1	4	4	8	16	16	32	64
2	4	8	16	16	32	64	128

Reduce precision of the higher-frequency terms

Figure 10.3   A possible quantization table

EXAMPLE SHOWING THE EFFECTS OF QUANTIZATION ON A DATA BLOCK

Original data block

50	43	53	50	56	43	56	61
50	48	58	50	56	58	56	58
53	45	45	40	45	61	50	61
45	58	50	58	56	50	50	61
81	48	38	-21	45	53	50	61
40	45	68	73	56	43	50	58
48	40	89	89	61	40	58	73
45	40	48	66	7	45	48	53

Data values after the FDCT

414	-14	14	-21	7	7	17	7
0	-8	6	28	-3	-21	-5	11
4	-1	-21	-29	5	30	-3	-16
10	2	-3	-1	7	-7	-1	27
-27	3	33	21	-7	-8	-2	-2
27	-2	-32	-30	16	8	-10	-2
-17	-2	-1	1	-2	5	-3	-15
-9	-2	35	24	-3	-9	16	19

Quantization Table 1

1	1	1	1	1	1	1	1
1	1	1	2	2	2	2	2
1	1	2	2	2	2	2	4
1	2	2	2	2	2	4	4
1	2	2	2	2	4	4	4
1	2	2	2	4	4	4	8
1	2	2	4	4	4	8	8
1	2	4	4	4	8	8	8

Quantization Table 2

1	1	1	1	1	1	1	2
1	1	1	2	2	2	4	4
1	1	2	4	4	4	4	8
1	2	4	4	8	8	8	16
1	2	4	8	8	8	16	16
1	2	4	8	8	16	16	32
1	4	4	8	16	16	32	64
2	4	8	16	16	32	64	128

Restored values from IDCT

50	44	53	50	57	43	57	60
50	47	58	50	57	58	56	58
52	45	46	39	43	63	50	61
45	59	50	57	57	49	51	60
82	49	37	-21	43	53	49	61
39	43	71	73	57	44	49	59
49	39	89	90	62	38	59	74
45	40	47	67	6	46	47	53

Restored values from IDCT

51	41	54	49	59	42	60	58
49	50	61	48	53	61	51	60
52	46	39	43	45	59	53	61
46	56	59	53	56	48	49	62
81	51	28	-15	44	58	49	58
40	41	80	61	64	38	48	63
48	43	80	101	54	39	63	69
45	39	50	63	9	46	46	54

Differences between the original data and the restored data (the error)

0	-1	0	0	-1	0	-1	1
0	1	0	0	-1	2	0	0
1	0	-1	1	2	-2	0	0
0	-1	0	1	-1	1	-1	1
-1	-1	1	0	2	-2	1	0
1	2	-3	0	-1	-1	1	-1
-1	1	0	-1	-1	2	-1	-1
0	0	1	-1	1	-1	1	0

Differences between the original data and the restored data (the error)

-1	2	-1	1	-3	1	-4	3
1	-2	-3	2	3	-3	5	-2
1	-1	6	-3	0	2	-3	0
-1	2	-9	5	0	2	1	-1
0	-3	10	-6	1	-5	1	3
0	4	-12	12	-8	5	2	-5
0	-3	9	-12	7	1	-5	4
0	1	-2	3	-2	-1	2	-1

The first example quantization table introduces minimal errors into the restored data. The second table introduces greater errors, though they are still small. The largest magnitude of error is 12, which is an error of 4.7% (i.e., $12/256 \times 100$). Most of the errors are less than 2%. These errors are not typically discernible by the human eye. By using the second quantization table, 15 of the high-frequency terms in the transformed data are zeroed out. These zeroed terms can be compressed more efficiently by the encoding process.

The amount of precision reduction that can be performed without affecting the visual quality of the image is data dependent. Some images can have no visible information loss even with more precision reduction than the examples above. To emphasize how data dependent quantization really is, the JPEG standard does not even define a default quantization table. Each application must define its own tables to best suit its needs.

A data set can be decoded successfully only if the encoder and decoder use identical tables. The tables can be included in the compressed data set or they can be predefined for a class of images and stored separately from the compressed data. The method used to initialize the quantization tables is application dependent. The JPEG standard allows for four different quantization tables to be stored at any one time during the decoding process. A different quantization table can be used for different components defined in a data stream. For example, one table could be used for the luminance values while another could be used for the chrominance values.

10.2.4   Coding

The *coding process* is performed after the quantization. This process is actually a combination of two transformations and then a code assignment. First the 8 × 8 block of data is transformed from a two-dimensional array of values into a sequential list of 64 values. Then this list is run-length encoded to minimize any redundancy. And finally, the run-length encoded list is coded using either a Huffman encoding or an arithmetic encoding. This is summarized in Figure 10.4.

The transformation from a data block to a sequential list is made using a zigzag scheme, as shown in Figure 10.5. The rationale behind the zigzag scheme comes from the importance and the magnitude of the cosine frequency values in the data block. The lower-order frequency values in the upper left tend to be larger in magnitude than the higher-order frequency values in the lower right due to the quantization process (or simply due to the nature of the data). The zigzag order produces a sequential list where, in many cases, the end of the list is predominantly zeroes.

An example showing the results of the zigzag transformation process is listed next. This is the same data block used in the example in Section 10.2.3 after it was quantized by Quantization Table 2.

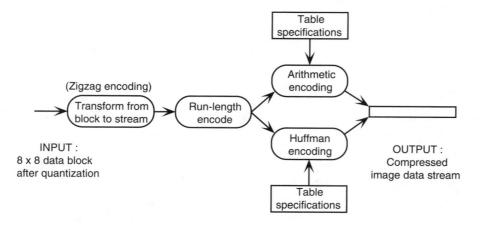

Figure 10.4   The JPEG encoding process

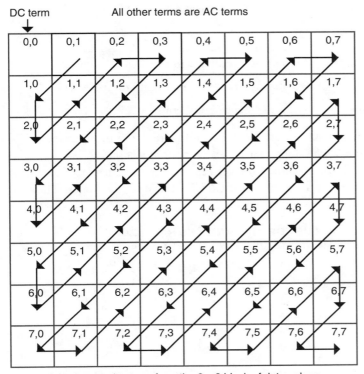

DC term — All other terms are AC terms

Ordering used to transform the 8 x 8 block of data values
into a linear sequence of 64 data values

Figure 10.5 The zigzag ordering used to order the 64 DCT values

The sequential list:

414	−14	0	4	−8	14	−21	6	−1	10	−27	1	−11	14
7	7	−2	−7	−1	2	27	−17	−1	8	0	1	−11	17
4	−1	8	1	3	−8	−1	−5	−1	0	−4	−1	−1	−1
3	−2	0	−1	2	0	4	2	0	1	0	2	0	−1
0	0	0	0	0	0	0	0						

This sequence of values is now run-length encoded. However, this run-length scheme is quite different from the schemes described previously. The intent here is to efficiently encode the runs of repeated zero values. The repetition of values other than zero is not run-length encoding. This scheme also minimizes the number of bits needed to encode each data value by using variable-length integers.

Each term in the run-length encoded sequence consists of three values: a RUN-LENGTH, a SIZE, and a DATA-VALUE. The RUN-LENGTH value represents the number of zero-value terms preceding this term, the SIZE value represents the number of bits used to represent the DATA-VALUE, and the DATA-VALUE is the actual value of the term. The following table summarizes this scheme.

DEFINITIONS OF THE FIELDS OF THE RUN-LENGTH ENCODING SCHEME

Field Name	# Bits Used	Description
RUN-LENGTH	4	Number of preceding zero terms
SIZE	4	Number of bits used to represent DATA-VALUE
DATA-VALUE	Variable	The actual value of this term

The DATA-VALUE is coded with only the number of bits required to represent it. The following table shows the range of values that can be represented for different values of SIZE. Notice that it is not a "normal" binary integer representation. There are gaps in the middle of each sequential range, and zero is not included in any of the ranges. The zero-valued terms are inferred by the run lengths.

CORRELATION BETWEEN THE VALUE FOR SIZE AND THE RANGE OF POSSIBLE VALUES THAT CAN BE ENCODED WITH THAT SIZE

SIZE	Range of Values Possible
1	−1, 1
2	−3, −2, 2, 3
3	−7..−4, 4..7
4	−15..−8, 8..15
5	−31..−16, 16..31
6	−63..−32, 32..63
7	−127..−64, 64..127
8	−255..−128, 128..255
9	−511..−256, 256..511
10	−1023..−512, 512..1023

The DATA-VALUEs are stored using the low-order bits of the actual data value (stored as 2's complement binary integers). The high-order bit can be restored in the decoding process from the SIZE value. SIZE number of low-order bits from the data value are used to represent the data. If the data value is negative, one is subtracted from the value before it is coded. The following chart gives an example of how this works for SIZE equal to 3. Notice that all of the negative numbers have a resulting high-order bit of 0 and that all of the positive numbers have a high-order bit of 1.

Let's transform the first few values from the zigzag sequence given above into this run-length format. The initial sequence is 414, −14, 0, 4, −8. The first value, 414, is the DC term of the data block, and it is encoded separately from the other terms because of its typically larger magnitude. Only the AC coefficients are encoded using the run-length scheme. The second value, 14, is encoded with a RUN-LENGTH of 0 and a SIZE of 4. Four bits are then used to represent the value 14. The next value is zero and it is not explicitly coded.

EXAMPLE ENCODING SCHEME WHERE SIZE EQUALS 3

Value to Be Coded	Conversion If Negative	8-bit 2's Complement Binary Representation	Bits Used for DATA-VALUE
−7	(−7 − 1) = −8	11111000	000
−6	(−6 − 1) = −7	11111001	001
−5	(−5 − 1) = −6	11111010	010
−4	(−4 − 1) = −5	11111011	011
4		00000100	100
5		00000101	101
6		00000110	110
7		00000111	111

This is a run of zero values of length 1. The next term has the value 4. It has a RUN-LENGTH of 1 (because of the previous 0) and a SIZE of 3. Notice that the DATA-VALUE is only 3 bits long. The run-length encoding continues this process for the entire sequence of data values (all 63 of them).

EXAMPLE ENCODING OF 4 DCT TERMS

Actual data values	14	0	4	−8
Encoding (in decimal)	0: 4: 14	—	1: 3: 4	0:4:7
Encoding (in binary)	0000:0100:1110	—	0001:0011:100	0000:0100:0111

It is typical of many data blocks to have a large run of zero values at the end of the sequence, as in the above example. A special RUN-LENGTH:SIZE encoding of 0:0 represents an end-of-block condition. This code can appear at any time in the sequence to indicate that the remaining data values are all zero. Another special RUN-LENGTH:SIZE encoding of 15:0 represents a run of 15 zeros and no data value. This code is used when run lengths greater than 15 are encountered.

Finally, this sequence of run-length encoded values is encoded with a Huffman encoding.[*] The DATA-VALUEs tend to be random for any given sequence of data, but certain pairs of RUN-LENGTH and SIZE values tend to be repeated more often than other pairs. This higher frequency of occurrence for certain pairs can be "exploited" by using a Huffman encoding. Again in this case the JPEG standard does not define a "default" Huffman coding. Each application must define their own coding tables. The tables can be stored with the data stream or stored separately, but in either case, the data cannot be decoded without access to the identical tables that were used by the encoder.

---

[*] The baseline sequential mode restricts the encoding to a Huffman encoding. The other modes allow either a Huffman encoding or an arithmetic encoding.

To summarize the JPEG coding process, the coded sequence results in a stream of variable-length coded data value pairs. The first value is a variable-length Huffman code that represents the RUN-LENGTH and SIZE associated with the current data item. The next value is a variable length integer value that represents the actual data value. The actual Huffman codes used are application and data set dependent.

10.2.5   Nuances and Conclusions

The JPEG standard is not a single encoding scheme but a suite of schemes, all but one of which are based on DCT. The technical documents on JPEG include the specifications and nuances associated with each mode of operation. It is possible that any given JPEG compliant decoder will not accept all possible variations of the JPEG standard. For example, a specific decoder might implement only Huffman encoding. Any data set that uses arithmetic encoding could not be decompressed by this specific decoder.

The JPEG standard does not define a color space for its pixel values. This is left to individual applications. In actuality, JPEG was designed with one specific color model in mind—the YC_rC_b color model. (Refer back to Chapter 6 for details on the color model and to Chapter 7 for details on the data organization.) Using this color model the color difference values C_r and C_b can be sampled at half the resolution of the luminance values Y while still maintaining good image quality. Taking an area of 16×16 pixels, this results in storing 384 values ($4 \times 64 + 64 + 64$) instead of 768 values ($4 \times 64 \times 3$) that would be required using the RGB color model. By simply converting pixels to the YC_rC_b color model we can compress the data stream by a ratio of 2:1.

In summary, compression is achieved in the JPEG standard by a combination of the following:

- Transform the pixel values into the YC_rC_b color model so that the color difference values can be sampled at half the resolution of the luminance values.

- Transform the data into another system of measurement where a majority of the critical information is stored in only a few of the terms. This new system is the discrete cosine frequency domain, and the critical information is contained in the low-order frequency terms.

- Reduce the precision of the less-critical terms. The quantization step lowers the precision of the higher-frequency cosine terms.

- Order and run-length encode the data to eliminate repetition. Given the precision reduction of the higher-order frequency terms, runs of zeros are common, and run-length encoding efficiently reduces the number of data values to code.

- Encode the values using a variable-length code that takes advantage of the more frequently occurring values. The run-length/size-values are Huffman encoded because certain pairs typically occur more often than others.

The combination of compression schemes used by the JPEG standard provide for a wide range of compression ratios. The amount of compression for any given data set is both data dependent and image-quality dependent. Typical compression ratios are listed below, but the ratios will vary from image to image.

TYPICAL COMPRESSION RATIOS PRODUCED BY JPEG COMPRESSION

Typical Compression Ratios	Compression Method	Reconstructed Image Quality	Comments
2:1	Predictive (Lossless)	Highest	No data loss
12:1	DCT (Lossy)	Excellent	Indistinguishable from the original
32:1	DCT (Lossy)	Good	Satisfactory for many applications
100:1	DCT (Lossy)	Low	Recognizable image inaccuracies

10.3 MPEG

MPEG uses basically the same compression scheme that JPEG uses except that it is designed for video sequences and not still images. MPEG differs from JPEG in the following key areas:

- MPEG makes explicit many of the options left open by JPEG; for example, MPEG *requires* the use of the YC_rC_b color model while JPEG does not, and MPEG *requires* the use of Huffman coding and predefines the coding tables while JPEG allows both Huffman and arithmetic coding and does not pre-specify their coding tables.

- MPEG does not encode every frame as a separate entity in a video sequence. Many of the frames are differenced with previous frames (or future frames) in the sequence to minimize the amount of data that must be encoded. This is called *inter-frame encoding* because it involves more than one frame. (Refer back to the discussion on three-dimensional differencing in Chapter 9.)

- MPEG is not just a graphical data encoder. It also defines a compression scheme for audio (sound) data. In addition, it defines a scheme that allows video data, audio data, and other types of data streams to be stored in a single data stream and then played back such that the audio, video, and other data streams are synchronized correctly. This process is called *multiplexing*. MPEG allows up to 32 audio and 16 video streams to be multiplexed simultaneously.

The MPEG standard is large and complex. It is beyond our scope to review the entire standard. Our remaining discussion focuses on the video stream encoding. For a discussion on the audio streams and the multiplexing scheme, refer to the original MPEG specification.

10.3.1   Users

MPEG was designed to accommodate synchronized digital video and digital audio at rates of up to 1.5 megabits per second. Most current implementations are hardware based, but some general-purpose RISC processors are capable of producing real-time playback of low-resolution MPEG video sequences in software. An MPEG data stream can be a stand-alone data format or it can be embedded within other data formats.

DATA FORMATS THAT ALLOW INCLUSION OF MPEG DATA STREAMS

Data Format	Name of Specific Implementation	Comments
IIF	MPEG-bitstream	
MPEG		Can be used independently of any other data format
QuickTime	MPEG	Not initially supported, but support is coming soon

10.3.2   Details

MPEG defines four distinct types of picture encodings. These are

- An *Intra-coded* (I) picture that is coded using information only from itself
- A *Predictive-coded* (P) picture that is coded using "motion-compensated prediction" from a *past* I-picture or P-picture
- A *Bidirectional predictive-coded* (B) picture that is coded using motion-compensated prediction from a *past* and/or a *future* I-picture or P-pictures
- A *DC-coded* (D) picture that is coded using information only from itself. A D-picture stores only the DC component of each discrete cosine transformed (DCT) block. A video sequence contains either all D-pictures or no D-pictures. A video sequence of D-pictures provides fast playback to facilitate video editing (and produces very lossy images)

Lets first discuss how I-, P-, and B-pictures relate to each other, and later we'll discuss the specific encoding used for each one.

A *group of pictures* is defined as a series of one or more pictures, the first of which is an I-picture. The first picture in a group of pictures is typically at a scene cut because differencing techniques between two totally different scenes provides little or no compression.[*] The remaining pictures in the group are encoded as differences from the I-picture. Figure 10.6 shows a possible sequence of pictures that compose a group of pictures. The number of pictures included is determined by the encoder, and there is no predefined limit. Shorter

---

[*] The choice of which frames to encode as I-pictures out of a video sequence is not defined by the MPEG standard. An encoder can arbitrarily choose any set of frames. (Ideally an encoder makes wise choices that maximize compression.)

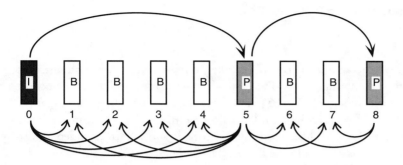

Figure 10.6 The dependencies between different types of picture encodings

sequences facilitate editing by allowing random access into a video sequence. Longer sequences typically produce better compression.

The number of P-pictures verses the number of B-pictures within a group of pictures is not specified by the MPEG standard and is left to the discretion of the encoder. For example, a group of pictures could look like Figure 10.6 or it could have all P-pictures and no B-pictures. Note, however, that you cannot have B-pictures without P-pictures. Typically B-pictures have the highest compression ratios, and by including more B-pictures, better compression is achieved.

The arrows in Figure 10.6 indicate the dependency between pictures. For example, consider picture 2, which is dependent on both Pictures 0 and 5. If we ordered the pictures in the data stream in the same order that they are displayed, we would have to read Pictures 2, 3, 4, and 5 before we could decode Picture 2 and display it. This would require large amounts of memory to store all of these pictures, and keeping up with the display frame rate would be difficult. Therefore, pictures are ordered in a data stream in the order in which they are needed, not their order of display. In Figure 10.6, we need Picture 5 to decode Pictures 1 through 4, so Picture 5 would follow picture 0 in the data stream. The pictures would be ordered in the data stream as 0, 5, 1, 2, 3, 4, 8, 6, and 7. An MPEG decoder must be able to store a minimum of three pictures at any one time: a previous picture, a future picture, and a current picture.

A group of pictures is segmented into individual encodings for each picture. Each picture encoding is made up of a picture header that contains timing, picture type, and coding information, followed by one or more *slices*. A slice is made up of a header that contains position and quantization information, followed by one or more *macroblocks*. (A macroblock covers exactly one 16×16 block of pixels) and consists of a header that contains "address," quantization, and motion-vector information, followed by exactly 6 *data blocks* (4 for luminance Y, 1 for chrominance C_r and 1 for chrominance C_b). For further discussion of this breakdown, refer to Chapter 7.

10.3.3   Picture Encoding According to Picture Type

I-Pictures

An intra-coded I-picture is encoded using only references to itself and no other pictures. Its encoding is basically a restricted version of a JPEG encoding with a few slight variations. An I-picture is broken into macroblocks of 16×16 pixels. Each 8×8 data block within the macroblock is transformed by a DCT, quantized, and transformed into a linear stream using the same zigzag order defined in JPEG. This stream of 64 terms is run-length encoded, and a variable-length Huffman code is assigned to each run-length data pair. The Huffman codes are pre-specified as is a standard set of quantization tables. No decoding tables are included within a MPEG data stream.

P-Pictures

A predictive-coded P-picture is based on a previously coded I-picture or another P-picture. All of the macroblocks in a P-picture do not have to reference other pictures. Some of them can be encoded totally by themselves using the DCT scheme just described above for I-pictures. If one or more of a picture's macroblocks reference a previous picture, then the entire picture is considered a P-picture. If a macroblock in a P-picture does reference a previous picture, it is decoded in two steps:

- The motion vector stored with the macroblock is used to reconstruct a "predicted" macroblock.
- The data blocks included in the macroblock are decoded, transformed using an inverse DCT, and then added to the already predicated macroblock. Notice that the data blocks contain only the differences between the predicated macroblock and the actual macroblock.

Let's discuss these two steps separately in some detail.

Information in a macroblock header indicates whether it references a previous picture. If it does, a motion vector is also included in the header. The motion vector determines which block of pixels from a previous picture are used to create a *prediction* of the current block. For example, consider Figure 10.7, which shows two possible prediction blocks and their associated motion vectors. The macroblock[*] indicated by the motion vector is the "closest match" to the macroblock in our current picture. The MPEG standard does not specify what *closest match* means.[†] An encoder can use any criteria it desires to determine the closest match. In general we want the differences between the predicated macroblock and the actual macroblock to be as small as possible. (Notice that a decoder does not care how the motion vector is selected or why!)

---

[*] Figure 10.7 shows only the luminance values for the macroblock, even though the 2-chrominance data blocks are also considered when searching for a "best match."

[†] The MPEG standard does offer a few suggested schemes for determining the "closest match," such as a "mean square error" or a "mean absolute difference," but these are not a formal part of the standard.

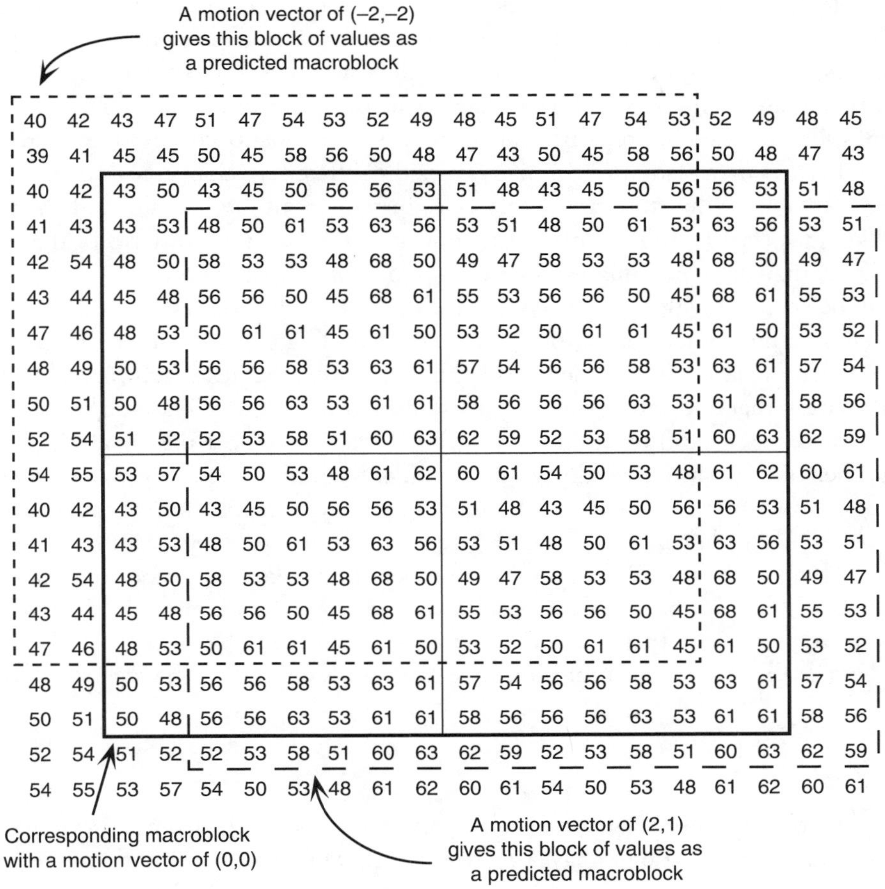

A motion vector of (−2,−2)
gives this block of values as
a predicted macroblock

```
40  42  43  47  51  47  54  53  52  49  48  45  51  47  54  53  52  49  48  45
39  41  45  45  50  45  58  56  50  48  47  43  50  45  58  56  50  48  47  43
40  42  43  50  43  45  50  56  56  53  51  48  43  45  50  56  56  53  51  48
41  43  43  53  48  50  61  53  63  56  53  51  48  50  61  53  63  56  53  51
42  54  48  50  58  53  53  48  68  50  49  47  58  53  53  48  68  50  49  47
43  44  45  48  56  56  50  45  68  61  55  53  56  56  50  45  68  61  55  53
47  46  48  53  50  61  61  45  61  50  53  52  50  61  61  45  61  50  53  52
48  49  50  53  56  56  58  53  63  61  57  54  56  56  58  53  63  61  57  54
50  51  50  48  56  56  63  53  61  61  58  56  56  56  63  53  61  61  58  56
52  54  51  52  52  53  58  51  60  63  62  59  52  53  58  51  60  63  62  59
54  55  53  57  54  50  53  48  61  62  60  61  54  50  53  48  61  62  60  61
40  42  43  50  43  45  50  56  56  53  51  48  43  45  50  56  56  53  51  48
41  43  43  53  48  50  61  53  63  56  53  51  48  50  61  53  63  56  53  51
42  54  48  50  58  53  53  48  68  50  49  47  58  53  53  48  68  50  49  47
43  44  45  48  56  56  50  45  68  61  55  53  56  56  50  45  68  61  55  53
47  46  48  53  50  61  61  45  61  50  53  52  50  61  61  45  61  50  53  52
48  49  50  53  56  56  58  53  63  61  57  54  56  56  58  53  63  61  57  54
50  51  50  48  56  56  63  53  61  61  58  56  56  56  63  53  61  61  58  56
52  54  51  52  52  53  58  51  60  63  62  59  52  53  58  51  60  63  62  59
54  55  53  57  54  50  53  48  61  62  60  61  54  50  53  48  61  62  60  61
```

Corresponding macroblock
with a motion vector of (0,0)

A motion vector of (2,1)
gives this block of values as
a predicted macroblock

Figure 10.7 Example macroblocks obtained using motion vectors

Motion vectors can be specified in full- or half-pixel increments. Each component of a motion vector (i.e., the horizontal and vertical component) can range in size from −512 to 511.5 (for half-pixel increments) or from −1,024 to 1,023 (for full-pixel increments). Doing a little math tells us that there are 9,437,184 [*] possible macroblocks we could use for a predication macroblock. In reality the number is smaller than this because motion vectors cannot represent offsets that go beyond the boundaries of a picture. An encoder must implement a search strategy to find the closest matching macroblock. The MPEG standard suggests several strategies such as a 2D search, a logarithmic search, or a telescopic search, but an encoder can use any strategy it desires. Obviously the longer an encoder searches, the longer it takes to produce the compressed data stream.

---

[*] There are 2,048 possible values in the range [−512, 511.5] using a step size of 0.5 between each value, and there are 1,024 possible values in the ranges [−1,024, −513] and [512, 1,024] when taking steps of 1.0 between each value. Therefore, we have 3,072 possible values per component or $3,072^2 =$ 9,437,184 possible motion vectors.

The 6 data blocks that follow a macroblock header contain only the differences between the predicted and the actual macroblock. Each data block is decoded from its Huffman run-length codes into a stream of 64 values. These values are used to reconstruct an 8×8 block of values that are then converted back into pixels using an inverse DCT. These new terms are multiplied by their appropriate scale factors (i.e., de-quantized) and then added to the predicted values we already had. In many cases the difference values are so small that the stream of 64 values is mostly zeros. Only the nonzero terms are actually coded. An encoder includes a special EOB (end-of-block) code after the last nonzero term of the 64 values to indicate that the remaining values are all zero. If *all* 64 values are zero, then the data block can be encoded with a single end-of-block code (which is only two bits, 10).

In the best case, a macroblock is identical to its corresponding previous-picture macroblock, and the macroblock is not encoded at all. This is possible because each macroblock contains an address that indicates where it fits within the picture. (The addresses are encoded as a difference in position from the last coded macroblock.) If the macroblock is not identical, then often a motion vector can make it identical. In this case, the macroblock can be encoded with basically two values, the horizontal and vertical components of the motion vector. (All of the data blocks must still be encoded, but since they are all zeros, this requires only 12 bits; six 2-bit EOB codes.) The number of bits required to code a macroblock grows as the differences between the predicated and actual values grow. In the worst case, an encoder can decide that the prediction of a particular macroblock does not facilitate compression at all, and the macroblock can be encoded using the scheme described for I-pictures.

B-Pictures

A bidirectional predictive-coded B-picture is based on two previously coded pictures. All of the macroblocks in a B-picture do not have to reference other pictures. Some of them can be encoded by themselves using the DCT scheme described previously for I-pictures. If one or more of a picture's macroblocks reference a next picture or a previous picture, then the entire picture is considered a B-picture. A B-picture macroblock that references other pictures is decoded in four steps:

- If a "forward-motion vector" is stored with the macroblock, it is used to reconstruct a predicted macroblock by retrieving pixels from a previous picture.

- If a "backward-motion vector" is stored with the macroblock, it is used to reconstruct a predicted macroblock by retrieving pixels from a "future picture" (i.e., a picture that has already been decoded but that has not been displayed).

- If both a forward- *and* backward-motion vector is present in the macroblock, the two predicted macroblocks are combined into a single "predicted" macroblock by averaging the corresponding values from each macroblock; i.e., Predicted-Pixel = (ForwardPixel + BackwardPixel)/2 for every pixel in the macroblock.

- The data blocks included in the macroblock are decoded, transformed using an inverse DCT, and then added to the already predicated macroblock. Notice that the data blocks contain only the differences between the predicated macroblock and the actual macroblock.

These encodings are basically identical to the P-picture macroblock encodings, with the exception that there are possibly two predicted macroblocks instead of just one. This potentially adds more burden on an encoder because now it is expected to find the best-matching macroblock by searching two pictures instead of one. Instead of 9,437,184 possible macroblocks, there are now possibly 18,847,184 to search, assuming that we use either a forward- or backward-motion vector but not both at the same time. If we use both types of motion vectors and average the predictions, there are too many possibilities to count (9 million times 9 million). Obviously an encoder would never examine all of the possible cases, but how the best-matching macroblock is found and how much time is spent doing so is left to the discretion of the encoder.

The standard defines either a fixed-length or a variable-length code for every type of data that could be included within a MPEG data stream. Each coding assignment defines the range of possible values for that particular piece of data and its meaning. For example, the standard defines eight distinct refresh rates as follows:

POSSIBLE REFRESH RATES DEFINED BY MPEG

Code	Pictures per Second	Comments
0000	Forbidden	
0001	23.976	
0010	24	Standard for movies
0011	25	Standard for PAL TV
0100	29.97	Standard for NTSC TV
0101	30	
0110	50	
0111	59.94	
1000	60	
1001–1111	Reserved for future use	

(Refer to the ISO IS 11172 document on MPEG for more details.)

10.3.4 Summary and Conclusions

MPEG encoding of video produces a compressed data stream using a combination of the following techniques:

- The YC_rC_b color model is used, and the chrominance values C_r and C_b are sampled at half the resolution of the luminance values Y.
- The pixels are transformed into discrete cosine space using the DCT and the precision of less-critical terms is reduced (i.e., quantization).
- A prediction scheme "guesses" the value of a pixel by referencing frames that have already been decoded. Only the differences between these predicted values

and the actual values are encoded. To make the prediction scheme as successful as possible, a motion vector indicates how to line up a block of data in one frame with a block from some previously decoded frame such that their differences are as small as possible (i.e., motion compensation). If we use pixels from both a past and a future frame, the technique is called *bidirectional prediction.*

- A variable-length coding is used to minimize the total number of bits needed to code the data (i.e., a Huffman encoding).

MPEG allows many options for an encoder. An encoder must decide the following:

- Which picture encoding to use for each frame (i.e., either I-picture, P-picture, or B-picture)

- How much quantization each frame should receive after the DCT to meet the goal of producing a compressed data stream under 1.5 megabits per second while still maintaining good image quality

- How much searching to do when looking for the best motion vector for each macroblock of data

For real-time applications, an MPEG encoder would typically minimize the amount of searching for motion vectors and use pre-specified sequences of I- and P-pictures. (A real-time encoder typically does not have the time to store a series of pictures and then find backward motion vectors.) For applications that require maximum compression but not real-time encoding, an encoder can perform a detailed analysis of frame sequences and make wiser choices on their encodings. Implementing a MPEG encoder is a complex and formidable task, whereas implementing a decoder is, by comparison, a straightforward task. A decoder has far fewer decisions to make. Its major concern is keeping up with the data stream and displaying the images as fast as the time stamps specify.

10.4 CCITT H.261 (VIDEOPHONE)

The CCITT H.261 standard was designed for encoding video data that is transmitted at rates of $p \times 64$ Kbit/s, where p is in the range 1 to 30 (i.e., 64 Kbit/s, 128 Kbit/s, 192 Kbit/s, ..., and 1.92 Mbit/s). It is designed for videophone and videoconferencing using Integrated Services Digital Networks (ISDN). The standard is similar to MPEG, but it is more restrictive in its options because of the lower-targeted bandwidth (i.e., the total number of bits per second that can be transmitted) and because it is a real-time application. The following chart provides a brief comparison between MPEG and H.261.

The CCITT H.261 standard is more restrictive than MPEG because it has to encode and decode in real time, approximately 30 times per second. At the macroblock level H.261 and MPEG use the same compression scheme. They both define a macroblock as six 8×8 data blocks (4 blocks of luminance values and 2 blocks of subsampled chrominance values). The 8×8 blocks are transformed using a DCT, quantized, converted to a stream of 64 values using the zigzag ordering, and then run-length encoded. The run-length pairs are then assigned variable-length Huffman codes. For intra-coded pictures, this process is done on the original picture data. For motion-compensated pictures, this

COMPARISON OF MPEG AND CCITT H.261

Topic	MPEG	CCITT H.261
Applications	Video editing Video storage Video playback	Real-time transmission
Image size	No restrictions	Only 352×288 (CIF) or 176×144 (QCIF)
Refresh rate	8 options ranging from 23.976 to 60 pictures per second	29.97 (i.e., a new picture every 1/1,29.97 of a second)
Picture encodings	Intra-coded (I) picture Predictive-coded (P) picture Bidirectional (B) picture DC coded (D) picture	Intra-coded picture Predictive-coded picture
Picture ordering	Pictures are ordered according to the needs of a decoder, which is not the display ordering if B-pictures are present in the data stream	Pictures are ordered according to their display time
Motion compensation	Forward motion vectors Backward motion vectors Bidirectional interpolation	Forward motion vectors
Color model	YC_rC_b	YC_rC_b
Data organization	Group of pictures Picture (1 or more slices) Slice (1 or more macroblocks) Macroblock (6 data blocks)	Picture (1 to 22 GOBs) GOB-group of blocks (1 to 33 macroblocks Macroblock (6 data blocks)

process is done on the difference values obtained by subtracting the predicted values from the actual values in each block.

MPEG defines the concept of a *slice* to be a group of one or more macroblocks. H.261 is less flexible and defines the concept of a group of blocks (GOBs), which is composed of exactly 33 macroblocks. Each macroblock contains an address that indicates its position within the GOB. Any macroblocks that remain unchanged from one picture to the next are not transmitted. Therefore, a GOB is conceptually 33 macroblocks, but in reality it can contain anywhere from 1 to 33 macroblocks. Each picture in CIF format contains exactly 12 GOBs, while each picture in the QCIF format contains only 3 GOBs. MPEG defined the *group of pictures* concept, but H.261 contains no such concept. The group of pictures was implemented to facilitate video editing, which is not a target application for H.261.

The H.261 standard defines some parameters not included in MPEG but which are important for videophone applications. Some examples include a split-screen indicator, a document-camera indicator, and a freeze-picture code.

MPEG and CCITT H.261 are more similar than different. The same hardware that is used to implement the MPEG standard could be used to implement the H.162 standard with some minor modifications.

10.5 SUMMARY AND CONCLUSIONS

We have discussed in detail three compression-encoding schemes that are quickly becoming the standard and preferred way of encoding compressed graphical data. They are all based on the DCT and operate on the same principle, which is to transform a data set into another set of values where the less-critical values can be dropped from the data stream with limited loss of visual information.

The new United States Federal Communications Commission (FCC) standard for High Definition television (HDTV) is reportedly based on DCT concepts, even though at the time of our publishing this book the standard had not been finalized. Assuming that this is true, DCT compression will be the dominant method used for raster-based compression for many years to come. Some researchers have recently argued that raster-based compression is too new a technology to standardize. Standardizing on the DCT now could potentially cause problems when better, more efficient, compression schemes are discovered in the future. One such example often cited is the wavelets transform, which reportedly can produce higher compression ratios than is possible using the DCT. There is always the possibility of new discoveries, but standards must be created in a timely fashion. Right or wrong, DCT has become today's standard for raster-data compression.

COMPARATIVE ANALYSIS

CONTENTS

11.1 INTRODUCTION

This chapter compares and classifies the 51 data formats that are explained in detail in the appendices. It is difficult to establish a single scheme to classify and compare graphical data formats; the number of issues that separate them is too large. Therefore, we have developed eight separate comparison schemes for doing so. These comparisons should help clarify what we have been discussing throughout the first 10 chapters of this book. There is little explanatory text in these sections because the topics have been explained in detail previously.

The intent of these comparisons is to show relationships between the various data streams, not to identify which is "best" or "worst." If you are looking for a data stream to satisfy a specific application, hopefully the comparisons will allow you to narrow your search. Once you have identified relevant formats, you will want to perform a detailed analysis to determine which format best meets the needs of your application.

11.2 ACCORDING TO ORIGIN

As we discussed in the history chapter, graphical data streams come from many different sources. The source of a data stream often explains many of its capabilities. Figure 11.1 gives you an overview of these origins. *Do not interpret the diagram literally.* It is for illustration purposes only.

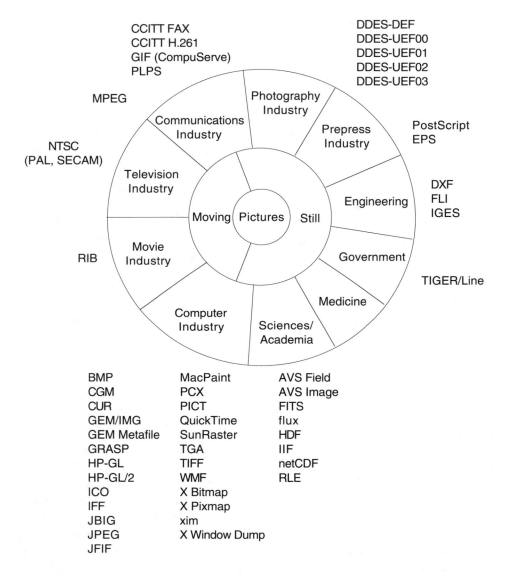

Figure 11.1　Illustrative (not literal) origin of data streams

11.3   ACCORDING TO STANDARDIZATION

Data streams are either "official" standards, de facto standards because of their widespread use, or simply a format that is widely (or not so widely) used. The following table categorizes the data streams into one of these three categories. The "Official Standards" column is straightforward. Whether a data format goes into the "De Facto Standards" column depends on whom you ask. The second and third columns in the table are subjective.

DATA STREAMS ORGANIZED ACCORDING TO THEIR STANDARDIZATION

Official Standards	Other	De Facto Standards
CCITT Fax	AVS Field	DXF
CCITT H.261	AVS Image	EPS
CGM	BMP	FITS
DDES-DEF	CUR	GIF
DDES-UEF00	FLI, FLC	HP-GL
DDES-UEF01	flux	HP-GL/2
DDES-UEF02	GEM/IMG	PICT
DDES-UEF03	GEM Metafile	PostScript
JBIG (encoding only)	GRASP	QuickTime
JPEG (encoding only)	HDF	RIB
IGES	ICO	TIFF
IIF	IFF	TIGER/Line
MPEG	JFIF	X Bitmap
NTSC (PAL, SECAM)	MacPaint	X Window Dump
PLPS	netCDF	
	PCX	
	RLE	
	SunRaster	
	TGA	
	WMF	
	X Pixmap	
	xim	

11.4   ACCORDING TO DATA TYPES

The types of information a data stream may represent is critical to its use in any particular application. The table on the following page separates the data streams according to their data types at a high level of abstraction: still versus moving pictures and 2D versus 3D data. The hybrid column lists those data streams that include both raster and geometric data.

DATA STREAMS THAT REPRESENT STILL PICTURES

Raster Data	Hybrids	Geometric Data
2-Dimensional Samples	CGM	**2-Dimensional Geometry**
AVS Image	EPS	DDES-UEF02
BMP	GEM Metafile	HP-GL
CCITT Fax	IFF	HP-GL/2
CUR	PICT	TIGER/Line
DDES-DEF	PLPS	
DDES-UEF00	PostScript	
DDES-UEF01	WMF	
DDES-UEF03		
EPS		
GEM/IMG		
GIF		
ICO		
IFF (ILBM)		
JBIG (encoding only)		
JFIF		
JPEG (encoding only)		
MacPaint		
PCX		
RLE		
SunRaster		
TGA		
TIFF		
X Bitmap		
X Pixmap		
xim		
X Window Dump		
Multidimensional samples	flux	**3-dimensional Geometry**
AVS Field		DXF
FITS		IGES
HDF		PHIGS
IIF		RIB
netCDF		

DATA STREAMS THAT REPRESENT MOVING PICTURES

Raster Data	Hybrids	Geometric Data
CCITT H.261	QuickTime	
FLI	GRASP	
IFF (ANBM)		
MPEG		
NTSC (PAL, SECAM)		

11.5 ACCORDING TO COLOR

The amount and type of color information within a data stream is critical to some applications but not so critical to others. The following table lists and groups the data streams according to the color models they support. Data streams that deviate from the "normal usage" are so indicated. For example, most lookup-table implementations support 256 entries. Data streams that support fewer entries are labeled with their maximum lookup-table size.

COLOR MODELS SUPPORTED BY EACH DATA STREAM

Data Stream	Monochrome	Lookup Table	RGB	CMYK	YC_bC_r	Others
CCITT Fax (I–IV)	•					
EPSI	• (gray)					
MacPaint	•					
X Bitmap	•					
CUR	•	• (8, 16)				
GIF	•	•				
ICO	•	• (8, 16)				
PCX	•	•				
DXF		•				
FLI, FLC		•				
HP-GL		• (pen)				
HP-GL/2		• (pen)				
IFF (ILBM)		•				
GRASP		•				
PLPS		• (16)				
X Pixmap		•				
DDES-UEF02		• (9)	•			
HDF		•	•			
RLE		•	•			
TGA		•	•			
xim		•	•			
X Window Dump		•	•			
AVS image			•			
IGES			•			
RIB			•			
GEM/IMG	• (gray)		•			
BMP	•	•	•			
flux	•	•	•			
PICT	•	•	•			
QuickTime	•	•	•			
SunRaster	•	•	•			
WMF	•	•	•			

COLOR MODELS SUPPORTED BY EACH DATA STREAM *(Continued)*

Data Stream	Monochrome	Lookup Table	RGB	CMYK	YC_bC_r	Others
DDES-UEF00			•	•		•
DDES-UEF03			•	•		•
DDES-UEF01		• (CMYK)	•			•
CCITT H.261					•	
JFIF					•	
MPEG					•	
CGM		•	•	•		•
DDES-DEF		• (CMYK)	•	•		•
EPS (Postscript)	•	•	•	•	•	•
IIF	•	•	•	•	•	•
PostScript	•	•	•	•	•	•
TIFF	•	•	•	•	•	•

Some data streams do not define a color model for their data. These data streams are shown in the following table. Data-visualization software must assign appropriate color values at rendering time under the control and discretion of a user.

DATA STREAMS THAT DEFINE NO COLOR MODEL

AVS Field
FITS
FITS
JBIG
JPEG*
netCDF
TIGER/Line

*JPEG does not define a color space, but currently most implementations use the YC_bC_r color space because it improves compression and it is used by video standards.

In addition to the importance of a color model, the number of samples and the number of bits per sample determines a raster data set's capacity to store data. Figure 11.2 classifies raster data streams accordingly.

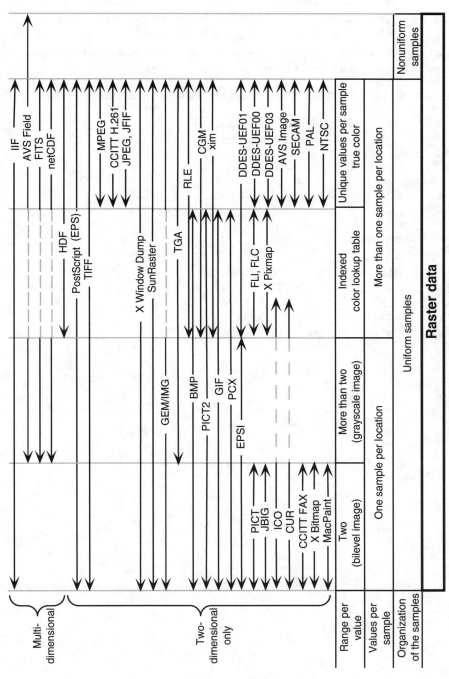

Figure 11.2 Raster data streams according to types of samples

11.6 ACCORDING TO ORGANIZATION SCHEMES

There are too many data-organization schemes to categorize in one simple chart. However, one important organization trend uses a "tagged" data structure that self-documents the data stream. (Unknown tagged blocks can be skipped.) In more advanced schemes, data blocks can be embedded within other data blocks to create hierarchical data associations. The table below categorizes data streams according to these ideas.

DATA STREAMS ORGANIZED ACCORDING TO THEIR ORGANIZATION*

Non-Self Documenting Data Streams	Self-Documenting Data Streams (Tagged Data Blocks)	
	No Hierarchies	Hierarchies
AVS Image	AVS Field	CCITT H.261
BMP	DXF	flux
CCITT Fax	FITS	IFF
CGM	FLI, FLC	IIF
CUR	GIF	MPEG
DDES-DEF	HDF	QuickTime
DDES-UEF00	JBIG	
DDES-UEF01	JFIF	
DDES-UEF02	JPEG	
DDES-UEF03	TIFF	
EPS		
EPSI		
GEM/IMG		
GEM Metafile		
GRASP		
HP-GL		
HP-GL/2		
ICO		
IGES		
MacPaint		
netCDF		
PCX		
PICT		
PLPS		
RLE		
SunRaster		
TGA		
TIGER/Line		
WMF		
X Bitmap		
X Pixmap		
xim		
X Window Dump		

*Note: PostScript and RIB are not self-documenting in the sense that data blocks can be skipped if they are not recognized, but they can form hierarchical data relationships.

11.7 DATA-ENCODING COMPARISONS

Data encodings affect a data stream's device independence and speed of access. Some data streams define only one encoding while others define multiple encodings. A bullet in the following table indicates the types of encodings defined for a particular data stream. Some data streams have mixed encodings. In these cases the type of data associated with each encoding is listed in the table. Even though some data formats define multiple encodings, in many cases only one encoding is used. In these cases the typical encoding is indicated.

**TYPES OF ENCODINGS DEFINED FOR
EACH DATA STREAM**

Data Stream	Text Encoding	Character Encoding	Binary Encoding
EPSI	•		
GRASP	•		
HP-GL	•		
HP-GL/2	•		
RIB	•		
TIGER/Line	•		
X Bitmap	•		
X Pixmap	•		
PLPS		•	
AVS Image			•
BMP			•
CCITT Fax			•
CCITT H.261			•
CUR			•
FLI, FLC			•
GEM/IMG			•
GEM Metafile			•
GIF			•
ICO			•
IFF			•
IIF			•
JBIG			•
JFIF			•
JPEG			•
MacPaint			•
MPEG			•
netCDF			• (XDR)
PCX			•
PICT			•
QuickTime			•
RLE			•
SunRaster			•
TGA			•

TYPES OF ENCODINGS DEFINED FOR
EACH DATA STREAM *(Continued)*

Data Stream	Text Encoding	Character Encoding	Binary Encoding
TIFF			•
WMF			•
X Window Dump			•
DXF	• (typical)		•
EPS	• (typical)		•
HDF	•		• (typical)
IGES	• (typical)		•
AVS Field (header;data)	header; *data*		data
	header		data
DDES-DEF	header		data
DDES-UEF00	header		data
DDES-UEF01	header		data
DDES-UEF02	header		data
DDES-UEF03	header		data
FITS	header; *data*		data
flux	• (typical)		•
PostScript xim	header		data
CGM	•	•	• (typical)

As the next table shows, the most common type of data stream encoding is binary. A common practice among more recently defined data streams is to encode the header information in ASCII text for readability and store the data values in binary format for efficiency.

ENCODING COMBINATIONS AND THEIR
PERCENTAGE OF OCCURRENCE

Encoding	How Many	Percentage
Text only	8	16%
Character only	1	2%
Binary only	27	53%
Text or character	0	0%
Character or binary	0	0%
Text or binary (separate)	4	8%
Text and binary (combined)	10	20%
Text or character or binary	1	2%

One of the most apparent distinctions between binary formats is the ordering of the bytes within individual data values. This is referred to as *Little-endian* or *Big-endian* byte ordering. Refer to Chapter 8 for a complete discussion. The following table lists data streams according to their byte orderings. The data streams in the Hybrids column allow data in either encoding.

CATEGORIZATION OF DATA FORMATS BY
BYTE ORDERINGS SUPPORTED

Little-endian	Hybrids	Big-endian
BMP	AVS Field	CGM
CUR	EPS	DDES-UEF02
FLI, FLC	flux	DXF
GIF	HDF	FITS
ICO	IIF	GEM/IMG
PCX	PostScript	GEM Metafile
RLE	TIFF	IGES
WMF	X Window Dump	JBIG
X Bitmap (version 10)		JFIF
		JPEG
		MacPaint
		netCDF
		PICT
		PLPS (character encoding)
		QuickTime
		SunRaster
		TGA

Some data encodings are bit ordered rather than byte ordered because of the variable-length codes used to accomplish data compression. Data steams that are bit ordered include CCITT Fax, CCITT H.261, and MPEG.

11.8 DATA-COMPRESSION COMPARISONS

COMPRESSION TECHNIQUES USED BY 2D RASTER DATA STREAMS

No Compression	Lossless Compression	Lossy Compression
AVS Image	**Run-length**	**DCT**
AVS Field	BMP	CCITT H.261
CGM	CCITT Fax	JPEG
CUR	DDES-UEF01	MPEG
DDES-UEF00	DDES-UEF03	JFIF
EPSI	FLI, FLC	IIF
FITS	GEM/IMG	PostScript (EPS)
flux	HDF	QuickTime
GEM Metafile	IIF	TIFF
GRASP	MacPaint	
ICO	PCX	
netCDF	PICT	
WMF	PostScript (EPS)	
X Bitmap	QuickTime	
X Pixmap	RLE	
X Window Dump	SunRaster	
	LZW	
	GIF	
	PostScript (EPS)	
	TIFF	
	Prediction/Differencing	
	FLI, FLC	
	JBIG	
	IIF	

**COMPRESSION TECHNIQUES USED BY
GEOMETRIC DATA STREAMS**

No Compression	Lossless Compression	Lossy Compression
DDES-UEF02	**Huffman encodings**	(Would anyone ever
DXF	CGM	do this? Probably not.)
HP-GL		
RIB	**Binary encodings**	
TIGER/Line	EPS	
	PostScript	
	base 64 encoding	
	HP-GL/2	
	A form of run-length	
	IGES	

11.9 STATIC VERSUS DYNAMIC DATA STREAMS

Data streams can be separated according to the methods they use to represent pictures. We distinguish the following three types of methods:

Actual Data Representation   A data stream contains every data value that defines a picture, either as raster samples or as geometric primitives. This is a static data stream that is consumed to create a picture.

Procedural Representation   A data stream is a sequence of procedure calls with appropriate parameters. When the procedures are executed in sequence, they create a picture. This is a more dynamic data set (depending on the range of parameters), but there is no control over the sequence of picture generation.

Algorithmic Representation   A data stream is a set of instructions that, when executed, creates a data stream that, in turn, creates a picture. In the general case, the data stream definition characterizes a general-purpose programming language that includes concepts such as iteration, recursion, and subprograms.

The following table categorizes the data formats according to these three representation schemes.

**DATA STREAMS CATEGORIZED ACCORDING TO HOW
THEY GENERATE A PICTURE**

Actual Data Representation	Procedural Representation	Algorithmic Representation
AVS Field	GEM Metafile	EPS
AVS Image	GRASP	PostScript
BMP	HP-GL	
CCITT Fax	HP-GL/2	
CCITT H.261	PICT	
CGM	RIB	
CUR	WMF	
DDES-DEF		
DDES-UEF00		
DDES-UEF01		
DDES-UEF02		
DDES-UEF03		
EPSI		
FITS		
FLI, FLC		
flux		
GEM/IMG		
HDF		
ICO		
IFF		
IGES		

**DATA STREAMS CATEGORIZED ACCORDING TO HOW
THEY GENERATE A PICTURE** *(Continued)*

Actual Data Representation	Procedural Representation	Algorithmic Representation
IIF		
JBIG		
JFIF		
JPEG		
MacPaint		
MPEG		
netCDF		
PCX		
PLPS		
QuickTime		
RLE		
SunRaster		
TGA		
TIFF		
TIGER/Line		
X Pixmap		
xim		
X Bitmap		
X Window Dump		

11.10 SUMMARY AND CONCLUSIONS

In many areas of study, classification is the starting point for understanding—as well as being a major challenge. In this chapter we have presented a few dimensions of the classification of data streams for graphical data. Though we may have not included the one chart that would help you identify the ideal format for your application, hopefully, the tables we did provide will help you narrow your possible choices. You can then study the potential candidate formats in the appendix. We wish you good hunting.

12

DATA CONVERSIONS

CONTENTS

12.1 INTRODUCTION

The conversion of data from one format to another ranges from the trivial to the impossible, with many levels of difficulty in-between. Volumes of books would be required to discuss every detail involved with every possible conversion. What we want to do here is explain the big picture and how graphical data formats relate to each other as a whole.

Consider Figure 12.1. As we have discussed earlier in this book, graphical data can be viewed as three distinct types: raster data, geometry data, and latent image data. For this discussion it is beneficial to view geometry data as distinctly 2D or 3D, since they can have distinctly different data representations. The thin arrows in Figure 12.1 represent the conversions that are "straightforward." These conversion processes can range from simple tasks, such as data reorganization, to more complex tasks that require a total transformation of the data. Do not confuse *straightforward* with *trivial.* Very few data conversion tasks are simple from a software-implementation viewpoint. Robust conversion programs that perform correctly, even when processing corrupt data streams, require large amounts of effort to implement.

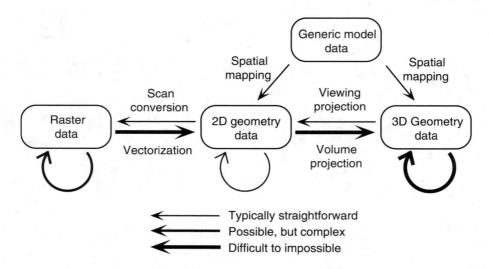

Figure 12.1   Difficulty of conversion between various types of graphic data

The boldest arrows in Figure 12.1 represent the difficult to impossible data conversions. In some cases various degrees of success can be achieved under controlled circumstances. However, in the general case, conversions are either theoretically impossible, or they produce data that is not in a form usable by actual applications. Why is this? Each data representation stores different types of *information*. Some data conversions can be performed without loss of information, but many of the conversions either lose information or they must infer missing information. In general, it is much easier to "throw out" information than it is to "find" information. The conversions that require the inference of missing data are marked with bold arrows.

To understand this idea of missing data, consider for example the conversion of 2D geometry data into 3D geometry data. The depth of objects is not contained in the 2D data and must be inferred from the available 2D data. Humans have the ability to infer depth from 2D data using their experience of the real world, which includes such things as knowing the normal size of toasters, cars, and trees, as well as having experiential knowledge of shadows, light intensities, and perspective projections. To give a conversion process these types of knowledge to convert 2D data to 3D data is currently beyond our technology. The converter would need "intelligence," and besides, even humans sometime make mistakes at inferring depth.

12.1.1   Conversion Categories

As discussed in Chapter 1, data formats involve two major ideas: the conceptual view of the data (its data types and data organization) and the data's actual representation (encoding and compression). A discussion of converting conceptual information between different data formats raises many problems, while the encoding issues are fairly mechanical to deal with. While they require a lot of attention when developing conversion software, there are not any difficult theoretical issues to tackle. On the other hand, our discussion of these issues is divided into the eight distinct categories that are listed in the following table. (In the table, 2D and 3D are abbreviations for 2D-geometry data and 3D-geometry data, respectively.)

DIFFICULTIES WITH CONVERSION BETWEEN DATA TYPES

Type of Conversion	Technique Used	List of Major Difficulties
Raster to Raster	Interpolation	• Different pixel sizes • Different color precisions • Different color models • Different data orderings
2D to Raster	Scan Conversion	• Straightforward
Raster to 2D	Vectorization	• Building the correct vectors (lines) from adjacent pixels • "Dirty" originals cause the creation of erroneous lines • Data organization after finding vectors
2D to 2D	Interpretation, then generation	• Similar data types represented in different ways • Conversion between curve definitions
3D to 2D	Viewing Projection	• Straightforward
2D to 3D	Volume Projection	• In the general case—impossible • In special cases, special purpose procedures can create approximations
3D to 3D	Interpretation, then generation	• Incompatible representations • Incompatible data types within similar representations • Conversion between curve definitions
Generic to 2D or 3D	Interpretation (execution)	• Requires special knowledge of the generic model

12.1.2   A General Conversion Strategy

Converting between two specific data formats is difficult in its own right. Add to this the problem of converting between *many* data formats and the conversion task can be overwhelming. Consider for example the problem of converting data between 10 different data formats. If we attempt to convert each format *directly* to each other's format, then we will need 90 different procedures (or programs). How did we get 90? Well, consider that for each data format we need a procedure that will translate it into the other 9 formats. Therefore, each of the 10 data formats needs 9 conversion procedures, and $10 \times 9 = 90$. In general, n data formats require $n(n-1)$ conversion procedures if we use the direct approach. However,

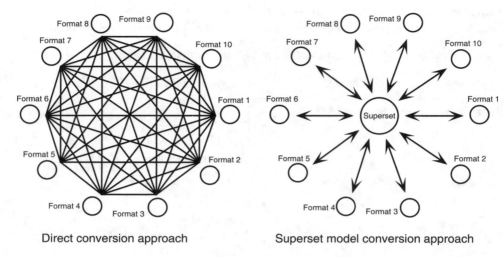

Direct conversion approach   Superset model conversion approach

Figure 12.2   How a superset approach reduces number of conversion routines

the direct approach becomes unmanageable when the number of required data conversions grows larger than three.

An efficient approach for data conversion is to define a data format that is a superset of all relevant data formats. Then, for each data format we want to support, we need only two procedures—one that will convert a given data set into the superset format and another one that will read data from the superset format and convert it into the desired data format. In the example of 10 data formats shown in Figure 12.2, this would cut our software development from 90 procedures to 20. In the general case, n data formats require $2n$ procedures. In the remainder of this discussion we will call such a superset format a *comprehensive data format*.

A comprehensive data format is related to a specific set of data types, not to the idea of a single format for *all* graphical data. In some conversion tasks there will be not one but several comprehensive formats, one for each specific type of data representation. For example, the pbmplus conversion software defines three distinct data formats for raster to raster conversions: one for 1-bit per pixel images, one for grayscale images, and one for color images.

It is common for software systems to treat their proprietary data structures as a comprehensive data format. In addition to reading and writing their own proprietary file formats, they also import (read) and export (write) other common data formats. Software developers include these features to enhance the usability of their systems. The result is that users get a data-conversion system along with the actual application software. However, users need to be aware that proprietary data formats are not necessarily comprehensive data formats. Data conversions made by application software sometimes ignore data in a file that is not relevant to its application or its software sophistication. Therefore, data can be lost between conversions. The average user is unaware that information has been lost because he or she did not know what information was in the original file.

An alternative approach to the comprehensive data format (i.e., the *superset model*) is a *subset model*. A subset model contains only the basic data elements that are common between all of the relevant data formats. It is a simpler approach to the conversion problem since it ignores any "extra" data that the various data sets might contain. This approach typically loses some data in the conversion process, which might be acceptable in some circumstances but unacceptable in others. An example of this approach is the pbmplus conversion package, which is discussed further at the end of this chapter. When the pbmplus software reads a TIFF file it ignores much of the extra data, such as title information, but in a research environment the loss of such information is not important. In a commercial environment the loss of such information could be important.

The remaining discussion in this chapter makes the assumption that a conversion process attempts to create the most accurate reproduction possible between data formats, with minimal loss of information. This implies the use of a comprehensive superset model for an intermediate data format. In some specific applications a less rigorous approach might suffice.

12.2 ENCODING PROBLEMS

Some differences between encodings require hardware solutions whereas others can be dealt with in software. Let's look briefly at some of the hardware issues.

The encoding of the television signals NTSC, PAL, and SECAM is in analog form. Each starts with the same conceptual data, but their encodings vary. Signal converters are available that take any of these signals as input and produce any of the signals as output. Although this might sound like a straightforward process at first, it is actually quite difficult. The decoding of the signals is the easy part. Each format uses different pixel resolutions that must be accommodated. But a more difficult problem is the frame rate. The NTSC signal sends 30 frames per second, while the others send 25 frames per second. Conversions that produce the best picture quality transform the color components of the original signal into a digital representation and then digitally interpolate and filter to produce the separate encodings. The increase in computational power of digital processors and the drop in integrated circuit costs have made the conversion between these television standards much more economical in recent years.

Different methods of representing numbers are used on different computers. The representation of integers is standardized on the 2's complement notation using a fixed number of bits. Bits are grouped into 8 bits per byte. What varies between computers is the order of these bytes. Two different byte orders are typically used. They are often referred to as the big endian or little endian approach. Consult Figure 12.3. The differences in byte order can be accommodated totally in software, assuming the software knows the byte ordering.

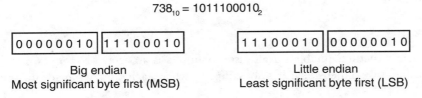

$$738_{10} = 1011100010_2$$

| 0 0 0 0 0 0 1 0 | 1 1 1 0 0 0 1 0 | | 1 1 1 0 0 0 1 0 | 0 0 0 0 0 0 1 0 |

Big endian
Most significant byte first (MSB)

Little endian
Least significant byte first (LSB)

Figure 12.3 Encoding byte order for different systems

The binary representation of floating point numbers differs from system to system as well. The ANSI/IEEE Binary Floating-Point Arithmetic standard defines a standard representation for binary floating point numbers, but it has not yet been universally adopted. The different formats can be handled totally in software, as long as the conversion process knows which representation is being used.

And finally, you need to remember that many of the data format specifications describe one conceptual data representation and more than one actual encoding representation. For example, the CGM standard has three defined encodings: Clear Text, Binary, and Character Encodings. To say, "I have a CGM file" is not enough. The type of encoding must be known as well. It would not be uncommon to have to convert a CGM file to a CGM file: that is, convert a Binary-Encoded CGM file to a Clear-Text Encoded CGM file. Even a conversion such as this is nontrivial due to the tremendous number of details involved in the encodings.

12.3 CONVERSIONS OF CONCEPTUAL DATA

The purpose of a conversion program is obviously to translate data from one representation encoding into another encoding, and to reorganize the data based on the new desired format. However, it is not so obvious what else the conversion program should do. When two different data formats are dissimilar in their information content, then accomplishing the conversion requires a transformation of the actual information of the file. When you get into the realm of data transformations, you become quickly involved with functions that are normally thought of as application functions. For example, converting raster data sets sometimes requires image processing techniques normally contained in *application tool-kits*.

Take another example, that of converting a 3D data set to a 2D image. In application terminology this is called *rendering*. Rendering software can be quite sophisticated. Should rendering programs be part of file conversion packages? Probably not. But if you have two file formats that are of different types, you will need application software that performs the transformations you require and that supports your file formats. Or, you can go through several stages of conversion—convert A to B, run it through application software C, which exports it as D, which can be converted to E, etc. This is the situation many users find themselves in today.

If we had a suite of standard data formats that most everyone could agree upon, then the decisions about what data format conversion consists of and what application data transformations consist of would become much clearer. A suite of such standards is proposed in Chapter 4. Until such a suite actually exists, the domain of conversion programs will be murky. The following discussion on data conversion may go beyond what some think data format conversion entails.

12.3.1 Raster to Raster

A comprehensive data structure suitable for all raster data sets is an array of samples. For images, this is typically a two-dimensional array of samples,[*] where each sample is made up of

---

[*] Or a three-dimensional array for volume data (i.e., voxels).

one or more data values. There is also a variety of related data that needs to be converted and translated correctly. This would include items like color lookup tables, gamma correction values, chromaticity information, pixel aspect ratio, etc., as well as any other documentation data such as the date of creation, author, title, etc.

Converting Differences in Color Accuracy

Two common differences between raster data formats is their physical organization of the data values and their method of data compression. Both of these differences are handled easily by the conversion of the data to a comprehensive data structure. What is not handled so easily is the differences in color accuracy (i.e., bits per pixel), resolution (i.e., pixels per inch), and pixel-aspect ratios. Consider Figure 12.4. Raster data has either one component value per pixel or multiple component values per pixel (e.g., red-green-blue), and the components can have different numbers of bits per value. If, during conversion, the number of bits used to represent each pixel is lowered, then data is lost in the process. It is easy to just "throw away bits;" it is more difficult to throw away bits and still retain "good" image quality. Conversions that go in the opposite direction—i.e., they gain pixel accuracy—can easily copy their data into the extended format, but they cannot typically add accuracy to the data.

There are simple schemes to reduce the color accuracy of pixels. (More involved schemes are presented after the discussion on resolution.) The most commonly used method of translating color data into grayscale values is the equation used by television signals for luminance:

$$Y(\text{grayscale}) = 0.299 \times \text{Red} + 0.587 \times \text{Green} + 0.114 \times \text{Blue}$$

This equation works well under most conditions. Under special coloring conditions the proportions might need to be adjusted to produce a more pleasing range of intensities (e.g., if shades of blue are the dominate color in the image or if nonstandard primary colors were employed in the original image). The simple method for reducing the accuracy of individual pixel component values is by dropping off lower-order bits. The technical name for this is *truncation*, although it is also known as *decimation*. By keeping the high-order bits of

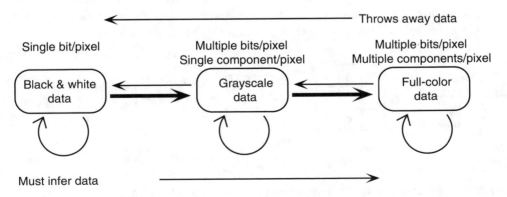

Figure 12.4 Conversion relationships between black & white, grayscale and color raster data

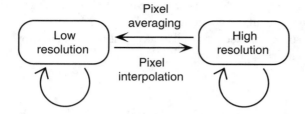

Figure 12.5   Effects of converting between low- and high-resolutions

each value we retain the overall magnitude of each value with as much accuracy as the new data format will allow. We'll come back to color accuracy after we discuss resolution.

Resolution Conversion

Data-format conversions must deal with differences in pixel resolution. Refer to Figures 12.5 and 12.6. One way to go from high resolution to low resolution is by pixel averaging. Pixel averaging calculates the average intensity value of a set of adjacent pixels and uses this value as a single pixel in the lower-resolution image. Going from a lower resolution to a higher resolution can be done by pixel replication, which takes one pixel at the lower resolution and makes it into multiple pixels in the higher-resolution image. This simplistic approach typically causes visible "jaggies" in the resulting image. A better approach uses pixel interpolation. Pixels from the original resolution are scaled to their appropriate positions in the new resolution. Then in-between pixels are assigned values based on the interpolation between these original pixels.

Color detail and resolution are interrelated to the human eye. When a group of light intensities are seen from a distance, the eye combines the intensities into a single value; the fine detail is lost.* Because of this, it is possible to make trade-offs between color accuracy and pixel resolution. There are nine different cases to handle, depending on whether the color precision becomes lower, remains the same, or increases, and whether the resolution increases, remains the same, or decreases. These are listed in Figure 12.7 along with a possible method of handling each conversion. The trade-offs between spatial resolution and color reproduction can be made automatically in some cases, but in certain situations user interaction is needed to arrive at acceptable compromises in image quality.

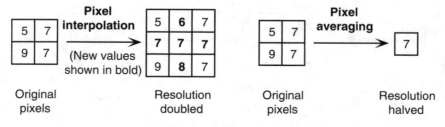

Figure 12.6   Effect of resolution conversion on example pixel values

---

* The technical name for this is *spatial integration*.

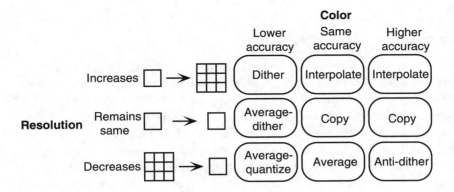

Figure 12.7   Strategies for handling coupled-spatial and color-resolution changes

In order to discuss these conversions we need to introduce the idea of *dithering*. It is common to have images represented using only 1 bit per pixel, especially in printing where it is common to print using only one color. In printing, varying intensities of grayscale can be achieved by printing different sizes of dots. This technique is called *halftoning*. Approximately the same effect can be achieved on raster devices by grouping clusters of dots, creating superpixels. The way in which dots are grouped together to form various level of intensity is called *dithering*. An example dither pattern is shown in Figure 12.8, where four adjacent pixels are used to represent five different intensity levels. There are, of course, four different ways that either one pixel or three pixels can be illuminated in a 2×2 superpixel, and six ways that two pixels can be illuminated. The challenge is in selecting a "random" order for adjacent superpixel patterns that minimizes artificial edges and other artifacts in the resulting grayscale image. In general, an $n \times n$ group of pixels that are either black or white can represent $n^2 + 1$ intensity values. If each pixel is represented with m bits, then an $n \times n$ group of pixels can represent $((2^m - 1) \times n^2) + 1$ levels of grayscale intensity. For a general overview to dithering refer to [Foley90], and for a complete discussion refer to [Ulichney87].

Now, back to the problem of converting between data formats. There are nine possibilities, as shown in Figure 12.7. Let's take each one in turn.

Intensities from halftoning   A 2 x 2 dither pattern resulting in five intensity levels

Figure 12.8   Sample 2×2 dither patterns to produce pseudo grayscale

Specific Cases

RESOLUTION IS RAISED, COLOR ACCURACY IS LOWERED

This is the ideal situation for dithering. The increase in resolution can make up for the decrease in color. But remember that the relationship between the size of the dither pattern and the number of approximation intensities is n^2. To approximate 256 shades of gray using 1 bit per pixel requires a dither pattern of 16×16, which means the resolution of the image must be raised by a factor of 16. Raising the resolution of a 512×512 image by a factor of 16 produces a 8192×8192 image. This is an unrealistic increase in resolution for most situations. In the typical case, the resolution of the target format is related to the capabilities of some output device. This output device determines the resolution of the target format and an appropriate dither pattern would be used related to the specific increase in resolution.

RESOLUTION REMAINS UNCHANGED, COLOR ACCURACY IS LOWERED

Several possibilities for conversion exist. A simple approach is to copy each pixel value from the original to the target format—truncated to the accuracy allowed by the target format. However, this approach will typically give less pleasing results than using some of the resolution to increase the perception of color. One option would be to combine a 2×2 block of pixels in the original data and calculate their average value. Then use this intensity value to create a corresponding dither pattern in the target format. This gives more intensities at less resolution, even though both data formats started with the same resolution.

RESOLUTION IS LOWERED, COLOR ACCURACY IS LOWERED

This is the worst of all possible conditions. The best you can do is calculate the average value of a cluster of pixels in the original format and truncate the value to the accuracy allowed by the target format. Because of the loss of resolution, dithering will typically not help in these situations.

RESOLUTION IS RAISED, COLOR ACCURACY REMAINS UNCHANGED

In these situations, the goal is to fill in the extra pixels created by the gain in resolution. The most visually pleasing approach is interpolation between the original values. Interpolation simply finds the difference between two values, divides this difference by the number of intervals between the numbers (+1), and increments the intermediate values accordingly. In mathematical form this looks like the following equation. Let A be the starting value and B be the ending value, with n values in-between, then each intermediate value is equal to

$$\text{Round}\left(A + k\left(\frac{B-A}{n+1}\right)\right), \quad k = 1 \text{ to } n$$

For example, given the values 10 and 27, and that 3 values are needed in between, the interpolated sequence would be 10, 14, 19, 23, and 27. A better solution is to average over several points and do cubic interpolation. In this way, edges can be detected and retained rather than averaged out. In fact, edge-sharpening algorithms can be applied, but this is more "image processing" than some people expect in data conversion. Finally, the process can be extended to two dimensions, using bicubic interpolation. A weighted average over a set of points provides a compromise in complexity and quality. Such techniques must be used with caution in images that contain texture patterns or other random color variations.

RESOLUTION REMAINS UNCHANGED, COLOR ACCURACY REMAINS UNCHANGED

This is straightforward—copy the pixels unchanged.

RESOLUTION IS LOWERED, COLOR ACCURACY REMAINS UNCHANGED

Calculate the average intensity of a cluster of pixels in the original format and use this as the intensity of a single pixel at the lower resolution. A weighted average can be used if desired.

RESOLUTION IS RAISED, COLOR ACCURACY IS RAISED

Use interpolation to calculate the extra pixels due to the increased resolution as described previously. However, because of the increased color precision, the interpolated values can be represented more accurately. The higher color accuracy allows the transitions between the original values to be smoother. Edge enhancement can be employed if appropriate for the image content.

RESOLUTION REMAINS UNCHANGED, COLOR ACCURACY IS RAISED

This is straightforward—copy the pixels unchanged.

RESOLUTION IS LOWERED, COLOR ACCURACY IS RAISED

There are two approaches that can be taken here. One approach is pixel averaging. Due to the lower resolution, the average intensity value of a cluster of pixels can be taken and transferred to a single pixel of the target format using no increase in color precision. Another approach is to treat the cluster of pixels as a dither pattern. In this case the sum of the intensities, and not the average, could be used as the single-pixel value in the target format, assuming that the increase in color precision allowed for a large value created by the summation. This approach would be the preferred method when taking a 1 bit per pixel image and creating a grayscale image at a lower resolution. The first approach would function best in cases where the increase in color accuracy is small.

The conversion of grayscale raster data from multiple bits per intensity value to single bit intensity values (bilevel values) has been studied and analyzed extensively because of its widespread use in printing. "Good" conversions require not only dithering but also *filtering*. Filtering distributes the errors introduced by the lose of accuracy so that the errors are not so visible. See [Ulichney87] for details. An alternative approach is known as *error diffusion* because it spreads the errors throughout the image.

Our discussion so far has been at a generic level, focusing on increases or decreases in resolution and color. Things get even more complicated when pixels are converted from full-color, red-green-blue values to a color index into a color lookup table. Typically a full-color image is still desired, but now dithering techniques must create a full range of colors using only those colors included in the color lookup table. The question of what colors to include in the lookup table to facilitate the dithering is a difficult one. For details refer to several schemes in [Heckbert82] and [Wan88].

Aspect Ratios and Pixel Size

Conversions between raster formats must also deal with differences in pixel aspect ratios. (In an ideal world all pixels would be square, but this is not an ideal world) When the pixels in two different formats have different aspect ratios (the ratio of their widths to their heights), then there is no one-to-one correspondence between pixels. The pixel overlap must be taken into account or the image will be scaled in one direction or the other by the conversion. The most accurate approach to this problem is to find the percentage of overlap between pixels and calculate an average intensity based on those proportions. Be aware that this can drastically change the color intensities of pixels when two pixels with different colors are averaged into a single color. For example, if a green pixel and a red pixel from the original data are overlapped halfway by the target pixel, then an average of the two pixels (50% red + 50% green) will produce yellow. New colors are introduced at the edges of objects where two colors meet. These new colors are often visible to the human eye in the converted image. This is one drawback to the comprehensive conversion format idea. If a conversion is being done between two formats that have nonsquare, but identical, ratio pixels, and if the conversion to the comprehensive format converts the nonsquare pixels to square pixels and then the square pixels get converted back to nonsquare pixels, erroneous colors are introduced into the target data format. For this reason, the initial conversion from the original format to the comprehensive format should not modify the pixel-aspect ratio. Adjustments in pixel ratios should be done while writing to the new format.

Color Conversions

Pixels can be represented in different color spaces. Refer to Chapter 6 for a thorough discussion. If the target data format does not support the representation used by the original format, then a color space conversion must be performed. Accurately matching colors requires the use of gamma correction values and color gamut information.

The above discussion concerning the conversion of raster data to raster data uses 2D raster data examples. All of the concepts apply to 3D raster data sets as well.

12.3.2   2D Geometry to Raster

The conversion of 2D geometry data to raster data is straightforward. Raster devices routinely convert 2D representations of lines, arcs, splines, and surfaces into sets of dots for raster display. This process is called *scan conversion*. To convert the data set, send the 2D data through a scan converter that will store the dots in a *frame buffer*. Then read the data out of the frame buffer into the raster data format. The only problem with this approach is that the scan-conversion might not be performed at the resolution you desire. If this is the case, then the scan conversion routines might have to be implemented separately from any particular device for the sole purpose of data conversion. It is important to realize that this conversion loses much of the information contained in the 2D representation. And more often than not, the information cannot be unambiguously regained through conversion back to 2D data.

12.3.3 Raster to 2D Geometry

The conversion of raster data to 2D geometry data is called *vectorization*. This process attempts to recognize when certain groups of pixels form geometric objects. It is typically done in several stages, with an initial cleanup stage.

If the raster data is coming from an optical scanning of a physical drawing, then the raster data often contains erroneous data from smudges or dirt on the original print. A thresholding process can eliminate some of the erroneous pixels by eliminating all pixels below a certain intensity level. In addition, *edge-enhancement* algorithms are sometimes used to clean up the edges found in the data in preparation for the next stage.

Feature-Extraction

This stage recognizes groups of pixels that form a linear path and creates a line segment defined by the endpoints of the path. If the data is "clean"—meaning there are no overlapping lines—then the process is fairly straightforward. Problems arise when the data contains lines of various widths, lines that cross, and solid-filled areas, especially if they are not filled with a solid color. Several examples of problem data are shown in Figure 12.9. The first example contains lines of various widths. The last line segment is very thick—or is a solid-filled rectangle. The conversion software can choose one over the other—but it will never be correct for every case without some user help. The second example contains text that slightly overlaps other line segments. This can break up the line segments into smaller fragments and make the next stage of pattern recognition more difficult. The third example contains shading which cannot be translated into line segments. The last example contains lines that intersect. If the thin line is recognized as two separate segments, then the positioning of their endpoints, is important. The wide line could cause them to have disjoint endpoints which can cause problems for the later pattern-recognition stage.

The next stage is pattern-recognition. This combines multiple line segments found in the previous stage into higher-order objects such as arcs and letters. The recognition of letters is often called OCR (optical character recognition). This recognition is not difficult under tightly-controlled circumstances, but it is very difficult in the general case (e.g., when there are many different letter fonts or letters written over other graphical elements).

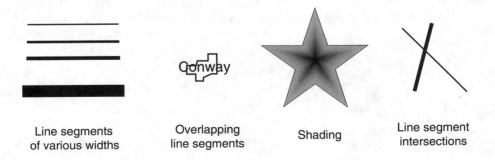

| Line segments of various widths | Overlapping line segments | Shading | Line segment intersections |

Figure 12.9 Problem areas for feature extraction from raster data

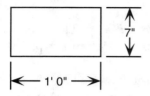

Figure 12.10 Example of the need for application
                  intelligence in data organization

Data Organization

This stage organizes the graphical objects into relevant data structures instead of one huge list of graphical primitives. Consider Figure 12.10. The previous stages of vectorization would have produced a list of line segments and the text strings. To get this data into a useful organization requires that we recognize which objects make up the dimensions and which compose the actual artifact. Most computer-aided design software systems manipulate and deal with dimensional data differently than they deal with other types of data. To prepare the data so that it can be manipulated according to user expectations, the data needs to be grouped into related sets and organized into relevant data structures. The type of desired data structures is often application specific. This is an "artificial intelligence" type of problem; it requires knowledge about how graphical data primitives combine into higher level abstract entities.

Summary

Capturing 2D data from raster data is possible under controlled situations but is difficult or impossible in the general case. For example, a general case might include the extraction of useful information from a rasterized photograph of a jungle forest. Perhaps research into fractal geometry will provide solutions to such problems, but in the meantime, conversion from raster to 2D geometry data is predominantly limited to simple line drawings. Vectorization-software products on the market have various levels of sophistication and require various levels of user intervention to finish or clean up the conversion.

Before we leave this subject, note that in all cases the rasterization of 2D geometry data loses information. It is possible to regain useful information through vectorization, but the original information is lost. Consider Figure 12.11. The original 2D geometry that created the figure was five connected line segments. Now suppose the shape is solid-filled and then

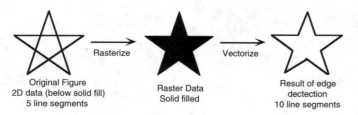

Figure 12.11 Example of information loss from vectorization

rasterized into a set of pixels. Edge detection can recover a 2D geometry description of the shape, but the result is 10 separate line segments. Sophisticated techniques could recognize that the line segments can be reconnected, but it is an arbitrary choice on whether they should be. Vectorization can produce useful 2D geometry data from raster data, but often the data is not combined or organized in ways consistent with the original 2D data. This change in structure and loss of information is important to some applications and makes vectorization impractical.

12.3.4 2D Geometry to 2D Geometry

The conversion of data between different 2D geometry data formats is often a straightforward process, though nontrivial. The major differences between 2D geometry data formats include:

- Schemes for combining, or linking graphical primitives
- Methods for relating attribute information to graphical primitives
- The organization of the data within the file
- The specific representations used for graphical primitives

Let's look specifically at each of these issues. As stated earlier, a comprehensive data format for 2D data is beneficial when more than two different data formats need conversion.

As Chapter 5 explains in detail, there are many representations possible even for simple entities such as line segments. Refer to that chapter for information on each graphical primitive. It is straightforward, though nontrivial, to take a given representation with its known values and calculate the unknown values needed to represent it in a different representation. Let's take the nine methods of circle representation as an example. Arbitrarily select one of the methods as the comprehensive method of representation. Then develop the equations that will convert between it and each of the other representations. These 16 sets of equations will handle conversions between all of the different formats, always being careful to include the nuances associated with each format. For example, the *arct* PostScript representation includes an initial line segment leading up to the arc. The line segment would be represented separately in most other formats. In some situations, some parameterizations may be less precise than others, such as a very large diameter circle defined by three nearly adjacent points, rather than a center and a radius.

There are several different representations for curves. Common representations include Bezier curves, *B*-spline curves, and NURBS (nonuniform rational *B*-splines). All of these representations are similar in that a curve is defined by a set of control points. The problem is that the control points must be positioned differently for each method to come up with the same identical curve. And in some cases it is impossible to position the control points such that identical curves are created. For example, it is possible to represent an exact circular arc using NURBS but impossible in the other methods. All you can do is get a close approximation. To convert data between formats that use different curve formulations requires a transformation of the control points. Sometimes additional points must be added to refine the curve approximation. Care must be taken to not move the reference points of other graphical elements or lose the connectivity of graphical elements when adding new points.

12.3.5   3D Geometry to 2D Geometry

The creation of a 2D representation from a 3D data set is well understood and straightforward to accomplish. There are a number of different viewing projections, such as parallel projections and perspective projections, that can move all of the 3D points in an object to a 2D viewing plane. See [Foley90].

12.3.6   2D Geometry to 3D Geometry

This conversion is another example of missing data. It is impossible for a computer program, an artificial intelligence, or even a human intelligence to create a unique 3D representation from a single 2D representation (except in the trivial case where the 3D representation lies entirely within a plane). If multiple 2D representations of an object exist, then it is possible to infer a 3D representation, given some additional information about the orientation of the 2-D representations. In the case of stereo "views," the viewing distance and view separation must be stated, and several common points must be identified in both representations. If the 2D representations correspond to front, end, and top views of an object, then the relative orientations of the three (or more) representations must be specified, and several common points in all three representations must be identified. There are several standard examples in mechanical drafting where even experienced students have problems inferring the true 3D form of an object from its front, top, and end views. A data conversion program cannot be expected to handle this general conversion case, even given multiple 2D representations.

12.3.7   3D Geometry to 3D Geometry

As Chapter 5 discusses, many different methods can be used to represent 3D data, ranging from polygonal boundary representations to procedural representations (e.g., fractals). The conversion of data between these representations is possible in some cases, impossible in other cases, and an open research question in still other cases. The following discussion categorizes these data conversions.

Consider Figure 12.12. It includes the traditional 3D data representations, and it indicates the potential data conversions between them. There are no arrows between the curved surface representation and the CSG representation because curved surfaces are typically used to model artifacts that cannot be usefully represented by CSGs (e.g., the panels of a car body). Given the four basic data representations, there are 10 possible conversions that might be desired between them. In addition, it is common to decompose any of these four into cell decomposition for a finite element analysis. Therefore, we have 14 different data conversions to discuss.

It is apparent from the figure that curved surfaces or constructive solid geometry primitives provide the most attractive representation for 3D data, since both can be easily mapped to either octrees or polygonal surfaces such as triangular patches. In any of the six relatively easy (or at least computationally possible) cases of conversion, the target representations provide only an approximation to the original specification of the surface (or volume).

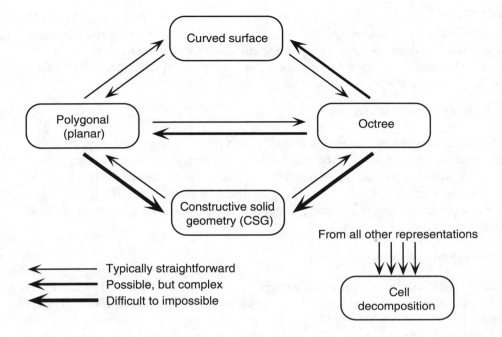

Figure 12.12 Difficulty of conversion between various 3D data formats

Polygonal to Curved Surface

A set of polygonal shapes with adjacent edges is referred to as a polygonal mesh. Polygonal meshes are often used as approximations to actual curved surfaces. When converting from a polygonal surface to a curved surface, an interpolating curved surface can be defined that goes through these points, such as a Hermite patch. The more common approach is to calculate new control points that define an approximate curved-surface definition that contains the polygon definition points, such as a Bezier surface or a *B*-Spline surface. Things get complicated when the original polygons have more than four sides. Consult the literature on high-order surface definitions for information on how to keep the error between the polygonal and curved surfaces within specified bounds.

Curved Surface to Octree

An octree representation involves subdividing a volume into eight octants and testing each octant for the presence of an element of the bounding surface of the object to be represented. Any of the eight octants that contain part of the surface of the object is subdivided into another eight octants. This process is continued recurrently until a predefined octant size (or resolution) is reached and all octants containing surface elements of the object are identified. These eight octants and their paths back to the initial root octant form the octree representation. A curved-surface object description uses a set of analytic expressions, such as Bezier surfaces or B-spline surfaces that are specified by polygon definition (or control) points. To convert from a curved-surface representation to an octree, an accuracy or resolution parameter must be defined. This determines how close source points on the curved surface must be in three-dimensional space. Then each source point on the curved surface is tested and its octree representation determined. The continuity of the curved surface can be used to shorten the octant search by using the octree representation of adjacent points on the surface as estimates of the representation of the new points to be converted.

Curved Surface to Polygonal (Planar)

To convert from a curved-surface representation to a planar representation, an accuracy or resolution parameter must be defined. This determines how close source points on the curved surface must be in three-dimensional space. Then each source point on the curved surface is used as a vertex in a polygon-mesh approximation to the surface. (It is possible to identify mesh points that result in a polygon approximation that does not exceed specified error limits.)

Constructive Solid Geometry to Polygonal

A constructive solid geometry representation uses the union, intersection, and difference of a small set of geometric solids together with cutting planes to describe an object. Typical basis objects include spheres, rectangular solids, cones, cylinders, pyramids, and plates. The surface of the modeled object is the set of surface pieces that remain visible after the collection of union and difference operations (each of which can have a scale and orientation associated with it) have been "executed." To convert from a CSG representation to a polygonal representation, an accuracy or resolution parameter must be defined. This determines how close source points on the CSG surface must be in three-dimensional space. Then each source point on the CSG surface is used as a vertex in a polygon-mesh approximation to the surface.

Constructive Solid Geometry to Octree

To convert from a CSG representation to an octree, an accuracy or resolution parameter must be defined. This determines how close source points on the CSG surface must be in three-dimensional space. Then each source point on the CSG surface is tested and its octree representation determined. The continuity of the CSG surface can be used to shorten the octant search by using the octree representation of adjacent source points on the surface as estimates of the representation of the new point to be converted.

Polygonal to Octree

To convert from a polygonal representation to an octree, an accuracy or resolution parameter must be defined. This determines how close source points on the polygonal surface must be in three-dimensional space. Then each source point on the polygonal surface is tested and its octree representation determined. The continuity of the polygonal surface can be used to shorten the octant search by using the octree representation of adjacent source points on the surface as estimates of the representation of the new points to be converted.

12.3.8 Procedural Representation Conversions

There is no general way to convert directly between procedural representations because the world views of different representations are totally different. The only technique to decode the source representation is by executing it and saving the results into some raster buffer.

12.3.9 Generic Model Data to 2D or 3D Geometry Data

What makes a model different from just a set of geometry information is the additional application- (or application-class) specific information it contains. This implies that application-specific knowledge is required to convert model data to 2D or 3D geometry data, even if the nongeometry information is to be discarded. The other potential difference between model data and strictly geometry data is structure information. This is related to the possible use of *references* to "subroutines" or (sub)parts of a model structure rather than simply replicating all of the geometry (and related information) for each occurrence of the (sub)part. It should be apparent that there can be no general solution for converting data from an arbitrary (generic) model into 2D or 3D geometry data.

For any given model, the conversion process to geometry data is relatively straightforward once it has been decided what to do with the additional (nongeometry) data that is encountered: whether any hierarchical structure in the model should be retained and whether or not the geometry data should retain any subroutine structure that might be present in the generic model.

12.4 DATA CONVERSION PROGRAMS

Numerous data conversion programs are available from commercial vendors, from public domain sources such as the Internet, and from bulletin boards that have downloadable shareware programs. The following list is a *sampling* of these conversion programs. If the list contains the particular file formats of interest to you, then you're in luck. If it does not, obtain more current information on the packages because they might have added support for that particular format. This list is curent as of June 1992. (To find other sources of data conversion, consult current trade magazines, industry publications, equipment vendors, and software vendors.)

The following conversion programs are not being endorsed or recommended by the authors. They are simply typical of the availability and functionality of data format conversion programs.

Name   pbmplus

Source   A public domain set of conversion programs written by Jeff Poskanzer and various other contributors. It is available from various archival sources on the Internet. In specific, it can be retrieved using FTP (File Transfer Protocol) from *wuarchive. wustl.edu* in the directory /graphics/graphics/packages/pbmplus. Retrieve the file named *pbmplus10dec91.tar.Z*. It is a little more than 600K in size. After transferring the file, do the following (assuming that you are on a Unix system): uncompress pbmplus10dec91.tar.Z, *tar -xvf pbmplus10dec.tar*

Executes on   The package includes source C code that could potentially, with modifications, be compiled on any system with a C compiler. It's primary intended environment is under Unix, but even on Unix machines, it requires some setup so that it can be compiled correctly

---

Name   Image Alchemy

Source   Handmade Software, Inc.; a shareware version with restricted functionality is also available on many bulletin boards.

Executes on   DOS systems

Name   PICTureThis

Source   A commercial package by FGM Inc.

Executes on   Macintosh

Name   HiJaak 2.1 (DOS), HiJaak for Windows 1.0

Source   Commercial package, $249; from Inset Systems, 71 Commerce Drive, Brookfield CT 06804-3405; (800)374-6738.

Executes on   PCs, under DOS or Windows

DATA FORMATS HANDLED BY FOUR DIFFERENT CONVERSION PACKAGES

R—Reads the format W—Writes the format	PICTure This	HiJaak	pbmplus	Image Alchemy
Black and white formats				
Andrew Toolkit raster *object*			R / W	
Autologic.gm and .gm2				R / W
ASCII graphics			W	
Atari Degas .pi3 format			R / W	
BBN BitGraph graphics			W	
Bennet Yee's "face" format			R / W	
CCITT Fax group 3			R / W	
CMU window manger format			R / W	
DCX (also for Fax use)				R / W
Epson printer format			W	
GEM .img format	R / W	R / W	R / W	R / W
Gemini 10x printer format		R / W	W	
GraphOn graphics			W	
HP LaserJet formats			W	R / W
MacPaint	R / W		R / W	
MGR format			R / W	
Printronix format			W	
Sun icon file			R / W	
X10 bitmaps	R / W		R / W	
X11 bitmaps	R / W		R / W	
Xerox doodle brushes			R	
Unix plot(5) file			W	
Zinc Interface Library icon			W	
Grayscale formats				
Autologic.gm4				R / W
FITS			R / W	
HIPS			R	
Lisp machine bit-array-file			R / W	
PostScript "image" data			R	
raw grayscale bytes			R	R / W
Usenix FaceSaver™ file			R / W	

**DATA FORMATS HANDLED BY FOUR DIFFERENT
CONVERSION PACKAGES** *(Continued)*

R—Reads the format W—Writes the format	PICTure This	HiJaak	pbmplus	Image Alchemy
Color formats				
Abekas YUV format			R / W	
ADEX.img and.rle				R / W
Agfa/Matrix Scodl				W
Amiga IFF ILBM	R / W	R / W	R / W	R / W
AT&T ATT		R / W		
Atari Degas.pi1 format			R / W	
Atari compressed Spectrum			R	
Atari uncompressed Spectrum			R	
CALS Raster			R / W	
Custom applications.fop				W
DEC pixel format			W	
DataBeam DBX			R / W	
Dr. Halo CUT	R / W	R / W		
GIF	R / W	R/ W	R / W	R / W
HP PaintJet format			R / W	R / W
Img-whatnot file			R	
JPEG/JFIF				R / W
Macintosh PICT		R	R / W	R
Motif UIL icon file			W	
MTV/PRT ray-tracer output			R	R
NCSA Interactive ColorRaster			W	
PC Paintbrush.pcx format	R / W		R / W	R / W
PCPAINT pictor page format				R
QDV				W
QO				R / W
QRT ray-tracer output			R	R / W
Stork (CMYK)				R / W
TrueVision Targa file	R / W		R / W	R / W
Vivid ray-tracer output				R / W
Wordperfect graphic file				R / W
X11 "puzzle" file			W	
Xim file			R / W	R
XBM (X Window ASCII pixmaps)	R / W		R / W	R / W

**DATA FORMATS HANDLED BY FOUR DIFFERENT
CONVERSION PACKAGES** *(Continued)*

R—Reads the format W—Writes the format	PICTure This	HiJaak	pbmplus	Image Alchemy
Formats containing the full range of raster data types				
Erdas LAN/GIS				R / W
EPS— Encapsulated PostScript	R / W	W	W	W
Portable Bit Map.pnm				R / W
Sun raster file	R / W		R / W	R / W
TIFF	R / W		R / W	R / W
Utah Raster Toolkit.RLE				R / W
Windows BMP				R / W
X10 window dump file	R / W		R	
X11 window dump file	R / W		R / W	
Vector Formats—2D geometry				
AutoCAD DXF		R / W		
CGM	R / W	R / W		
Digital Research GEM		R / W		
EPS—Encapsulated PostScript	R / W	R / W		
HPGL		R / W		R / W
IBM GOCA BCA		R / W		
Inset IGF		R / W		
Lotus PIC	R / W	R / W		
Macintosh PICT 2		R / W		R / W
Micrographx DRW (vector only)		R / W		
WMF—Windows Metafile		R / W		
WordPerfect WPG		R / W		
PM Metafile MET		W		
MathCAD MCS		W		
Tektronics Plot 10		R		

APPENDICES

INTRODUCTION TO DATA FORMATS

The following appendices provide an overview of individual data formats discussed throughout the chapters of this book. The intent of these appendices is to provide a consist and uniform set of information about each data format. The synthesized information follows the format shown below. The appendices are ordered alphabetically. For a classification and comparison *between* data formats refer to Chapter 11.

Purchasing the documentation for multiple data formats can become quite expensive. Hopefully the summaries provided in these appendices will allow the reader to make well-educated decisions on which documents to purchase.

DATA FORMAT NAME

Acronym	If the name is an acronym, the full name is given. Some data formats are known by their "common name" and not their "technical name." If a technical name exists it is given here as well
Origin	Describes the organization or individuals who created the data format. If the authority or control of the data format has changed hands from the original developers, these parties are also listed
	All organization names, addresses, telephone numbers, Fax numbers, and e-mail addresses were correct at the completion of this manuscript. Obviously this information can become quickly outdated. If you find that the information is no longer correct, it should still provide you with a starting point from which to contact them
Motivation	Data formats are created to meet specific goals for specific applications. Any motivations that drove the development of the data format are listed here
Users	Often a data format is widely used for some applications and never used by others. The typical users are listed
Control	Copyrighted by The name of organization holding the copyright
	Trademarks Lists the data format name if it is a registered trademark, and any other trademarks associated with the data format
	Royalty fees Lists any fees required to legally use the data format

DATA FORMAT NAME   *(Continued)*

Versions Lists the major versions of a data format, along with adoption dates and a description of how the format was modified between versions

Overview Summarizes the following five major features of the data format:

Major Type of Data
Color Representation
Data Organization
Data Encoding
Data Compression

Data Types Lists the major types of data that the data format supports. This list will hopefully allow the reader to make an educated decision concerning whether the data format will support their desired application. The intent of the list is *not* to include every data type the data format defines

Color Discusses the color models used by the data format (if the overview summary needs more explanation)

Data Organization Data formats are organized in many ways, but they eventually end up as a sequential stream of bytes. This section includes a diagram that captures the essence of a data format's data stream. Four basic symbols are used in each diagram as follows:

A rectangle represents a *data block*. The label describes its general contents

A downward pointing arrow indicates the *sequence* of the data blocks; the block above the arrow comes before the data block below the arrow within the data stream

An arrow that loops down (and to the right) around one or more data blocks indicates that the data blocks are *optional;* they may or may not be present in a particular data stream

An arrow that loops up (and to the left) around one or more data blocks indicates that the data blocks are *repeated* within the data stream

These types of diagrams capture the ordering of a data stream, but they do not necessarily capture the "higher level" nature of some organization schemes (such as hierarchical relationships). For the sake of consistency and comparison, all of the diagrams are drawn using this simple scheme. Where appropriate, higher level organizational relationships are mentioned in text below the diagram

DATA FORMAT NAME *(Continued)*

Data Encoding	This section lists and describes the byte encodings used for the major data blocks of the data stream. In many cases the limitations of the data format can be inferred by observing the number of bytes reserved for particular data values. The intent is to show the complexity and design of the data stream. Again, this should help the reader discern whether the data format will meet the needs of a desired application • It is not the intent of this section to include all of the details needed to program software to read and write each format. *Please refer to the appropriate references to discover all of the nuisances associated with each individual data format.*
Data Compression	Discusses the compression schemes used by the data format (if the overview summary needs more explanation)
Example	Several of the formats contain a small sample data stream. Examples like these are practical only for text-encoded (ASCII) data streams
File Name Suffix	Lists the standard file name extensions used with files of this data stream type. Where appropriate, these are separated into DOS, Macintosh, and Unix file extensions
References	Lists source documents that provide a detailed description of the data format. Where available, readers are directed to resource files on publicly accessible networks such as the Internet or CompuServe

In some instances information concerning a particular category was not available to us. In those instances the section is marked with an *NA* which stands for not available.

And finally, as we said in Chapter 1, it is not our goal to duplicate information that is currently spread over a wide variety of sources. To duplicate such information would produce a multivolume set of text that accomplishes little except duplicating information. Our goal is a comprehensive resource on the essence of graphical data streams—their history, what the issues are, how they are similar, and how they are different. *Therefore, do not hold us liable when attempting to write software from the information contained in this book.* In some cases software implementations might be possible, but that was not our goal in recording and organizing the information. *Please refer to the original source documents on each format before attempting software implementations of that format.*

AVS FIELD

Acronym	AVS (Application Visualization System) Field data
Origin	Stardent Computer, Inc.

Development, sales, and support of AVS was split off into a separate company in January, 1992:
Advanced Visual Systems Inc.
300 Fifth Avenue
Waltham, MA 02154
Tel. (617) 890-4300
Fax. (617) 890-8287

Motivation	A simple data structure to hold general multidimensional data
Users	AVS software systems that run on workstations and supercomputers

Control	Copyrighted by	Advanced Visual Systems Inc.
	Trademarks	AVS
	Royalty fees	None on the data format; use of AVS requires a license

Versions NA

Overview	Major Type of Data	Raster
	Color Representation	None
	Data Organization	N-dimensional vector array; column major order
	Data Encoding	ASCII header; binary or ASCII data
	Data Compression	None

Data Types	Dimensional specifications	Specifies the number of dimensions for the field and the number and data type for the values in each field location
	Field data	The specific value (or values) associated with each field position (i.e., raster samples)
	Coordinate data	Maps each field to a specific physical point (typically either 2 or 3 dimensions, but there is no restriction)

Data Organization

General syntax of data stream

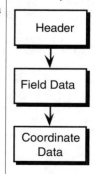

AVS FIELD *(Continued)*

Signature
First 5 bytes must be "# AVS" in ASCII

Header
The header contains a group of keyword = value pairs. The data is represented in ASCII text, one pair per line. Any text between a # character and the end of a line is a comment. Comments are optional and there is no limit on their number. The following keywords are recognized:

Required tokens:

ndim	The number of dimensions in the field
dim1, dim2, dim3, …	The size of each dimension in the field. There must be one value specified for each dimension. For example, if ndim = 2 then specify dim1 and dim2; if ndim = 4 then specify dim1, dim2, dim3, and dim4. Elements in the field are identified using subscripts beginning at 1 and going to dimX where X is the size of the particular dimension
veclen	The number of data values for each field element
data	The data type of each data value in a field element vector. All data in a single field must have the same data type. Options include: byte, integer, float, double, xdr_integer, xdr_float, and xdr_double
nspace	The number of dimensions of the physical space that the field coordinates are mapped to (typically 2 or 3)
field	Specifies how the field values are mapped to physical space. Options are: *uniform* No mapping specified; the field values are assumed to be uniform distances apart in each dimension of the field *rectilinear* A value is associated with each position of each dimension that creates nonuniform spacing between field elements. The elements are still assumed to be in a orthogonal axis system where each axis is 90 degrees to all other axes *irregular* Each position in the field is given a specific location in the physical space

Optional tokens:

min_ext	Coordinate space extent
max_ext	Coordinate space extent
label	Text label associated with a specific value of the vector
unit	Describes the unit of measure for a particular value of the vector

AVS FIELD   *(Continued)*

min_val	Minimum data values per component of the vectors
max_val	Maximum data values per component of the vectors
variable	For each value in the vector, describes where to find the data and how to read it
coord	For each dimension in the N-dimensional array, describes where to find the coordinate data and how to read it

The file header is terminated by two ASCII form-feed characters (0C in hex, 12 in decimal). This scheme is used so that the header of the file can be viewed with the Unix *more* utility. The more utility stops at the form-feed characters and allows the header to be viewed before entering the binary data section of the file. (The more program is typically terminated at this point, since display of the following binary data is typically meaningless.)

Field Data

This section of the file is stored in a binary format. It can be a machine-dependent binary format or the XDR binary interchange format. Machine-dependent binary data is typically not portable from machine to machine. The data is stored in the same fashion as a FORTRAN multidimensional array, which is referred to as "column major order." Using this scheme, the left most field subscript varies the quickest. All of the values for each field position are stored contiguously. Consider the example below where each field position has three values (veclen = 3), and the field is 3D of size (10, 12, 5)

DATA(1,1,1)	Value 1
DATA(1,1,1)	Value 2
DATA(1,1,1)	Value 3
DATA(2,1,1)	Value 1
DATA(2,1,1)	Value 2
DATA(2,1,1)	Value 3
...	
DATA(10,12,5)	Value 1
DATA(10,12,5)	Value 2
DATA(10,12,5)	Value 3

Coordinate Data

This section of the file is stored in a binary format analogous to the Field Data. If the field type is uniform, then this section of the file is empty. If the field type is rectilinear, then this section of the file contains a single value for each possible subscript along each possible dimension of the field. If the field type is irregular then this section of the file contains a position in physical space for each element in the field. Consider the following example where a 3D field is mapped to a 2D physical space in an irregular fashion

DATAPOSITION(1,1,1)   ← (35,42)   (i.e., *x, y* coordinate)
DATAPOSITION(2,1,1)   ← (10,5)
DATAPOSITION(3,1,1)   ← (10,8)
...
DATAPOSITION(10,12,5)   ← (3,25)

Example   The following is an example header. The comments included below are not typical of a real world application data file, but they are included here to help further explain the meaning of each specification

```
# Field data from collection station.....
# Collected by....
#
# Specify the size, structure, and data types for the field data.
#
ndim = 3        # This field is 3-dimensional.
dim1 = 10       # The field has dimensions 10 by 10 by 5.
dim2 = 10
dim3 = 5
veclen = 4      # The data at each field location is defined by 4
                     values.
data = byte     # Each individual data value is of type byte,
#
# Specify the mapping to a physical coordinate system that is desired.
#
nspace = 2      # This field is mapped to 2 dimensions in physical
                     space.
field = uniform # No coordinate mapping information is included.
                #
                # This 3-dimensional data will be mapped to a 2-
                # dimensional physical space, using equal spacing on
                # each axis.
```

File Name   Unix   .fld
Suffix

References   *AVS Users Guide, Release 4*, May 1992, Advanced Visual Systems Inc., Waltham, MA, Part # 320-0011-02 Rev B

AVS Module Reference, Release 4, May 1992, Advanced Visual Systems Inc., Waltham, MA, Part # 320-0014-02 Rev B

AVS IMAGE FILE

Acronym	AVS (Application Visualization System) Image File
Origin	Stardent Computer, Inc. (1989)
	Development, sales, and support of AVS was split off into a separate company in January, 1992: Advanced Visual Systems Inc. 300 Fifth Avenue Waltham, MA 02154 Tel. (617) 890-4300 Fax. (617) 890-8287
Motivation	Simple raster image file format
Users	AVS software systems that run on workstations and supercomputers
Control	Copyrighted by Advanced Visual Systems, Inc. Trademarks AVS Royalty fees None on the data format; use of AVS requires a license
Versions	NA
Overview	Major type of data 2D raster Color representation ARGB uncalibrated Data organization Sequential; 2D array; row major order Data encoding Binary Data compression None
Data Types	Image size # of samples in the horizontal and vertical direction 4 bytes for each pixel Pixel data
Data Organization	General syntax of data stream

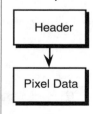

Signature
None

AVS IMAGE FILE *(Continued)*

Header

Byte#	Data	Details
1–4	*X*-size	Number of pixels in *X* direction
5–8	*Y*-size	Number of pixels in *Y* direction

Pixel Data

The pixel values are stored in rows, with the top row first. Each row is stored from left to right. There is *no* compression, and the data is *not* broken into blocks

Byte#	Data	Details
9	Auxiliary	
10	Red	
11	Green	RGB for Pixel 1 (4 bytes)
12	Blue	
…	…	
n–3	Auxiliary	
n–2	Red	RGB for the last pixel (last row, far right)
n–1	Green	
n	Blue	$n = 4\ (X\text{-size})(Y\text{-size}) + 8$

The auxillary byte in the pixel data is typically used to store opacity (alpha) information on a pixel by pixel basis

File Name Suffix	Unix .x
References	*AVS Users Guide, Release 4,* May 1992, Advanced Visual Systems Inc., Waltham, MA, Part # 320-0011-02 Rev B

BMP

Acronym	BitMaP format
Origin	Windows Marketing Group Microsoft Corporation 16011 NE 36th Way Box 97017 Redmond, WA 98073-9717 Tel. (206) 882-8080

BMP   *(Continued)*

Motivation	To storage raster image data in a format that is independent of the color specification scheme used on any single hardware device
Users	Microsoft Windows 3.0 (or higher) users and application programs running under the Windows 3.0 (or higher) environment

Control

Copyrighted by	Microsoft Corporation
Trademarks	Microsoft, Windows, Windows/286, Windows/386
Royalty fees	None

Versions Version 1

Overview

Major Type of Data	2D raster
Color Representation	Monochrome, Color lookup table, RGB
Data Organization	Sequential; 2D array of pixel values
Data Encoding	Binary
Data Compression	None, run-length

Data Types

Image size	Width and height
Bits per pixel	
Type of compression	
Resolution	Pixels per meter
Color palette	
Raster data	

Data Organization

General syntax of the data stream

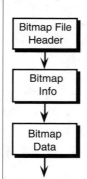

Signature
First two bytes, must be BM, in ASCII, Hex(42 4D)

BMP *(Continued)*

Bitmap File Header
All data values are in LSB first format

Byte#	Data	Details
1–2	File type	Must be ASCII text "BM"
3–6	Size of the file	In double words (32-bit integers)
7–10	Reserved for future use	Must be zero
11–14	Byte offset to bitmap data	Offset from the Bitmap File Header (i.e., the start of the file)

Bitmap Information

Byte#	Data	Details
1–4	Number of bytes in header	Currently 40 bytes
5–8	Width of bitmap	In pixels
9–12	Height of bitmap	In pixels
13–14	Number of color planes	Must be set to 1
15–16	Number of bits per pixel	Valid choices are 1, 4, 8, 24; if not 24, determines the size of the palette
17–20	Type of compression	0: No compression; 1: run length (8 bits per pixel); 2: run length (4 bits per pixel)
21–24	Size of image	In bytes
25–28	Horizontal resolution	In pixels/meter
29–32	Vertical resolution	In pixels/meter
33–36	Number of color indexes used by the bitmap	Zero indicates all colors are important
37–40	Number of color indexes important for displaying bitmap	A value of zero indicates all colors are important
41	Blue color value	Beginning color palette (entry 0) (Notice RGB values are reversed from typical order)
42	Green color value	
43	Red color value	
44	Reserved for future use	Must be zero
…	… Remaining color palette entries	4 bytes per palette entry, the number of entries is based on the bits per pixel value above. Colors should be listed in order of importance

BMP   *(Continued)*

Bitmap Data

The pixels are stored by rows, left to right within each row. *The rows are stored bottom to top;* the origin of the bitmap is the lower-left corner. The bits of each pixel are packed into bytes and each scan line is padded with zeros, if necessary, to be aligned with a 32-bit word boundary

File Name Suffix	DOS, OS/2	.BMP

References   *Microsoft Windows Programmer's Reference*, New for Version 3, edited by Microsoft Corporation, Microsoft Press, Redmond, WA, 1990, ISBN 1-55615-309-0

Microsoft Windows Software Development Kit
Call the Microsoft Information Center at (800) 426-9400 for further information

---

CCITT FAX

Acronym   International Telegraph and Telephone Consultative Committee (CCITT) Facsimile (Fax) transmission data formats

Origin   International Telegraph and Telephone Consultative Committee (CCITT)
International Telecommunications Union (ITU)
Place des Nations
CH-1211 Geneva, Switzerland

Motivation

Format	Description
Group I	Transmits a document over standard telephone wires in approximately 6 minutes when either or both stations are unattended
Group II	Identical to Group I except that it transmits the document in approximately 3 minutes. The lower transmission time is accomplished by compression modulation
Group III	Transmits a document over standard telephone wires in approximately 1 minute. Digital compression is used to reduce the amount of data to be transmitted. A modem converts the data to an analog signal for transmission
Group IV	Transmits a document over digital public data networks (PDNs) in a digital 2D compressed format. Optional encoding schemes in the future will allow for not only black and white images, but also for grayscale and color images

CCITT FAX   *(Continued)*

Users | Fax machines worldwide

Fax machines support up to a certain "group" performance. It will initially attempt to send data at its highest possible speed. If the receiving Fax cannot accept the particular data format, the originating system "drops" to the next lower group and tries again. Any Fax machine that adheres to at least one of these standards should be able to send and receive data to any other machine that supports one or more of the standards

Control | Copyrighted by   CCITT
Trademarks
Royalty fees   None

Versions | Group I   1968
Group II   1976
Group III   1980
Group IV)   1988 (monochrome only)

Overview | Major Type of Data   2D raster
Color Representation   Group I, II, and III: Monochrome
                                Group IV: Monochrome, grayscale, and color
Data Organization   Sequential; 2D array of pixels
Data Encoding   Binary
Data Compression   Group I: (No compression)
                                Group II: (No compression)
                                Group III: 1D, run-length, Huffman; 2D, form
                                  of differencing
                                Group IV: (Similar to Group III)

Data Types | Runs of black dots
Runs of white dots

Data Organization | General syntax of data stream

Signature
Device to device communication protocols establishes a link and negotiates a data format. These "handshaking" protocols are outside the realm of our discussion. They do however act as a signature for the data formats

CCITT FAX   *(Continued)*

Summary

The following table summarizes their resolution, transmission speeds and transmission types

Type	Horizontal resolution (scan lines per mm)	Vertical resolution (elements per scan line)	Transmission rate (scan lines per minute)	Transmission type
Group I	3.85	1144	180	Analog
Group II	3.85	1144	360	Analog
Group III	3.85 or 7.7	1728	3000[*]	Analog
Group IV	3.85 or 7.7	1728	3000	Digital

Notes:

3.85 scan lines per mm	≈ 98 pixels per inch
7.7 scan lines per mm	≈ 196 pixels per inch
1144 elements per scan line	≈ 138 pixels per inch
1728 elements per scan line	≈ 209 pixels per inch

[*] The minimum transmission time per scan line is optionally 5, 10, 20, or 40 milliseconds per scan line. The recommended standard is 20, which translates into 3000 scan lines per minute

File Name Suffix	None
References	International Telegraph and Telephone Consultative Committee (CCITT) Blue Book Volume VII—Fascicle V11.3 Terminal Equipment and Protocols for Telematic Services Recommendations T.0–T.63

CCITT H.261

Acronym	None Technical name: Video Codec for Audiovisual Services at $p \times 64$ kbits/s
Origin	International Telegraph and Telephone Consultative Committee (CCITT) Geneva, Switzerland

CCITT SG XV (Study Group 15) Subgroup—Specialist Group on Coding for Visual Telephony |

CCITT H.261   *(Continued)*

Motivation	To create an international standard for videophone and videoconferencing

The following assumptions were made while designing the standard:
- The transmission of the data would be over the Integrated Services Digital Network (ISDN)
- The bandwidth of the transmission channels will vary in capacity. The capacity of the channels is measured in increments of 64 Kbits/ second (i.e., 65,536 bits/s, where K = 1,024). Potential channel bandwidths are $p \times$ 64 Kbits/s where p = 1, 2, 3, …, 30 (i.e, 64 Kbits/s, 128 Kbits/s, 192 Kbits/s, …, 1.92 Mbits/s)

Users	Videophone and videoconferencing applications

Control		
Copyrighted by	ITU (International Telecommunications Union)
Trademarks	None
Royalty Fees	None

Versions	First approved at the 1990 CCITT Plenary Assembly on December 14, 1990

Overview	
Major Type of Data	2D raster; real-time video
Color Representation	YC_BC_R (CCIR Recommendation 601)
Data Organization	Sequential
Data Encoding	Binary
Data Compression	Intraframes use DCT (Discrete Cosine Transform)
	Interframes use Predictive-coded pictures
Refresh Rate Resolution	30000/1001 approximately 29.97 frames/s
	Two options: the Common Interface Format (CIF) or the Quarter Common Interface Format (QCIF)

	CIF		QCIF	
Sample Type	Lines/ Frame	Pixels/ Line	Lines/ Frame	Pixels/ Line
Luminance *(Y)*	288	352	144	176
Chrominance *(C_B)*	144	176	72	88
Chrominance *(C_R)*	144	176	72	88

Compression	Uncompressed bit rates required for transmitting data at 29.97 frames/s

At CIF resolution	36.45 Mbits/s
At QCIF resolution	9.115 Mbits/s

CCITT H.261   *(Continued)*

Compression ratios required for given resolutions:

Bandwidth

P	Kbits/s	CIF	QCIF
1	64	570:1	142:1
6	320	95:1	24:1
15	960	38:1	10:1
30	1920	19:1	5:1

Data Organization   General syntax of data stream

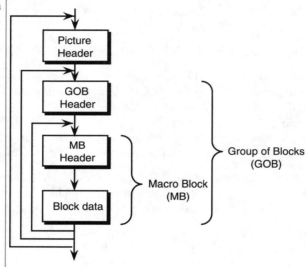

File Name Suffix   None

References   *Video Codec for Audiovisual Services at p × 64 kbit/s*
CCITT Recommendation H.261
International Telegraph and Telephone Consultative Committee,
August 1990

Liou, Ming, "Overview of the *p* × 64 kbit/s Video Coding Standard," *Communications of the ACM,* Vol. 34, No. 4, April 1991, pages 60–63

CGM
(ISO/IEC 8632-1992)

Acronym	Computer Graphics Metafile
Origin	American National Standards Institute, Inc. (ANSI) 1430 Broadway New York, NY 10018

Original author	Technical Committee X3H3 (Computer Graphics Programming Languages) of Accredited Standards Committee X3, Project 347I P. Bono, Chair; B. Shepherd, Vice-Chair, plus a 50-member committee
Current support	ISO International Register of Graphical Items, maintained by the Registration Authority, which is the US National Institute of Science and Technology (formerly the National Bureau of Standards)

Motivation	A device- and operating system-independent file format suitable for the storage, retrieval, and interchange of *picture* information
Users	Software systems based on the GKS (Graphical Kernel System—ISO 7942), and other CAD systems. CGM is slowly spreading beyond the CAD market (e.g., Harvard Graphics will import CGM files)
	Its use is mandated by the CALS program (i.e., the Computer Assisted Logistics Support program that is part of the US Department of Defense (DOD)

Control		
	Copyrighted by	ISO/IEC and ANSI
	Trademarks	None
	Royalty Fees	None

Versions		
	ANSI X3.122-1986	Version 1, August 1986 (Started in March 1981)
	ANSI X3.122-1992	Version 2, 1992; totally replaces the 1986 document; this version includes the functionality of the 1986 version as a proper subset
	ISO/IEC 8632:1992	(Identical to ANSI X3.122-1992)

Overview		
	Major Type of Data	2D geometry; 2D raster
	Color Representation	Color table lookup; RGB; CMYK, CIE LUV, CIE LAB; RGB related
	Data Organization	Sequential; *graphic state* based
	Data Encoding	ASCII text or Binary or Character
	Data Compression	In general—none, except for raster data; Huffman encoding of Point List Parameters in Character Encoding

CGM
(ISO/IEC 8632-1992) *(Continued)*

Each metafile contains zero or more "picture" descriptions. A picture includes a "window" extent description in which graphical elements can be displayed. Attribute parameters are set to specify a *current state*. The current state defines how each element is displayed on the graphic device. The final display of the picture will be affected by the interpreter and characteristics associated with each physical device

Data Types	Basic Graphical Primitives	
	Polyline	List of points, connected consecutively by line segments
	Disjoint Polyline	List of points, each pair connected by a line segment
	Polymarker	List of points where the current "marker type" is to be drawn
	Text	A position point and text string
	Restricted Text	A position point and text string that is restricted to lie within a parallelogram
	Append Text	Text string to be appended to a previously defined text
	Polygon	List of points, connected by line segments, closed shape
	Polygon Set	Polygon with "holes"
	Tile Array	Tiled compressed raster
	Cell Array	Device-independent pixel map
	Generalized Drawing Primitive	An identifier, list of points, and parameter data; specifies user-definable "primitives"
	Rectangle	Defined by two points
	Circle	Defined by a center point and a radius
	Circular Arc 3-point	Defined by a starting point, intermediate point, and an ending point
	Circular Arc 3-point	Closed 3-point arc, either a pie shape or a line segment connects the start and end points (chord)
	Circular Arc Center	Defined by a center point, a starting and ending vector, and a radius
	Circular Arc Center	Closed circular arc, either a pie shape or a line segment connects the start and end points (chord)
	Ellipse	Defined by a center point and a point on each axis
	Ellipse Arc	Defined like Ellipse, along with start and end vectors
	Ellipse Arc Close	Closed elliptical arc, either a pie shape or a line segment connects start and end points (chord)
	Hyperbolic Arc	Defined by a center point, and a start and end point
	Parabolic Arc	Like Hyperbolic arc, plus transverse and conjugate radii end points
	Nonuniform *B*-Spline	Parameters include spline order, number of control points, list of knots, and start and end parameter values
	Nonuniform Rational *B*-Spline	Like nonuniform *B*-spline, with the addition of weights for the control points

CGM
(ISO/IEC 8632-1992)   *(Continued)*

PolyBezier	If discontinuous, then 4 control points for each Bezier curve; if continuous, then 3 control points for each curve, plus one additional point

Data Organization

General syntax of the data stream

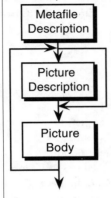

Signature

Character Encoding	First 2 bytes, hex(30), hex(20)
Binary Encoding	First byte hex(00), 3 high-order bits of second byte (001)
Clear Text Encoding	BEGMF

All of the details of these three separate encodings are too numerous to be discussed in this overview. Refer to the CGM standard document for complete details

Metafile Description

This section contains information related to all of the pictures in the file, and contains the following data

Metafile Version	Version of CGM this file conforms to
Metafile Description	Descriptive text, e.g., author, origin, etc.
VDC Type	Data type of the Virtual Device Coordinates
Integer Precision	Precision of integer data in file
Real Precision	Precision of real data in file
Index Precision	Range of values valid for indexes
Color Precision	Maximum value used to represent color components (i.e., max red, max green max blue)
Color Index Precision	Maximum value for an index into the color table
Maximum Color Index	Specifies color table size
Color Value Extent	Specifies values for black and white
Metafile Element List	Lists all nonmandatory elements used in the file
Metafile Defaults Replacement	Change default values of status and modes
Fonts List	List of fonts (by name) used in the file
Character Set List	List of character set encodings used in the file
Character Coding Announcer	Indicates the character set encoding used to specify text for the Text graphical primitives

CGM
(ISO/IEC 8632-1992) *(Continued)*

Picture Description

This section contains information related only to the immediately following picture data. It contains the following data:

Scale Mode	Abstract (no dimensions), or metric
Color Selection Mode	Indexed (palette), or direct (full RGB)
Line Width Specification Mode	Absolute or scaled
Marker Size Specification Mode	Absolute or scaled
Edge Width Specification Mode	Absolute or scaled
VDC Extent	Rectangular extent of picture window, specified in Virtual Device Coordinates
Background Color	Color of picture background
VDC Integer Precision	Precision of values used to specify locations in the Virtual Device Coordinates
VDC Real Precision	Precision of values used to specify locations in the Virtual Device Coordinates
Auxiliary Color	Background color used when Transparency is off
Transparency	On or off, affects the background of several graphical primitives (e.g., text)
Clip Rectangle	Specifies rectangular clipping region
Clip Indicator	Turns clipping on and off

Picture Body

This section contains the picture data, which is made up of a list of graphical primitives with associated parameters (See previous Data Types section)

Example

```
(Clear Text Encoding)

BEGMF "Koch Curve Example"
    mfversion 1; mfdesc"May 28, 1993";vdctype real;
    indexprec -127,127;
    maxcolrindex 7; mfelemlist drawingplus;
    font_list "Helvetica","Courier";

BEGDEFAULTS;
    VDCEXT 0,0,1,1;
    text_font_index 2;
    int_style solid;
ENDDEFAULTS;
BEGPIC "Koch curve"
    marker_size_mode abs;
BEGPICBODY;
    % curve%
    line (0,0) (1,0) (1,1).... (5,0);% the continuation.... dots
                                are not a valid part of the syntax,
                                but they shorten this example%

    % label%
    char_height 0.04;
    text_align ctr, bottom, 0, 0;
    text (0,5,0) final "KochCurve";
ENDPIC;
ENDMF
```

CGM
(ISO/IEC 8632-1992)   *(Continued)*

References	American National Standard for information systems—Computer Graphics—Metafile for the storage and transfer of picture description information, ANSI X3.122-1992, Published by American National Standards Institute, 1992, 293 pages (Can only be purchased through ANSI)

Part 1	Semantic Specification	332 pages
Part 2	Character Encoding	88 pages
Part 3	Binary Encoding	72 pages
Part 4	Clear Text Encoding	56 pages

ISO/IEC 8632:1992 (also available through ANSI)

CUR

Acronym	CURsor resource file
Origin	Windows Marketing Group Microsoft Corporation 16011 NE 36th Way Box 97017 Redmond, WA 98073-9717 Tel. (206) 882-8080
Motivation	The storage of multiple bitmaps in a resolution-independent format for the display of cursors
	The intent is to store bitmap representations of the same cursor at different resolutions. A specific application searches for the most appropriate representation given its current device
Users	Microsoft Windows 3.0 (or higher) users and application programs running under the Windows 3.0 (or higher) environment

Control	Copyrighted by	Microsoft Corporation
	Trademarks	Microsoft Windows, Windows/286, Windows/386
	Royalty Fees	None

Versions	Version 1

Overview	Major Type of Data	2D raster
	Color Representation	Monochrome; Limited color table (8 or 16 entries)
	Data Organization	Sequential; multiple bitmaps per file
	Data Encoding	Binary
	Data Compression	None

CUR   *(Continued)*

Contains 2 bitmaps per cursor:
1. A color bitmap which supplies the XOR mask for the icon
2. A monochrome bitmap which provides the AND mask that defines the transparent portion of the icon

Data Types   Bitmap data
Bitmap size
Hotspot, the "center" of the bitmap

Data Organization   General syntax of the data stream

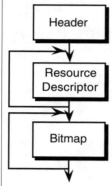

Signature
The 3rd and 4th bytes are hex(02 00), respectively, This is the resource type number (2 in LSB first format)

File Header

Byte#	Data	Details
1–2	Reserved	Must be set to zero
3–4	Reserved type	Set to 2 for a CURsor resource
5–6	# of cursor descriptions	Contained in the file

Resource Directory
There is one resource descriptor for each cursor defined in the file

Byte#	Data	Details
1	Cursor width	In Pixels
2	Cursor height	In Pixels
3	Number of Colors used	Acceptable values are 2, 8, or 16
4	Reserved	Must be set to zero
5–6	Horizontal hotspot position	In pixels
7–8	Vertical hotspot position	In pixels
9–12	Size of pixel array	In bytes
13–16	Byte offset to bitmap	From the beginning of the file

CUR   *(Continued)*

Bitmap
The bits of each pixel are packed into bytes and each scan line is padded with zeros, if necessary, to align with a 32-bit word boundary. The origin of the bitmap is the lower-left corner (Same format as BMP type files)

File Name Suffix   DOS   .CUR

References   *Microsoft Windows Programmer's Reference,* New for Version 3, edited by Microsoft Corporation; Microsoft Press, Redmond, WA, 1990, ISBN 1-55615-309-0

Microsoft Windows Software Development Kit
Call the Microsoft Information Center at (800) 426-9400 for further information

---

DDES-DEF
(IT8.4-1989; ISO 10758)

Acronym   Digital Data Exchange Standard—Device Exchange Format

Origin   IT8 (Image Technology Committee)
An accredited committee of ANSI (American National Standards Institute)
American National Standards Institute, Inc.
11 West 42nd St., 13th Floor
New York, NY 10036

The Secretariat of the IT8 Committee is:
NPES (The Association for Suppliers of Printing and Publishing Technologies)
1899 Preston White Drive
Reston, VA 22091-4367
Tel. (703) 264-7200

Motivation   To define the mechanical, electrical, protocol, and data format characteristics to allow on-line transfer of digital color proof data between Color Electronic Prepress Systems (CEPS) and Direct Digital Color Proofing (DDCP) systems

Users   Prepress systems

Control   Copyrighted by   NPES
Trademarks   None
Royalty Fees   None

Versions   IT8.4-1989   (also ISO 10758)
IT8.4a-1990   Addendum 1 for IT8.4
                    Extensions for Other Hardcopy Color Devices
IT8.4-199x   Revision currently in working group

DDES-DEF
(IT8.4-1989; ISO 10758)   *(Continued)*

Overview | Major Type of Data   2D raster
Color Representation   CMYK or color table
Data Organization   Sequential
Data Encoding   ASCII headers; binary data
Data Compression   None for color pictures; run-length for line art

This format contains data basically identical to the DDES standards UEF00 for Color Picture Data and the DDES standard UEF01 for "line art" data. The differences include the following:

- This defines a protocol for on-line device to device communications (instead of a magnetic tape file structure)

- The magnetic tape standards (UEF00 and UEF01) are based on 80-byte blocks of data. This on-line data transfer protocol is based on 128-byte blocks. The data organization is changed accordingly. Refer to the standard document for details

- Job, proof, image set, and separation information are included to allow construction of a complete proof

References | *Device Exchange Format for the On-Line Transfer of Color Proofs from Electronic Prepress Systems to Direct Digital Color Proofing Systems*, October 27, 1989, ANSI, 28 pages

Addendum 1 to ANSI IT8.4, Device Exchange Format for the On-Line Transfer of Color Proofs from Electronic Prepress Systems to Direct Digital Color Proofing Systems: Extensions for Other Hardcopy Devices, September 14, 1990, ANSI, 1 page

---

DDES-UEF00
(IT8-1988; ISO 10755)

Acronym | Digital Data Exchange Standard—User Exchange Format 00

Full name: User Exchange Format (UEF00) for the Exchange of Color Picture Data between Electronic Prepress Systems via Magnetic Tape (DDES00)

Origin | IT8 (Image Technology) Committee
An accredited committee of ANSI (American National Standards Institute)
American National Standards Institute, Inc.
11 West 42nd St., 13th Floor
New York, NY 10036

DDES-UEF00
(IT8-1988; ISO 10755)   *(Continued)*

The Secretariat of the IT8 Committee is:
NPES (The Association for Suppliers of Printing and Publishing Technologies)
1899 Preston White Drive
Reston, VA 22091-4367
Tel. (703) 264-7200

Motivation | To exchange color pictures between electronic prepress systems via magnetic tape

Users | Prepress systems

Control

Copyrighted by	NPES
Trademarks	None
Royalty Fees	None

Versions | IT8.1-1988   (Also ISO 10755)

Overview

Major Type of Data	2D raster
Color Representation	CMYK; RGB; UVL (CIE 1961 U, V, and photopic luminance); user-definable
Data Organization	Sequential
Data Encoding	ASCII header; Binary data
Data Compression	None

Data Types | Raster data
Parameters that define the order and meaning of the raster data

Data Organization | This standard specifies the overall structure of a magnetic tape, including all of the directories and headers required to store multiple files on a single tape volume

General syntax of the data stream (not including the magnetic tape file structure):

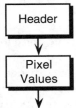

Header
Each data set contains a parameter block that defines its color picture data. This is referred to in the standard as User Header Label 3 (UHL3) (Parameter Block). Its contents are shown below. All values are coded as ASCII text (EUEF stands for Extended User Exchange Format)

DDES-UEF00
(IT8-1988; ISO 10755)   *(Continued)*

Byte#	Data	Details
1–4	Tag	"UHL3"
5–6	Format of data	The pixel order (see below)
7–8	Number of color separations (values/entry in color tables)	Always "04" for UEF "01 to "16" allowed in EUEF
9–12	Sequence of colors	e.g., "CMYK" or "YMCK" or "RGB"
13–24	Sequence of colors (Continued)	Not used for UEF—all blanks; allows for up to 16 color separations in EUEF
25–28	Color value for 0% dot	
29–32	Color value for 100% dot	
33–42	Length of line	In millimeters
43–52	Breadth of area	In millimeters
53–58	Number of pixels/line	
59–64	Number of lines	
65–66	Orientation	9 possible (See below)
67	Units of resolution (line)	"I" pixels per inch; "M" pixels per mm
68	Units of resolution (breadth)	"I" pixels per inch; "M" pixels per mm
69–74	Resolution of line	Optional
75–80	Resolution of breadth	Optional

Format of Data (pixel order)

00: Pixel Interleaving	Color values for each pixel are stored together
01: Line Interleaving	Values for color separation 1 of line 1 are stored together; values for color separation 2 line 1 are stored next; color separation 3 line 1, etc.
02: Color Interleaving	All values for the first color separation are stored first, then all values of the second separation, etc.

The ordering of the data values in the "sequence of color" field above determines what each color separation "means." For example, if the field contains "CMYK," then the pixel values represent cyan, magenta, yellow, and black. If the field contains "YMCK" then the values represent yellow, magenta, cyan, and black

Color Values
The color values are unsigned bytes in the range from 0 to 255. The 0% and 100% dot values specified in the header create a linear scale in which all color values are interpreted

DDES-UEF00
(IT8-1988; ISO 10755)   *(Continued)*

Picture Orientation

There are nine pixel orderings defined. Support of the last 04–08 is optional. Note that the meaning of "line" and "breadth" is different for different orientations

Orientation Code	"Line"	"Breadth"
00: Load from top left, horizontally	Horiz.-left to right	Top-bottom
01: Load from top left, vertically	Vert.-top to bottom	Left-right
02: Load from bottom left, horizontally	Horiz.-left to right	Top-bottom
03: Load from bottom left, vertically	Vert.-bottom to top	Left-right
04: Load from top right, horizontally	Horiz.-right to left	Bottom-top
05: Load from top right, vertically	Vert.-top to bottom	Right-left
06: Load from bottom right, horizontally	Horiz.-right to left	Bottom-top
07: Load from bottom right, vertically	Vert.-bottom to top	Right-left
09: Orientation unknown		

References | *User Exchange Format (UEF00) for the Exchange of Color Picture Data between Electronic Prepress Systems via Magnetic Tape (DDES00)*, July 5, 1988, ANSI, 11 pages

---

DDES-UEF01
(IT8.2-1988; ISO 10756)

Acronym | Digital Data Exchange Standard—User Exchange Format 01

Full name: User Exchange Format (UEF00) for the Exchange of *Line Art Data* between Electronic Prepress Systems via Magnetic Tape (DDES00)

Origin | IT8 (Image Technology) Committee
An accredited committee of ANSI (American National Standards Institute)
American National Standards Institute, Inc.
11 West 42nd St., 13th Floor
New York, NY 10036

The Secretariat of the IT8 Committee is:
NPES (The Association for Suppliers of Printing and Publishing Technologies)
1899 Preston White Drive
Reston, VA 22091-4367
Tel. (703) 264-7200

Motivation | The exchange of raster images that have a limited number of colors, and have contiguous areas of pixels with the same color. The exchange is targeted for data exchange between prepress systems via magnetic tape

Users | Prepress systems

DDES-UEF01
(IT8.2-1988; ISO 10756) *(Continued)*

Control	Copyrighted by	NPES
	Trademarks	None
	Royalty Fees	None
Versions	IT8.2-1988	(Also ISO 10756)
Overview	Major Type of Data	2D raster
	Color Representation	CMYK in a Color Table; RGB; UVL (CIE 1961 U, V, photopic luminance); user-definable
	Data Organization	Sequential
	Data Encoding	ASCII header; Binary data
	Data Compression	Run-length

Data Types Raster data
Parameters that define the order and meaning of the raster data
Color table

Data Organization This standard specifies the overall structure of a magnetic tape, including all of the directories and headers required to store multiple files on a single tape volume

General syntax of the data stream (not including the file structure of the magnetic tape):

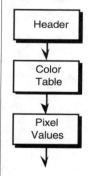

Header
Each data set contains a parameter block that defines its raster data. This is referred to in the standard as User Header Label 3 (UHL3) (Parameter Block). Its contents are shown below. All values are coded as ASCII text (EUEF stands for Extended User Exchange Format)

Byte#	Data	Details
1–4	Tag	"UHL3"
5–6	Format of data	Always "30"—color line art data
7–8	Number of color separations (values/entry in color tables)	Always "04" for UEF "01 to "16" allowed in EUEF
9–12	Sequence of colors	e.g., "CMYK" or "YMCK" or "RGB"
13–24	Sequence of colors (Continued)	Not used for UEF—all blanks; allows for up to 16 color separations in EUEF
25–28	Color value for 0% dot	
29–32	Color value for 100% dot	
33–42	Length of line	In millimeters
43–52	Breadth of area	In millimeters
53–58	Number of pixels/line	
59–64	Number of lines	
65–66	Orientation	9 possible (See below)
67	Units of resolution (line)	"I" pixels per inch; "M" pixels per mm
68	Units of resolution (breadth)	"I" pixels per inch; "M" pixels per mm
69–74	Resolution of line	Optional
75–80	Resolution of breadth	Optional

Picture Orientation

There are nine pixel orderings defined. Support of the last five (04–08) is optional. Note that the meaning of "line" and "breadth" is different for different orientations

Orientation Code	"Line"	"Breadth"
00: Load from top left, horizontally	Horiz.-left to right	Top-bottom
01: Load from top left, vertically	Vert.-top to bottom	Left-right
02: Load from bottom left, horizontally	Horiz.-left to right	Top-bottom
03: Load from bottom left, vertically	Vert.-bottom to top	Left-right
04: Load from top right, horizontally	Horiz.-right to left	Bottom-top
05: Load from top right, vertically	Vert.-top to bottom	Right-left
06: Load from bottom right, horizontally	Horiz.-right to left	Bottom-top
07: Load from bottom right, vertically	Vert.-bottom to top	Right-left
09: Orientation unknown		

DDES-UEF01
(IT8.2-1988; ISO 10756) *(Continued)*

Color Table

Each data set contains a parameter block that defines its color table. This is referred to in the standard as User Header Label 4 (UHL4). Its contents are shown below. All values are coded as ASCII text

Byte#	Data	Details
1–4	Tag	"UHL4"
5–8	Last valid color number used	Possible values (1–255)
9–12	Number of bits for each color number	"0008"
13–16	Number of bits for short run-length	"0008"
17–20	Number of bits for extended run-length	"0000" or "00016"
21–80	Reserved for expansion	Set to all blanks

Following the color table header is the color table. It uses one 8,192-byte data block on the tape. The block contains from 1 to 256 color entries, each 20 bytes long as shown below

Byte#	Data	Details
1	Reserved	For future DDES use
2	Color number (index)	Binary value between 1 and 254; 0 and 255 are reserved for the run-length encoding scheme
3–4	Transparency flags	UEF: only bits 0–3 of byte 4 are used; EUEF: 1 flag per color value (up to 16)
5–20	Color values	UEF: only bytes 5–8 are used; EUEF: up to 16 color values are possible

The ordering of the data values in each entry of the color table is determined by the "sequence of color" field in the header. For example, if the field contains "CMYK," then the pixel values represent cyan, magenta, yellow, and black. If the field contains "YMCK" then the values represent yellow, magenta, cyan, black

Color Values

The color values are unsigned bytes in the range from 0 to 255. The 0% and 100% dot values specified in the header create a linear scale from which all color values are interpreted

DDES-UEF01
(IT8.2-1988; ISO 10756)   *(Continued)*

Pixel Data Values

The pixel indexes into the color table are ordered according the picture orientation described above. A run-length encoding scheme is used to compress the data

File Name Suffix	NA
References	*User Exchange Format (UEF00) for the Exchange of Line Art Data between Electronic Prepress Systems via Magnetic Tape (DDES00)*, December 14, 1988, ANSI, 14 pages

---

DDES-UEF02
(IT8.3-1990; ISO 10757)

Acronym	Digital Data Exchange Standard—User Exchange Format 02
	Full name: User Exchange Format (UEF02) for the Exchange of *Geometric Data* between Electronic Prepress Systems via Magnetic Tape (DDES00)
Origin	IT8 (Image Technology) Committee An accredited committee of ANSI (American National Standards Institute) American National Standards Institute, Inc. 11 West 42nd St., 13th Floor New York, NY 10036
	The Secretariat of the IT8 Committee is: NPES (The Association for Suppliers of Printing and Publishing Technologies) 1899 Preston White Drive Reston, VA 22091-4367 Tel. (703) 264-7200
Motivation	The exchange of geometric data that consists of page geometry, image placement data, and simple geometric page elements. The exchange is targeted for data exchange between prepress systems via magnetic tape
Users	Prepress systems
Control	Copyrighted by NPES Trademarks None Royalty Fees None
Versions	IT8.3-1990 (Also ISO 10757)

DDES-UEF02
(IT8.3-1990; ISO 10757) *(Continued)*

Overview
Major Type of Data	2D geometry data
Color Representation	RGB or Color Table (9 predefined entries)
Data Organization	Sequential
Data Encoding	ASCII headers; binary data
Data Compression	None

Data Types The following types of IGES defined entities are supported. The data types place some restrictions on the original IGES definitions. For example, the *Z* values for all entities must be zero; only 2D data is allowed. Refer to the IGES data format for a brief description of these data types

Point	Rectangle
Circular Arc	Line
Offset Curve	Composite Curve
Copious Data	Conic Arc
Transformation Matrix	Parametric Spline
Line Font	General Note
Associativity Instance	Color
Properties	

(Implementor-defined entity developed by the IT8 committee)

Data Organization This standard specifies the overall structure of a magnetic tape, including all of the directories and headers required to store multiple files on a single tape volume. These details are outside the range of our discussion here

General syntax of the data stream (not including the magnetic tape file structure):

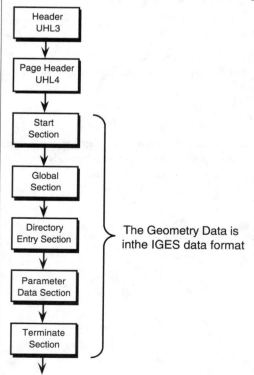

DDES-UEF02
(IT8.3-1990; ISO 10757) *(Continued)*

Header

Each data set contains a parameter block that identifies this as geometry data and establishes the page size. This is referred to in the standard as User Header Label 3 (UHL3) (Parameter Block). Its contents are shown below. All values are coded as ASCII text

Byte#	Data	Details
1–4	Tag	"UHL3"
5–6	Format of data	Always "40"—geometry data
7–32	Reserved	Set to all blanks
33–42	Length of page	In millimeters (untrimmed)
43–52	Breadth of page	In millimeters (untrimmed)
53–64	Reserved	Set to all blanks
65–66	Orientation	Same as UEF00 (Refer to its description)
67–80	Reserved	Set to all blanks

Header (page layout)

The User Header Label 4 (UHL4) contains the following data. All values are coded as ASCII text. A description of the data is shown in the diagram below

Byte#	Data	Details
1–4	Tag	"UHL4"
5–10	UEF flag	"UEF 02" or "EUEF02"
11–20	Page trim size X	
21–30	Page trim size Y	
31–36	Head margin	
37–42	Foot margin	
43–48	Left margin	
49–54	Right margin	
55–60	Head bleed	
61–66	Foot bleed	
67–72	Left bleed	
73–78	Right bleed	
79	Page type	0: undefined; 1: left handed; 2: right handed
80	Reserved	For future use; set to blank

DDES-UEF02
(IT8.3-1990; ISO 10757)   *(Continued)*

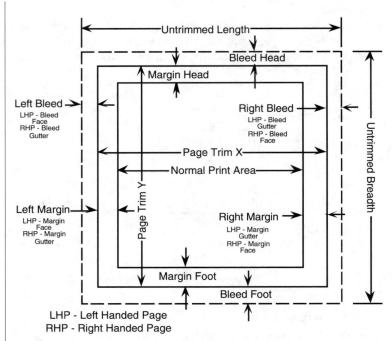

Page Dimensions

Geometry Data

The geometry data is stored in a IGES data format and supports the limited number of data types listed above in the Data Types section. Refer to the IGES data format for a description

File Name Suffix	NA
References	*User Exchange Format (UEF02) for the Exchange of Geometric Data between Electronic Prepress Systems via Magnetic Tape (DDES00)*, March 9, 1990, ANSI, 28 pages

---

DDES-UEF03
(IT8-1988; ISO 10759)

Acronym	Digital Data Exchange Standard—User Exchange Format 03
	Full name: User Exchange Format (UEF03) for the Exchange of *Monochrome Image Data* between Electronic Prepress Systems via Magnetic Tape (DDES00)

DDES-UEF03
(IT8-1988; ISO 10759)   *(Continued)*

Origin	IT8 (Image Technology) Committee
	An accredited committee of ANSI (American National Standards Institute)
	American National Standards Institute, Inc.
	11 West 42nd St., 13th Floor
	New York, NY 10036
	The Secretariat of the IT8 Committee is:
	NPES (The Association for Suppliers of Printing and Publishing Technologies)
	1899 Preston White Drive
	Reston, VA 22091-4367
	Tel. (703) 264-7200
Motivation	To exchange monochrome images between color and monochrome electronic pre-press systems of different manufacture via magnetic tape
	A monochrome image is defined as a rectangular array of picture elements (pixels) with varying grades of intensity of a single color (which is not necessarily black or white)
Users	Prepress systems
Control	Copyrighted by NPES
	Trademarks None
	Royalty Fees None
Versions	IT8.5-1990 (also ISO 10759)
Overview	Major Type of Data 2D raster
	Color Representation · CMYK; RGB; UVL (CIE 1961 U, V, photopic luminance); user-definable
	Data Organization Sequential
	Data Encoding ASCII header; Binary data
	Data Compression None for Monochrome Pictures and Binary Pictures; run-length for Binary Line Art
Data Types	Raster data
	Parameters that define the order and meaning of the raster data
Data Organization	This standard specifies the overall structure of a magnetic tape, including all of the directories and headers required to store multiple files on a single tape volume

DDES-UEF03
(IT8-1988; ISO 10759)   *(Continued)*

General syntax of the data stream (not including the magnetic tape file structure):

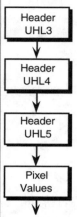

Header (UHL3)

Each data set contains a parameter block that defines its picture data. This is referred to in the standard as User Header Label 3 (UHL3) (Parameter Block). Its contents are shown below. All values are coded as ASCII text. (EUEF stands for Extended User Exchange Format.)

Byte #	Data	Details
1–4	Tag	"UHL3"
5–6	Format of data	"20": Monochrome picture format; "21": Binary picture format; "22": Binary line art format
7–8	Number of color separations	Always "04" for UEF
9–12	Sequence of colors	e.g., "CMYK", "YMCK", or "RGB"
13–24	Sequence of colors (Continued)	Not used for UEF—all blanks; allows for up to 16 colors separation in EUEF
25–28	Color value for 0% dot	
29–32	Color value for 100% dot	
33–42	Length of line	In millimeters
43–52	Breadth of area	In millimeters
53–58	Number of pixels/line	
59–64	Number of lines	
65–66	Orientation	The pixel order (See description in UEF00)
67	Units of resolution of line	"I" pixels per inch; "M" pixels per mm
68	Units of resolution (breadth)	"I" pixels per inch; "M" pixels per mm
69–74	Resolution of line	Optional
75–80	Resolution of breadth	Optional

DDES-UEF03
(IT8-1988; ISO 10759)   *(Continued)*

Image Color Header (UHL4)

Byte #	Data	Details
1–4	Tag	"UHL4"
5	Image color indicator	"0": Color not defined in header; "1": Color defined in header; "2": Full transparency: color not defined in header
6	Background color indicator	Same as above; 0, 1, or 2
7–22	Image color values	4 values as designated by "sequence of colors" above
23–70	Image color values	Not used for UEF—all blanks; allows for up to 16 values in EUEF mode
71–73	Value for 0% pixel intensity	
75–78	Value for 100% intensity	
79–80	Reserved	For future use

Background Color Header (UHL5)

Byte #	Data	Details
1–4	Tag	"UHL5"
5–20	Background color values	4 values as designated by "sequence of colors" above
21–68	Background color values	Allows for EUEF (up to 16)
69–80	Reserved	For future use

Pixel Data

Three different types of data are defined:
- Monochrome Pictures   One 8-bit intensity value per pixel
- Binary Pictures   One bit per pixel (0: background; 1: image)
- Binary Line Art   One bit per pixel; run-length encoded

File Name Suffix   NA

References   *User Exchange Format (UEF03) for the Exchange of Monochrome Image Data between Electronic Prepress Systems via Magnetic Tape (DDES00)*, December 15, 1989, ANSI, 12 pages

DXF

Acronym	Drawing eXchange File
Origin	Autodesk Inc. 2320 Marinship Way Sausalito, CA 94965 Tel. (415) 332-2344
Motivation	The interchange of "drawing" data produced by AutoCAD software with other application programs
Users	It is the most widely used CAD interchange format, and is supported by virtually every CAD software vendor

Control		
	Copyrighted by	Autodesk Inc.
	Trademarks	AutoCAD, AutoCAD 2, AutoCAD-80, AutoCAD-86, 3D Level 1, CAD/camera
	Royalty Fees	None

Versions	NA

Overview		
	Major Type of Data	3D and 2D geometry
	Color Representation	Indexed (256 values; indexes 0–7 are predefined)
	Data Organization	Sequential
	Data Encoding	ASCII text; alternate binary format
	Data Compression	None

Data Organization

General syntax of the data stream:

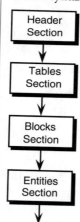

The file is composed of a stream of data groups. Each group is composed of two lines of ASCII text. The first line is a single integer code value which identifies the data value on the second line. The data value on the second line can be an integer, floating-point, or string value. Using this scheme, data groups that are not recognizable by a DXF software decoder can be easily skipped and ignored

DXF *(Continued)*

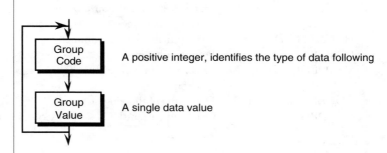

Group Code — A positive integer, identifies the type of data following

Group Value — A single data value

An example of 3 groups that define a variable in the header section is shown below. The comments to the right are not part of the file and would not be included in the file

9	Group code: string data follows—a variable name identifier
$VIEWCTR	Group value: the variable name identifier (center point of a view)
10	Group code: floating point value follows—primary *X* coordinate
7.38	Group value: *X* coordinate of viewing center point
20	Group code: floating point value follows—primary *Y* coordinate
4.5	Group value: *Y* coordinate of viewing center point

Signature

None prespecified, but the following are unique enough to function as a signature

ASCII encoding — Look for first group code:
0
SECTION
i.e., in ASCII, 2 blanks, zero, carriage return, 'SECTION'.
in Hex 20 20 30 13 53 45 43 54 49 4F 4E 0D

Binary encoding — First 22 bytes is the following ASCII string:
"AutoCAD Binary DXF<CR><LF><SUB><NUL>"

Header Section

Contains setting of variables associated with the drawing. The variables can be listed in any order. The following lists ten arbitrary examples of the possible 136 different variables

$ANGDIR	Angle direction; 1: clockwise, 0: counterclockwise
$AXISUNIT	Axis *X* and *Y* tick spacing
$DIMRND	Rounding value for dimension distances
$FILLETRAD	Fillet radius

DXF   *(Continued)*

$HANDLING	Handles enabled if nonzero; allows the tagging of elements to represent associations
$HANDLSEED	Next available handle number
$PDMODE	Point display mode
$SHADEDIF	Percent of ambient/diffuse light, range 1–100, default 70
$TDCREATE	Date/time of drawing creation
$UCSORG	Origin of current UCS—User Coordinate System

Tables Section

Contains zero to 8 tables. The tables are as follows:

LTYPE	Line-type definitions: dash spacing, patterns, etc.
LAYER	Layers definitions: color for layer, line-type for layer, etc.
STYLE	Text font definitions: font name, height, width, obliquing angle
VIEW	Viewport definitions: window size, front and back clipping planes, twist angle
VPORT	Viewport definitions: same as VIEW, but includes grids, snapping, and zoom information
DIMSTYLE	Dimension style definitions
UCS	User Coordinate System definition
APPID	Maintains a unique index for a given registered application name, used to resolve external references to other drawing files

Blocks Section

Contains block definitions, which are simply groups of entities. A BLOCK and ENDBLK group delimit the entities in each group. The entities are defined in the same format as in the Entities Section

Entities Section

Contains the descriptions of the drawing primitives. The following primitives are supported: (each description lists the typical parameters)

Line	A start point and end point
Point	x, y, and z coordinates, (plus orientation of UCS)
Circle	Center point, radius
Arc	Center point, radius, start angle, end angle
Trace	A wide line; defined by 4 points
Solid	A solid filled planar region; either a quadrilateral region (4 points) or a triangular region (3 points)
Text	Text to display; insertion point, height, rotation angle, font style, other various attributes
Shape	A predefined entity composed of lines, arcs, and circles (they are optimized blocks); insertion point, size, shape name, rotation angle, X-scale factor

DXF   *(Continued)*

	Insert	Attributes, block name, insertion point, *X*-scale factor, *Y*-scale factor, *Z*-scale factor, rotation angle, column and row counts, column and row spacing (an instance of a block entity)
	Attdef	Sets up a template to define the attributes of blocks;
	Attrib	Attribute definition; text start, text attributes, etc.
	Polyline	A group of line and arc segments treated as a single entity; vertices list, various attributes
	Vertex	A point on a curve, spline, or polyface
	Seqend	Ends a sequence of entities (such as a sequence of vertices or attributes
	3Dface	Four points defining the corners of a three-dimensional face
	Viewport	A rectangular region for clipping the drawing to a particular area of the "paper"; center point, width, height
	Dimension	One of five different types: linear, angular, angular (3-point), diameter, radius, ordinate; (too many details to list here)
	Extended Entity Data	Application specific data; not predefined
File Name Suffix	DOS	.DXF
References	*AutoCAD Users manual,* Version 11, Appendix C, pages 527–557 Contact AutoDesk	

EPS (EPSF)

Acronym	EPS—Encapsulated PostScript or EPSF—Encapsulated PostScript File
Origin	Adobe Systems Incorporated 1585 Charleston Rd. P.O. Box 7900 Mountain View, CA 94039-7900
Motivation	The description of a *single picture* (which can be a whole page) that can be included, or "encapsulated," in another PostScript file or that can be "read into" an application specific program (e.g., a paint program, or a document editor) for combination with the content of an application
Users	Programs that share "single pages" of graphical data with other programs. EPS data sets are widely supported by both paint programs (raster-based) and CAD programs (geometry-based)

EPS (EPSF) *(Continued)*

Control	Copyrighted by	Adobe Systems Incorporated
	Trademarks	PostScript, Display PostScript, Adobe, Adobe Illustrator
	Royalty Fees	The trademark, PostScript, cannot be used to identify any product not originating from or licensed by Adobe. No royalties are required to write programs in the PostScript language, or to write drivers which generate PostScript output, or to write PostScript interpreters

Versions	Version 1.0
	Version 2.0
	Version 3.0

Overview	Major Type of Data	2D geometry; 2D raster; text
	Color Representation	All PostScript supported color spaces
	Data Organization	Sequential
	Data Encoding	ASCII; binary encoding possible but discouraged
	Data Compression	All PostScript supported filters; more portable if no compression is used

Data Types See the PostScript description for a list of data types and operators

Data Organization An EPS file is identical to a PostScript file with the following exceptions

One critical aspect of an EPS data set is that it must leave the definition of all variables and the contents of all stacks unchanged after it is processed. Because of this, some PostScript operators cannot be included in an EPS data set; using them modifies the PostScript environment in such a way that it can not be restored. The following operators are *illegal* in an EPS file:

banddevice, clear, cleardictstack, copypage, erasepage, exitserver, framedevice, grestoreall, initclip, initgraphics, initmatrix, quit, renderbands, setglobal, setpagedevice, setshare, startjob

The following operators are *restricted.* They must be used to restore the state of the PostScript environment

nulldevice, setgstate, sethalftone, setmatrix, setscreen, settransfer, undefinefont

There are two required header comments as shown below. For a discussion of PostScript comments, refer to the PostScript Appendix

```
%!PS-Adobe-3.0 EPSF-3.0
%%BoundingBox: lower-left-x lower-left-y upper-right-x upper-right-y
```

An EPS data set may optionally include a preview raster which may be a Macintosh PICT resource, a TIFF file, a device dependent hex bitmap, or an EPSI

File Name Suffix	DOS	.EPS	(If no preview image exists in the file)
		.EPI	(If a preview image exists in the file)

EPS (EPSF) *(Continued)*

Macintosh	file type EPSF	
All other Systems	.epsf	No preview image exists in the file
	.epsi	Interchange format

References | Adobe Systems Incorporated, *PostScript Language Reference Manual, Second Edition*, Addison-Wesley, Reading, MA, 1990, Appendix H, pages 709–736, ISBN 0-201-18127-4

EPSI

Acronym | EPSI—Encapsulated PostScript Interchange format

Origin | Adobe Systems Incorporated
1585 Charleston Rd.
P.O. Box 7900
Mountain View, CA 94039-7900

Motivation | A simple encoding of a "preview" image of a EPS data set.

Users | Files that contain both a EPS data set and a preview image of the data

Control | Copyrighted by | Adobe Systems Incorporated
| Trademarks | PostScript, Display PostScript, Adobe, Adobe Illustrator
| Royalty Fees | The trademark, PostScript, cannot be used to identify any product not originating from or licensed by Adobe. No royalties are required to write programs in the PostScript language, or to write drivers which generate PostScript output, or to write PostScript interpreters

Versions | NA

Overview | Major Type of Data | 2D raster
| Color Representation | Monochrome or grayscale
| Data Organization | Sequential; 2D array
| Data Encoding | ASCII text (of hexadecimal digits)
| Data Compression | None

Data Types | Raster samples

Data Organization | The preview section of an EPSI data set is composed of a single header line followed by the raster samples. The header line is

```
%%BeginPreview: width height depth lines
```

EPSI *(Continued)*

where, *width* is the number of samples in the horizontal direction, *height* is the number of samples in the vertical direction, *depth* is the number of bits per sample value (typically 1, 2, 4, or 8),and *lines* is the number of ASCII text lines that contain the data (included so that the data can be skipped if it is unwanted)

The sample values are packed into consecutive bytes and encoded as ASCII characters that represent hexadecimal digits (2 per byte)

The samples are ordered by rows from left to right and each row is ordered from bottom to top

Example   The following example contains a simple data set that represents a 16 × 16 monochrome image (1 bit per pixel) with a line around its boundary. (Note: a hexadecimal F represents 1111, an 8 represents 1000, and 1 represents 0001)

```
%%BeginPreview: 16 16 1 2
%FFFF8001800180018001800180018001
%8001800180018001800180018001FFFF
%%EndPreview
```

File Name   DOS   .EPS   No preview image exists in the file
Suffix   .EPI   Preview image exists in the file

              Macintosh   File type EPSF

              All other systems   epsf   No preview image exists in the file
                                           epsi   Interchange format

References   Adobe Systems Incorporated, *PostScript Language Reference Manual, Second Edition*, Addison-Wesley, Reading, MA, 1990, Appendix H, pages 730–732, ISBN 0-201-18127-4

FITS

Acronym   Flexible Image Transport System

Origin   International Astronomical Union (IAU)

Later formalized as a standard by:
NASA Science Data Systems Standards Office (NSDSSO)
National Space Science Data Center (NSSDC)
National Aeronautics and Space Administration (NASA)
NASA Goddard Space Flight Center
Greenbelt, MD 20771

Motivation   To transfer astronomical data from one installation to another

FITS *(Continued)*

Users	All spacecraft projects and astrophysics data archives under the management of the Astrophysics Division of NASA are required to make processed data available to users in the FITS data format	
Control	Copyrighted by	IAU
	Trademarks	None
	Royalty Fees	None
Versions	1982	Initial specification
	1988	IAU ASCII Tables extension
	1990	NASA specification
Overview	Major Type of Data	Raster; N-dimensional ($N \le 999$)
	Color Representation	None
	Data Organization	Sequential; N-dimensional array—column major order
	Data Encoding	ASCII text header; binary data values
	Data Compression	None

Data Types The primary data keywords are listed to indicate the range of data that can be represented (The extension keywords are not listed here)

Mandatory principle keywords:

BITPIX	Bits per pixel; one of 8, 16, 32, or 64
NAXIS	Number of axes; the number of dimensions of the data array
NAXISn	The number of positions along axis n; this is defined for each separate axis

Optional data array keywords:

BSCALE	Used when the array pixel values are not the true physical values; used with the BZERO value
BZERO	Same as BSCALE; used in the equation: physical-value = BZERO + BSCALE * array-value
BUNIT	The name of the physical units associated with the data values
BLANK	Defines a special integer value that is used to represent data values that are undefined
CTYPEn	The physical coordinates of axis n
CRPIXn	The location of a reference point along axis n
CROTAn	A rotation from a standard coordinate system to the data values coordinate system
CRVALn	The value of the coordinate specified by the CTYPEn keyword at the reference pixel CRPIXn
CDELTn	The partial derivative of the coordinate specified by CTYPEn
DATAMAX	The maximum physical value represented in the array
DATAMIN	The minimum physical value represented in the array

FITS *(Continued)*

Optional documentation keywords

AUTHOR	Individual who compiled the header information
COMMENT	General comments
DATE	Date of data creation
DATE-OBS	Day when the data was observed
EQUINOX	Equinox for the celestial coordinate system in which positions given in the data are expressed
HISTORY	History of steps and procedures associated with the data processing
INSTRUME	Instrument used to acquire the data
OBJECT	The name of the objects observed
OBSERVER	Individual who acquired the data
ORIGIN	Organization creating the data
REFERENC	Any references to published portions of the data
TELESCOP	The telescope used to acquire the data

Data Organization

General syntax of data stream

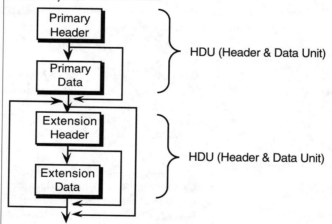

Signature
None

Primary Header
Data parameters are stored as (keyword, value) pairs, one per 80 character line. All data in the header is ASCII text and is positioned in fixed column fields as shown

Columns:	1–8	9	10	11–80
Data:	Keyword	"="	blank	value associated with keyword

A group of 36 "card images," each 80 bytes long, make up a single logical record (This comes from the time when FITS's data was stored on magnetic tape using 2,880 byte blocks). If there are more than 36 keywords, subsequent logical records are used. All unused bytes must be set to ASCII blanks (character code 32)

FITS *(Continued)*

Primary Data
The data values are encoded in binary representations specified by the BITPIX (bits per pixel) keyword. The encoding options include 8-bit, 16-bit, or 32-bit integers, or 32-bit or 64-bit IEEE-754 floating point. All values within a particular data set use the same data type and precision. They are organized in column major order (FORTRAN style). Nothing separates one data value from the next

Extended Header and Data
There are several defined extensions to this data model, including the ASCII Table Extension, the Random Groups Extension, and the Binary Table Extension. Related keywords are defined for each one. Other, user specific extensions can be defined and registered with the NSDSSO. The registration guarantees uniqueness

File Name Suffix	None—the storage on individual systems is system dependent
References	Wells, D.C., Greisen, E.W., and Harten, R.H., "FITS: a flexible image transport system," *Astronomy and Astrophysics Supplement Series,* Vol. 44, pages 363–370, 1981
	A copy of the FITS Draft Standard by NASA is available by anonymous FTP from *nssdca.gsfc.nasa.gov,* in the subdirectory FITS

FLI, FLC

Acronym	FLI—Flic Files: Autodesk Animator FLC—Flic Files: Autodesk Animator Pro, 3D Studio
Origin	Autodesk Animator Autodesk Inc. 2320 Marinship Way Sausalito, CA 94965 Tel. (415) 332-2344 Original Author: Jim Kent Current Support: Autodesk Multimedia Developer Support
Motivation	Efficient storage of a series of frames (i.e., images) that create an animation. Only the differences between frames is stored
Users	Autodesk Animator software users
Control	Copyrighted by None Trademarks Autodesk Animator, Autodesk Animator Pro Royalty Fees None

FLI, FLC   *(Continued)*

Versions	Version 1.0 FLI	Supports only 320 × 200 pixel images
	Version 1.0 FLC	Supports any size image and 256 entry color tables
Overview	Major Type of Data	2D raster; animation
	Color Representation	Color table
	Data Organization	Sequential
	Data Encoding	Binary
	Data Compression	None, run-length delta encoding
Data Types	Number of frames in animation sequence	
	Size of images	
	Speed of display	
	Raster image data	

Data Organization   General syntax of the data stream:

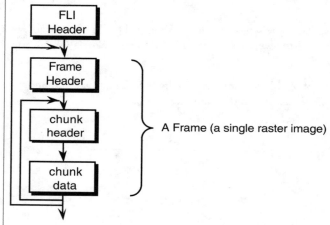

Signature
Bytes 5 and 6 set to hexadecimal AF11

FLI Header
A 128-byte header with the following data values (stored in LSB first)
Note: This is the FLI header which is a subset of the FLC header

FLI, FLC *(Continued)*

Byte#	Data	Details
1–4	Size	Length of file in bytes
5–6	Magic	Hex AF11 for FLI files Hex AF12 for FLC files
7–8	Frames	Number of frames (maximum = 4000)
9–10	Width	Screen width FLI:320; FLC:320,640, 800, 1280
11–12	Height	Screen height FLI: 200; FLC:200, 480, 600, 1024
13–14	Depth	Bits per pixel (always 8)
15–16	Flags	Always 0 in a FLI file
17–18	Speed	Number of video ticks between frames; each tick is 1/70 of a second.
19–22	Next	Set to 0
23–26	Frit	Set to 0
27–128	Expand	All zeroes; for future expansion

The big idea is to store only the differences between consecutive frames and not the entire contents of each frame

Frame Header

Byte#	Data	Details
1–4	Size	Length of frame in bytes (must be ≤ 64K)
5–6	Magic	Always hex F1FA
7–8	Chunks	Number of chunks in frame
9–16	Expand	Space for future enhancements (all 0s)

The data for a frame is divided into *chunks* of data. If the color table changes from one frame to the next, then the first chunk contains a color table. The second chunk contains the pixel data in one of several different possible formats

Chunks

Byte#	Data	Details
1–4	Size	Length of chunk in bytes
5–6	Type	Type of chunk (see below)
7–Size	Data	The color or pixel data

FLI, FLC *(Continued)*

Type	Name	Description
4	FLI_COLOR256	Compressed color table (color range from 0 to 255)
7	FLI_SS2	Word-oriented delta compressed line data (FLC only)
11	FLI_COLOR	Compressed color table (color range from 0 to 63)
12	FLI_LC	Byte-oriented delta compressed line data
13	FLI_BLACK	Set whole screen to background color (color 0)
15	FLI_BRUN	Byte run-length compression (1st frame only)
16	FLI_COPY	Uncompressed pixels; 64,000 bytes (320 × 200)
18	FLI_PSTAMP	Postage stamp sized image (FLC only)

All chunks are aligned to word (even address) byte offsets

FLI_COLOR and FLI_COLOR256 chunk

A color chunk is divided into packets. A packet is composed of a skip value, a change value, and a set of RGB values as shown below. The RGB values in the FLI_COLOR chunk are limited to a range from 0 to 63. The RGB values in the FLI_COLOR256 chunk are limited to a range from 0 to 255

Byte#	Data	Details
1–2	Size	Number of packets in chunk
3	Skip	Number of colors to skip in the color table
4	Change	Number of color RGB values that follow (0 means 256)
5	Red	
6	Green	New entry for color table
7	Blue	
...	...	More RGB values
...	...	Possibly more packets (i.e., skip, change, RGB values)

FLI_LC (Line Coded) (FLI only)

Byte#	Data	Details
1–2	Unchanged lines	Number of lines in this frame that are unchanged from the previous frame
3–4	Number of changed lines	Number of scan lines in this chunk
5	Set of compressed lines:	Compressed pixel data
...	...	

Compressed Line

Byte#	Data	Details
n	Starting *x* position	Starting position on this scan line for data
n	Packet count	Number of packets for this scan line
n+1 ...	Set of run-length packets ...	0 or more run-length packets

Run-length Packet

Byte#	Data	Details
n	Skip count	Number of pixels to skip on a scan line from current location
n+1	Size count	>0: *count* bytes follow <0: one byte follows; repeat |*count*| times
(*n*+2) –	Data	

FLI_SS2
This chunk is similar to the FLI_LC chunk except it is word-oriented (2 bytes) instead of byte-oriented

FLI_BLACK
No data is stored in this chunk; it is used to clear the screen to the background color (index 0)

FLI_BRUN (Byte Run-length)
Exactly like the FLI_LC chunk above—except there are no "skip count" values in each run-length packet. The entire image is run-length encoded

FLI_COPY
There is no compression. The chunk contains exactly (image width) × (image height) bytes that define an image in scan-line order from left to right and top to bottom. For FLI files the chunk contains 64,000 bytes for a 320 × 200 pixel image

File Name Suffix	DOS	.FLI .FLC
References	Autodesk Animator Pro Flic Files (FLC), Autodesk Animator Pro Manual, Autodesk	
	A document that summarizes the FLI format can be accessed from the Internet. Using anonymous FTP connect to *zamenhof.cs.rice.edu* and access the subdirectory /pub/graphics.formats	

FLUX

Acronym	None
Origin	apE—Software for Visualization The Ohio Supercomputer Center 1224 Kinnear Road Columbus, OH 43212 Currently sold and supported by: TaraVisual Corporation 929 Harrison Avenue Columbus, OH 43215 Tel. (800) 458-8731
Motivation	A flexible data description language that supports hierarchical data relationships and that is portable to many computing platforms
Users	Users of the apE software system
Control	Copyrighted by The Ohio State University Trademarks apE Royalty Fees None
Versions	NA
Overview	Major Type of Data 2D raster; 3D raster; 3D geometric Color Representation Monochrome; 256 colormap; RGB; RGB + matte Data Organization Sequential; hierarchy of "groups" Data Encoding ASCII text headers; ASCII or binary data Data Compression None

Data Types   The data language supports the following major data types:

Comments	User comments, not interpreted as data
Command/Field	A call to a command (procedure) along with its associated arguments
Array	N-dimensional arrays stored in row major order
Group	A collection of Flux entities (including other groups)
Reference	A pointer to one or more instances of other groups

Predefined groups include the following

Colormap group	Defines a set of 245 color tuples (red, green, blue)
Grid group	Provide a geometric layout that determines how variable values are mapped spatially; three types: *uniform:* equal spacing, uniform distance grid *scatter:* equal spacing, nonuniform distance grid *hybrid:* nonequal spacing, nonuniform distance grid
Image group	2D raster data; supports 1, 8, 24, and 32 bits per pixel
Light group	The color, position, and characteristics of lights in a digital scene

FLUX   *(Continued)*

Object group	Allows lower-level physical structures (e.g., part, sphere, or grid) to be grouped in a hierarchical structure and positioned relative to their parents
Part geometry group	Geometric objects (e.g., points, vectors, or polygons)
Property group	Define the physical and appearance characteristics of an object (e.g., color, Phong shading coefficients)
Scene group	Define the physical characteristics of a digital image for photo-realistic imagery
Transfer group	Re-maps a set of values in a variable group from one range of values to another range
Variable group	Represents a named block of data of a certain type
View group	Defines the directional and view aspects of the camera position

Data Organization

The Flux data format is not considered a file format—it is a data structure that supports a *dataflow* model of computation where data moves systematically through a communications pipeline between computational modules

The data groups defined above can be nested inside of each other to represent hierarchical relationships to any arbitrary level. The data is consumed sequentially during processing

Data Encoding

The encoding of the *structure* of the data is always in ASCII text. Groups of data values can be encoded in ASCII or binary formats. The native binary format is XDR, but other formats can be defined by users. Each data section is labeled with its corresponding encoding. The example below uses ASCII text; note the keyword "ascii" above the data

Example

This example defines an instance of a "variable group"

```
begin variable "Temperature"
    range 2 3
    data[6] float ascii
        37.1
        16.2
        11.14
        90.234
        17.4
        13.1
end variable
```

File Name Suffix

Unix   .flx

References

apE Version 2.0 User's Manual, The Ohio Supercomputer Graphics Project, 1990, pp. 25–28

apE Version 2.0 Reference Manual, The Ohio Supercomputer Graphics Project, 1990

apE Version 2.0 Programmer's Manual, The Ohio Supercomputer Graphics Project, 1990, pp. 49–94

GEM/IMG

Acronym	GEM IMaGe format
Origin	Digital Research, Inc. Box DRI 70 Garden Court Monterey, CA 93942 Tel. (800) 274-4374 Fax. (408) 649-8209
Motivation	To provide raster image data exchange between Digital Research's product line of application programs: GEM Artline™ , GEM Draw Plus, GEM Scan, and GEM Paint
Users	GEM window environment and desktop publishing applications (e.g., Ventura Publisher) Since Novell purchased of Digital Research, Inc., GEM is no longer being sold or supported. It is still used as part of a GUI for their Dr. DOS and Multiuser DOS operating systems
Control	Copyrighted by Digital Research, Inc. Trademarks GEM, Digital Research Royalty Fees None
Versions	NA
Overview	Major Type of Data 2D Raster Color Representation Monochrome, grayscale, RGB Data Organization Sequential Data Encoding Binary Data Compression Run-length encoding
Data Types	Image size Pixel representation and characteristics Pixel data
Data Organization	General syntax of the data stream 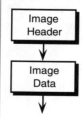

Signature
None

Image Header
All values have their MSB first

Byte#	Data	Details
1–2	Image file version number	
3–4	Header length	Specified in eight or nine 2-byte words
5–6	Bits per pixel	
7–8	Number of bytes in image data	
9–10	Pixel width	On source device (in microns)
11–12	Pixel height	On source device (in microns)
13–14	Scan line width	In pixels
15–16	Number of scan lines	
17–18	Bit image flag (optional)	Only uses bit 0, byte 18; 0: print planes as colors, 1: print planes as gray levels

Image Data
The data values are organized left to right in each row. The rows are ordered from top to bottom. The run-length compression scheme is given in Chapter 9

File Name Suffix	DOS, Unix .IMG
References	GEM Programmer's Toolkit (Not Available) Digital Research Inc. Rimmer, Steve, *Bit-Mapped Graphics,* Windcrest Books, Blue Ridge Summit, PA, pp. 55–89

GEM METAFILE

Acronym	None
Origin	Digital Research, Inc. Box DRI 70 Garden Court Monterey, CA 93942 Tel. (800) 274-4374 Fax. (408) 649-8209

GEM METAFILE *(Continued)*

Motivation To exchange graphical primitives data between Digital Research's of application programs: GEM Draw Plus™ , GEM Output, and GEM Artline™

Users GEM window environment and GEM CAD type application programs

Since Novell purchased Digital Research, Inc., GEM is no longer being sold or supported. It is still used as part of a GUI for their Dr. DOS and Multi-user DOS operating systems

Control

Copyrighted by	Digital Research, Inc.
Trademarks	GEM, Digital Research, Artline, Draw Plus
Royalty Fees	None

Versions NA

Overview

Major Type of Data	2D geometry; raster (bitmap)
Color Representation	NA
Data Organization	Sequential
Data Encoding	Binary
Data Compression	None

Data Types The following two-dimensional graphical primitives are supported:

Polymarker	Rounded Rectangle
Polyline	Filled, Rounded Rectangle
Circle	Bar
Arc	Pie
Ellipse	Bit Image
Elliptical Arc	Text
Elliptical Pie Slice	Justified Graphics Text

The following operations are also included:

Open, Update, and Close a workstation
Printer control, such as 'Form Advance'
Graphics mode control, such as Set Color, Set Clipping Rectangle, Set Polyline
    Line Type, Set Text Font, etc.

Data Organization General syntax of the data stream:

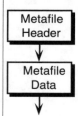

Signature
The first two bytes of the file, hexadecimal FF FF

GEM METAFILE   *(Continued)*

Metafile Header
All values have their MSB first

Byte#	Data	Details
1–2	Signature	Hexadecimal FF FF
3–4	Header length	Specified in words (a word is 2 bytes)
5–6	Version	$100 \times$ major version number + minor version number
7–8	Coordinate system orientation	0: origin lower-left corner ($+y$ up) 2: origin upper-left corner ($+y$ down)
9–10	Minimum x extent of metafile data	The next four values specify the limits of the data in the entire file. These are set to zero if undefined
11–12	Minimum y extent of metafile data	
13–14	Maximum x extent of metafile data	
15–16	Maximum y extent of metafile data	
17–18	Physical page width	In tenths of millimeters
19–20	Physical page height	In tenths of millimeters
21–22	Lower left x value	The next 4 values specify the coordinate system for the viewing window
23–24	Lower left y value	
25–26	Upper right x value	
27–28	Upper right y value	
29–30	Bit image opcode flag	Uses only bit 0, byte 30; 0: no bit image opcode in file, 1: bit image opcode in file

GEM METAFILE   *(Continued)*

Metafile Data

Data is encoded using a unique opcode for each operation the metafile supports.
Each opcode can have a variable number of parameters, as specified by the
counters which follow the opcode

Byte#	Data	Details
1 2	Opcode	Specifies type of operation to perform
3 4	Vertex count	Number of vertices
5 6	Integer parameter count	
7 8	Sub-opcode	Specifies options related to this specific operation, set to zero if not needed
9 ...	Vertices	Bytes not used if vertex count is zero
...	Integer parameters	Bytes not used if integer parameter count is zero

File Name Suffix   NA

References   GEM Programmer's Toolkit (Not available)
Digital Research, Inc.

GIF

Acronym	Graphics Interchange Format™ GIF is pronounced 'jif'
Origin	CompuServe Incorporated Graphics Technology Department 5000 Arlington Centre Blvd. Columbus, OH 43220 Tel. (614) 457-8600

	Original author	Steve Wilhite
	Current support	John Harper, CompuServe, technical support Larry Wood, PICS forum manager on CompuServe

Motivation	CompuServe is a telephone-based information source. Efficient transmission of image data over telephone lines is a major criteria for this format
Users	CompuServe users, other bulletin board users, commercial businesses, etc. This format has widespread usage

Control	Copyrighted by	CompuServe Incorporated
	Trademarks	Graphics Interchange Format™
	Royalty Fees	GIF is based on LZW compression which is patented. The legal use of LZW compression requires a license fee. It is unclear how this affects the use of GIF

Versions	Version 87a	May 1987
	Version 89a	July 1989

Overview	Major Type of Data	2D Raster
	Color Representation	Monochrome, color table (up to 256 entries)
	Data Organization	Sequential
	Data Encoding	Binary
	Data Compression	LZW compression

Data Types	Screen Descriptor (screen width, height, etc.) Image Descriptors (image width, height, etc.) Color Maps (color lookup tables) Raster pixel data User definable functions and data (extension blocks)
Data Organization	All of the following information relates to Version 89a. Refer to the original documentation for Version 87a variances

GIF   *(Continued)*

General syntax of data stream:

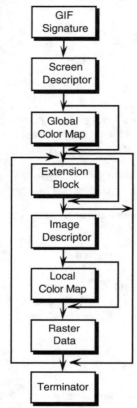

GIF Signature
First 6 bytes in the file (in ASCII), the last 3 of which are a version identifier
Examples: G I F 8 7 a   or   G I F 8 9 a

Logical Screen Descriptor
All data values are stored LSB first

Byte#	Data								Details
	7	6	5	4	3	2	1	0	
0	Logical screen width								In pixels
1									
2	Logical screen height								In pixels
3									
4	M	Cr			S	P			See below
5	Background color								Index into global color map
6	Pixel aspect ratio								= (byte_value + 15)/64

GIF *(Continued)*

M	Global color Map	0: No map
		1: Map immediately follows this header
Cr	Color resolution	$(Cr + 1)$: Number of bits per pixel
S	Sort Flag	0: Color table is not ordered
		1: Color table is ordered (most used colors first)
P	Global color map size	Global color map size = $2^{(P+1)}$

Color table (map) (both Global and Local)

The number of color map entries (3 bytes each) is equal to $2^{(P+1)}$ Each intensity value is a single unsigned byte (0 ... 255)

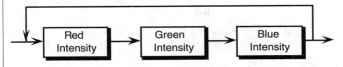

Image Descriptor

Byte#	Data								Details
	7	6	5	4	3	2	1	0	
0	0	0	1	0	1	1	0	0	Image code; ASCII ',' hex(2C)
1	Start of image from the								In pixels
2	left side of screen								
3	Start of image from the								In pixels
4	top side of screen								
5	Width of the image								In pixels
6									
7	Height of the image								In pixels
8									
6	M	I	S	0	0		P		See below

M	Global color (map)	0: Use global color map
		1: Local color map immediately follows
I	Interlaced	0: No interlace; rows in sequential order: top to bottom
		1: Interlaced image rows
S	Sort Flag	0: Local color table is not ordered
		1: Local color table is ordered (most used colors first)
P	Bits per pixel	Bits per pixel = $2^{(P+1)}$

Raster Data

Conceptually each pixel value is stored in row major order (left to right, and top to bottom) for a total of ImageWidth × ImageHeight pixel values. In actuality this stream of pixel values are encoded using the LZW compression algorithm using variable-length codes. The data is divided into sub-blocks of 255 bytes or less

GIF   *(Continued)*

Byte#	Data	Details
	7 6 5 4 3 2 1 0	
1	LZW minimum code size	# of bits used for beginning codes
2	Data sub-block size	Value between (0–255)
3 ...	Raster data	Encoded using LZW compression
... ...	Repeat data sub-blocks as needed	
...	0 0 0 0 0 0 0 0	Zero-size sub-block terminates

Application Extension Blocks

Application extension blocks contain application-specific information. Application codes can be registered through CompuServe. These allow for orderly extensions to the GIF format. The bytes can be ignored (skipped) if the function code is not recognized by the application reading the file

Byte#	Data	Details
	7 6 5 4 3 2 1 0	
1	0 0 1 0 0 0 0 1	Extension code, '!' hex(21)
2	1 1 1 1 1 1 1 1	Extension label, always hex(FF)
3	Header block size	Currently 11
4–11	Application Identifier	Eight printable ASCII characters identifying who owns the extension
12–14	Application authentication code	
15	Data sub-block size	Value between (0–255)
16 ...	Extension data	
... ...	Repeat extension data sub-blocks as needed	
...	0 0 0 0 0 0 0 0	Zero-size sub-block terminates

Terminator

Marks the end of the file. A single ASCII byte ';' hex(3B)

Other optional data (not documented herein)

Graphic Control Extension blocks contain presentation parameters
Comment Extension blocks contain ASCII text related to the image
Plain Text Extension blocks contain ASCII text and the parameters necessary to render that text as part of the image

GIF *(Continued)*

References	From CompuServe about GIF: Download document *gif.doc* from the GIF subdirectory while accessing CompuServe *or* write and request information from the above address About LZW compression: Terry A. Welch, "A Technique for High Performance Data Compression," IEEE Computer, **17**, 6 (June 1984) About the LZW patent: United States patent number 4,558,302 Owned by the Sperry Corporation (which is now the Unisys Corporation) Welch Licensing Department, Law Department, M/SC2SW1, Unisys Corporation, Blue Bell, PA 19424-0001

GRASP

Acronym	GRAphical System for Presentation	
Origin	Microtex Industries, Inc. 2091 Business Center Drive Irvine, CA 92715 Efforts to contact Microtex Industries, Inc. were unfruitful and we assume the company no longer exists	
Motivation	A simple graphics programming pseudo-language that can be used to create and run animated graphics demonstrations (on IBM PC or compatible machines)	
Users	NA	
Control	Copyrighted by	Microtex Industries, Inc.
	Trademarks	NA
	Royalty Fees	NA
Versions	Version 1.10	May 1986
	Version 2	
	Version 3.1	
Overview	Major Type of Data	2D raster; 2D geometric; animation control
	Color Representation	Color Table
	Data Organization	Animation language is random access
	Data Encoding	ASCII
	Data Compression	None for animation language
Data Types	The GRASP language accepts the following commands. The commands are divided according to function	

GRASP *(Continued)*

Graphic commands

CLEARSCR	Clear screen
POINT $x,y,<x2,y2>$	Draw a point
LINE $x,y,x2,y2$	Draw line
BOX $x,y,x2,y2,<width>$	Draw a box
CIRCLE $x,y,rx,<ry>$	Draw an ellipse
TEXT $x,y,$"some text",$<delay>$	Put up text @ x,y
COLOR color1,<color2>	Set color1 and color2
FGAPS <char_gap, space_gap>	Set text gaps
FSTYLE style	Set text style
OFFSET x,y	Set x and y for relative addressing
WINDOW $x0,y0,x1,y1$	Set clip window

Animation commands

CFADE #,$x,y,<buffer>,<speed>,<delay>$	Fade a clipping to screen
FLOAT $xs,ys,xe,ye,$step,delay,clp1...	Float clip across screen
FLY xs,ys,xe,ye,step,delay,clp1 ...	Fly clip across screen
PFADE #,<buffer>,<speed>,<delay>	Fade a picture to the screen
PUTUP $x,y,<buffer>,<delay>$	Put a clip to the screen
TRAN on/off, color	Transparent mode on/off

Memory commands

CFREE buffer,<buffer>,...	Free up clipping buffers
CLOAD clipping filename, <buffer>	Load a clipping
FFREE	Free the font buffer
FLOAD character set filename	Load a font
PFREE buffer,<buffer>,...	Free up picture buffers
PLOAD picture filename, <buffer>	Load a picture

Device commands

CHGCOLOR from,to,,from,to>, ...	EGA, change color index
MODE border color, <palette>	CGA border and palette set
PALETTE buffer	EGA mode set palette
NOISE freg1,freq2,duration	Make some noise
PAN $x0,y0,x1,y1,<buffer>$	EGA pan image
RESETSCR	Reset screen to default
SETCOLOR c1, c2, c3, ..., c16	EGA mode set 16 colors
VIDEO videomode	Set video mode

GRASP   *(Continued)*

Program control commands

EXEC program,<parameters>	Execute program from GRASP
EXIT	Quit program
GOSUB	Execute a subroutine
GOTO label	Go to a labeled statement
IFKEY label	If key match, goto label
LINK textfile filename	Link to another text file
LOOP	Loop to a previous statement
MARK loop count	Mark for looping
RETURN	Return from subroutine
WAITKEY <timeout>,<label>	Wait for a key press

Data Organization

The language is line oriented. Each line contains one of the following:

1) A GRASP command with associated parameters
2) A comment: The line must start with a semicolon
3) A label: A continuous string of ASCII characters (no spaces) terminated with a colon

The language definition includes jumps (goto), looping (mark/loop), and subprograms (gosub). The data stream must be random access to support these constructs

Example

```
; Slideshow demo for GRASP
;
; This program will load and display pictures, alternating between fade #1
; and fade #2, waiting for a count of 500 between each fade.
;
video a;                set medium res, 4 color, CGA mode
;
pload pic1;             load the first picture named pic1
pfade 1;                fade horizontal left to right wipe
waitkey 500
;
pload pic2;             load the second picture named pic2
pfade 2;                fade horizontal right to left wipe
waitkey 500
;
; continue as many pictures as desired
;
exit
```

File Name Suffix

DOS		
	.txt	The GRASP command file
	.pic	An image
	.clp	An image with no color map
	.set	A font
	.fnt	A font
	.GL	A combined archive of all of the above

References

The GRASP's Users Manual
Available from various bulletin boards and from anonymous FTP on the Internet at *zamenhof.cs.rice.edu* in the directory /pub/graphic.formats

HDF

Acronym	Hierarchical Data Format
Origin	National Center for Supercomputing Applications (NCSA) at the University of Illinois at Urbana-Champaign NCSA Software Development Group HDF 152 Computing Applications Bldg. 605 E. Springfield Ave. Champaign, IL 61820 E-mail: *softdev@ncsa.uiuc.edu*
Motivation	HDF is a multi-object file format for transferring graphical and scientific data between machines. The design of this format allows for self-definition of data contents, and easy extensibility for future enhancements or compatibility with other standard formats
Users	Users of NCSA Visualization software, supercomputing centers, NASA EOSDIS Project, National Labs, several commercial firms, and the medical community

Control

Copyrighted by	None; in the public domain
Trademarks	None
Royalty Fees	None

Versions

Version 1.0	
Version 2.0	
Version 3.0	
Version 3.1	July 1990
Version 3.2	August 1992

Overview

Major Type of Data	2D raster images; N-dimensional raster fields
Color Representation	Color Table; RGB
Data Organization	Random Access
Data Encoding	Binary; ASCII
Data Compression	Run-length; IMCOMP

Data Types   The following types of data are currently supported:

RIS8—8-bit raster image set

Image data	2D array of 8-bit numbers
Dimensions	x and y dimensions of image
Compression scheme	None or run-length or IMCOMP
Color palette	256 RGB entries (exactly 768 bytes)

RIS24—24-bit raster image set

Image data	2D array of 24-bit numbers (each with three 8-bit components—RGB)
Interlace scheme	*Pixel:* RGB values for each pixel stored together
	Scan-line: red values for line 1 together, green values for line 1 together, blue value for line 1 together; continued for each line
	Scan-plane: all the red values, all the blue values, then all the green values
Dimensions	*x* and *y* dimensions of the image
Compression scheme	None (compression will be included in future releases)

SDS—Scientific DataSet

(The first two types of data are mandatory; the others are optional)

Actual data	*N*-dimensional array (8-, 16-, or 32-bit integers; 32- or 64-bit floats)
Dimensions	Number of dimensions (rank) and the size of each dimension
Vsets	Provides a generalized grouping structure; allows storage of unstructured grids and other non-Cartesian aggregates
Coordinate system	To be used when interpreting or displaying the data
Scales	To be used along each dimension
Labels	For all dimensions
Units	For all dimensions
Format specifications	To be used when displaying the values
Limits	The maximum and minimum values of the data

Annotations—descriptive text associated with other data objects in a file

Label	A single null terminated string of characters
Description	More than one null terminated string of characters

HDF *(Continued)*

Data Organization

General organization of data stream:

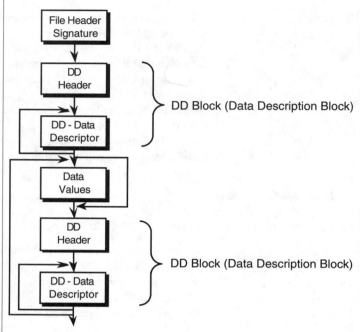

Signature
First four bytes: hexadecimal value 0E031301

Data Descriptor
There is a data descriptor for each *data object* in the file

Byte#	Data	Details
1–2	Tag	Designates the type of data
3–4	Reference number	Uniquely distinguishes this data element from others with the same tag
5–8	Data offset	To the location of the data from the beginning of the file (in bytes)
9–12	Data length	In bytes

The tag and reference number uniquely identify a data object and the tag/ref combination is called a *data identifier*

Data Descriptor Block
This is simply a group of Data Descriptors

Byte#	Data	Details
1–2	Block size (*n*)	Number of data descriptors in the block
3–6	Next block	Location of the next DD block (in bytes from the beginning of the file)
7–18	Data descriptor 1	
19–30	Data descriptor 2	
...		A sequential list of *n* data descriptors
	Data descriptor *n*	

Overall Organization
The data elements can occur anywhere within a file, except within a Data Descriptor Block. The first Data Descriptor Block must immediately follow the 4-byte signature. Other Data Descriptor Blocks can be positioned anywhere within the file. The "next block" value in the DD header forms a linked list of DD Blocks. The last DD Block has a next block value of zero

Data Compression

The run-length scheme is similar to Packbits, except the count bytes are not stored as 2's compliment numbers. The 8-bit count value is broken into a high order "flag" bit and a 7-bit unsigned integer (*n*). If the high-order bit is 1, the next byte is replicated *n* times. If the high-order bit is zero, the next *n* bytes are actual data values

The IMCOMP compression scheme is truly unique. The raster data is segmented into 4 × 4 arrays of pixels. Two colors are selected to represent all 16 pixels within the 4 × 4 block and these two colors are placed in a color lookup table. Each of the pixels is then assigned one of the two colors chosen using one bit of memory (0 for the first color; 1 for the second color). Now the 16 pixels can be stored using only 16 bits. Two 1-byte indexes into the color lookup table must also be stored for each 4 × 4 block. Therefore each block is represented by 4 bytes of data, whereas the original block would have required 16 bytes. IMCOMP always produces a 4:1 compression ratio

File Name Suffix   NA

References   *NCSA HDF, Calling Interfaces and Utilities*, Version 3.1, NCSA, University of Illinois at Urbana-Champaign, July 1990

NCSA HDF Specifications, NCSA, University of Illinois at Urbana-Champaign, March 1989

NCSA HDF Vset, Version 2.0, NCSA, University of Illinois at Urbana-Champaign, Nov. 1990

These documents are available by anonymous FTP at *zaphod.ncsa.uiuc.edu*

HP-GL

Acronym	Hewlett Packard Graphics Language
Origin	Hewlett Packard Company 16399 W. Bernardo Drive San Diego, CA 92127-1899 Tel. (800) 752-0900
Motivation	A simple language for sending graphical commands to plotters and other graphical output devices
Users	Software systems that drive Hewlett Packard plotters
Control	Copyrighted by Hewlett Packard Company Trademarks HP-GL, HP-GL/2 Royalty Fees None
Versions	There are over 25 different implementations of HP-GL. The differences in implementation include: • The number of commands supported by each plotter • Parameter ranges supported by each plotter • Placement of the origin (small format plotters use the lower left; large format plotters use the center of the page) • Positioning of P1/P2 in relationship to the hard-clip limits
Overview	Major Type of Data 2D geometry; plotter device control Indexed (pen Color Representation numbers) Data Organization Sequential Data Encoding ASCII text Data Compression None
Data Types	The following commands make up the language. Not all commands are supported by all plotters. The list is divided according to function

HP-GL *(Continued)*

Commands to draw graphical primitives:

PU (x,y(,...))	Pen up
PD x,y (,...))	Pen down
PA x,y (x,y (,..))	Plot absolute to x,y (line)
PR x,y(,x,y(,...))	Plot relative from current pen (line)
AA x,y,arc angle(,chord angle)	Arc absolute
AR x,y,arc angle(,chord angle)	Arc relative
CI radius(,chord angle)	Circle of specified radius
EA x,y	Edge rectangle absolute
ER x,y	Edge rectangle relative
EP	Edge polygon
EW radius, start angle, sweep angle,(,chord angle)	Edge wedge
FP	Fill polygon
WG radius, start angle, sweep angle(,chord angle)	Fill wedge of circle
RR x,y	Fill rectangle relative
RA x,y	Fill rectangular absolute
XT	Draw X-axis tick
YT	Draw Y-axis tick

Commands to set the attributes of graphical primitives

PC	Pen color
SP pen number	Select pen
SG group number	Select pen group
GP (group number, (pen number (,number of pens) (,length))))	Designate group starting with pen of specified pens changing at interval
LT pattern number (,pattern length)	Set line type and pattern length
CT n	Set chord tolerance mode
FT type(,spacing (,angle))	Fill type with spacing and angle
UF gap1(,gap2,...gap20)	Create user-defined fill type
TL tp(,tn)	Set tick length
PM n	Enable polygon mode n

HP-GL *(Continued)*

Commands to display text

LB label characters	Label ASCII string
WD labeling characters	Write to display
PB	Plot label from buffer
BF label characters	Buffer label
CS set	Designate character set
CA set	Designate alternate character set
SS	Select standard character set
SA	Select alternate character set
DI run,rise	Set absolute label direction
DR run,rise	Set relative label direction
CM switch mode (,fallback mode)	Character selection mode
DV	Set label direction
CC chord angle	Set character chord angle
DL character number (,pen control), x,y(,...)(,pen control)(,...)	Define downloadable font
UC (pen control,)x,y (,pen control)(,...)	Plot user-defined character
CP spaces, lines	Character plot
DS slot,set	Designate character set into slot
DT label terminator	Define label terminator
ES spaces(,lines)	Set extra spacing between characters or lines
SI width,height	Set absolute character size
SR width, height	Set relative character size
SL tan theta	Set character slant from vertical
SM c(c)	Specify character for symbol mode plotting
IC c	Input character for sizing
IV slot(,left)	Invoke slot into character table
LO position number	Set label origin

Coordinate system control

RO n	Rotate coordinate system
SC xmin,xmax,ymin,ymax	User-unit scaling
IW x1,y1,x2,y2	Input window
IP x1,y1,x2,y2	Input corner limit points

HP-GL   *(Continued)*

Device control

IN	Initialize plotter
PG *n*	Advance page
AF	Advance full page
AH	Advance half page
FR	Advance frame
AP *n*	Automatic pen operations
AS pen acceleration(,pen number)	Select pen acceleration
PT thickness	Select pen thickness
VS pen velocity(,pen number)	Set velocity for pen
VA	Activate adaptive velocity
FS pen force(,pen number)	Select tip force for pen
DF	Set default values
IM e(,s(,p))	Set e-, s-, and p- masks
EC (*n*)	Enable cutter
PS paper size	Select paper size
RP *n*	Replots buffered plot *n* times
CV *n*(,input delay)	Enables curved line generator for delay
DC	Digitize clear
DP	Digitize point
GC count number	Set count number
KY key(,function)	Assign function to key
NR	Not Ready

Commands to query the device

OA	Output actual position & pen status
OB	Output box dimensions of character from IC
OC	Output commanded position & pen status
OD	Output digitized point & pen status
OE	Output error
OF	Output factors
OG	Output count number & escape status
OH	Output hard-clip limits
OI	Output identification
OK	Output function key
OL	Output length of buffered label
OO	Output options
OS	Output P1 and P2 (limits of plotting area)
OT	Output carousel status
OW	Output window

HP-GL   *(Continued)*

Data Organization	The syntax of the language is described by the following

```
OSep X OSep X OSep Parameter RSep Parameter OSep Terminator
```

where, *OSEP* is an optional separator (zero or more commas or spaces), *X* is a single letter (the two Xs make up the command mnemonic), *Parameter* is either an integer, decimal or character as required by the command, *RSep* is a required separator (one or more commas or spaces), and *Terminator* is a termination character (typically a semicolon ";" or line feed or the next mnemonic). The requirements vary between devices

Example	The following draws a box with a circle inside touching at the edges. The label "example" is drawn inside the box

```
IN; SP 1; PU; PA 0,0,PD, 0,100, 100,100, 100,0, 0,0;
PU; PA 100,50; CI 50; PA 15,40; LBexample<ETX>;
```

File Name Suffix	NA

References	*Hewlett-Packard HP-GL Product Comparison Guide,* Hewlett-Packard Company, 1987

Interfacing and Programming Manual, HP 7475A Graphics Plotter, Hewlett-Packard Company

HP-GL vs. HP-GL/2 Language Comparison Guide, Rev 1.0, Hewlett-Packard Company, 1991

There are 11 individual manuals that relate to the individual types of HP plotters. Manuals cannot typically be purchased separately

---

HP-GL/2

Acronym	Hewlett Packard Graphics Language 2
Origin	Hewlett Packard Company 16399 W. Bernardo Drive San Diego, CA 92127-1899 Tel. (800) 752-0900
Motivation	A standardized vector graphics language with a common implementation across all HP-GL/2 language products

HP-GL/2   *(Continued)*

It is a simplification/refinement/enhancement of HP-GL. HP-GL/2 is neither a subset nor a superset of HP-GL, but a little of both. The command set is reduced to 86 commands, parameter ranges and functionality are consistent for all HP-GL/2 devices, and the origin is always in the lower left corner. Data compression was also added to reduce transmission times

Users	Software systems that drive Hewlett Packard plotters

Control	Copyrighted by	Hewlett Packard Company
	Trademarks	HP-GL, HP-GL/2
	Royalty Fees	None

Versions	NA

Overview	Major Type of Data	2D geometry; plotter device control
	Color Representation	Indexed (pen numbers); RGB table lookup
	Data Organization	Sequential
	Data Encoding	ASCII text
	Data Compression	None; base 64 or base 32 encoding

Data Types The following commands make up the language. The parameters to each command are shown after each 2-letter mnemonic. Parameters shown in parenthesis are optional

Note the following comparisons between HP-GL and HP-GL/2:
- 30 new commands were added to HP-GL/2 (these are italicized below)
- 37 commands defined in HP-GL were removed from HP-GL/2

Commands to draw graphical primitives

PU $(x,y(,...))$	Pen up
PD $x,y (,...))$	Pen down
PA x,y $(x,y (,..))$	Plot absolute to x,y (line)
PR $x,y(,x,y(,...))$	Plot relative from current pen (line)
PE (flag) (value/x,y) ...	Polyline Encoded (compressed form of PR)
AA $x,y,$arc angle(,chord angle)	Arc absolute
AR $x,y,$arc angle(,chord angle)	Arc relative
AT xi,yi,xe,ye(,chord angle)	Arc (3 points)
RT xi,yi,xe,ye(,chord angle)	Relative Arc (3 points)
CI radius(,chord angle)	Circle of specified radius
EA x,y	Edge rectangle absolute
ER x,y	Edge rectangle relative
EP	Edge polygon
EW radius, start angle, sweep angle,(,chord angle)	Edge wedge
FP	Fill polygon

WG radius, start angle, sweep angle(,chord angle)	Fill wedge of circle
RR *x,y*	Fill rectangle relative
RA *x,y*	Fill rectangular absolute

Commands to set the attributes of graphical primitives

AC (x,y)	Anchor corner of fill pattern
PC	Pen color
PW (width)(,pen)	Pen width
WU (type)	Pen width units (millimeters or %)
SP pen number	Select pen
GP (group number, (pen number (,number of pens) (,length))))	Designate group starting with pen of specified pens changing at interval
LA (kind,value)	Line end Attributes (butt, square, round, mitered, etc.)
LT pattern number (,pattern length)	Set line type and pattern length
UL (index(,gap1,.. gapn))	User-defined line type
CT *n*	Set chord tolerance mode
FT type(,spacing (,angle))	Fill type with spacing and angle
RF (index(,width,height, pen(,..)))	Raster fill definition
PM *n*	Enable polygon mode *n*

Commands to display text

LB label characters	Label ASCII string
AD (kind,value,…(,kind, value))	Alternate font definition
CF (file mode (,edge pen))	Character fill mode (for outline fonts)
SS	Select standard character set
SA	Select alternate character set
SD (kind,value(,…(,kind, value)))	Standard font definition
DI run,rise	Set absolute label direction
DR run,rise	Set relative label direction
DV	Set label direction
CC chord angle	Set character chord angle
DL character number (,pen control), *x,y*(,...)(,pen control)(,...)	Define downloadable font

HP-GL/2 *(Continued)*

CP spaces, lines	Character plot
DT label terminator	Define label terminator
ES spaces(,lines)	Set extra spacing between characters or lines
SI width,height	Set absolute character size
SR width, height	Set relative character size
SL tan theta	Set character slant from vertical
SM c(c)	Specify character for symbol mode plotting
LO position number	Set label origin

Coordinate system control

RO *n*	Rotate coordinate system
SC xmin,xmax,ymin,ymax	User-unit scaling
IW x1,y1,x2,y2	Input window
IP x1,y1,x2,y2	Input corner limit points
IR x1,y1,x2,y2	Input relative limit points

Device control

IN	Initialize plotter
BP (kind,value(,...(,kind, value)))	Begin plot
MC (mode)	Merge control (how overlapping pixels are plotted)
MT (type)	Media type (e.g., paper, vellum)
QL (quality level)	Quality level (draft or final)
ST (switches)	Sort (how plotter sorts vectors)
PG *n*	Advance page
FR	Advance frame
VS pen velocity(,pen number)	Set velocity for pen
DF	Set default values
EC (*n*)	Enable cutter
PS paper size	Select paper size
RP *n*	Replots buffered plot *n* times
DC	Digitize clear
DP	Digitize point
NR	Not Ready
TD (mode)	Transparent data (how to handle control characters)

Color (Palette) Extension

CR (br,wr,bg,wg,bb,wb)	Set color ranges for RGB values
NP (n)	Number of pens
PC (pen(,red,green,blue))	Pen color assignment
SV (screen type(,option1 (,option2)))	Screened (area fill) vectors
TR (n)	Transparency mode (defines how the color white is plotted)

HP-GL/2   *(Continued)*

Dual-Context Extension

Esc%#A	Enter the PCL mode (interpret subsequent instructions as PCL commands)
EscE	Reset (restore device defaults)
FI FontID	Primary font selection
FN FontID	Secondary font selection
SB (n)	Scalable or bitmap fonts

Commands to query the device:

OD	Output digitized point & pen status
OE	Output error
OH	Output hard-clip limits
OI	Output identification
OP	Output P1 and P2 (limits of plotting area)
OS	Output decimal value of status byte

Data Organization   The syntax of the language is described by the following:

```
OSep XX OSep Parameter RSep Parameter OSep Terminator
```

where, *OSep* is an optional separator (zero or more spaces), *X* is a single letter (the two Xs make up the command mnemonic), *Parameter* is either an integer, decimal or character as required by the command, *RSep* is a required separator (one or more commas or spaces) *Terminator* is a termination character (typically a semicolon or line feed or the next mnemonic). Some commands require a semicolon as a terminator

Data Compression   HP-GL/2 is an ASCII encoded data stream. Instead of using the normal base 10 representation of numbers, the PE command uses numbers represented in base 64 (or base 32). For example, $10234_{10} = 2\,VS_{64}$ (assuming that $A = 10$, $B = 11$, $C = 12, \ldots, S = 28, \ldots V = 31$, etc.) The original five bytes can now be encoded in 3 bytes. The code used to represent these digits are listed below. The last digit of a number is coded differently than the other digits to indicate its end. These are called terminating digits

Compression Mode	Range of Digits	Codes Nonterminating	Codes Terminating
Base 64 (8 bits per byte)	0–63	63–126	191–254
Base 32 (7 bits per byte)	0–31	63–94	95–126

Example   See example in HP-GL

File Name Suffix   NA

References   Hewlett-Packard, *The HP-GL/2 Reference Guide, A Handbook for Program Developers,* Addison-Wesley, Reading, MA, 1990, 295 pages (ISBN 0-201-56308-8)

HP-GL vs. HP-GL/2 Language Comparison Guide, Rev 1.0, Hewlett-Packard Company, 1991

ICO

Acronym	ICOn resource file
Origin	Windows Marketing Group Microsoft Corporation 16011 NE 36th Way Box 97017 Redmond, WA 98073-9717 Tel. (206) 882-8080
Motivation	To store multiple bitmaps in a format independent of pixel resolution and color scheme
	The intent is that a file of this type contains icon bitmap representations of the same icon at different resolutions and with different levels of color. A specific application searches for the most appropriate representation given its current device
Users	Microsoft Windows 3.0 users and application programs running under the Windows 3.0 environment

Control

Copyrighted by	Microsoft Corporation
Trademarks	Microsoft, Windows, Windows/286, Windows/386
Royalty Fees	None

Versions Version 1

Overview

Major Type of Data	2D Raster
Color Representation	Monochrome; Color table (limited to 8 or 16 colors)
Data Organization	Sequential
Data Encoding	Binary
Data Compression	None

Data Types

Bitmap
Bitmap mask
Bitmap size
Color resolution (bits per pixel)

Data Organization

General syntax of the data stream:

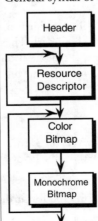

ICO   *(Continued)*

The data set can contain multiple images. Each icon image is defined by two bit-maps:
- A color bitmap that supplies the XOR mask for the icon
- A monochrome bitmap that provides the AND mask that defines the transparent portion of the icon

Signature
The 3rd and 4th bytes are hex(01 00), respectively (i.e., a 1 with the LSB first)

File Header
All data values are stored in LSB first format

Byte#	Data	Details
1–2	Reserved	Must be set to zero
3–4	Resource type	Set to 1 for a Icon resource
5–6	Number of images	Contained in the file

Resource Descriptor
There is one resource descriptor for each icon image defined in the file

Byte#	Data	Details
1	Image width	In pixels (only 16, 32, or 64 allowed)
2	Image height	In pixels (only 16, 32, or 64 allowed)
3	Number of colors used	Acceptable values are 2, 8 or 16
4	Reserved	Must be set to zero
5–6	Reserved	Must be set to zero
7–8	Reserved	Must be set to zero
9–12	Size of pixel array	In bytes
13–16	Byte offset to bitmap data	Offset from the beginning of the file

Bitmaps (Color and Monochrome)
The bits of each pixel are packed into bytes and each scan line is padded with zeros, if necessary, to be aligned with a 32-bit word boundary. The origin of the bitmap is the lower left corner. (Same format as BMP type files). The Color bitmap comes first, immediately followed by the Monochrome bitmap

File Name Suffix   DOS   .ICO

References   *Microsoft Windows Programmer's Reference,* New for Version 3, edited by Microsoft Corporation, Microsoft Press, Redmond, WA, 1990, ISBN 1-55615-309-0

Microsoft Windows Software Development Kit
Call the Microsoft Information Center at (800) 426-9400 for further information

IFF (EA IFF 85)

Acronym	Electronic Arts' Interchange File Format
Origin	Electronic Arts 1820 Gateway Dr. San Mateo, CA 94404

Original authors	Bob "Kodiak" Burns, R.J. Mical, Jerry Morrison, Greg Riker, Steve Shaw, Barry Walsh

Motivation To establish a standard file format that includes diverse kinds of data such as plain and formatted text, raster and structured graphics, fonts, music, sound effects, musical instrument descriptions, and animation

The goals of the data format include portability, simplicity, and efficiency

Users IFF is used predominantly on Amiga computers (though it is designed to be easily portable to other systems)

Control

Copyrighted by	None
Trademarks	Electronic Arts
Royalty Fees	None

Versions

Version 1	1985

Overview IFF is a "wrapper" around all types of data, each encoded in a different way. The characteristics listed below are related to the definition of "interleaved bit map" data. The IFF data specification does not specify specific data encodings

"ILBM"—interleaved bitmap data chunk

Major Type of Data	2D Raster
Color Representation	Color Table
Data Organization	Sequential (broken into data chunks)
Data Encoding	Binary
Data Compression	None

Note: other raster data formats and encodings can be defined and included in an IFF data set

Data Types Data is divided into "chunks." (Refer to the Data Organization section for the definition of a data chunk). The following "group" chunks provide a structure for the entire data set

FORM	A data section composed of zero or more data chunks
CAT	A concatenation (or group) of data chunks, typically of the same type (but not required)
LIST	The same as a CAT except that it provides a scope for properties that apply to more than one data chunk
PROP	Properties definitions that can be used by more than one FORM data chunk; properties only appear in LIST data chunks

IFF (EA IFF 85)   *(Continued)*

The following group chunk "names" are reserved for future revisions:
FOR1 thru FOR9, CAT1 thru CAT9, and LIS1 thru LIS9

Currently defined FORMs include the following:

8SVX	8-bit sampled sound voice
ANBM	Animated bitmap
FNTR	Raster font
FNTV	Vector font
FTXT	Formatted text
GSCR	General-use musical score
ILBM	Interleaved raster bitmap image
PDEF	Deluxe Print page definition
PICS	Macintosh picture (in PICT format)
PLBM	(Obsolete)
USCR	Uhuru Sound Software musical score
UVOX	Uhuru Sound Software Macintosh voice
SMUS	Simple musical score
VDEO	Deluxe Video Construction Set video

Currently defined PROP LIST IDs

OPGM	Properties originating program
OCPU	Processor family
OCMP	Computer type
OSN	Computer serial number or network address
UNAM	User name

Data Organization   The general syntax of the data stream:

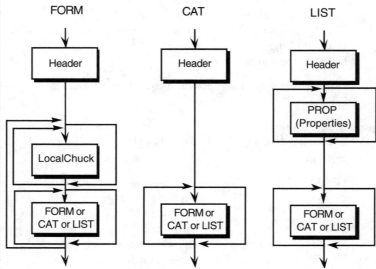

IFF (EA IFF 85)   *(Continued)*

The LIST syntax implements the idea of "scope." The PROP data basically defines variables and gives them values. These variables retain their values unless they are redefined by imbedded LISTs. For example, a color map can be defined and then applied to more than one image, unless a "lower-level" LIST redefines it

FORM, CAT, or LIST Header

Byte#	Data	Details
1–4	Identification (ID)	ASCII; either FORM, CAT, or LIST
5–8	Chunk size	In bytes; not including ID or this size value
9–12	Type	ASCII string; e.g., ILBM or ANBM
13– (8 + size)	Data	Data values in the chunk

LocalChunk

Byte#	Data	Details
1–4	Identification (ID)	ASCII string; e.g., ILBM or ANBM
5–8	Chunk size	In bytes; not including ID or this size value
9– (8 + size)	Data	Data values in the chunk; the semantics and encoding depend on the ID value

PROP

Byte#	Data	Details
1–4	Identification (ID)	ASCII string; "PROP"
5–8	Chunk size	In bytes; not including ID or this size value
9–12	Type	ASCII string; a FORM type; e.g., ILBM or ANBM
13– (8 + size)	Data	ASCII text in the form of: variable = value

Example	Single purpose files	None specified	
	Scrap files	Macintosh File Type	"IFF"
		DOS	.IFF

References "EA IFF 85" Standard for Interchange Format Files
Available from Commodore Business Machines, Dept. C, 1200 Wilson Drive, West Chester, PA 19380, for a small fee

IGES

Acronym	Initial Graphics Exchange Specification
Origin	U.S. Department of Commerce National Bureau of Standards National Engineering Laboratory Gaithersburg, MD 20899

	Original author	Bradford Smith
	Current support	IGES/PDES Organization (Initial Graphics Exchange Specification / Product Data Exchange Specification Organization)

Motivation	To provide for the exchange of data "required to describe and communicate the essential engineering characteristics of physical objects as manufactured products." This data includes both geometric and nongeometric information
Users	CAD/CAM systems (almost exclusively), some publishing systems (e.g., Interleaf)
	The United Stated government initiated the IGES format and mandates that all U.S. government contracts related to product development support it

Control	Copyrighted by	ANSI
	Trademarks	None
	Royalty Fees	None

Versions	1.0 1980	(Also ANSI Y14.26M-1981)
	2.0 1982	Enhanced geometric entities
		Added Rational *B*-spline curves and surfaces
		Added larger set of text fonts
		Included node data for finite element modeling
		Included electronic printed wiring board product data
		A binary format (in addition to the ASCII format)
	3.0 1986	(Also ANSI Y14.26M-1987)
		New entity capacities (Offset Curves, Offset Surfaces, Curves on a Parametric Surface)
		Included a larger range of annotation styles
		Enhanced user-defined MACROs for standard parts libraries
		A compressed ASCII format encoding
	4.0 1988	Constructive Solid Geometry representation
		Inclusion of electrical/electronic attributes and properties
		Ability to define attribute tables
		Added FEM (finite element model) results data
	5.2 1994	(Estimated release)

IGES *(Continued)*

Overview	Major Type of Data	3D geometry
	Color Representation	RGB (values between 0.0 and 100.0)
	Data Organization	Sequential
	Data Encoding	ASCII; optional binary encoding
	Data Compression	None (the binary encoding does produce smaller data sets)

Data Types	Geometric entities

Graphical Primitive Entities
Transformation Matrix (a 3×3 matrix multiplication followed by a vector addition)
Point (3D, *xyz*)
Line
Copious Data (nonsolid lines, e.g., center lines, section lines)
Circular Arc (defined in a reference plane called the *definition space*)
Conic Arc (i.e., ellipse, parabola, hyperbola)
Parametric Spline Curve
Rational *B*-spline Curve
Offset Curve (define a new curve as an offset from an existing curve)
Composite Curve (an ordered list of entities which define a continuous curve)
Plane
Ruled Surface
Surface of Revolution
Tabulated Cylinder
Parametric Spline Surface
Rational *B*-spline Surface
Offset Surface (define a new surface as an offset from an existing surface)
Trimmed Parametric Surface (surface with interior "holes")
Curve on a Parametric Surface
Connect Point (point of connection for zero, one, or more entities)
Flash (simple planar predefined shapes, e.g., circle, donut, rectangle)

Finite Element entities
Node
Finite Element
Nodal Displacement and Rotation
Nodal Load/Constraint
Nodal Results
Element Results

IGES   *(Continued)*

Constructive Solid Geometry entities
Block (a rectangular parallelepiped)
Right Angular Wedge
Right Circular Cylinder
Right Circular Cone Frustum
Sphere
Torus
Solid of Revolution
Solid of Linear Extrusion
Ellipsoid
Boolean Tree (describes the union, intersection, and difference of primitives)
Solid Assembly (collection of items which share a fixed geometric relationship)
Solid Instance (a pointer to a solid, with an associated transformation)

Nongeometric data

Annotation entities
Leader (lines or curves with arrows used for dimensioning and textual pointers)
Linear Dimension
Ordinate Dimension (dimensions from a common base line)
Point Dimension (associate text with a single point)
Angular Dimension
Diameter Dimension
Radius Dimension
General Note (text, including font size and angle of rotation)
General Label (a General Note with associated Leaders)
Flag Note (a General Note surrounded by a "box" with associated Leaders)
General Symbol (a General Note with associated geometric entities and Leaders)
Text Display Template (text created from parameter values (integer, real, or logical
     data) stored in other entities)
Sectioned Area (a boundary curve filled with a pattern of lines)

Structure entities (to establish relationships between entities)
Associativity Definition (schemes for combining entities)
Associativity Instance
Subfigure Definition (a set of associated entities)
Subfigure Instance (a Subfigure Definition with a translation and scale factor)
Network Subfigure Definition (a Subfigure with specified Points of Connection)
Network Subfigure Instance (Network Subfigure with a translation, scale factor,
     and Points of Connection)
Rectangular Array Subfigure Instance (copies of a Subfigure equally spaced along a
     set of rows and columns)
Circular Array Subfigure Instance (copies of a Subfigure equally spaced around an
     imaginary circle)
External Reference (using entities in other files)

IGES *(Continued)*

Attribute entities

Attribute Table Definition (define a tables of attributes)

Attribute Table Instance (a specific Attribute Table with associated table values)

Color Definition (a red, green, blue color specification)

Property (various properties of other entities, e.g., how to draw the end points of lines, electrical component pen numbers, etc.)

Text Font Definition (description of characters in a font)

Line Font Definition (specification of how lines and curves are displayed, e.g., arbitrary dashed lines)

View (specify a viewing orientation and projection onto a viewing plane)

Drawing (set of views with their positioning on a "page," and associated annotation)

Misc. entities

Null (an easy method to temporarily ignore entities in a file, i.e., mark them as Null)

MACRO definition

MACRO instance

Data Organization   Complete details of the IGES format are too numerous to cover in the context of this discussion. This is related to the large number of data types supported and to the three different encoding schemes for the same data. A brief overview of the data organization is presented here

General syntax of the data stream

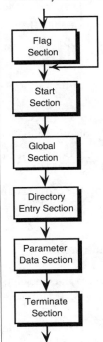

IGES *(Continued)*

Signature
There is no unique signature identifying an IGES file. One possible way to recognize the file is to examine byte 73 and test for the character *S, C* or *B*

Byte 73	Encoding Format
S	ASCII Format
C	Compressed ASCII Format
B	Binary Format

Flag Section
This is included in the file *only* if it is Binary-encoded. It is eighty bytes long and specifies the precision and encoding format for the binary data (e.g., the number of bits in a single precision integer.). It also specifies the number of bytes included in each major section of the file

Start Section
This section contains any information in a textual format that a user might wish to include with the file. It is typically skipped (ignored) by an IGES decoder

ASCII and Compressed ASCII formatted files are made up of a sequence of 80 character records having the following syntax

Byte#	Data	Details
1–72	ASCII text	Free format
73	*S*	Marks line as part of the Start Section
74–80	Sequence number (in ASCII text)	Right justified in the field; e.g., 0000001

Binary formatted files have the following single structure for the Start Section

Byte#	Data	Details
1	*S*	ASCII, Start Section identifier
2–5	Number of bytes in this section	The count does not include the first five bytes, i.e., the *S* and byte count
6–	Text	Can include carriage return characters

Global Section
This section specifies 24 parameters, a few of which are:

Parameter Delimiter Character (separates parameter values, default: comma)
Record Delimiter Character (allows line continuation, default: semicolon)
File name (of IGES file)
System ID (information about vendor system which created the file)
Preprocessor version (version of IGES used to create the file)

IGES *(Continued)*

Directory Entry Section

Each entity in the file has a directory entry which consists of 20 values, not all of which are valid for each entity. The details are entity specific, but a general entity record follows. It is made up of 20 eight-character fields spread across two 80-byte records. (The notation "→" means "pointer")

Byte#	Data	Details
1–8	Entity type number	
9–16	→ To parameter data	Actual values which define the entity
17–24	→ To structure	Pointer to "parent" entity
25–32	Line font pattern	Pattern to be used to display entity
33–40	Level	Grouping of entities by "level"
41–48	→ To view	Which views display the entity
49–56	→ To transformation matrix	How to position the entity
57–64	→ Label display associativity	How to display any entity labels
65–72	Status number (encoded)	4 values, e.g., visible versus blank
73–80	Sequence number	Line # from start of Directory Section

Byte#	Data	Details
1–8	Entity type number	Same number as field 1–8 above
9–16	Line weight number	Thickness used to display the entity
17–24	Color number	Color used to display the entity
25–32	Parameter line count	# of data lines in parameter section
33–40	Form number	Different formulations of basic entity
41–48	Reserved	Reserved for future use
49–56	Reserved	Reserved for future use
57–64	Entity label	Application specific name of entity
65–72	Entity subscript number	Used to make the entity label unique
73–80	Sequence number	Line # from start of directory section

The entity-specific requirements, details, and nuances associated with the Directory Entries are numerous and their implementation is nontrivial

Parameter Data Section

This section contains the actual data that defines each entity. Each entity has a unique set of definition parameters. For a complete description of entity parameters refer to the original IGES specification. A sample parameter record for a line entity is shown next to indicate the type of record this section contains

A Line Entity is specified by 6 real numbers, the starting point $(x1, y1, z1)$ and the terminating point $(x2, y2, z2)$. The line can be associated with other entities through a list of pointers. The list is prefixed by the number of pointers in the list (denoted NV below). The line can also have a list of pointers to associated attributes and properties. This list is prefixed by the number of pointers in the list (denoted NA below). The data can be on a single line or multiple lines. Each value is separated by the "Parameter Delimiter Character" as specified in the Global Section of the file, which is typically a comma. The general syntax for a Line Entity is:

```
entity #, x1, y1, z1, x2, y2, z2, NV..., NA...      Sequence #
```

If the first record in the Parameter Data Section was a Line Entity, it might look like the following, where the Entity Number associated with the Line Entity is 110. The line entity shown is not associated with any other entities, nor does it have any associated attributes or properties

```
110, 1.0, 1.025, 1.0, 3.2, 4.0, 3.5325,0,0        P0000001
```

Terminate Section

A single line contains a summary of the number of lines in each Section of the file

Byte#	Data	Details
1–8	# of lines in Start Section	e.g., S0000020, number right justified
9–16	# of lines in Global Section	e.g., G0000003
17–24	# of lines in Directory Entry	e.g., D0000532
25–32	# of lines in Parameter Data	e.g., P0000261
33–72		Not used (ignored)
72–80	Sequence Number	T0000001

References Order document NBSIR 88-3813 (for version 4.0) from
U.S. Department of Commerce
National Technical Information Service
Springfield, VA 22161
Tel. (703) 487-4650
Fax. (703) 321-8547

IIF
(ISO 12087 — Part 3)

Acronym	Image Interchange Facility
	Full name: Computer Graphics and Image Processing—Image Processing and Interchange (IPI)—Part 3: Image Interchange Facility (IIF)
Origin	ISO/IEC JTC1/SC 24/WG 1 Rapporteur Group on Imaging, since 1989
	The preparation of the IIF documents has been promoted by previous work on image formats in the international computer graphics and image processing community
Motivation	The Image Processing and Interchange (IPI) international standard was developed to provide common definitions, common functionality, and data interchange between digital image processing systems. The three-part standard is divided as follows:

Part 1	Common Architecture for Imaging (CAI) defines a common architecture and nomenclature for the discussion of imaging and image processing
Part 2	Programmer's Imaging Kernel System (PIKS) defines a programmer's imaging kernel system along with an applications program interface (API)
Part 3	Image Interchange Facility (IIF) defines a standard data format for the interchange of imaging data between application programs

Users	This is a new standard. Its future use will depend on its adoption and implementation by software developers	
Control	Copyrighted by	ISO/IEC JTC1
	Trademarks	None
	Royalty Fees	None
Versions	Committee Draft (CD)	May 1992
	Draft International Standard (DIS)	December 1992
	International Standard (IS)	December 1993 (estimated)

Overview	The comments in this appendix are based on a May 4, 1992 committee draft (CD). Some of the details are probably changed in the final international standard (IS)

The IIF specification allows for a very broad range of raster data types and organizations, even more than the imaging kernel (PIKS) defines. For this reason IIF defines three *conformance profiles* that reduce the complexity of an IIF data stream for certain classes of data. (This is very similar to the classes defined by the TIFF standard). This allows software developers to use the IIF specification without the massive overhead that would be required to implement the entire standard. Three conformance profiles are defined:

IIF
(ISO 12087 — Part 3)   *(Continued)*

IIF boolean image profile	Supports only bi-level (monochrome) image data
IIF color image profile	Meets the requirements of most desktop publishing systems (i.e., 24-bit color, 8-bit color, lookup tables, grayscale images, etc.)
IIF PIKS profile	Supports all image data objects defined in PIKS

The following discussion covers the IIF PIKS profile, of which the other two are subsets

Major Type of Data	Raster (5-dimensional)
Color Representation	CIE 1931 color space, including: CIE XYZ, CIE RGB, CIE L*a*b*, CIE L*u*v*, YCrCb, UVW, Yxy, YUV, IHS, CCIR RGB, EBU RGB, NTSC RGB, SMPTE RGB
	CIE 1964 color space $X_{10}Y_{10}Z_{10}$
	Uncalibrated linear RGB and video-gamma RGB
	Uncalibrated linear CMY and linear CMYK
Data Organization	Sequential (file); "Tree" (data structures)
Data Encoding	Binary (ANS.1 using BER)
Data Compression	Run-length (FAX group 3 and 4)
	Prediction (JBIG)
	DCT (JPEG)
	DCT (MPEG)

Data Types   The data types are categorized into the following four groups:

Image Data

An image is composed of a group of pixels. The basic structure of the pixel values is an array. All data elements in an image array are the same type. The elements can be of a simple data type (e.g., a boolean, integer, real, complex, or enumerated type) or each element can be a compound data type (i.e., another array, a record, or a list). The formal definition of an image array is recursive. The structure of an image array can be arbitrarily complex

Conceptually images are viewed as 5-dimensional arrays which have the following dimensions:

X for spatial columns (horizontal direction)
Y for spatial rows (vertical direction)
Z for depth (i.e., volumes)
T for temporal pixel planes (e.g., moving images)
B for color bands, spectral bands, or generic pixel planes

All of the dimensions are not required for every image. The following classes of images are identified in the standard:

Dimensions	Description
X, Y, 1, 1, 1	2D Monochrome
X, Y, 1, 1, *B*	Color (3- or 4-color bands)
X, Y, Z, 1, 1	Volume (monochrome)
X, Y, 1, 1, *B*	Spectral (with *B* spectral bands)
X, Y, 1, *T*, 1	Temporal (a grayscale movie))
X, Y, Z, 1, *B*	Volume-color (multiple color values per "voxel")
X, Y, Z, 1, *B*	Volume-spectral
X, Y, Z, T, 1	Volume-temporal (a series of volumes over time)
X, Y, 1, *T, B*	Temporal-color (e.g., a color movie)
X, Y, 1, *T, B*	Temporal-spectral
X, Y, Z, T, B	Volume-temporal-color (a volume color movie)
X, Y, Z, T, B	Volume-temporal-spectral

Image Attributes

Channel	Channel type (one of: bi-level, halftone, gray-value, color, transparency, feature, application-specific) and scanning characteristics (e.g., scan type, gamma correction, quantization depths, transfer function)
Color	Color model used, the white point specification in the CIE Yxy space, and a sequence of test colors associated with particular regions of the image
Free-form	A character string; its interpretation is application-dependent
Representation	A description of the coordinate system in which the image is represented, a specific description of each dimension (axis) of the coordinate system, and a transformation matrix that relates the image data to the coordinate system

Image Annotations

Text, graphics, audio or other application-related data can be associated with an image. The exact encoding of such data is not specified by this standard; its encoding is application dependent

Image-related
Non-image data

Histogram	A table that defines the number of pixels that lie within specified value ranges
Lookup table (LUT)	A general structure for mapping a set of input vectors to a set of output vectors
Neighborhood	A region that is not referenced to a particular position within the image
Region of interest (ROI)	A general mechanism for pixel-by-pixel selection; it can be implemented by an area boundary (e.g, an ellipse), a set of coordinates, or a bit-array
Value list	A list of features; each feature is associated with a specific pixel in the image

IIF
(ISO 12087 — Part 3) *(Continued)*

Data Organization

The data organization is defined using the Abstract Syntax Notation One (ANS.1)—ISO 8824. The syntax definition for IIF is recursive. Arbitrarily complex data structures can be built from the combination of lower-level primitives. The data structures can be conceptualized as a "tree"

The data stream is sequential. The actual pixel values associated with an image can be stored with an image description, or separately at the end of the file. If they are stored separately, they are associated by a unique label

The following is a simplified diagram of the data stream:

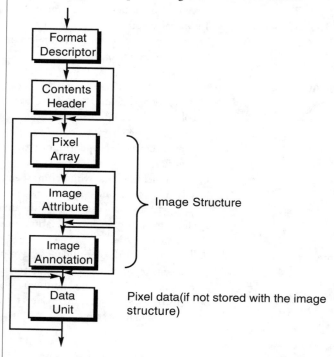

The encoding of the data follows the Basic Encoding Rules (BER) associated with ANS.1 defined in ISO 8825. Due to the variable length encoding scheme used by the BER, no byte offsets are shown in the following data descriptions

Format Descriptor

Byte#	Data	Details
—	Self identification	ISO standard 12087 Part 3; 1.0.12087.3
—	Conformance profile	Defines the level of implementation needed to interpret this data set
—	Version number	Will not be included in final standard

Only the first field is required

Contents Header

All of these fields are optional. The ASCII strings have no predefined structure or interpretation

Byte#	Data	Details
—	Title	ASCII string
—	Owner	ASCII string
—	Data and time	Generalized time
—	Message	ASCII string

Pixel Array

This is a description of the image data. The order of the values in the array is determined by the ordering of the dimension descriptions. The first dimension indicates the outermost loop over the array (i.e., the left-most subscript). The last dimension indicates the innermost loop over the array (i.e, the right-most subscript). This is "column major order" where the right-most array subscript varies the fastest

Byte#	Data	Details
—	Number of dimensions	Of the array

The following two fields are repeated for each dimension of the array

Byte#	Data	Details
—	Dimension identifier	ASCII string
—	Index range	Either a single integer that specifies the size of the interval or two integers: a lower and upper bound of the interval

Byte#	Data	Details
—	Pixel data type	Either a simple data type (e.g., real, integer) or a compound data type (e.g., record, array, list).
—	Data placement	Either the actual pixel data values or a label reference to the data (which is stored later in the data stream)
—	Attributes	A sequence (list) of attributes

IIF
(ISO 12087 — Part 3) *(Continued)*

Image Attributes
Refer to the ISO documents for details of the attribute data. Attributes can be one the following types:

Metric-attributes
Band-attributes
Capture-attributes
Freeform-description

Image Annotation
Any type of data, identified simply as a "text-structure," a "graphics-structure," an "audio-structure," or as "application-specific" data

Data Unit
A data unit is a set of data values that define the pixels of an image. Four major encodings are allowed. Each major encoding has optional sub-encodings

BuiltinEncodedDataUnit	The ANS.1 primitives: bitstring, octet string, integer, real, complex number defined as two reals, and an enumerated value defined as ASCII text
ExternallyDefinedDataUnit	Defines 8-, 16- and 32-bit integers (in both MSB and LSB forms and both signed and unsigned) and IEEE single- and double-precision floating point encodings
CompressedDataUnit	One of "faxg3-1d-field," "faxg3-2d-field," "faxg4-2d-field," "jbig-bilevel-image-entity," "jpeg-intermediate-format," or "mpeg-bitstream"
ANY	An undefined encoding; application-dependent

File Name Suffix None

References ISO/IEC 12087
Computer Graphics and Image Processing
Image Processing and Interchange (IPI)

Part 1	12087-1	A Common Architecture for Imaging, 70 pages (DIS)
Part 2	12087-2	Programmer's Imaging Kernel System Application Program Interface, 952 pages (DIS)
Part 3	12087-3	*Image Interchange Facility*, 167 pages (DIS)

Available through ANSI and most standards making bodies

JBIG
(ISO 11544; CCITT T.82)

Acronym	Joint Bi-level Experts Group
	Real Title: Coded Representation of Picture and Audio Information—Progressive Bi-level Image Compression
Origin	ISO/IEC committee JTC1/SC2/WG9 (before Nov. 1991)
	ISO/IEC committee JTC1/SC29/WG9 (current)
	There was close collaboration with CCITT SGVIII
Motivation	To create an international standard for digital encoding and lossless compression of one-bit-per-pixel (monochrome) still images
	During development it was also determined that this compression scheme produces good lossless compression ratios for grayscale and color images by coding them as a series of bit-planes
Users	This is a new standard and its range of use will be determined by its acceptance into various applications

Control	Copyrighted by	ISO
	Trademarks	None
	Royalty Fees	There are 24 patents identified in Annex E of the standard that *possibly* apply to the use of the JBIG compression scheme. Twelve are owned by IBM, seven by AT&T, two by Mitsubishi, two by KDD, and one by Canon. The exact set of licenses required to use JBIG is not specified by the standard
Versions	CD (Committee Draft)	October 1991
	DIS (Draft International Standard)	May 1992
	IS (International Standard)	October 1993
Overview	Major Type of Data	2D Raster
	Color Representation	None specified
	Data Organization	Sequential data stream
		Pixel data—progressive-hierarchical
	Data Encoding	Binary; arithmetic coding
	Data Compression	Predictive (lossless encoding)

JBIG is a data encoding format and not a file format. It is expected that JBIG-encoded data will be encapsulated within other data formats. For example, IIF supports JBIG encodings

The data is compressed in layers using a "resolution-reduction" method that repeatedly reduces the resolution of an image by a factor of 2 in both horizontal and vertical dimensions. This reduces the number of pixels in each layer by a factor of four. The following diagram represents this scheme

JBIG
(ISO 11544; CCITT T.82) *(Continued)*

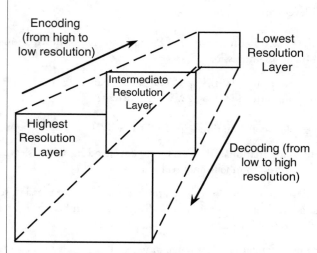

Each layer's resolution is 1/2
of the previous layer's

Progressive Encoding

Data Types | Image size | Number of samples per line, number of lines, number of bit-planes (1 for bilevel images)

Compression parameters — Number of differential layers in the compression, which schemes are used, which decoding tables to use, etc.

Prediction table — (Optional); used to predicate the value of a pixel given the value of surrounding pixels

Pixel data — Pixel values, encoded at different resolutions

JBIG
(ISO 11544; CCITT T.82)   *(Continued)*

Data Organization | General syntax of the data stream:

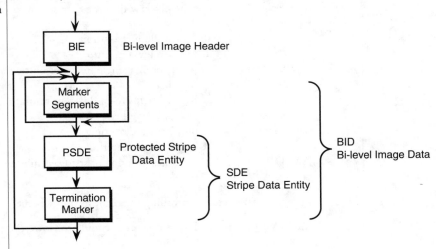

Signature
None

BIE: Bilevel Image Header
All values are stored with the MSB first

Byte#	Data	Details
	7 6 5 4 3 2 1 0	
1	Lowest resolution layer	Typically 0 (unless it references a previous BIE)
2	Number of resolution layers	In this BIE
3	Number of bit planes	This is 1 if the image is bilevel
4	Fill	Always 0
5–8	Horizontal dimension	Of the highest resolution image
9–12	Vertical dimension	Of the highest resolution image
13–16	# of scan lines per strip	In the lowest resolution image
17	Maximum horizontal offset	For the AT (adaptive templates) pixel
18	Maximum vertical offset	For the AT (adaptive templates) pixel
19	0 0 0 0 b_3 b_2 b_1 b_0	Bit flags (See description below)
20	0 c_6 c_5 c_4 c_3 c_2 c_1 c_0	Bit flags (See description below)
21–1748	Deterministic prediction table	0 or 1728 bytes; optional; if absence the default table is used

JBIG
(ISO 11544; CCITT T.82)   *(Continued)*

Bit flag descriptions

Flags b_3–b_0 specify the order of the pixels within the data stream

b_3	HITOLO	0: Low to high resolution
		1: High to low resolution
b_2	SEQ	0: All strips of a single image resolution are grouped together;
		1: Related strips from different resolutions are grouped together
b_1	ILEAVE	0: bit planes are contiguous
		1: bit planes are interleaved
b_0	SMID	Determines ordering of strips within the stream (see text)

Flags c_6–c_0 specify parameters controlling the compression scheme

c_6	LRLTWO	0: The template for coding the lowest resolution layer has 3 lines
		1: The template for coding the lowest resolution layer has 2 lines
c_5	VLENGTH	0: No NEWLEN marker segments in the data stream
		1: The data stream may or may not contain NEWLEN markers
c_4	TPDON	0: Disable differential-layer TP (typical prediction)
		1: Enable differential-layer TP
c_3	TPBON	0: Disable lowest-resolution-layer TP (typical prediction)
		1: Enable lowest-resolution-layer TP
c_2	DPON	0: Disable deterministic prediction (DP)
		1: Enable deterministic predication
c_1	DPPRIV	0: Use the default deterministic prediction (DP) table
		1: Use a private deterministic prediction (DP) table
c_0	DPLAST	0: The private DP table is included in the header
		1: Use the last loaded private DP table

Marker Segments

Three types of data can be included between the strips of data

JBIG
(ISO 11544; CCITT T.82)   *(Continued)*

The ATMOVE marker (Adaptive-Template AT movement) allows the relocation of a special pixel within the predictive template. Moving this location can sometimes produce better predications and hence better compression

The NEWLEN marker, redefines the image length. This allows compression to begin before the length of the image is known

The COMMENT marker allows the inclusion of any number of application-dependent bytes between the strips of data

PSCD—Protected Strip Data Entity

This is the compressed data values for a single strip of the image. A strip is composed of one or more scan lines. The data is called "protected" because any data bytes that contain all 1s (i.e., hexadecimal FF) have a stuffed zero byte following them. This distinguishes them from a marker segment

Termination Marker

This marks the end of the strip data and it also indicates whether the decoder should be re-initialized to its start-up state

Byte#	Data	Details
1	Escape byte	Always hexadecimal FF
2	End flag	2: SDNORM —normal end 3: SDRST—reset after strip is processed

File Name Suffix	None	
References	CCITT Recommendation T.82 ISO/IEC International Standard 11544 Coded Representation of Pictures and Audio Information—Progressive Bi-Level Image Compression	
	The document can be purchased from ANSI or other standards bodies	

JFIF

Acronym	JPEG File Interchange Format
Origin	C-Cube Microsystems 1778 McCarthy Blvd. Milpitas, CA 95035
	C-Cube Microsystems developed JFIF with input from all of the major vendors of JPEG-related products
Motivation	A minimal file format that enables JPEG bitstreams to be exchanged between a wide variety of platforms and applications
Users	This is such a new data format that its amount of use is not currently known

Control	Copyrighted by	NA
	Trademarks	NA
	Royalty Fees	Same restrictions that apply to JPEG

Versions	Version 1.01	December 10, 1991

Overview	Major Type of Data	JPEG bitstream plus parameters
	Color Representation	YC_rC_b
	Data Organization	Sequential data stream
	Data Encoding	Binary
	Data Compression	Normal JPEG options

Data Types	JPEG bitstream	Identical to the JPEG standard

An application data block with the following data:

Identifier	Uniquely identifies this application data block; "JFIF"
Version	The version of JFIF used to create the data
Units	Units for density values (i.e., none, inches, cm)
Xdensity	Pixels per unit of measurement in the horizontal direction
Ydensity	Pixels per unit of measurement in the vertical direction
Xthumbnail	Number of pixels in preview image in horizontal direction
Ythumbnail	Number of pixels in preview image in vertical direction
$(RGB)n$	Pixels of "thumbnail" image (preview image)

Two assumptions are made about the data that are not explicitly required by the JPEG standard. These are:

- The color values represent a YC_rC_b color space. The transformation between RGB values and YC_rC_b values is defined according to the CCIR Recommendation 601 (normalized to values in the range 0–255)

JFIF   *(Continued)*

$$Y = 0.299 \quad R + 0.587 \quad G + \ 0.114 \ B$$
$$C_b = -0.1687 \quad R - 0.3313 \quad G + \quad 0.5 \ B$$
$$C_r = 0.5 \quad\quad R - 0.4187 \quad G - 0.0813 \ B$$

$$R = Y \quad\quad\quad\quad\quad\quad + 1.402 \quad\quad C_r$$
$$G = Y \quad - 0.34414 \quad C_b - 0.71414 \quad C_r$$
$$B = Y \quad + 1.772 \quad\quad C_b$$

- When the components of an image are sampled at different resolutions, the JPEG standard does not specify the alignment of the different resolutions. JFIF assumes that components sampled at a lower resolution (as compared to the highest-resolution component) are centered within their respective sub-blocks. To calculate the offset of the upper-left-hand corner sample within any component, use the following equations:

$$X\text{offset}_i[0,0] = (N\text{samples}_{ref}/N\text{samples}_i)/2 - 0.5$$
$$Y\text{offset}_i[0,0] = (N\text{lines}_{ref}/N\text{lines}_i)/2 - 0.5$$

where, $N\text{samples}_{ref}$ is the number of samples per line in the largest component, $N\text{samples}_i$ is the number of samples per line in the ith component, $N\text{lines}_{ref}$ is the number of lines in the largest component, and $N\text{lines}_i$ is the number of lines per line in the ith component

Data Organization

General (simplified) syntax of the data stream:

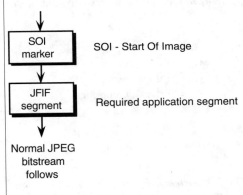

SOI - Start Of Image

Required application segment

JFIF *(Continued)*

To conform to the JFIF format the first bytes of the data stream must be as follows:

Byte#	Data	Details
1–2	SOI: Start Of Image	Hex FFD8
3–4	APP0: Application segment 0	Hex FFE0
5–6	Length	In bytes; length includes these 2 bytes but not the previous 2
7–11	Identifier	"JFIF"; hex 4A46494600
12–13	Version	Currently 1.01; hex 0101
14	Units	0: no units; 1: inch; 2: cm
15–16	Xdensity	Horizontal pixel density
17–18	Ydensity	Vertical pixel density
19	Xthumbnail	Thumbnail horizontal pixel count
20	Ythumbnail	Thumbnail vertical pixel count
21–(20 + 3n)	(RGB)n	3n bytes of red, green, blue values; $n = X$thumbnail $\times Y$thumbnail

Frame Header

In the frame header the following values must be set to conform to the JFIF format:

Number of components $Nc = 1$ or 3
1st component $C_1 = 1$; the Y component
2nd component $C_2 = 2$; the C_b component
3rd component $C_3 = 3$; the C_r component

File Name Suffix   Unix   .jpg

References   Hamilton, Eric, *JPEG File Interchange Format,* Version 1.01, December 10, 1991, C-Cube Microsystems, 1778 McCarthy Blvd., Milpitas, CA 95035

Independent JPEG Group
A volunteer organization to prompt and support the use of JPEG
Organized by Tom Lane
E-mail: *jpeg-info@uunet.uu.net*

JPEG
(ISO 10918)

Acronym	Joint Photographic Experts Group Real Title: Digital Compression and Coding of Continuous-Tone Still Images
Origin	ISO/IEC committee JTC1/SC2/WG8 (before 1990) ISO/IEC committee JTC1/SC2/WG10 (before Nov. 1991) ISO/IEC committee JTC1/SC29/WG10 (current) There was close collaboration with CCITT SGVIII Special Rapporteur committee Q.16
Motivation	To create an international standard for the digital encoding and compression of continuous-tone still images (both grayscale and color) JPEG was designed to satisfy the needs of a broad range of applications. Its specific design goals were: • High compression ratios along with high image fidelity (a comparison of the original image to the decompressed image reveals little loss of image quality) • An application (or user) can select from a broad range of compression ratios, trading off image quality for higher compression to meet the specific needs of an application • No restrictions on the image contents (such as, image complexity and range of colors) • No restrictions on the image characteristics (such as, resolution and pixel aspect ratios) • A manageable computational complexity that would allow for reasonable software implementations and fast hardware implementations • A lossless encoding mode for exact image reproduction • A sequential encoding mode for image reproduction using a single pass through the data • A progressive encoding mode for image reproduction using multiple passes through the data (the image is initially presented blurry and each pass through the data adds further clarity to the image) • A hierarchical encoding mode for image reproduction using a sequence of frames, each at different resolutions
Users	This is a new standard and its range of use will be determined by its acceptance into various applications. Its intended use includes, but is not limited to, facsimile, videotex, audiographic conferencing, desktop publishing, graphics arts, medical imaging, and scientific imaging

JPEG
(ISO 10918) *(Continued)*

Control	Copyrighted by	ISO/IEC
	Trademarks	None
	Royalty Fees	There are 10 patents related to arithmetic encoding identified in Annex L of the standard. Of these, some are owned by IBM, some by AT&T and one by Mitsubishi. The use of arithmetic encoding in a JPEG data set probably requires some set of license fees, but the exact requirements are unclear
Versions	Committee Draft (CD)	June 1991
	Draft International Standard (DIS)	June 1992
	International Standard (IS)	June 1993
Overview	Major Type of Data	2D Raster
	Color Representation	None specified; (YC_rC_b typically used)
	Data Organization	Sequential data stream
		Pixel data
		Sequential mode: DCT or predictive
		Progressive mode: DCT
		Hierarchical mode: DCT or predictive
	Data Encoding	Binary
	Data Compression	Predictive (lossless encoding); DCT (lossy encoding)

JPEG is not one standard but a suite of standards—29 distinct coding processes in all. These are shown in the following diagram. The "baseline sequential" mode is the basis of the majority of JPEG implementations. The support of all 29 encodings by a single implementation will probably be rare

JPEG is an encoding format and not an actual file format. JPEG does not include some of the "normal" information associated with raster images, such as the definition of a color space to interpret the pixel values. One advantage to this is that a JPEG encoding can be used in many different application-dependent data streams. Five data formats covered in the appendices of this book support the JPEG encoding: IIF, JFIF, JTIFF (a class of TIFF file), QuickTime, and Postscript Level 2

JPEG
(ISO 10918) *(Continued)*

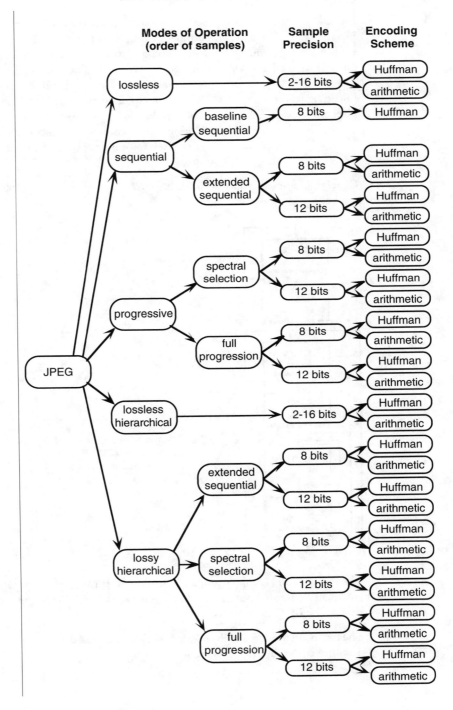

JPEG
(ISO 10918) *(Continued)*

Data Types	Mode of operation	Lossless, sequential, progressive, or hierarchical
	Image size	Number of samples per line, number of lines, etc.
	Compression parameters	Which decoding tables to use, etc.
	Quantization tables	Defines an array of 64 values used to limit (or restore) the precision of the sample values
	Encoding tables	Defines the Huffman and arithmetic coding tables
	Pixel data	Pixel sample values, possibly at different spatial resolutions; monochrome images contain one sample per pixel; color images contain three samples per pixel

Data Organization General, simplified syntax of the data stream (for sequential and progressive modes):

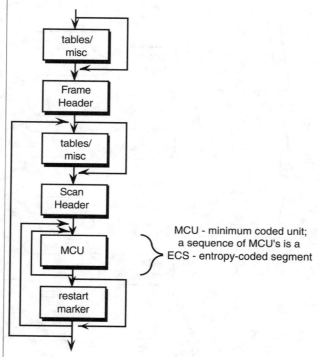

The organization, compression, and encoding of JPEG's *baseline sequential* mode are discussed throughout this book. For a detailed discussion of the other modes, refer to the JPEG documents

The two main headers are given here for insight into the data format. For complete details refer to the JPEG documents

JPEG
(ISO 10918)   *(Continued)*

Frame Header

Byte#	Data	Details
1–2	SOFn (tag)	Encoding type (e.g., baseline sequential)
3–4	Lf (header length)	In bytes
5	P (sample precision)	Number of bits per sample
6–7	Y (number of lines)	In largest component of image
8–9	X (number of samples)	Per line, in the largest component of image
10	Nf (# of image components)	i.e., Samples per pixel

The following set of parameters are repeated Nf times; one set for each component of the image

Byte#	Data	Details
	7 6 5 4 3 2 1 0	
1	Ci	Component identifier; a unique label
2	Hi | Vi	Horizontal and vertical sampling factors
3	Tqi	Quantization table selector for component

Scan Header

Byte#	Data	Details
1–2	SOS	Start of scan: hex FFDA
3–4	Ls (length of header)	In bytes
	Ns (number of components)	In scan

The following set of parameters are repeated Ns times; one set for each component included in the scan

Byte#	Data	Details
	7 6 5 4 3 2 1 0	
1	Csi	Scan component selector
2	Tdi | Tai	DC and AC entropy coding table selectors

JPEG
(ISO 10918) *(Continued)*

The scan header ends with the following parameters:

Byte#	Data		Details
1	*Ss*		Start of spectral selection
2	*Se*		End of spectral selection
3	*Ah*	*Al*	Used for progressive and lossless mode only

File Name Suffix
None

References
ISO/IEC 10918, Digital Compression and Coding of Continuous-Tone Still Images

| Part I | 10918-1 | Requirements and Guidelines, 198 pages (DIS) |
| Part II | 10918-2 | Compliance testing, 43 pages (CD) |

These can be purchased from ANSI, or from other standards bodies

---

MACPAINT

Acronym
Macintosh Paint format

Origin
Apple Computer, Inc.
20525 Mariani Avenue
Cupertino, CA 95014-6299
Tel. (408) 996-1010

Motivation
To provide a common raster data format for Macintosh applications

Users
Macintosh applications, as well as the exchange of raster based images on bulletin boards

Control

Copyrighted by	Apple
Trademarks	NA
Royalty Fees	None

Versions
NA

MACPAINT *(Continued)*

Overview	Major Type of Data	2D Raster (fixed size: 576 × 720)
	Color Representation	Monochrome; (0: white, 1: black)
	Data Organization	Sequential
	Data Encoding	Binary
	Data Compression	Run-length encoding (PackBits)

Data Types Monochrome raster image data, (fixed size of 575 across × 720 down)
Monochrome raster pattern data (38 patterns, 8 × 8 bitmaps)

Data Organization General syntax of data stream

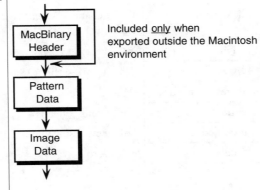

Included <u>only</u> when
exported outside the Macintosh
environment

Signature
On a Macintosh system
bytes 1–4; hex (00000002)

On a nonMacintosh system (file contains a MacBinary header)
bytes 67–70 contain ASCII 'PNTG,' hex (504E5447)

MACPAINT   *(Continued)*

MacBinary Header
Included only when exported outside the Macintosh environment. Contains exactly 128 bytes

Byte#	Data	Details
1	First byte	Always zero
2–3	Length of file name (L)	Possible values 0–31, MSB first
4–66	File name	ASCII characters
67–70	File type	ASCII characters, 'PNTG'
71–74	File creator	ASCII characters (e.g., 'MPNT' for MacPaint)
75–84	Filler	Set to zero
85–88	# of bytes in data	(Not counting this 128 byte header)
89–92	Length of "resource" fork	Typically zero
93–96	Creation date	# of seconds since Jan. 1, 1904
97–100	Last modified date	# of seconds since Jan. 1, 1904
101–128	Filler	Set to zero

Pattern Data (512 bytes)

Byte#	Data	Details
1–4	Pattern data signature	Hex(00000003)
5–12	Pattern one	8 bytes, 8×8 bit encoded bitmap pattern
…	Patterns 2–38	Remaining bitmap patterns in order
308–512	Filler	204 bytes of filler, set to zero

Raster Data
The data is stored in rows from left to right. The rows are ordered from top to bottom. Each scan line of the image is encoded separately (the equivalent of 72 bytes ($8 \times 72 = 576$ pixels). Run lengths do not cross scan-line boundaries. The data is compressed using the PackBits run-length encoding scheme

References

Hogan, Thom, *The Programmer's Apple Mac Sourcebook: Reference Tables for Apple Macintosh Hardware and System Software,* Microsoft Press, Redmond, WA, 1989, p. 91

Rimmer, Steve, *Bit-Mapped Graphics,* Windcrest Books, Blue Ridge Summit, PA, pp. 27–54

MPEG
(ISO 11172)

Acronym	Moving Picture Experts Group
	Formal Title: Coded Representation of Picture, Audio and Multimedia/ Hypermedia Information
	ISO CD 11172 Title: Information Technology—Coding of moving pictures and associated audio—For digital storage media at up to about 1.5 Mbit/s
Origin	ISO/IEC JTC1/SC 2/WG 11 (before Nov. 1991) ISO/IEC JTC1/SC 29/WG 11 (current)
Motivation	To create an international standard that combines digital video data, digital audio data, and timing data into a single sequential data stream
	The data is compressed to create acceptable video and audio performance within a limited data rate of up to 1.5 Mbits/s
Users	This is a new standard and its range of use will be determined by its acceptance into various applications. Its intended use is with devices that can support a data rate of approximately 1.5 Mbits/s, such as Compact Disc, Digital Audio Tape, and magnetic hard disks

Control	Copyrighted by	ISO/IEC
	Trademarks	None
	Royalty Fees	Approximately 30 patents which may be relevant for implementing an MPEG system have been identified. The implications of this are unknown at this time

Versions	Committee Draft (CD)	November 1991
	Draft International Standard (DIS)	March 1992
	International Standard (IS)	March 1993

Overview	MPEG defines three distinct functions:	
	• System layer	Synchronization of multiple compressed streams on playback
		Interleaving of multiple compressed streams into a single stream on creation
		Initialization of buffering for playback start up
		Continuous buffer management
		Time identification
	• Digital video codec	Encoding and decoding of sequences of 2D raster images or traditional video
	• Digital audio codec	Encoding and decoding of sound or audio
	The following discussion summarizes the system layer and the video codec in two separate sections	

MPEG
(ISO 11172   *(Continued)*)

Overview | Major Type of Data   Timing and synchronization; data packets
(System | Color Representation   None
Layer) | Data Organization   Sequential
               | Data Encoding   Binary
               | Data Compression   None

Up to 32 audio and 16 video streams may be multiplexed simultaneously, along with up to 16 "private" data streams

Data   The general syntax of the data stream:
Organization

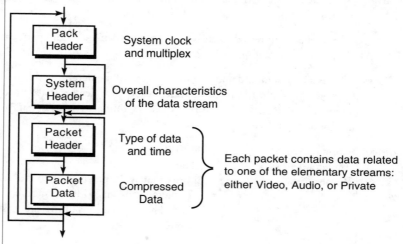

For the exact encodings of these fields, see the MPEG specification

Pack Header
Includes the following:

System clock reference   Indicates the intended time of arrival of the last byte
                              of the "system clock reference field" at the input of
                              the system target decoder
Multiplex rate   The rate at which the system target decoder receives
                              the data stream during the pack; measured in 50
                              bytes/s (rounded up)

System Header
Includes the following:

Rate bound   The maximum multiplex rate of any pack in the data
                              stream
Audio bound   The maximum number of audio streams (up to 32
                              allowed)

MPEG
(ISO 11172   (Continued))

Fixed flag	Indicates a fixed bit-rate or a variable bit-rate operation mode
CSPS flag	Indicates whether the data stream is a "constrained system parameters stream"
System audio lock flag	Indicates whether there is a specified, constant harmonic relationship between the audio sampling rate and the system clock
System video lock flag	Indicates whether there is a specified, constant harmonic relationship between the video sampling rate and the system clock
Video bound	The maximum number of video streams (up to 16 allowed)

For each stream (i.e., video, audio, or private), buffer requirements may be specified as follows. STD stands for "standard target decoder"

STD buffer bound scale	0: Indicates units of 128 bytes; 1: Indicates units of 1,024 bytes
STD buffer size bound	The required input buffer size for decoding the data stream

Overview (Video Data)

Major Type of Data	Raster (2D digital video)
Color Representation	YC_rC_b (4:1:1)
Data Organization	Sequential
Data Encoding	Binary
Data Compression	DCT: for individual frame images
	Differencing (with motion compensation)—for temporal compression (between frames)

The size of the pictures and the frame rate is not mandated by the MPEG standard. However the target data rate of 1.5 Mb/s effectively limits these parameters. The practical limits are approximately 350×250 pixels displayed at 24 to 30 pictures per second. MPEG does not support scan-line interlacing

Data Types (Video Data)

Three types of picture encodings are defined:

Intra *(I)* Pictures

These pictures are encoded without references to any other pictures. They are compressed by using DCT and by sub-sampling the chrominance information (C_rC_b) of the picture at half the spatial resolution of the luminance information (Y)

MPEG
(ISO 11172 *(Continued)*)

Predicted (P) Pictures

These pictures are encoded in reference to a previous "I picture" (or another "P picture"). Only the differences between the current picture and the previous reference picture are stored. Typically the differences are small. To reduce the differences even further, "motion vectors" are stored to indicate shifts in the horizontal or vertical directions between the pictures. Offsetting a 16×16 macroblock of pixels by a motion vector "lines up" the values so that their differences are as small as possible (and often zero)

Bidirectional (B) Pictures

These pictures are encoded in reference to either previous or future pictures ("I" or "P" pictures). *Forward motion vectors* reference previous pictures and *backward motion vectors* reference future pictures

Data Organization (Video Data)

The *conceptual* organization of the data stream (in terms of picture order):

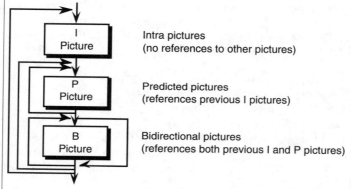

Note: The order of the pictures in the data stream does not match the order in which they are displayed. They are ordered in the data stream to simplify decoding. During video playback, the B pictures are displayed before the P pictures

The number of P pictures and B pictures included in the data stream is not specified by the standard. More P and B type encodings produces better compression at the cost of poorer image quality. Limiting the P and B type encodings typically increases image quality at the cost of higher data rates (i.e., lower compression)

MPEG
(ISO 11172 *(Continued)*)

The actual syntax of the data stream:

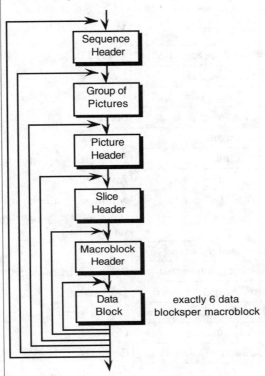

exactly 6 data
blocksper macroblock

MPEG
(ISO 11172 *(Continued)*)

Sequence Header
Contains information related to one or more "group-of-pictures"

Byte#	Data	Details
1–4	Sequence header code	In hex 000001B3
(12 bits)	Horizontal size	In pixels
(12 bits)	Vertical size	In pixels
(4 bits)	Pel aspect ratio	See below
(4 bits)	Picture rate	See below
(18 bits)	Bit rate	In units of 400 bits/s (rounded up)
(1 bit)	Marker bit	Always 1
(10 bits)	VBV buffer size	Minimum buffer needed to decode this sequence of pictures; in 16-KB units
(1 bit)	Constrained parameter flag	
(1 bit)	Load intra quantizer matrix	0: false; 1: true (matrix follows)
(64 bytes)	Intra quantizer matrix	Optional
(1 bit)	Load nonintra quantizer matrix	0: false; 1: true (matrix follows)
(64 bytes)	Nonintra quantizer matrix	Optional
—	Sequence extension data	Optional
—	User data	Optional application-dependent data

MPEG
(ISO 11172 *(Continued)*)

The following aspect ratios are defined:

Code	Height/Width	Examples
0000	Undefined	Forbidden: cannot be used
0001	1.0000	VGA, most computer monitors
0010	0.6735	
0011	0.7031	16:9 ratio, 625 lines
0100	0.7615	
0101	0.8055	
0110	0.8437	16:9 ratio, 525 lines
0111	0.8935	
1000	0.9375	CCIR 601, 625 lines; 720×576 at 4:3 ratio
1001	0.9815	
1010	1.0255	
1011	1.0695	
1100	1.1250	CCIR 601, 525 lines; 720×485 at 4:3 ratio
1101	1.1575	
1110	1.2015	
1111	Undefined	Reserved for future definition

The following picture rates are defined:

Code	Pictures/Second	Examples
0000	Undefined	Forbidden: cannot be used
0001	23.976	
0010	24	Film
0011	25	PAL/SECAM video (noninterlaced)
0100	29.97	NTSC video (noninterlaced)
0101	30	
0110	50	PAL/SECAM video (interlaced)
0111	59.94	NTSC video (interlaced)
1000	60	
1001	Undefined	
...		Reserved for future definition
1111	Undefined	

MPEG
(ISO 11172 *(Continued)***)**

Group of Pictures Header
A group-of-pictures contains one "I picture" and zero or more B and P pictures

Byte#	Data	Details
1–4	Group start code	In hex 000001B8
(25 bits)	Time code	Time synchronization for the first picture of the group
(1 bit)	Closed group of pictures?	Set to 1 if this group of pictures does not reference the previous group of pictures
(1 bit)	Broken link	Always set to 0 during encoding; set to 1 if editing of the group makes it non-decodeable
—	Sequence extension data	Optional
—	User data	Optional application-dependent data

Picture Header
One picture of the video sequence

Byte#	Data	Details
1–4	Picture start code	In hex 00000100
(10 bits)	Temporal reference	Counter that orders the picture in display order (modulo 1024)
(3 bit)	Picture coding type	Coded (See below)
(16 bit)	vbv_delay	Decoder buffer control
(4 bits)	Forward vector coding scheme	Only present in data stream for P or B pictures
(4 bits)	Backward vector coding scheme	Only present in data stream for type B pictures
(1–40 bits)	Extra information	5 optional data values, each 8 bits; a flag bit precedes each value
—	Sequence extension data	Optional
—	User data	Optional application-dependent data

MPEG
(ISO 11172 *(Continued)*)

Code	Picture coding type
000	Undefined (forbidden)
001	Intra-coded (I Picture)
010	Predicative-coded (P Picture)
011	Bidirectionally-predicative-coded (B Picture)
100	DC-intra-coded (D Picture)
101	Undefined (reserved for future use)

...

Slice Header
A slice contains one or more macroblocks

Byte#	Data	Details
1–4	Slice start code	In hex 000001 followed by a "slice vertical position" in the range 01 to AF
(5 bits)	Quantizer scale	Used to increase the amount of quantization for this slice
Min 1 bit	Extra information	Optional data values, each 8 bits; a flag "1" bit precedes each value

Macroblock Header
A macroblock is data for a 16 × 16 pixel area of the picture. It contains 6 data blocks with 64 values in each one (i.e., an 8 × 8 array). The first four blocks are the luminance values. The last two are the chrominance values sampled at one-half the spatial resolution. The following diagram indicates this scheme

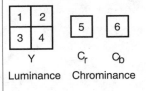

Y C_r C_b
Luminance Chrominance

MPEG
(ISO 11172 *(Continued)***)**

The data is encoded using variable-length (Huffman) codes. Therefore the following list of data values does not include bit or byte counts

Address increment	Indicates the number of skipped macroblocks (macroblocks which are not changed from the previous picture may be skipped)
Macroblock type	Indicates whether the quantization for this block is changed and whether forward or backward motion prediction was used to code it
Quantizer scale (optional)	Used to increase or decrease the quantization level for the 6 data blocks that make up the macroblock
Motion vectors	(Forward horizontal, forward vertical) (Backward horizontal, backward vertical)
Coded block pattern	Determines which of the 6 data blocks are actually present in the macroblock (data blocks which are not changed from the previous picture do not need to be coded)

Data Block

This contains the Huffman-encoded coefficients of an 8×8 block of pixel values after being transformed by a DCT. The coefficients are stored in zigzag order and run-length encoded

File Name Suffix

Unix   .mpg

References

ISO/IEC 11172 Title: Information Technology—Coding of moving pictures and associated audio—For digital storage media at up to about 1.5 Mbit/s

Part 1	11172-1	Systems	57 pages (DIS)
Part 2	11172-2	Video	115 pages (DIS)
Part 3	11172-3	Audio	164 pages (DIS)
Part 4	CD 11172-4	Conformance Testing	

Available through ANSI and most standards making bodies

netCDF (CDF)

Acronym	netCDF: Network Common Data Form CDF: Common Data Format
Origin	netCDF is an extended and modified version of CDF by: Unidata Program Center University Corporation for Atmospheric Research (UCAR) P.O. Box 3000 Boulder, CO 80307-3000 CDF is a data format developed by: NASA Science Data Systems Standards Office (NSDSSO) National Space Science Data Center (NSSDC) National Aeronautics and Space Administration (NASA) NASA Goddard Space Flight Center Greenbelt, MD 20771
Motivation	The netCDF library provides an application and machine-independent interface to self-describing, multidimensional scientific data Its initial target was National Weather Service (NWS) data
Users	Several software systems use netCDF and are included in a composite package of software called *Unidata's Scientific Data Management system (SDM)*. Other software packages have also made use of netCDF

Control	
Copyrighted by	UCAR
Trademarks	
Royalty Fees	None

Versions	
Version 1.0	1988
Version 1.06	1990

Overview	
Major Type of Data	Raster (*N*-dimensional)
Color Representation	None
Data Organization	Sequential
Data Encoding	Binary (XDR format)
Data Compression	None

The actual data format of a netCDF data set is hidden from the user by the library interface. Users are expected to access the data only through the library interface routines. The specifications for the data format are not documented by UCAR. The following specifications comes from a reverse engineering of the data format

netCDF (CDF)   *(Continued)*

Data Types	Dimension	One axis of a multidimensional array. It has a descriptive name and a size
	Attribute	Contains information about the entire file or a single variable (i.e., an array). It is metadata. It can be a descriptive text string, a scalar value, or a vector
	Variable	A multidimensional array of values (all of the same data type). It has a name, a data type, and a shape described by its list of dimensions
	Record Variable	A variable with the size of its first dimension undefined. It has a variable size

Data Organization   The general syntax of the data stream:

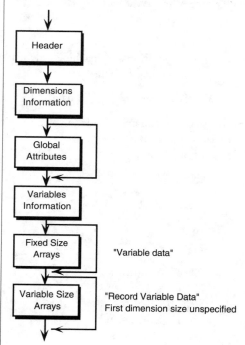

Header

Byte#	Data	Details
1–4	Signature	ASCII string "CDF1"
5–8	Number of records	

Dimension Information

Byte#	Data	Details
1–4	Dimension indicator	Hexadecimal 0000000A
5–8	Number of dimensions	

The following 3 fields are repeated for each separate dimension defined

Byte#	Data	Details
(4 bytes)	Length of name	In bytes
(Varies)	Name of dimension	ASCII text; aligned to 4-byte boundaries
(4 bytes)	Size	Number of values along dimension

Attributes

The presence of attributes is optional. If there are no attributes, the "attribute indicator" is not included in the data set

Byte#	Data	Details
1–4	Attribute indicator	Hexadecimal 0000000C
5–8	Number of attributes	

The following 3 fields are repeated for each separate attribute defined

(4 bytes)	Length of name	In bytes
(Varies)	Name of attribute	ASCII text; aligned to 4-byte boundaries
(4 bytes)	Type of values	
(4 bytes)	Size	Text—size is the number of bytes in string. Other data types—number of data values
(Varies)	Values	Actual attribute data

Variables

Byte#	Data	Details
1–4	Variable indicator	Hexadecimal 0000000B
5–8	Number of variables	

netCDF (CDF)   *(Continued)*

The following 8 fields are repeated for each separate variable defined

Byte#	Data	Details
(4 bytes)	Length of variable name	In bytes
(Varies)	Name of variable	ASCII text; aligned to 4-byte boundaries
(4 bytes)	Number of dimensions	
(Varies)	Dimension array	A 4-byte integer index for each dimension; indexes one of the dimensions defined in the "dimension information" section
(Varies)	Attributes	Any attributes associated with this variable; an "attribute indicator" is used to mark the presence of attributes; see the attributes section above
(4 bytes)	Variable type	Data type for values in the array
(4 bytes)	Size	Number of bytes used to store the array
(4 bytes)	Offset	In bytes, from the beginning of the file where the array data is stored

Data (fixed-size arrays)

The data values for fixed-size arrays are stored in this section. The size of a data set is the product of its dimension sizes and the number of bytes used for each data value

Data (variable-size arrays)

The data values for variable-size arrays are stored last in the file. The size of the first dimension of the array is inferred by the physical size of the stored data set

File Name Suffix   NA

References   *netCDF User's Guide, An Interface for Data Access,* Version 1.06, June 1990. (available from UCAR or by anonymous FTP from *unidata.ucar.edu* in the file *netcdf.tar.Z*)

Private research notes documenting the internal data format for netCDF, by Mike Folk, Senior Software Engineer, Software Development Group, National Center for Supercomputing Applications (NCSA), 152 Computing Applications Building, 605 East Springfield Avenue, Champaign, IL 61820

PCX

Acronym	None
Origin	PC Paintbrush file format ZSoft Corporation 450 Franklin Rd. Suite 100 Marietta, GA 30067 Tel. (404) 428-0008
Motivation	Storage of images for ZSoft Corporation's paint programs: PC Paintbrush, PC Paintbrush +, PC Paintbrush for Windows, and Publisher's Paintbrush
Users	Users of PC Paintbrush software

Control

Copyrighted by	ZSoft Corp. (now Word Star Atlanta Technology Center)
Trademarks	NA
Royalty Fees	None

Versions

Version 2.5	
Version 2.8	Included color palette
Version 3.0	
Version 5.0 (1991)	Includes support for 24-bit (RGB) color images

(See version field in data organization section below)

Overview

Major Type of Data	2D Raster
Color Representation	Monochrome; Color table (16 or 256 entries)
Data Organization	Sequential
Data Encoding	Binary
Data Compression	Run-length

Data Types

Raster Data
Color table
Image size, resolution
Pixel value characteristics

Data Organization

General syntax of the data stream:

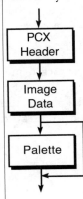

PCX *(Continued)*

PCX Header

Byte#	Data	Details
1	Signature	Hex A0
2	Version	See below
3	Compression scheme	1: run-length
4	Bits per pixel	Per color plane
5–6	Xmin	Screen upper left corner (in pixels)
7–8	Ymin	Screen upper left corner (in pixels)
9–10	Xmax	Screen lower right corner (in pixels)
11–12	Ymax	Screen lower right corner (in pixels)
13–14	Horizontal resolution	
15–16	Vertical resolution	
17–64	Palette	
65	Reserved	For future use
66	Number of color planes	
67–68	Bytes per line	Buffer space needed for decoding
69–70	Palette type	1: grayscale; 2: color
71–128	Filler (not used)	

The version field can contain one of the following:
0: Version 2.5
2: Version 2.8 (contains palette)
3: Version 2.8 (no palette)
4: PC Paintbrush for Windows (Plus for Windows users Version 5)
5: Version 3.0 and greater of PC Paintbrush and PC Paintbrush +

Image Data
The image pixels are ordered from left to right and from top to bottom. Each scan line of the image is encoded separately; run-lengths do not cross scan-line boundaries

Monochrome data is stored as bitmaps (1-bit per pixel packed into bytes). The 16-color data (i.e., 4 bits per pixel) is stored as scan-line bit planes (e.g., line 1, bit plane 1, line 1 bit plane 2, line 1 bit plane 3, line 1 bit plane 4, then line 2). The 256-color data is stored as contiguous values, one byte per pixel (e.g., line 1 pixel 1 (byte), line 1 pixel 2 (byte))

PCX   *(Continued)*

Palette (769 bytes)

The palette defines exactly 256 RGB colors and is always exactly 769 bytes long

Byte#	Data	Details
1	Signature	Hex 0C
2	Red	Palette index 0
3	Green	
4	Blue	
…	…	
767	Red	Palette index 255
768	Green	
769	Blue	

File Name Suffix	DOS	.PCX

References   Rimmer, Steve, *Bit-Mapped Graphics,* Windcrest Books, Blue Ridge Summit, PA, pp. 91–126

Technical Reference Manual from ZSoft Corporation. This can be downloaded from ZSoft's Bulletin Board at (404) 514-6332 or by contacting the "Code Librarian" at the address given above

---

PICT

Acronym	PICTure data format	
Origin	Apple Computer, Inc. 20525 Mariani Avenue Cupertino, CA 95014-6299 Tel. (408) 996-1010	
Motivation	To capture a picture as a set of Macintosh QuickDraw library function calls	
Users	Software systems that run on a Macintosh	
Control	Copyrighted by	Apple Computer, Inc.
	Trademarks	Apple®, Mac®, Macintosh®, QuickDraw™
	Royalty Fees	None
Versions	PICT1	
	PICT2	Added support for additional QuickDraw functions

Overview	Major Type of Data	2D Geometry; 2D Raster
	Color Representation	Monochrome; Color table; RGB
	Data Organization	Sequential
	Data Encoding	Binary
	Data Compression	Run-length (PackBits) for raster data only

Data Types A PICT data set can include any of the following set of QuickDraw commands (organized according to graphical primitives):

Lines	line, line from, short line, short line from
Text	long text, DH text, DV text, DHDV text, ChExtra
Rectangles (square corners)	frameRect, paintRect, eraseRect, invertRect, fillRect, frameSameRect, paintSameRect, eraseSameRect, invertSameRect, fillSameRect
Rectangles (rounded corners)	frameRRect, paintRRect, eraseRRect, invertRRect,fillRRect, frameSameRRect, paintSameRRect, eraseSameRRect, invertSameRRect, fillSameRRect
Ovals	frameOval, paintOval, eraseOval, invertOval, fillOval, frameSameOval, paintSameOval, eraseSameOval, invertSameOval, fillSameOval
Arcs	frameArc, paintArc, eraseArc, invertArc, fillArc, frameSameArc, paintSameArc, eraseSameArc, invertSameArc, fillSameArc
Polygons	framePoly, paintPoly, erasePoly, invertPoly, fillPoly
Region	frameRgn, paintRgn, eraseRgn, invertRgn, fillRgn
Bitmaps	BitsRect, BitsRgn, PackBitsRect, PackBitsRgn
Graphic state	clipRgn, bkPat, txFont, txFace, txMode, spExtra, pnSize, pnMode, pnPat, thePat, ovSize, origin, txSize, fgColor, bkColor, txRatio, BkPixPat, PnPixPat, FillPixPat, PnLocHFrac, BkPixPat, PnPixPat, FillPixPat, PnLocHFrac, RGBFgCol, RGBBkCol, HiliteMode, HiliteColor, DefHilite, OpColor
Misc. commands	HeaderOp, picVersion, Version (PICT2), shortComment, longComment, EndOfPicture

PICT *(Continued)*

<table>
<tr><td>Data
Organization</td><td>General syntax of the data stream:</td></tr>
</table>

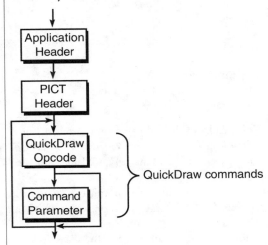

Byte#	Data	Details
1–512	Header	Application-specific header information
513–514	Length of the picture	Obsolete; use the length of the data fork
515–522	Picture bounding frame	4 integers; top, left, bottom, right
... ...	Picture data ...	Opcodes for calls to QuickDraw commands plus any associated data for each function call

A 1-byte opcode is associated with each possible QuickDraw command in the PICT1 data format. The PICT2 version contains some 2-byte opcodes

Each QuickDraw command has a pre-specified number of parameters that defines the number of bytes each command uses in the data stream. Refer to the references for details

File Name Suffix   Macintosh file type   PICT

References   Apple Computer, Inc. *Inside Macintosh, Volume V,* Addison-Wesley, Reading, MA, 1988, pp. 93–105

Hogan, Thom, *The Programmer's Apple Mac Sourcebook: Reference Tables for Apple Macintosh Hardware and System Software,* Microsoft Press, Redmond, WA, 1989, pp. 92–97, 195–214

(NA) PLPS

Acronym	North American Presentation Level Protocol Syntax (for Videotex/Teletext systems)
Origin	American National Standards Institute, Inc. (ANSI) 1430 Broadway New York, NY 10018 Canadian Standards Association (CSA) 178 Rexdale Boulevard Rexdale (Toronto), Ontario M9W 1R3 Original author: Joint effort of the following three groups: • ANSI X3L2.1 Standing Task Group on Videotex/Teletext Coded Character Sets, ANSI committee, E. Lohse, Chair; W. C. Rinehuls, Vice-Chair, and a 40-member committee • The Canadian Videotex Consultative Committee/Canadian Standards Association/Working Group (CVCC /CSA/ WG) on Videotex, CSA committee, P. Bowers, Chair, and a 35-member committee • The Electronic Industries Association (EIA) Broadcast Television Systems, Teletext Steering Committee, Special Working Group
Motivation	Specification of a standard interchange format for videotex and teletext services Teletext services provide a one-way communications link to "pages" or "frames" of alphanumeric and graphic information (typically using broadcast television). It differs from "teletex," which is a terminal-to-terminal text communication service Videotex services are similar to teletext, but they are two-way communication links that allow user interaction The international community could not agree on a world-wide Videotex standard and currently there are three different major standards used worldwide: • North American Videotex (NAPLPS) • French Videotex, Acquisition Numerique et Televisualisation d'Images Organisees en Pages d'Ecriture (ANTIOPE) • Japanese Videotex (CAPTAIN)
Users	Anyone with a TV or computer monitor who wishes to subscribe to these services. NAPLPS forms the basis for Prodigy's presentation support
Control	Copyrighted by ANSI and CSA Trademarks None Royalty Fees Part of the standard is covered by a patent and requires a license from the patent holder. Contact ANSI or CSA for details
Versions	ANSI X3.41-1974 CSA Z243.35-1976 ISO 2022-1982 ANSI X3.110-1983 CSA T500-1983

Overview	Major Type of Data	2D geometry; raster (very coarse)
	Color Representation	RGB color table (minimum support of 16 colors out of a palette of 512 possible colors, 3 bits per RGB value)
	Data Organization	Sequential
	Data Encoding	Character-based; 7-bit or 8-bit codes
	Data Compression	None for raster data; (character-based encoding is a form of compressed data)

PLPS is based on the Open Systems Interconnection (OSI) reference model. It defines the presentation layer protocols and some specific semantics for use at the application layer

Data is transmitted by sending 7-bit or 8-bit "character codes" from predefined and user defined "character sets." The standard 7-bit ASCII code table is used to transmit textual information, another code table is used to invoke macros, and two other code tables are used to transmit graphical data. The Mosaic character set can be used to display coarsely defined graphical objects. The Picture Description Instructions character set can be used to display high-resolution graphical objects. Codes are interpreted according to the active character set. The active character set is selected (or switched) by transmitting designated 3-byte escape sequences

Data Types　Graphical data is encoded using one of the following:

Picture description instructions (PDIs)

Point	Sets a drawing point, establishes the "last-referenced point"
Line	Draws a line, based on two endpoints
Arc	Draws a circular arc, based on two endpoints, and an intermediate point
Rectangle	Rectangular outline or filled area; based on length and width
Polygon	Polygon outline or filled area; based on a series of points
Incremental	Draws a point, line, or polygon incrementally; an incremental point is essentially a pixel map
Control	Sets drawing mode and environment, (e.g., precision of operands, logical pixel size, text orientation and spacing, cursor styles, line patterns, fill textures, color)

Mosaic set

A set of sixty-five predefined 2 × 3-block mosaic characters make up the mosaic character set. These are only suitable for coarse pixel maps because of the large size of each "dot" in each block mosaic character. They are best used for drawing horizontal or vertical lines and borders. (Refer to the diagram of the character codes in the encoding chapter.)

(NA) PLPS   *(Continued)*

Dynamically redefinable character set (DRCS)

A custom-defined character set of up to 96 displayable patterns can be downloaded and used in the same fashion as other 7-bit character sets

Data Organization

PLPS is a communication standard and not a file format. Information and commands are transmitted as streams of either 7-bit or 8-bit characters. There is no pre-specified sequence in which the information must be transmitted

Example

Encoding of a line

To allow for variable precision in the specification of coordinate data (and other types of data as well), most values are encoded "down the columns" of consecutive bytes. Using the encoding of a line as an example, the x and y components of each end point are encoded using 3 bits per byte. The most significant bits are encoded first. Individual receivers can truncate the bits to the precision needed for their device. In the following table, an X indicates that the bit is not part of the data, and a 0 or 1 indicates mandatory bit setting. All operands in PLPS have bit 6 set to 1 and only bits 5 through 0 contain valid data

Byte#	7	6	5	4	3	2	1	0	Details
1	X	0	1	0	1	0	1	0	Code for Set and Line (Absolute)
2	X	1							Starting point coordinates
...	X	1							Uses as many bytes as needed for the desired precision, 3 bits per byte for each of the x and y coordinates
...	X	1							Endpoint coordinates
...	X	1							Uses as many bytes as needed for the desired precision, 3 bits per byte for each of the x and y coordinates
			x			y			

References

Videotex/Teletext Presentation Level Protocol Syntax, North American PLPS, ANSI X3.110-1983, CSA T500-1983, published by American National Standards Institute, Inc. and Canadian Standards Association, December 1983, 158 pages

NAPLPS: "A New Standard for Text and Graphics, Part 1: Introduction, History, and Structure," by Jim Fleming and William Frezza, *BYTE,* **8**, 2, Feb. 1983, pp. 203–254 (See also Parts 2–4 in the March, April, and May 1983 issues of BYTE)

PostScript

Acronym	None
Origin	Adobe Systems Incorporated 1585 Charleston Rd. P.O. Box 7900 Mountain View, CA 94039-7900 Original authors: John E. Warnock and Charles M. Geschke Current support: Adobe Systems Developer Support staff
Motivation	A high-level, device-independent page description language for output to raster-based graphics devices High-level refers to the use of abstract graphical entities (such as lines, arcs, cubic curves) as opposed to a raster-based description. Device independence means the description is not restricted to any single raster resolution or device
Users	Many application software packages generate PostScript as a generic output that can then be processed for a particular output device. Example applications include word processing (Microsoft Word), mathematical symbolic manipulation (Mathematica), and desktop publishing (PageMaker). Many printers accept PostScript as direct input (e.g., Apple LaserWriter)

Control	Copyrighted by	Adobe Systems Incorporated
	Trademarks	PostScript, Display PostScript, Adobe, Adobe Illustrator
	Royalty Fees	The trademark, PostScript, cannot be used to identify any product not originating from or licensed by Adobe. No royalties are required to write programs in the PostScript language, or to write drivers which generate PostScript output, or to write PostScript interpreters; the language description is copyrighted by Adobe

Versions	Level 1, 1985	Original language specification
	Level 2, 1990	Extensions for device-independent color specification, patterns, composite fonts, forms, file system support, binary encodings, compression schemes, and Display Postscript

SPDL (Standard Page Description Language) is based on a subset of Level 2 Postscript in which the structuring conventions have been formalized and encoded in SGML for cleartext or ASN.1 for binary representations. SPDL is formally called ISO/IEC 10180. It was created by ISO/IEC JTC1 SC18

Overview	Major Type of Data	2D geometry; raster; text; fonts
	Color Representation	DeviceGray (grayscale) DeviceRGB (red, green, blue) HSB (hue, saturation, brightness) DeviceCMYK (cyan, magenta, yellow, black)

PostScript   *(Continued)*

CIEBasedABC, some examples include the following:
X, Y, and Z in the CIE 1931 (XYZ)-space
R, G, and B in a calibrated RGB space
l*, a*, and b* in the CIE 1976 (L*a*b*)-space
Y, I, and Q in the NTSC space
Y, U, and V in the SECAM and PAL spaces

CIEBasedA, some examples include the following:
Luminance Y component of CIE 1931 (XYZ)-space
Gray component of a calibrated gray space
CIE 1976 psychometric lightness l* component of the
    CIE 1976 (L*a*b*)-space
Luminance Y component of the NTSC, SECAM, and
    PAL television color spaces

Indexed color space (color lookup table)
Pattern color space (painting with patterns)
Separation color space (color separation for a single
    color print, apart from the CMYK separations)

Data Organization	Sequential
Data Encoding	ASCII; binary tokens can be mixed with ASCII; binary object sequence encoding (fully- and partially-precompiled sequences of objects)— emphasizes efficient interpretation.
Data Compression	ASCII85—similar to public domain utilities *btoa* and *atob;* LZW; run-length; CCITT Group 3 and Group 4; DCT (JPEG standard)

PostScript can be viewed as a general-purpose programming language with powerful built-in graphics primitives, *or* as a page description language that includes programming language features, *or* as an interchange format

PostScript is an interpreted language that includes more than 300 predefined operators. It contains the programming constructs of variables, stack-based execution, conditional branching, looping, subprograms and recursion. (The Postscript language can be used interactively, but those issues are beyond the scope of this discussion.)

PostScript *(Continued)*

Data Types

Simple "objects"
Simple atomic entities that have a constant value:

integer	
real	Floating-point numbers
boolean	True or false
name	An identifier for referencing variables, procedures, etc.
operator	Built-in action (a simple action, e.g., addition, or a procedure invocation, e.g., drawing a line)
FontID	Used in the construction of fonts
save	A snapshot of the state of a PostScript interpreter's memory
mark	'Mark' a position on the operand stack
null	Used to fill empty or uninitialized positions in composite objects

Composite "objects"
Entities having internal modifiable substructures

dictionary	Associative table of (keyword,value) pairs
array	Heterogeneous,1D (higher-dimensional arrays are created by nesting arrays within arrays)
packedarray	An array 'packed' into less memory than a normal array
string	An array of integers in the range from 0 to 255
file	A readable or writable stream of characters transferred to or from a PostScript interpreter
gstate	Represents an entire graphics state
condition, lock	Used to synchronize multiple execution contexts in a Display PostScript system

Graphical Operators
As a general programming language, PostScript has over 300 predefined operators. Of major interest are those operators that represent graphical types of data. The list below shows the basic graphical "ideas" built into PostScript, and the operators which create or manipulate them

PostScript   *(Continued)*

Transformations	matrix, initmatrix, identmatrix, defaultmatrix, currentmatrix, setmatrix, translate, scale, rotate, concat, transform, dtransform, itransform, idtransform, invertmatrix
Path construction	newpath, currentpoint, moveto, rmoveto, lineto, rlineto, arc, arcn, arct, arcto, curveto, rcurveto, closepath, flattenpath, reversepath, strokepath, ustrokepath, charpath, uppend, clippath, setbbox, pathbbox, upath, initclip, clip, eoclip, rectclip, ucache
Painting	erasepage, fill, eofill, stroke, ufill, ueofill, ustroke, rectfill, rectstroke, image, colorimage, imagemask
Color	setcolor, currentcolor, setcolorspace, currentcolorspace, setgray, currentgray, setrgbcolor, currentrgbcolor, sethsbcolor, currenthsbcolor, setcmykcolor, currentcmycolor, setpattern
Graphics state (device-independent)	gsave, grestore, grestoreall, initgraphics, currentgstate, setgstate, setlinewidth, currentlinewidth, setlinecap, currentlinecap, setlinejoin, currentlinejoin, setmiterlimit, currentmiterlimit,setstrokeadjust, currentstrokeadjust, setdash, currentdash, (color commands above)
Graphics state (device-dependent)	sethalftone, currenthalftone, setscreen,currentscreen, setcolorscreen, currentcolorscreen, settransfer, currenttransfer, setcolortransfer, currentcolortransfer, setblackgeneration, currentblackgeneration, setundercolorremoval, currentundercolorremoval, setcolorredering, currentcolorrendering, setflat, currentflat, setoverprint, currentoverprint
Fonts	definefont, undefinefont, findfont, scalefont, makefont, setfont, currentfont, rootfont, show, ashow, widthshow, awidthshow, xshow, xyshow, yshow, glyphshow, stringwidth, cshow, kshow, FontDirectory, GlobalFontDirectory, StandardEncoding, ISOLatin1Encoding, findencoding, setcachedevice, setcachedevice2, setcharwidth

Fonts in PostScript are defined using an outline of each character in the font. Therefore fonts are treated similar to any other graphical objects; they can be modified using any combination of linear transformations, including translation, scaling, rotation, reflection, and skewing

PostScript   *(Continued)*

Raster images are stored as rectangular arrays of sampled values. Each sample consists of a specified number of bits (1, 2, 4, 8, or 12). Sample data values are stored as a sequence of 8-bit integers, each in a range from 0 to 255. Sample values are packed if the number of bits per sample is not equal to 8. Transformations can be applied to images

Data Organization

Signature
The first two bytes of the file are the ASCII characters "%!" (hex 2521)

Language syntax
All operations in PostScript are performed on operands placed on a stack. The language syntax is in postfix notation (i.e., the operation comes after its data). The ASCII text encoding is line oriented and has the following general syntax:

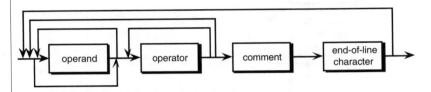

Note: the comment section begins at the first % sign on the line

For example, the following PostScript commands draw a line from (0,0) to (10,20)
```
0 0 moveto 10 20 lineto                    % line from (0,0) to (10,20)
```

These commands do the same thing:
```
10 20 0 0 moveto lineto                    % line from (0,0) to (10,20)
```

Drawing a square box 10 units on each side might look like the following, where the operand *rlineto* draws a line relative to the last current position.
```
0 0 moveto 10 0 rlineto 0 10 rlineto -10 0 rlineto 0 -10 rlineto closepath
```

A final example draws a square of any size starting at any position. The commands assume that the square size and starting position are already on the operand stack (i.e., size, start_x, start_y). Note that operators "use up" the values on the stack. The *dup* operator duplicates the top item on the stack. The *exch* operator exchanges the top two items on the stack. The *neg* operator takes the negative of the top item on the stack and pushes it back on the stack

```
moveto                   % moves to start of box; uses start_x start_y on
dup 0 rlineto              stack
dup 0 exch rlineto       % duplicates size of box, moves relative to
                           (size, 0)
dup neg 0 rlineto        % duplicates size of box, moves relative to
                           (-size, 0)
dup neg 0 exch rlineto   %duplicates size of box, moves relative to
                           (-size,0)
closepath                % ends the path that creates the box
pop                      % removes size of the box from the stack
```

PostScript   *(Continued)*

File structure

There is no required structure for a PostScript language program. There is, however, a set of Document Structuring Conventions (DSC) that, if followed, make the PostScript program more device-independent and more manipulatable by document managers (e.g., spool managers). The general structure of a file adhering to the Document Structuring Conventions, Version 3.0, is shown below

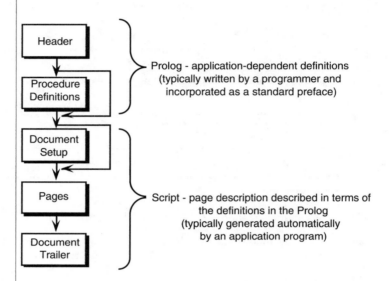

DSC comments are specified by 2 percent characters (%%) as the first characters on a line (no leading space). Refer to the example file below for examples

Example

```
%!PS-Adobe-2.0
%%Creator: Wayne Brown
%%Title: Koch Curve
%%CreationDate: 5-21-93

/inch { 72 mul } def
/depth 0 def
/maxdepth 4 def
/down {/depth depth 1 add def} def
/up   {/depth depth 1 sub def} def

/CurveForward
    { depth maxdepth eq
    { 288 0 rlineto stroke } if
    288 0 translate
    0 0 moveto} def
```

PostScript *(Continued)*

```
/KochCurve
    gsave
    .25 .25 scale
    down
    depth maxdepth le
    {   KochCurve CurveForward
          90 rotate KochCurve CurveForward
         -90 rotate KochCurve CurveForward
         -90 rotate KochCurve CurveForward
           0 rotate KochCurve CurveForward
          90 rotate KochCurve CurveForward
          90 rotate KochCurve CurveForward
         -90 rotate KochCurve CurveForward } if
    up
    grestore } def

1 inch 3 inch translate
0 0 moveto KochCurve

/Courier findfont 16 scalefont setfont
1.5 inch -1.7 inch moveto
(Koch Curve) show
showpage
%%EOF
```

References	Adobe Systems Inc., *PostScript Language Reference Manual, Second Edition,* Addison-Wesley, Reading, MA, 1990, 764 pages, ISBN 0-201-18127-4
	Adobe Systems Inc., *PostScript Language Tutorial and Cookbook,* Addison-Wesley, Reading, MA, 1985, 243 pages, ISBN 0-201-10179-3
	Adobe Systems Inc., *PostScript Language Program Design,* Addison-Wesley, Reading, MA, 1988, 224 pages, ISBN 0-201-14396-8

QuickTime

Acronym	None
Origin	Apple Computer, Inc. 20525 Mariani Avenue Cupertino, CA 95014-6299 Tel. (408) 996-1010
Motivation	The storage, retrieval and manipulation of compressed time-based data—often referred to as movies (spelled Moov in QuickTime). This is typically a sequence of video with synchronized sound
Users	Software systems that run on a Macintosh or other compatible platforms. The QuickTime architecture is open for use by other users on other computer platforms via the QuickTime Movie Exchange Toolkit

QuickTime *(Continued)*

Control	Copyrighted by	Apple Computer, Inc.
	Trademarks	QuickTime™ , Apple®, Mac®, Macintosh®, QuickDraw™
	Royalty Fees	None
Versions	Initial release	May 1992
Overview	Major Type of Data	2D Raster, 2D geometric data in PICT files, digitized compressed video, digitized sound, timing information
	Color Representation	Monochrome; Color table; RGB
	Data Organization	Sequential; references to other data streams
	Data Encoding	Binary
	Data Compression	Photo Compressor (DCT; JPEG standard), RPZA (i.e., Road Pizza) (an Apple scheme), Animator Compressor (Apple scheme: Run-length—PackBits; both lossless and lossy), other compression schemes can be integrated

Data Types A QuickTime movie is made up of two parts (known as a two-fork movie). The media-data part contains the actual images and sound data. The other part contains the control information for the movie. The media data can be scattered over many separate files and can be referenced by more than one movie. The control information for a single movie is always together in a single file

Media Data

Video images
- PICT data format (either raster data or 2D geometry data or a combination of both)
- JPEG compressed raster images
- BCT: Block Color Transform compressed video (i.e., RPZA)
- Other user-defined data formats (such as compact video) can be used with the QuickTime architecture if the appropriate software is added

Sound
- 8- or 24-bit digitized sound data

QuickTime   *(Continued)*

Control Information

Timing scale	Units per second for "clock ticks" and the length of the entire movie
Preview	Specifies a portion of the movie for previewing
Poster	Specifies a single frame of the movie for "still viewing" when the movie is not active
Selection	Used for movie editing
Spatial	Specifies how to map the video images onto the screen; it include a clipping region
Playback settings	Specifies the preferred video rate and sound volume
Tracks	A movie is composed of 1 or more tracks; each track is a single video sequence, audio sequence, or other user-specified data. This specifies the location of the track data, its timing information, and other relevant information.
User data	Any data the user wishes to include with the movie

Data Organization

Movies are stored differently on Macintosh and nonMacintosh systems. On a Macintosh system, the "control information" is stored in the "resource fork" of the file, and the "data fork" is empty (if the actual video and sound data are in separate files). A special file format is defined to allow all of the data associated with a movie to be stored in one large file. These are called *single-fork movie files*. NonMacintosh systems require single-fork movies

The data file is organized into *atoms*. Each atom contains a size, a type, and some data. Atoms can be nested within other atoms. Atoms that are not recognized by their type field are simply skipped

Byte#	Data	Details
1–4	Size of the atom	In bytes, including the size and type fields
5–8	Type	4 ASCII characters; e.g., "moov"
9–"size"	Data	

QuickTime *(Continued)*

The general syntax of the data stream for a single-fork movie file follows. All of the data is imbedded within atoms, but the atoms are not shown in the diagram

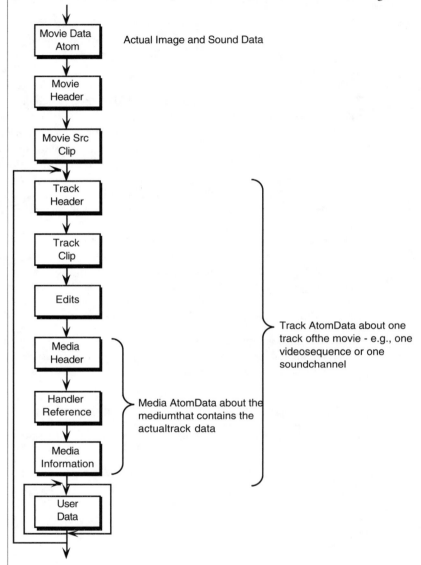

Signature
Bytes 5–8 of the file will be the ASCII characters "mdat"

QuickTime *(Continued)*

Movie Header

Byte#	Data	Details
1–4	Flags	1 byte of version; 3 bytes of flags
5–8	Creation time	Seconds since January 1, 1904
9–12	Modification time	
13–16	Time scale	Units per second (e.g, 1, 60, 1000)
17–20	Duration	How long the movie lasts (total time)
21–24	Preferred rate	The most natural rate for playback
25–26	Preferred volume	The preferred volume for sound tracks
27–30	Reserved 1	For future use
31–34	Reserved 2	
35–38	Reserved 3	
39–74	Transformation matrix	(3 × 3); used to map images to the screen
75–78	Preview time	Start position of preview section of movie
79–82	Preview duration	Length of preview section of movie
83–86	Poster time	Which image to use as a poster
87–90	Selection time	Start of movie segment for editing calls
91–94	Selection duration	Length of movie segment for editing calls
95–98	Current time	
99–102	Next track ID	

The remaining details of the QuickTime single-fork movie data format are too numerous to include here. Refer to the QuickTime documentation for the remaining details

File Name Suffix Macintosh file type   MooV

References Apple Computer, Inc. *QuickTime Documentation,* Preliminary release, 5/6/91. (available from Apple)

MoviesFormat.h   A C source-code header file that defines the exact structures of the data format. This file is part of the "Interfaces" information available about QuickTime from various Bulletin Boards and anonymous FTP sites

"What is QuickTime?," *Developer Magazine,* March 1992, Apple Computer, Inc.

RIB

Acronym	RenderMan Interface Byte-stream
Origin	Pixar 1001 W. Cutting Blvd. Richmond, CA 94804-9984 Tel. (510) 236-4000
Motivation	A software-independent protocol for "modelers" to communicate with "renderers" *Modeling* software is used to create a description of a scene, including the exact geometry, location in space, and visual properties of all objects in the scene. The characteristics of all light sources and the "camera" must be specified before viewing *Rendering* is the process of generating a visual image from a precise description of a scene
Users	Modeling software systems that use RenderMan software for rendering

Control	Copyrighted by	Pixar
	Trademarks	MacRenderMan, PhotoRealistic RenderMan, RIB, RenderMonitor, RenderApp, ShaderApp, Reyes
	Royalty Fees	The following patents apply to RenderMan: US 4,897,806; UK 2,177,577; Canada 1,256,244. Consult Pixar for royalty fees

Versions	Version 1	1990

Overview	Major Type of Data	3D geometry; viewing information
	Color Representation	RGB (values 0.0 to 1.0)
	Data Organization	Sequential
	Data Encoding	ASCII text
	Data Compression	None

RIB data streams contain model data that describe a scene and rendering specifications that determine how the scene is rendered. In simplified terms, an RIB file is a set of procedure calls that transform 3D data into a photorealistic 2D image

Data Types	An RIB data set can contain the following commands (listed according to type):

RIB *(Continued)*

Rendering Parameters
Format
FrameAspectRatio
ShadingRate
PixelSamples
ScreenWindow
Display
LightSource
Projection   Type, e.g., perspective, other parameters

Geometry Primitives
Quadratic surfaces   (Surfaces of revolution): Cylinder, Sphere, Disk
Patch   Bilinear

Transformations
Translate dx, dy, dz
Rotate   Angle, (x, y, z)
Scale sx, sy, sz
Transform   A 4×4 transformation matrix

Assigning Attributes
Attribute   Uniquely name an attribute block, identify attribute
                                 type
Surface   Identify surface characteristics, e.g., oak, carpet
Color   Red, Green, Blue

Grouping into Hierarchies
FrameBegin; FrameEnd   One image
WorldBegin; WorldEnd   All of the geometry elements for an image
AttributeBegin;   One set of attributes to more than one geometry
   AttributeEnd   element
TransformBegin;   One set of transformations to more than one
   TransformEnd   geometry element

Shaders
Surface Shaders   Constant, matte, metal, shinymetal, plastic, painted-
                                 plastic
Light source shaders   Ambientlight, distantlight, pointlight, spot light
Atmosphere shaders   Depthcue, fog, bumpy
Other shaders   Carpet, finemetal, finite, potwood, realwood,
                                 rmarble, spatter, stone, transpmap

RIB   *(Continued)*

Resource Manager Hints
```
##RenderMan RIB-Structure
##Scene
##Creator
##CreationDate
##For
##Frames
##Shaders
##Textures
##CapabilitiesNeeded
##CameraOrientation
```

Data
Organization

A RIB data set is a sequence of RIB commands. Each command consists of a one-word identifier that may be followed by arguments. The arguments can be in one of two forms:

• A list of values   When the arguments are required
• Keyword-value pairs   When only some of the arguments are required (and the others retain default values). The keyword identifier is encoded in quotes. The value is encoded in brackets

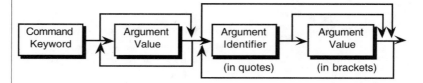

For example:
```
Translate   0    1.5    3.7      # i.e., dx, dy, dz
Surface "wood" "grain" [5] "darkcolor" [0.4 0.027 1]
```

Any text between a single # symbol and an end-of-line character is a comment

RIB *(Continued)*

General syntax of the data stream (according to the optional, but highly-recommended, RIB File structuring conventions):

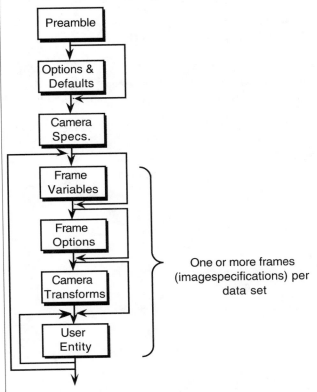

Signature
The first line of the file must be the following (in case-sensitive ASCII text):

```
##RenderMan RIB-Structure 1.1
```

The version number will vary according to the release of the software that creates the data

Preamble
This section contains hint statements (that start with ##). The hints are used to allow a resource manager to route a data set to an appropriate renderer. It also includes the declaration of global variables

Options and Defaults
Contains image, display and camera options

Camera Specifications
Contains the camera location and orientation

Frame Variables
Contains the declaration of frame-specific variables

Frame Options
Contains the declaration of any variable options or default attributes

Camera Transformations
Specific changes in the global camera specification for this frame

User Entities
The geometry elements that make up the scene, along with their associated transformations and attributes. These are typically grouped into hierarchies

Example

This example comes from the *MacRenderMan User's Guide*, 1990, pp. 93–94

```
##RenderMan RIB-Structure 1.1
##Frames 1
##CapabilitiesNeeded ShadowDepthMapping
version 3.03

Declare "shadowname" "uniform string"

Display "tempshadow" "zfile" "z"
Format 256 256 1
ShadingRate 1
PixelSamples 2 2

Rotate 62 -12 12 0
Translate -12 -12 9
Translate 0 -5 0
ScreenWindow -8 8 -8 8

WorldBegin

AttributeBegin
Attribute "identifier" "name" "middlegroup"
Rotate -90 1 0 0
Translate 0 0 5
    Sphere 1 -1 1 360
    Disk -1 1.7 360
    Cylinder 1.7 -1.4 -1 360
    Cylinder 1 -5 -1.4 360
AttributeEnd

# other attribute blocks ...

WorldEnd
```

References

MacRenderMan User's Guide (packaged with RenderMan software)

The following three documents are available by ordering the *MacRenderman Developer's Stuff* package from Pixar:

- The RenderMan Companion, A Programmer's Guide to Realistic Computer Graphics, 475 pages
- The RenderMan Interface, Version 3.1
- PhotoRealistic RenderMan Application Notes

RLE

Acronym	Run Length Encoded format
Origin	University of Utah Department of Computer Science
Motivation	To provide a data format that is efficient and device-independent for the storage of multilevel raster images. It is not designed for monochrome (1 bit per sample) images
Users	RLE-formatted files have been used predominantly in university and research environments that are accessible to the Internet. It has been used on a variety of different computers and displays

Control	Copyrighted by	None
	Trademarks	None
	Royalty Fees	None

Versions	First appeared in 1986 Basic file format is stable, but enhancements are added occasionally

Overview	Major Type of Data	2D raster
	Color Representation	Color table (grayscale or RGB); RGB (plus alpha)
	Data Organization	Sequential
	Data Encoding	Binary
	Data Compression	Run-length encoding (obviously)

Data Types	Image characteristics	Width, height, starting position, flags, etc.
	Color Map (optional)	
	Comments	ASCII text in null-terminated strings
	Raster pixel data	

Data Organization	General syntax of the data stream:

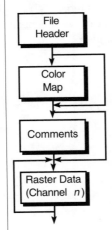

RLE   *(Continued)*

File Header
Data values are stored LSB first

Byte#	Data	Details
0–1	Magic number	CC52 (hex)
2–3	Xpos	In pixels; lower-left corner (X coordinate)
4–5	Ypos	In pixels; lower-left corner (Y coordinate)
6–7	Xsize	# of pixels in the X direction (horizontal)
8–9	$y$size	# of pixels in the Y direction (vertical)
10	Flags	See below
11	Ncolors	# of color channels (0 to 254 allowed)
12	Bits per pixels	Currently only 8 bits/pixel is supported
13	Ncmap	# of color channels in the color map
14	Cmaplen	Stored as $\log_2$ of the color table length
15	Red background	Red component of background color
16	Green background	Green component of background color
17	Blue background	Blue component of background color

Options included in flag field above:

ClearFirst	Clear to the background color before reading the scan-line data
NoBackground	No background color is supplied
Alpha	Indicates the presence of an "alpha" channel (always stored as channel number 255)
Comments	Indicates the presence of comments immediately following the color map

RLE *(Continued)*

Color map

The color map is optional. If it is present, each color map value is a 16-bit quantity, left justified in the word (low-order byte first). The entries for each channel are stored contiguously

Byte#	Data	Details
18–19	Color value 0	Channel 0
20–21	Color value 1	Channel 0
	...	Continued for $2^{cmaplen}$ values
	Color value 0	Channel 1
	Color value 1	Channel 1
	...	Continued for ncmap channels

Comments

Comments are optional. If they are present, an initial 16-bit quantity gives the length of the comment block. The comments contain any number of null terminated strings. The standard convention is to have strings of the form "name = value," but there are no restrictions on the kinds of text included in this section

Raster Data

The image coordinate system assumes that the positive x axis points to the right and the positive y axis points up; the origin is the lower-left corner

The raster data consists of a sequence of operators and associated data. There are currently 6 operators defined. The operators manipulate 3 variables that keep track of where the next data values should be placed in the image data. These variables are:

Current channel	Indicates which color is currently active
Scan-line number	The Y position of the scan line in the image
Pixel index	The X position in the current scan line

RLE   *(Continued)*

The operators that manipulate these variables are as follows:

SkipLines	Increments the current scan-line number by the operand value. The pixel index is reset to the xpos value
SetColor	Sets the current channel to the operand value. The pixel index is reset to the xpos value
SkipPixels	Increments the pixel index by the operand value. This skips pixels in the current scan line and leaves them in the background color
PixelData	The operand value specifies a length. A sequence of data values of this length follows the operation. The sequence is copied into the current scan line in increasing *x* order. If the sequence length is odd, a filler byte is appended to keep the data on word (2-byte) address boundaries
Run	Two operands follow, a length value and a pixel value. The pixel value is replicated length number times into the current scan line. The operator and its operands require 3 bytes of memory. A filler byte is added to maintain word alignment
EOF	This operator indicates the end of the file. It is not required for files that contain single images, but can be used to separate multiple images included in a single file. It has no operands

If an operation has a single operand that fits into 1 byte, the operation is coded using only 2 bytes of memory as follows. This is the *short* operand syntax

Byte#	Data									Details
	7	6	5	4	3	2	1	0		
n	0	0		Opcode						6-bit operation code
n + 1				Operand						Operand

If an operation requires two operands or if an operand requires more than one byte of memory, the operation is coded using 4 bytes as follows. This is the *long* operand syntax

RLE   *(Continued)*

Byte#	Data	Details
	7 6 5 4 3 2 1 0	
n	`0` `1` Opcode	6 bit operation code
n + 1	(Filler - not used)	To maintain even word boundaries
n + 2	Operand low byte	
n + 3	Operand high byte	

References | Documentation for the RLE format and access to the Utah RLE toolkit source code can be obtained by anonymous FTP from *cs.utah.edu*. Refer to the files /pub/urt-*

Thomas, S. G., "Design of the Utah RLE Format," Technical Report 86–15, Alpha-1 Project, CS Department, University of Utah, November, 1986

SunRaster

Acronym	Sun Raster Data Format	
Origin	Sun Microsystems 2550 Gracia Avenue Mountain View, CA 94043 Tel. (415) 960-1300 Fax. (415) 969-9131	
Motivation	A simple format for raster data	
Users	Predominantly applications that run on Sun Workstations	
Control	Copyrighted by Trademarks Royalty Fees	NA NA NA
Versions	NA	
Overview	Major Type of Data Color Representation Data Organization Data Encoding Data Compression	2D raster Monochrome; Color table RGB; RGB and XRGB Sequential Binary None; run-length

SunRaster   *(Continued)*

Data Types	Image Width Image Height Image Depth Image Length Raster Type Raster Color Map Type Map Color Map Length Raster Data
Data Organization	General syntax of the data stream:

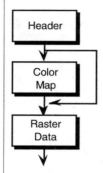

Signature

The first 4 bytes of the data stream (in hexadecimal—59A66A95)

Header

The data is assumed to be in Big Endian format (MSB first)

Byte#	Data	Details
1–4	Magic Number	Must be hex 59A66A95
5–8	Image width	In pixels
9–12	Image Height	In pixels
13–16	Image Depth	Bits per pixel: 1, 8, or 24
17–20	Image Length	# of bytes of image data (always 0 for Version 1)
21–24	Raster Type	Format of raster data, See below
25–28	Raster Color Map Type	0: no color map; 1: RGB; 2: RAW mode
29–32	Color Map Length	# of byte that make up the color table

Color Map

If a color map exists, it contains exactly "Color Map Length" bytes as indicated in the header. The individual values of the table are always single-byte unsigned characters in the range from 0 to 255. All red values are stored first, then all green values, and finally all blue values

Raster Data

The raster data can be of the following types, as indicated by the "Raster Type" value in the header. Raster Type equals:

0 (RAS_OLD)	No compression
1 (RAS_STANDARD)	No compression (Same as type 0)
2 (RAS_BYTE_ENCODED)	RLE compression (See Chapter 9)
FFFF (RAS_EXPERIMENTAL)	

The pixel values are ordered from left to right on each scan line and the scan lines are ordered from top to bottom. Stored scan lines are always rounded to multiples of 16 bits. If the data type is RAS_BYTE_ENCODED, the data values are run-length encoded

File Name Suffix   No standard file extension is specified by Sun. The following file extensions are used by the Image Alchemy conversion program when dealing with Sun Raster files

.rast
.ras
.im
.im1
.im8
.im24
.im32

References   The above information was gathered from a variety sources, including files and Email messages from the Internet. To the author's knowledge there is no *official* documentation of the SunRaster format

TGA

Acronym	None
Origin	Truevision, Inc. 7340 Shadeland Station Indianapolis, IN 46256-3925 Tel. (317) 841-0332 Fax. (317) 576-7700
Motivation	A "true-color" raster-based data format that can be easily parsed with a small amount of program memory
Users	Application programs that use Truevision's products for displaying raster graphics data

Control

Copyrighted by	Truevision, Inc.
Trademarks	Truevision, TARGA, TrueVista, ATVista, NuVista, TIPS, TGA
Royalty Fees	None

Versions

1.0,1984

2.0, November 1989	Optional extensions included the following (they are downward-compatible extensions): 'Comment' information Gamma correction values Pixel aspect ratio

Overview

Major Type of Data	2D raster
Color Representation	Color table (Pseudo-Color); separate color tables (for each RGB) (Direct-Color); full color, ARGB, (True-Color)
Data Organization	Version 1: sequential Version 2: random access
Data Encoding	Binary
Data Compression	No compression; three types of run-length encoding

Data Types

Parameters that define raster data
Raster data
Color tables
Color correction tables (gamma correction)
Application specific data

TGA   *(Continued)*

Data Organization   (All of the following specifications refer to Version 2.0)
General syntax of the data stream:

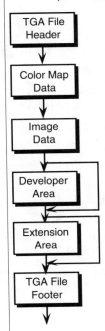

Signature
The signature is at the *end of the file* (it was added in Version 2). The last 18 bytes of the file should contain the null terminated ASCII string "TRUEVISION-XFILE." (Note the period as the last character in the string)

TGA *(Continued)*

TGA File Header

Byte#	Data	Details
	7 6 5 4 3 2 1 0	
0	ID Length	# of bytes used for Image ID, max 255
1	Color Map Type	0: no color map, 1: color map in file
2	Image Type	7 types defined, specifies color and compression schemes
3–4	Color Map Specification First Entry Index	Color table index to associate with first entry of file color map
5–6	Color Map Specification Color map Length	Total number of color map entries in file
7	Color Map Specification Color map Entry Size	Number of bits per entry, typically 15, 16, 24, or 32 bits
8–9	*X*-origin of Image	Horizontal coordinate for the lower-left corner of the image
10–11	*Y*-origin of Image	Vertical coordinate for the lower-left corner of the image
12–13	Image Width	In pixels
14–15	Image Height	In pixels
16	Pixel Depth	Bits per pixel, typically 8, 16, 24, or 32
17	0 0 Origin Alpha bits	See below
18–	Image ID	Optional ASCII text, 0–255 bytes

Origin   Bottom left, bottom right, top left, top right;
Alpha bits   Attribute bits per pixel, either Alpha channels bits or overlay bits

Color Map Data

Byte#	Data	Details
	Color Map Data	Variable amount of data, determined by the Color Map Specification above. Bits are packed if bits per color value are less than 8

Image Data

This contains Width × Height pixels values. Each pixel is specified in one of the following formats:

For Pseudo-Color	A single color-map index
For True-Color	Attribute (Alpha), Red, Green, Blue
For Direct-Color	Three independent color-map indices

Developer Area (optional)

Application-specific information that does not match any other TARGA pre-defined data item is included in this section of the file. A directory of 'tags' indicates the type, location, and size of data blocks

Byte#	Data	Details
0–1	# of Tags in the Directory	
2–3	1st Tag	Identifies information type and format
4–7	Byte offset to data	From the beginning of the file
8–11	Field size	In bytes
...	Further tags	3 values (10 bytes) per tag

TGA *(Continued)*

Extension Area (optional)

Byte#	Data	Details
0–1	Extension Size	In bytes, currently 494 for Version 2.0
2–42	Author Name	ASCII text, the last byte must be null
43–366	Author Comments	ASCII text, (324 bytes divided into 4 80-byte lines, where each byte 81 is always null
367–378	Date/Time Stamp	6 16-bit values that represent month, day, year, hour, minute, second
379–419	Job Name / ID	ASCII text, last byte must null
420–425	Job Time	3 16-bit values which represent hours, minutes, seconds
426–466	Software ID	ASCII text, the last byte must be null
467–469	Software Version	3 bytes, bytes 0–1, Version number × 100, byte 2, ASCII version letter
470–473	Key Color	'Background' or 'transparent' color, 4 bytes, alpha channel, then RGB
474–477	Pixel Aspect Ratio	2 16-bit values, pixel width, pixel height
478–481	Gamma Value (value 0.0 to 10.0)	2 16-bit values, gamma numerator, gamma denominator
482–485	Color Correction Offset	Offset from the beginning of the file to the Color Correction table
486–489	Postage Stamp Offset	Offset from the beginning of the file to the Postage Stamp image
490–493	Scan Line Offset	Offset from the beginning of the file to the Scan Line Table
494	Attributes Type	Specifies the type of Alpha channel data contained in the file
...	Scan Line Table	A table of 4-byte offset values; each offset specifies the byte offset from the beginning of the file to the beginning of a scan line
...	Postage Stamp Image	A smaller version of the original image (less than 64 × 64 pixels); noncompressed, 1st byte: *X*-size in pixels, 2nd byte: *Y*-size in pixels, then pixel map
0...2047	Color Correction Table	256 × 4, 16 bits values, which specify the Alpha, Red, Green, Blue values for a color correction lookup table

TGA File Footer (optional)

The presence of this footer indicates that the file may contain the extensions defined in Version 2 (i.e., the Extension Area and the Developer Directory)

Byte#	Data	Details
1–4	Extension Area Offset	Offset (in bytes) from the start of the file
5–8	Developer Directory Offset	Offset (in bytes) from the start of the file
9–24	The Signature	ASCII text: TRUEVISION-XFILE
25	Period	ASCII character "."; hex(2E)
26	String Terminator	Binary zero; hex(00)

File Name Suffix	
DOS, Unix, XENIX	.TGA
Macintosh file type	TPIC

Old extensions used, but no longer encouraged, are: VDA, ICB, VST

References	Truevision TGA™ File format specification, Version 2.0 Available from Truevision, see address above

---

TIFF

Acronym	Tag Image File Format
Origin	Aldus Corporation 411 First Ave. South Suite 200 Seattle, WA 98104 Tel. (206) 622-5500

The development was a cooperative effort between Aldus, Datacopy, DEST Corporation, Hewlett-Packard Company, Microsoft Corporation, Microtek International Inc., and New Image Technology, Inc.

Original author: The TIFF Advisory Committee (chaired by Aldus)
Current support: Bulletin board forums on CompuServe and AppleLink

Motivation	To provide for the exchange of raster image data between application programs and raster scanning devices

TIFF   *(Continued)*

The design goals were:

Extensibility	Accommodate new images without invalidating older images
Portability	Independent of hardware and operating systems
Revisability	Data can be revised "in place" without having to read the entire file

Users   Desktop publishing was the initial area of greatest use, but TIFF's usage has spread to video applications, facsimile transmission, medical imaging, satellite imaging, and document storage and retrieval

Control

Copyrighted by	Aldus Corporation, 1987, 1988, 1990
Trademarks	None
Royalty Fees	None

To request allocation of private TIFF tags, Fax inquiries to the Aldus Developer's Desk at (206) 343-4240

Versions

1.0 1986	
2.0	
3.0	
4.0	
5.0 1988	Compression of gray scale and color images
	TIFF classes (helps simplify TIFF reader implementation)
	Support for color pallet images
	Colorimetry information (for better color reproduction)
6.0 June 1992	Compression using horizontal differencing
	Methodology for 4-color print images (i.e., CMYK)
	Digital video support (YC_bC_r)
	Support for CIE L*a*b color model
	Storing pixels in tiles (instead of rows)
	New tag for "subimage" pointers
	Support of JPEG compression

Overview

Major Type of Data	2D raster
Color Representation	Black and White
	Grayscale: 16–256 gray values (4–8 bits per pixel)
	Palette color
	Full color: 24 bits per pixel, 8 bits per RGB
Data Organization	Random access
Data Encoding	Binary

Data Compression	No compression
	CCITT Group 3 (Modified Huffman run length)
	CCITT Group 3 standard
	CCITT Group 4 standard
	run-length (PackBits)
	LZW: for grayscale, palette-color and full-color images
	JPEG (in Version 6; see JTIFF)

Each data item has a unique "tag" associated with it. Only those data items pertaining to an image needed to be included in a particular file

A large and diverse combination of raster image formats and resolutions are supported through the proper specification of image parameters. To simplify TIFF readers somewhat, TIFF classes define the required and recommended types of "tags" needed for certain types of images. Current TIFF classes include:

Class B for bilevel images
Class G for gray scale images
Class P for color palette images
Class R for RGB full color images
Class X
Class Y for YC_bC_r full color images (compression: none, JPEG or LZW)

Data Types	Basic raster data	(As of Version 5)
	ImageWidth	Number of pixels in the horizontal direction
	ImageLength	Number of pixels in the vertical direction
	BitsPerSample	# of bits used to represent each pixel sample
	SamplesPerPixel	e.g., 1 sample for monochrome images, 3 for RGB
	RowsPerStrip	The image is typically divided into horizontal strips
	StripByteCounts	# of bytes in each strip, after compression
	StripOffsets	Where each image strip data is located in the file
	PlanarConfiguration	Single- or multiple-image planes
	PhotometricIntrepetation	Is bit 0 black or white?, color palette or full color?
	GrayResponseUnit	Accuracy of values in the GrayResponseCurve
	GrayResponseCurve	Grayscale lookup table that specifies dot densities
	ColorMap	A color palette for color table lookups
	ColorResponseCurves	"Gamma" correction lookup tables for RGB values
	ResolutionUnit	Dots per inch or dots per centimeter
	XResolution	Dots per unit in the ImageWidth direction
	YResolution	Dots per unit in the ImageLength direction
	Compression	Type of compression used
	NewSubfile Type	Specifies relationships of an image to other images in the same file, e.g., a low-resolution image of a larger image

TIFF *(Continued)*

Information Data

Artist   Person who created the image
DateTime   Date and time of image creation
ImageDescription   User comments about image, image subtitle, etc.
HostComputer   Computer system used to create the original image
Make   Manufacturer of the scanner, video digitizer, etc.
Model   Model name/number hardware
Software   Name and version of software that created the image

Facsimile data

Group3Options   Bit-encoded parameters controlling compression
Group4Options   Bit-encoded parameters controlling compression

**Document Storage and
Retrieval data**

DocumentName   Document name from which this image was scanned
PageName   Page name from which this image was scanned
PageNumber   Page # of multiple-page documents (e.g., facsimile)
XPosition   Offset to left side of image from left side of page
YPosition   Offset to top of image from top of page

There are several old data types that are no longer recommended for general data
   interchange use

There are several new data types included in Version 6.0. See the 6.0 specification
   for details

Users can create and register their own data types (i.e., tags) as needed

**Data
Organization**

General syntax of the data stream:

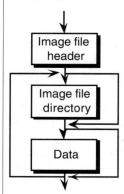

Signature

First two bytes of the file are either
   'II,'   hex(4949)   *I* stands for Intel, LSB first
   'MM,' hex(4D4D)   *M* stands for Motorola, MSB first

TIFF   *(Continued)*

Image File Header

Byte#	Data	Details
1–2	Specifies byte order	Either 'II' or 'MM' (see above)
3–4	Version number	Always 42, hex(2A): never changes
5–8	Offset of the first IFD (Image file directory)	Offset (in bytes) from the beginning of the file, zero subscripted

Image File Directory (IFD)

Byte#	Data	Details
0–1	Number of directory entries	
2–3	Tag	Defines the type of data this directory entry contains (or points to)
4–5	Type	Data type (see possible types below)
6–9	Length	The number of data values this tag "points to"
10–13	Data value (if ≤ 4 bytes) or Value Offset	Data value left justified within the 4 bytes *or* The offset (in bytes) from the beginning of the file where the data is located
...	Further directory entries	Each entry is 12 bytes and includes a Tag, Type, Length, and Value Offset Entries in the directory are sorted in ascending order by their Tag numbers
L $L+1$ $L+2$ $L+3$	Offset of next Image File Directory	The offset (in bytes) from the beginning of the file, zero subscripted $L = 2 + ($Number of directory entries$) \times 12$

Possible data types include:
1: BYTE, 8-bit unsigned integer
2: ASCII string; the last byte must be null (zero)
3: SHORT, 16-bit unsigned integer
4: LONG, 32-bit unsigned integer
5: RATIONAL, fraction made up of two LONGs

Data
All of the data in a TIFF file is located through the "Value Offsets" stored in the directory entries. The data has no prespecified order and can appear anywhere in the file, even before the Image File Directory entry that points to it. Reading a TIFF file typically requires random access to the data stream

TIFF *(Continued)*

File Name	DOS, Unix	.TIF
Suffix	Macintosh file type	TIFF

References	*TIFF 6.0 Specification,* can be ordered for $25 (plus local sales tax)
	Tel. (800) 831-6395 Fax. (414) 631-1425
	The specification can be downloaded free from the following sources:
	CompuServe: DataLibrary 10 of the ALDSVC forum
	AppleLink: Aldus icon in the 3rd party folder
	Internet: site *sgi.com* in the graphics/tiff directory

TIGER/LINE Census Files

Acronym	Topologically Integrated Geographic Encoding and Referencing/Line Census Files
Origin	Bureau of the Census
	United States Department of Commerce
	Washington, DC 20233
	Tel. (301) 763-1580
	Current support: Data User Services, Bureau of the Census
Motivation	To provide users with the final 1990 census boundaries (including voting districts), and to support the 1990 Census Data Products Program. The sole purpose of the data is for statistical analysis
Users	Anyone interested in the locations of people and the physical geographic features of the United Stated and its territories. This includes such groups as the Census Bureau, postal service, marketing firms, geographers, and demographers

Control	Copyrighted by	Bureau of the Census
	Trademarks	TIGER/Line
	Royalty Fees	None
Versions	Version 0	TIGER/Line Initial Voting District Files, 1990
	Version 1	TIGER/Line Precensus Files, 1990
	Version 2	TIGER/Line Prototype Files, 1990
	Version 3	TIGER/Line Census Files, 1990
Overview	Major Type of Data	2D geometry; Census data
	Color Representation	None
	Data Organization	Sequential
	Data Encoding	ASCII text (fixed field records)
	Data Compression	None

The data in the files are obtained from U.S. Geological Survey 1:100,000-scale maps (i.e., where 1 "on the map equals 100,000" in actual distance), and the Census Bureau's 1980 GBF/DIME-Files. It is not suitable for high-precision measurement applications such as engineering problems

TIGER/LINE Census Files *(Continued)*

A single TIGER/Line file covers one county (or statistically equivalent area). Each file ranges in size from less than 1 MB up to 125 MB. The average file is 7.5 MB. The estimated size of all files for all areas covered is 25,000 MB

Data Types

The data defines the location and relationship of streets, rivers, and railroads to each other, and to the numerous geographical areas for which the Census Bureau tabulates data. Each record represents a feature traditionally found on a paper map

There are 12 different types of records in a TIGER/Line data set. These records types are:

Record Type 1	Basic Data Record (a line with associated attributes)
Record Type 2	Shape coordinate points
Record Type 3	Additional decennial census geographic area codes
Record Type 4	Index to alternate feature names
Record Type 5	Feature name list
Record Type 6	Additional address range and ZIP Code data
Record Type 7	Landmark features
Record Type 8	Area features
Record Type A	Additional polygon geographic area codes
Record Type I	Area boundaries
Record Type P	Polygon location
Record Type R	Record number range

Lines (straight and curved)

Record Types 1 and 2 are used to store lines. A straight line segment is represented by a Type 1 record only. A curved line is represented by a Type 1 record plus one or more Type 2 records. A Type 2 record contains the intermediate points that define points along the curve

Points

Record Type 7 contains a single point designation (and information about what the point locates)

Polygons

There is one "P" record for each polygon in the database. Every Type 1 record has an associated type "I" record that links its line segment to the polygon record

Data Organization

The order of the data records is not defined in the data format description; they can appear in any desired order

Every line segment in the data base is defined by a Type 1 record that includes the following data. It is beyond our discussion to define each individual field in detail. Notice that the last 38 bytes of the record define the actual line segment; all other data defines attributes associated with the line segment. All fields are coded as ASCII text

TIGER/LINE Census Files *(Continued)*

Byte#	Data	Details
1	Record type	Always "1"
2–5	Version number	Currently "0003"
6–15	Record number	A unique number for each record in the database
16	Single-side segment code	1: one side only
17	Source code	
18–19	Feature direction (prefix)	
20–49	Feature name	
50–53	Feature type	
54–55	Feature direction (suffix)	
56–58	Census feature class code	
59–69	From address left	
70–80	To address left	
81–91	From address right	
92–102	To address right	
103	From address flag left	Imputed
104	To address flag left	Imputed
105	From address flag right	Imputed
106	To address flag right	Imputed
107–111	ZIP code left	(Only when addresses are present)
112–116	ZIP code right	
117–121	FIPS PUB 55 code left	
122–126	FIPS PUB 55 code right	
127–128	Alaska code left	Native regional corporation code
129–130	Alaska code right	Native regional corporation code
131–132	FIPS state code left	
133–134	FIPS state code right	
135–137	FIPS county code left	
138–140	FIPS county code right	
141–145	FIPS PUB 55 code left	MCD/CCD
146–150	FIPS PUB 55 code right	MCD/CCD
151–155	FIPS PUB 55 code left	sub-MCD
156–160	FIPS PUB 55 code right	sub-MCD

TIGER/LINE Census Files   *(Continued)*

Byte#	Data	Details
161–165	FIPS PUB 55 code left	Place
166–170	FIPS PUB 55 code right	Place
171–174	Census tract/BNA code left	Basic number
175–176	Census tract/BNA code left	Suffix
177–180	Census tract/BNA code right	Basic number
181–182	Census tract/BNA code right	Suffix
183–185	Tabulation block # left	Collection block number (numeric)
186	Tabulation block # left	Tabulation suffix (alphabetic)
187–189	Tabulation block # right	Collection block number (numeric)
190	Tabulation block # right	Tabulation suffix (alphabetic)
191–200	Longitude from	Starting position of line segment
201–209	Latitude from	
210–219	Longitude to	Ending position of line segment
220–228	Longitude to	

Coordinates are expressed in standard Federal Information Processing Standards (FIPS) notation, where a negative latitude represents the southern hemisphere, and a negative longitude represents the western hemisphere. All coordinates are expressed as signed integers with six decimal digits implied. For example, Longitude 131° East is represented by + 131,000,000, which implies a coordinate value of +131.000000

A Type 2 record stores intermediate points along a curved line. This is a fixed-length record that allows for 10 point definitions. If more points are needed extra Type 2 records are defined

Byte#	Data	Details
1	Record type	Always "2"
2–5	Version number	Currently "0003"
6–15	Record number	A unique number for each record in the database
16–18	Record sequence number	
19–28	Longitude for point 1	
29–37	Latitude for point 1	
...	...	...
190–199	Longitude for point 10	
200–208	Latitude for point 10	

TIGER/LINE Census Files   *(Continued)*

File Name Suffix	NA
References	*TIGER/Line Census Files,* 1990 Technical Documentation/prepared by the Bureau of the Census—Washington: The Bureau, 1991
	Addition information can be obtained from the Data User Services Division, TIGER Staff, Bureau of the Census, Washington, DC 20233, Tel. (301) 763-1580

WMF

Acronym	Windows MetaFile
Origin	Windows Marketing Group Microsoft Corporation 16011 NE 36th Way Box 97017 Redmond, WA 98073-9717 Tel. (206) 882-8080
Motivation	Convenient storage of images that appear repeatedly in applications
Users	Microsoft Windows 3.0 (or higher) users and application programs running under the Windows 3.0 (or higher) environment

Control	Copyrighted by	Microsoft Corporation
	Trademarks	Microsoft, Windows, Windows/286, Windows/386
	Royalty Fees	None

Versions	Version 1	Metafiles prior to Windows 3.0
	Version 2	Metafiles for Windows 3.0 and later

Overview	Major Type of Data	2D geometry; 2D raster
	Color Representation	Monochrome, Color lookup table, RGB
	Data Organization	Sequential (a list of function calls)
	Data Encoding	Binary
	Data Compression	None

Data Types	The data is a set of Windows' graphical-device-interface (GDI) function calls. The following list of supported functions are divided according to functionality

WMF *(Continued)*

Graphical primitives	SetPixel, LineTo, MoveTo, Rectangle, RoundRect, Polygon, PolyPolygon, PolyLine, Arc, Ellipse, Pie, Chord, FloodFill
Text	DrawText, TextOut, ExtTextOut, SetTextAlign, SetTextCharExtra, SetTextColor, SetTextJustification, CreateFontIndirect
Bitmap primitives	BitBlt, PatBlt, StretchBlt, StretchDIBits, SetDIBitsToDevice, SetStretchBl
Color	CreatePalette, SelectPalette, SetPaletteEntries, AnimatePalette, RealizePalette, ResizePalette
Regions	CreateRegion, SelectClipRegion, ExcludeClipRect, IntersectClipRect, OffsetClipRgn, OffsetViewportOrg, OffsetWindowOrg, ScaleViewportExt, ScaleWindowExt, SetViewportExt, SetViewportOrg, SetViewportExt, SetWindowOrg
Graphics State	CreateBrushIndirect,CreatePatternBrush, CreatePenIndirect, RestoreDC, SaveDC, SetBkColor, SetBkMode, SetMapMode, SetMapperFlags, SetPolyFillMode, SetROP02
Misc.	SelectObject, DeleteObject, Escape

Data Organization General syntax of the data stream:

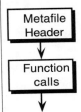

Signature
None

Metafile Header
All data values are in LSB first format

Byte#	Data	Details
1–2	Type	1: data in memory; 2: data in on disk
3–4	Size of the header	In 16-bit words
5–6	Version number	e.g., 0300 (hex)
7–10	Size of the file	In 16-bit words
11–12	Number of objects	Maximum number at one time
13–16	Size of maximum record	In 16-bit words
17–18	Not used	

WMF   *(Continued)*

Function Calls

This section contains references to GDI function calls and appropriate parameters for each call. Each record contains one function call. A typical record is as follows:

Byte#	Data	Details
$n -$ $(n + 3)$	Size of record	In words (16 bits)
$(n + 4) -$ $(n + 5)$	Function number	Unique for each function in the GDI
$(n + 6) -$	Array of parameters (one word per value)	In the reverse order they are passed to the function

File Name Suffix	DOS, OS/2	.WMF

References   *Microsoft Windows Programmer's Reference,* New for Version 3, edited by Microsoft Corporation, Microsoft Press, Redmond, WA, 1990, ISBN 1-55615-309-0

Microsoft Windows Software Development Kit
Call the Microsoft Information Center at (800) 426-9400 for further information

---

X Bitmap

Acronym	X Window System Bitmap
Origin	Project Athena Massachusetts Institute of Technology MIT's Laboratory for Computer Science Boston, MA 02139
	With support from the Digital Equipment Corporation (DEC)
	Original Author: Robert Scheifler, Ron Newman, and Jim Gettys Current Support: X Windows Consortium (of hardware and software vendors)
Motivation	A data format for bitmaps (1 bit per pixel) that can be included into a C source program and compiled without modification
Users	Applications using the X Window System (Xlib)
Control	Copyrighted by MIT and DEC Trademarks X Window System (owned by MIT) Royalty Fees None

X Bitmap *(Continued)*

Versions	Versions prior to Version 10 were used within MIT and DEC. Version 10 was the first version released to the general public

	Version 10	Stores data as 2-byte "short" integers
	Version 11	Stores data as 1-byte characters

Overview

Major Type of Data	2D Raster (1 bit per pixel only)
Color Representation	Monochrome
Data Organization	Sequential
Data Encoding	ASCII
Data Compression	None

Data Types

Image width
Image height
Image data

Data Organization

General syntax of the data stream:

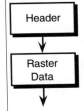

The data is encoded using the C language syntax. Refer to a description of the C language for details related to the following discussion

Header
The beginning of the data stream contains two *define statements* that define the width and height of the bitmap. The order of the statements is not important. One of the defined names must end with the characters "_width"; the other name must end with the characters "_height." These statements define the number of pixels in the horizontal (width) and vertical (height) directions

If the bitmap represents a cursor, two *define statements* also specify a "hot stop." They must have the form *name*_x_hot and *name*_y_hot, where the user provides any appropriate *name* desired

Following the define statements is an array declaration. If the array is declared of type "short," the data is represented as 2-byte integers (in Little Endian format). This is the technique used in Version 10. Version 11 declares a "char" array and represents the data as single bytes. The array should be of type "static"

X Bitmap *(Continued)*

Raster Data

The bits are ordered left to right in each scan line and the scan lines are ordered top to bottom. The bits are packed within bytes. The high-order bits represent the left most pixels. Version 10 pads each row to a 16-bit word boundary. Version 11 pads each row to a 8-bit byte boundary. The data is encoded as hexadecimal characters

Example

```
/* a version 10 bitmap of a simple outlined rectangle */
#define SimpleBox_width          16
#define SimpleBox_height         8
static short SimpleBox[] = {   0xFFFF,
                               0x0180,
                               0x0180,
                               0x0180,
                               0x0180,
                               0x0180,
                               0x0180,
                               0xFFFF  };

/* a version 11 bitmap of the same data */
#define SimpleBox_width          16
#define SimpleBox_height         8
static char SimpleBox[] = { 0xFF,    0xFF,
                            0x80,    0x01,
                            0x80,    0x01,
                            0x80,    0x01,
                            0x80,    0x01,
                            0x80,    0x01,
                            0x80,    0x01,
                            0xFF,    0xFF    };
```

File Name Suffix

Unix	.bitmap
DOS	.xbm
	.bm

References

X User's Group (XUG)
c/o Integrated Computer Solutions
163 Harvard Street
Cambridge, MA 02139

Actual software and release notes can be downloaded from various anonymous FTP Internet sites

---

X Pixmap

Acronym

X Window System Pixel Map

Origin

Project Athena
Massachusetts Institute of Technology
MIT's Laboratory for Computer Science
Boston, MA 02139

X Pixmap *(Continued)*

With support from the Digital Equipment Corporation (DEC)

Original Author: Robert Scheifler, Ron Newman, and Jim Gettys
Current Support: X Windows Consortium (of hardware and software vendors)

Motivation	A data format for pixmaps (i.e., an array of pixels) that can be included into a C language source program and compiled without modification
Users	Applications using the X Window System (Xlib)

Control	Copyrighted by	MIT and DEC
	Trademarks	X Window System (owned by MIT)
	Royalty Fees	None

Versions	Format	1

Overview	Major Type of Data	2D Raster
	Color Representation	Color Table
	Data Organization	Sequential
	Data Encoding	ASCII
	Data Compression	None

Data Types	Data format (version)
	Image width
	Image height
	Color Table
	Image data

Data Organization	General syntax of the data stream:

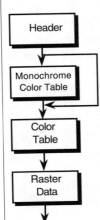

The data is encoded using the C language syntax. Refer to a description of the C language for details related to the following discussion

X Pixmap   *(Continued)*

Header

The beginning of the data stream contains five *define statements,* as indicated below. The italicized terms are user-specified. All other characters must appear exactly as shown. The order of the statements is not important

```
#define name_format     Version
#define name_width      Width
#define name_height     Height
#define name_ncolors    ColorTableLength
#define name_pixel      BytesPerPixel
```

Monochrome Color Table

```
static char name_mono[] = { /* data /*}
```

Color Table

The color table is declared as an array of pointers to strings. Each string contains the definition of one color in the table. The number of strings is determined by the "ncolors" value in the header. For example:

```
            /* one string per color entry in the table */
static char *name[] = { "     ", "     ",...}
```

Each string defines an index and a color specification. The index is specified in hexadecimal digits. The color specification is given in one of five possible formats shown below (in C format notation):

`rgb:%x/%x/%x`	Three values in hex notation separated by slashes (with "rgb:" in front of the values)
`rgbi:%f/%f/%f`	Three values in decimal notation separated by slashes (with "rgbi:" in front of the values). The values must be in the range from 0.0 to 1.0
`#%x`	Three values in hex notation with no separations between them (with a "#" character in front). The number of hex digits must by 3, 6, 9, or 12
`%f,%f,%f`	Three decimal values between 0.0 and 1.0, separated by commas
`%s`	A string of characters (with no blanks) that matches a color name in a specially-formatted file (typically called "rgb.txt")

Raster Data

The pixel values are stored in rows from left to right. The rows are ordered from top to bottom

The data is encoded as an array of pointers to strings. Each string contains an array of bytes. The number of bytes per pixel is determined by the "BytesPerPixel" value from the header. The number of bytes per string is not important. (But each ASCII line should not be longer than 256 bytes and strings cannot cross line boundaries)

X Pixmap   *(Continued)*

Example

```
/* a light red rectangle with a dark red border
        Note: ~ is a hex 7E (decimal 126)
             ? is a hex 3F (decimal 63)                        */

#define SimpleBox_format      1
#define SimpleBox_width       16
#define SimpleBox_height      8
#define SimpleBox_ncolors     256
#define SimpleBox_pixel       1

static char *ShadesOfRed[] = {
                       "00 rgb:00/00/00",
                       "01 rgb:01/00/00",
                       "02 rgb:02/00/00",
                       /* rest of colors here */
                       "FF rbi:FF/00/00"};

static char *SimpleBox[] = {    "~~~~~~~~~~~~~~~~",
                                "~??????????????~",
                                "~??????????????~",
                                "~??????????????~",
                                "~??????????????~",
                                "~??????????????~",
                                "~??????????????~",
                                "~~~~~~~~~~~~~~~~"   };
```

File Name Suffix   NA

References   X User's Group (XUG)
c/o Integrated Computer Solutions
163 Harvard Street
Cambridge, MA 02139

Actual software and release notes can be downloaded from various anonymous FTP Internet sites

---

X Window Dump

Acronym   X Window System Window Dump file

Origin   Project Athena
Massachusetts Institute of Technology
MIT's Laboratory for Computer Science
Boston, MA 02139

With support from the Digital Equipment Corporation (DEC)

Original Author: Robert Scheifler, Ron Newman, and Jim Gettys
Current Support: X Windows Consortium (of hardware and software vendors)

X Window Dump   *(Continued)*

Motivation	A single data format to support all types of raster data within the X Window System
Users	Applications using the X Window System (Xlib)

Control

Copyrighted by	MIT and DEC
Trademarks	X Window System (owned by MIT)
Royalty Fees	None

Versions

X10WD_FILE_VERSION
X11WD_FILE_VERSION   (This is the one discussed below)

Overview

Major Type of Data	2D Raster
Color Representation	Color Table; RGB
Data Organization	Sequential
Data Encoding	Binary
Data Compression	None

Data Types

Data format (version)
Image width
Image height
Bits per pixel
Ordering of bits within the data stream (XYBitmap, XYPixmap, ZPixmap)
Byte order (LSB or MSB)
Bitmap (1 bit per pixel) structure information
Bit masks (to determine which bits within a pixel value are valid)
Window information (size and location of window; border width)
Color Table
Image data

Data Organization

General syntax of the data stream:

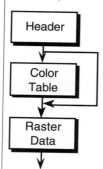

Header

All values in the header are unsigned long integers (4 bytes), except the "window x" and "window y" values which are signed long integers

X Window Dump *(Continued)*

Byte#	Data	Details
1–4	Header size	In bytes
5–8	File version	X11WD_FILE_VERSION
9–12	Pixmap format	See below
13–16	Pixmap depth	Number of bits per pixel
17–20	Pixmap width	In pixels
21–24	Pixmap height	In pixels
25–28	Bitmap *x*offset	
29–32	Byte order	MSB first or LSB first
33–36	Bitmap unit	Typically 8, 16 or 32
37–40	Bitmap bit order	MSB first or LSB first
41–44	Bitmap Pad	
45–48	Bits per pixel	
49–52	Bytes per scan line	
53–56	Visual class	See below
57–60	Z red mask	
61–64	Z green mask	
65–68	Z blue mask	
69–72	Bits per RGB	Log base 2 of distinct color values
73–76	Color map entries	Number of entries in color map
77–80	Ncolors	Number of color structures
81–84	Window width	
85–88	Window height	
89–92	Window *x*	Upper left *X* coordinate
93–96	Window *y*	Upper left *Y* coordinate
97–100	Window border width	

The pixmap format type is one of the following:

XYPixmap	1	The first bit of each pixel is stored in a rectangular bit-map array, then the second bit of each pixel, etc., until all bit-planes are stored
ZPixmap	2	All bits of each pixel are stored contiguously

The Visual class of the data is one of the following:

X Window Dump *(Continued)*

StaticGray	0	Only one sample per pixel; predefined colors
GrayScale	1	Only one sample per pixel; color table included
StaticColor	2	Indexes into a color table; predefined color table
PseudoColor	3	Indexes into a color table; color table included
TrueColor	4	RGB (typically)
DirectColor	5	More than one sample per pixel; each value indexes into a different color table

Color Table

The color table is stored as an array of color structures. Each color entry consists of the following:

Byte#	Data	Details
1–4	Number	Index position within the color table
5–6	Red	
7–8	Green	
9–10	Blue	
11	Flags	Determines which colors are actually used
12	Pad	

Raster Data

The pixel values are stored in rows from left to right. The rows are ordered from top to bottom

File Name Suffix

| Unix | .wd |
| DOS | .xwd |

References

X User's Group (XUG)
c/o Integrated Computer Solutions
163 Harvard Street
Cambridge, MA 02139

Actual software and release notes can be downloaded from various anonymous FTP Internet sites

xim

Acronym	X Window System IMage file
Origin	Project Athena Massachusetts Institute of Technology MIT's Laboratory for Computer Science Boston, MA 02139 With support from the Digital Equipment Corporation (DEC) Original Author: Robert Scheifler, Ron Newman, and Jim Gettys Current Support: X Windows Consortium (of hardware and software vendors)
Motivation	A data format to support full-color and color-table images within the X Window System
Users	Applications built on top of the X Windows System (Xlib)

Control	Copyrighted by	MIT and DEC
	Trademarks	X Window System (owned by MIT)
	Royalty Fees	None

Versions	IMAGE_VERSION	3

Overview	Major Type of Data	2D raster
	Color Representation	Color Table; RGB (plus optional Alpha)
	Data Organization	Sequential
	Data Encoding	ASCII header; binary data
	Data Compression	Run-length option

Data Types	Data format (version)
	Image width
	Image height
	Bits per channel (sample value)
	Number of channels (number of distinct sample values per pixel)
	Documentation data (author, comments, date, etc.)
	Color Table
	Image data

xim   *(Continued)*

Data Organization

General syntax of the data stream:

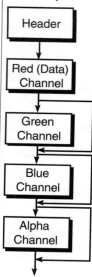

Header

All data in the header is encoded as ASCII character strings, except the color table, which is in binary. Data values within each string are in decimal notation. The header is always 1024 bytes long, even if a color map is not included with the data

xim   *(Continued)*

Byte#	Data	Details
1–8	File version	Header version
9–16	Header size	In bytes
17–24	Image width	In pixels
25–32	Image height	In pixels
33–40	Number of colors	Actual number of valid colors in color map
41–43	Number of channels	0 or 1 → pixmap; 3 → RGB
44–48	Bytes per scan line	
49–52	Number pictures	In this file (currently not used)
53–56	Bits per channel	Usually 1 or 8
57–60	Alpha channel flag	
61–64	Run-length flag	
65–112	Author	Name of creator
113–144	Date	Date and time the image was made
145–160	Program	Program used to create the image
161–256	Comments	Other viewing info
257–1024	Color map	256 entries; 3 bytes per entry; RGB1, RGB2, RGB3, etc.

Raster Data

The pixel values are stored in rows from left to right. The rows are ordered from top to bottom

If the *number of channels* is 1, the data is assumed to be indexes into the color map. All of the data values are stored as a single "channel"

If the *number of channels* is 3, the data is stored as three separate channels. All red values are in the first channel, all green values are in the second channel, and all blue values are in the third channel

The *alpha channel flag* specifies whether a fourth channel of data is included in the file for *alpha values*

Each channel is run-length encoded if the *run-length flag* is set. The following scheme is used:

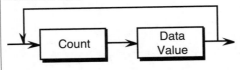

xim   *(Continued)*

Each data value is replicated (Count + 1) number of times until the correct number of pixel values are placed into the channel buffer (i.e., width × height number of values). There is no provision for non-run-length data

Example	Unix .xim
References	X User's Group (XUG) c/o Integrated Computer Solutions 163 Harvard Street Cambridge, MA 02139 Actual software and release notes can be downloaded from various anonymous FTP Internet sites

Amanatides90   Amanatides, John and Mitchell, Don P., "Antialiasing of Interlaced Video Animation," SIGGRAPH '90 Conference Proceedings, *Computer Graphics,* **24** (4), 77–85, 1990.

Barnsley89   Barnsley, Michael F. and Sloan, Alan D., "Fractal Image Compression," In *Proceedings,* Scientific Data Compression Workshop, Snowbird, Utah, May 3–5, 1988, Ramapriyan, H. K., ed., NASA Conference Publication 3025, pp. 351–365.

Barnsley93   Barnsley, Michael F., *Fractal Image Compresssion,* AK Peters, Ltd., Wellesly, MA, 1993 (244 pages).

Becker91   Becker, Richard A. and Cleveland, William S., Take a Broader View of Scientific Visualization, *Pixel,* July/August 1991, pp. 42–44.

Britannica90   *The New Encyclopedia Britannica,* 15th Edition, Encyclopedia Britannica, Inc., Chicago, 1990.

Cargill89   Cargill, Carl F., *Information Technology Standardization, Theory, Process, and Organizations,* Digital Press, 1989.

Cogoli73   Cogoli, John E., *Everything To Know About Photo Offset,* North American Publishing Co., Philadelphia, 1973.

Costigan71   Costigan, Daniel M., *FAX, The Principles and Practice of Facsimile Communication,* Chilton Book Company, Philadelphia, 1971.

CCITT89   *Blue Book, Volume VII — Fascicle VII.3,* The International Telegraph and Telephone Consultative Committee, 1989, pp. 3–57.

Durrett87   Durrett, H. John, ed., *Color and the Computer,* Academic Press, Orlando, 1987 (299 pages).

Foley90   Foley, James D., van Dam, Andries, Feiner, Steven K., and Hughes, John F., *Computer Graphics Principles and Practice,* Second Edition, Addison-Wesley, Reading, 1990.

Gonzalez87   Gonzalez, Rafael C., *Digital Image Processing,* Second Edition, Addison-Wesley, Reading, 1987.

Heckbert82   Heckbert, P., Color Image Quantization for Frame Buffer Display, Proceeding of SIGGRAPH '82, *Computer Graphics,* **16** (3), 297–307, 1982.

Hill90   Hill, Francis S., *Computer Graphics,* Macmillan, New York, 1990.

Huffman52   Huffman, D.A., A Method for the Construction of Minimum Redundancy Codes, *Proc. IRE*, **40** (10), 1098–1101, 1952.

Jacobson76   Jacobson, Kurt I. and Jacobson, Ralph E., Imaging Systems, *Mechanisms and Applications of Established and New Photosensitive Processes,* John Wiley and Sons, New York, 1976 (319 pages).

Kaufman92   Kaufman, Arie, slides for "Volume Synthesis," in Introduction to Volume Visualization, Course Notes, ACM SIGGRAPH '92, pp. 151–168.

MacLennan83   MacLennan, Bruce J., *Principles of Programming Languages: Design, Evaluation, and Implementation,* Holt, Reinhart and Winston, New York, 1983.

NASA89   Ramapriyan, H. K., ed., *Proceedings,* Scientific Data Compression Workshop, Snowbird, Utah, May 3–5, 1988, NASA Conference Publication 3025.

Netravali88   Netravali, Arun N. and Haskell, Barry G., *Digital Pictures, Representation and Compression,* Plenum, New York, 1988.

Poe86   Poe, Daryl Thomas, "One- and Two-Pass Color Quantization Methods in Computer Graphics," Master Thesis, The Ohio State University, 1986.

Quinn89   Quinn, Gerald V., *The Fax Handbook,* Tab Book, Blue Ridge Summit, 1989.

Rao90   Rao, K. R. and Yip, P., *Discrete Cosine Transform: Algorithms, Advantages, and Applications,* Academic Press, San Diego, 1990.

Rose90   Rose, Marshall T., *The Open Book, A Practical Perspective on OSI,* Prentice Hall, Englewood Cliffs, 1990, pp. 225–336.

SMPTE89   *4:2:2 Digital Video, Background and Implementation,* Pensinger, Glen, ed., SMPTE, White Plains, New York, 1989.

Southworth79   Southworth, Miles, *Color Separation Techniques,* 2nd Edition, Graphics Arts Publishing, Livonia, 1979.

Storer88   Storer, James A., *Data Compression,* Computer Science Press, Rockville, 1988.

Treinish91   Treinish, Lloyd A., "Data Structures and Access Software for Scientific Visualization," *Computer Graphics,* **25** (2), April 1991, ACM SIGGRAPH, New York, pp. 104–118.

Ulichney87   Ulichney, Robert, *Digital Halftoning,* The MIT Press, Cambridge, 1987.

Unicode90   The Unicode Consortium, *The Unicode Standard,* Addison-Wesley, Reading, 1991.

Wan88   Wan, S., Wong, K., and Prusinkiewicz, P., "An Algorithm for Multidimensional Data Clustering," *ACM Transactions on Mathematical Software,* **14** (2), 153–162, 1988.

INDEX